TREASURY CONTROL OF THE CIVIL SERVICE
1854–1874

TREASURY CONTROL
OF THE
CIVIL SERVICE
1854–1874

BY

MAURICE WRIGHT

CLARENDON PRESS · OXFORD

1969

Oxford University Press, Ely House, London W. 1

GLASGOW NEW YORK TORONTO MELBOURNE WELLINGTON
CAPE TOWN SALISBURY IBADAN NAIROBI LUSAKA ADDIS ABABA
BOMBAY CALCUTTA MADRAS KARACHI LAHORE DACCA
KUALA LUMPUR HONG KONG TOKYO

Printed in Great Britain by
Alden & Mowbray Ltd
at the Alden Press, Oxford

FOR MY MOTHER AND FATHER

PREFACE

THE focus of this book is the Treasury; its subject-matter, Treasury control. Little is known in detail about the Treasury in the nineteenth century, less about its control of public expenditure. Falling into the no-man's-land of recent administrative history dividing historians from political scientists, the Treasury has attracted the attention of few scholars from either discipline. One consequence of this neglect has been the acceptance, *faut de mieux*, of a familiar hypothesis, which assigns to the Treasury the role of chief villain of the mid-nineteenth-century piece. It is alleged that, in the relentless pursuit of stringent economy, it exercised an inflexible and, sometimes, capricious control of public expenditure; that it dealt autocratically, at times despotically, with other departments; and that, before departmental accounts were scrutinized and reported on by the Public Accounts Committee and the Comptroller and Auditor-General, it was largely ill-informed of the work done by other departments.

'The account of the past which satisfies a particular generation must be regarded as a working hypothesis, no more', Dr. Kitson Clark has warned, writing of the 'task of revision' in *The Making of Victorian England*. 'We can use what we have received to give form and direction to our thought, but we have no right to regard it as an unquestionably and exhaustively correct view of what actually happened, or of the meaning of what happened.' In attempting to follow this advice, it is less my intention to offer an alternative hypothesis than to test the validity of that which has been handed on to us for one particular aspect of public expenditure.

The book deals principally with the Treasury's control of the public money spent by central government departments under the general head of 'establishments'—staff complements, pay, pensions, and so on; it does not deal with other types of public expenditure controlled by the Treasury, such as the administration of poor relief, education, or law and justice. Nor does it deal with the control of naval and military expenditure, other than that money spent on the civil establishments of the Admiralty and War Office departments.

In dealing with only a part of the Treasury's general financial control I have separated establishments' from supply and other types of expenditure. In practice the distinction was much less sharp than it appears from this study. Establishments, supply and all other business belonging to a particular department was dealt with by the same Treasury officials in the same division. In consequence, their advice on establishments' questions was often influenced or reinforced by their knowledge of what was happening or had happened on the supply side, and vice versa. Ideally, but impossibly, each piece of establishments business which was dealt with by the Treasury would have been considered here in the context, not only of all other establishments' decisions, but all other decisions as well. A further limiting factor is that focus upon a particular decision tends to obscure the dynamic element in decision-making, and the fact that an official was dealing concurrently with several other questions as well.

Although establishments' expenditure was a very much larger proportion of total civil expenditure than it is now—in 1854 the Government spent approximately £10 million on civil and revenue services, more than a half of which was establishments' expenditure—my conclusions relate only to the Treasury's control of establishments' expenditure. Without further study, it is impossible to tell whether what I have said here about the nature, method, and effectiveness of that control applied equally to the control of money spent on new buildings, education, or the colonies. At best, I may have provided a starting point for further research.

The period 1854–74 embraces both the last years of a fragmented and departmentalized Service with roots in the eighteenth century, and the first years of a new unified Service looking forward to the twentieth century. The link between them was provided by Northcote and Trevelyan, who, in their *Report on the Organisation of the Civil Service* published in 1854, laid down the guide-lines upon which the development of the Service was to proceed: open competitive examinations, division of labour, promotion by merit, and uniform conditions of service. The extent to which the Treasury influenced the acceptance of these general principles and their translation into the particular practice of departments during the next twenty years provides the subject-matter of the second main

theme. It is closely linked with the first, for the Treasury's ability
to influence the development of the Service derived from its control
of establishments' expenditure. As it slowly grasped the relationship between economy and efficiency, it began to turn increasingly
to a consideration of problems of organization and structure, and
to accept that as a central department it had an overall responsibility for the Service.

Focusing narrowly upon the Treasury, I have not dealt with the
Parliamentary and political context within which the department
operated, except where it appeared to relate directly to a particular
issue, such as competitive examinations. In a bigger book there
would have been room to deal with other individuals and groups
who were pressing for administrative reform of many different
kinds at this time, and whose influence and activity, both inside
and out of Parliament, provided the climate within which the
Treasury worked.

Throughout the book I am concerned mainly with that part of
the Civil Service to which Northcote and Trevelyan referred in
their report, namely, those civil servants whose functions may be
broadly described as administrative and clerical. I do not deal
explicitly with the diplomatic and consular services; the inspector-
ates and other 'field executives'; professional officers, such as
doctors and surgeons; and technical and industrial civil servants
such as engineers, shipwrights, postmen, and manual workers.

Why I have chosen to begin at 1854 is self-evident: to end at
April 1874 is perhaps less obvious. The time-span is a convenient
one, roughly a generation, long enough to reveal the nature and
extent of any changes which were taking place after the publication
of the report, and to identify some of the forces which inspired
them. But it is not principally on that account that I have made my
choice; nor have I been particularly influenced by the political
events which followed the dissolution of Parliament in January
1874. My main consideration has been an administrative one. On
25 April 1874 a commission under the chairmanship of Lyon Playfair was appointed by the new Conservative Government to
inquire into the condition of the Civil Service. It signalled the end
of the furious debate sparked off by Northcote and Trevelyan.
Subsequently, argument was less concerned with the validity of
their general principles than with the most practical and economic
way to give effect to them.

The book is divided into four parts. Part I describes the organization and procedure of the Treasury, drawing particular attention to the dominant and dominating position of the Assistant (later Permanent) Secretary, the key figure in the decisions discussed in the chapters that follow. Part II deals with the Treasury's control of establishments—recruitment, division of labour, and staff complements; Part III, with control of conditions of service—salaries, allowances, promotion, leave, discipline, and pensions. In the two concluding chapters of Part IV I deal separately with each of the two principal themes, in an attempt to evaluate the purpose, methods and effectiveness of the Treasury's control of establishments' expenditure, and to assess the Treasury's influence upon the changes which had taken place in the organization and structure of the Service between 1854 and 1874.

In preparing this book I have been helped by many colleagues and friends. I owe a particular debt of gratitude to Mr. D. N. Chester, Warden of Nuffield College, Oxford, and to Miss Betty Kemp for their guidance and wise counsel in the early stages. Subsequently my main debt is to Professor W. J. M. Mackenzie and Professor H. J. Hanham, who took great pains with the final draft of the manuscript and contributed many valuable ideas and suggestions for its improvement; their comments and criticisms have saved me from the embarrassment of numerous errors and solecisms. My thanks are due also to Dr. Henry Parris who read and commented on the final draft; and to Dr. Henry Roseveare who read an earlier draft of the chapters on the Treasury, and generously made available biographical material on some of the senior Treasury civil servants which he had collected for his own book on the Treasury. Needless to say, none of them bears any responsibility for what flaws may remain.

I am grateful to H.M. Treasury for allowing me to examine papers then in the possession of the Chief Registrar, and to Professor C. J. Hughes for the loan of an unpublished memoir of his great-grandfather, Philip Hughes, who served in the Treasury and the Commissariat during the first half of the nineteenth century.

Victoria University of Manchester   M. W. WRIGHT

CONTENTS

APPENDICES

INTRODUCTION

THE NORTHCOTE–TREVELYAN REPORT

ON 23 November 1853, four months before the outbreak of
the Crimean War, Sir Stafford Northcote and Sir Charles
Trevelyan reported to Gladstone, then Chancellor of the
Exchequer in Aberdeen's Government, the results of their inquiry
into the organization of the Civil Service. For a document later to
be recognized and revered as the greatest single influence upon
the development of the modern Service, the Northcote–Trevelyan
Report is brief and unprepossessing in appearance, its twenty-
three quarto pages unsupported by any independent and expert
testimony, written evidence or statistical appendices. More was
not to be expected from an inquiry lasting less than eight months;
nor was it intended. Gladstone had not commissioned them to
conduct an intensive and exhaustive investigation of the whole
Service, but had invited them to reflect upon the series of departmental inquiries which they had recently completed, and to distil
from them conclusions of general validity.

These inquiries had begun in response to general alarm at the
growth of public expenditure in the 1840s, the result of an increase
in the scope and intensity of government activity and the rise in
the number of civil servants.[1] In 1848 a Select Committee of the
House of Commons examined Civil Service expenditure, but
after an exhaustive inquiry, in which many departments were
called upon to give evidence, made no specific recommendations.
As permanent head of the Treasury, Sir Charles Trevelyan had
been called before the Committee, but his proposals for reorganizing the Treasury establishment by dividing the intellectual and
mechanical work were rejected. Soon after he participated in an
inquiry at the Colonial Office, which established the precedent for
the series of Treasury inquiries which followed in the next five
years. Between 1849–54 he inquired into no fewer than thirteen

---

[1] Thirty years later, Trevelyan claimed that 'the revolutionary period of 1848
gave us a shock, and created a disposition to put our house in order'. P[arliamen-
tary] P[apers], 1875, XXIII, Appendix F to 2nd Report, CSC, p. 100.

different departments, in nine, assisted by Sir Stafford Northcote. Their work was summarized by Gladstone in the Treasury Minute commissioning them to inquire into the whole Service.

The Chancellor of the Exchequer states to the Board, that his attention has been called to the inquiries which are in progress under the super-intendence of the Treasury into the establishment of various depart-ments, for the purpose of considering applications for increase of salary, abolishing or consolidating redundant offices, supplying addi-tional assistance where it is required, getting rid of obsolete processes, and introducing more simple and compendious modes of transacting business, establishing a proper distinction between intellectual and mechanical labour, and, generally, so revising and readjusting the public establishments as to place them on the footing best calculated for the efficient discharge of their important functions, according to the actual circumstances of the present time. . . .

The general result of these inquiries and of the proceedings which will be taken on them, will, undoubtedly, be that the public service will be conducted in a more efficient manner by a smaller number of persons than is the case at present. The gain in point of economy will probably be important. . . .

The object is, that the business of the public should be done in the best and most economical manner, and that arrangement of the public establishments which most conduces to this result will, in almost every case, be the most economical.[1]

The Civil Service inquiry was the culmination of these investiga-tions, and the report was intended to be Northcote's and Trevel-yan's general reflections and conclusions on the state of the Service derived from their first-hand knowledge and experience of more than a dozen departments. Most of the criticisms and recommenda-tions which appeared in the general report were not, therefore, new. As Trevelyan said later

We found, as we went on, the same evils and circumstances pointing to the same remedies, with reference to every department; so that when we came to make our general report we had arrived at an ample induction, and our premises were so large, and we had gone with such detail into the state of the different establishments, that the conclusions arrived at in our report were the necessary logical inference of what had preceded.[2]

[1] T[reasury] M[inute] 12 April 1853, P.P., 1854–5, XXX.
[2] *2nd Report of the Civil Service (Playfair) Inquiry Commission*, 1875, P.P., 1875, XXIII, Appendix F, paragraph 1.

To emphasize this, the general report was published together with the reports of all the separate departmental inquiries as a Parliamentary Paper.[1]

The purpose of their report was less to inform or persuade by argument than to point the way forward; it was a 'reformer's tract or pamphlet', a 'broadsheet or broadside', a manifesto of Civil Service reform. Certainly there is little of that scrupulous objectivity and consistent understatement characteristic of so many official reports. The tone is strident, the authors asserted rather than argued coolly and rationally—in short, they had written a polemic, the opening shot in a sustained attack upon incompetence and inefficiency. More significantly, they had produced a perceptive blueprint of principles of organization and conditions of employment, 'an uncanny prophetic vision' of the Civil Service the country would need in conditions which were not yet wholly perceived.

The report opens with a passing reference to the need and importance of a permanent Civil Service, but almost immediately launches into a blistering and not wholly fair or impartial attack upon the imperfect organization of the Service and the quality of the civil servants, a 'large proportion' of whom were stigmatized as 'unambitious, incapable or indolent', attracted to the Service by the 'comparative lightness of the work, the security of tenure, and the prospects of a substantial pension on retirement, whether through infirmity or incapacity'.[2] Writing to Delane, the editor of *The Times*, six months later, Trevelyan said

There can be no doubt that our high Aristocracy have been accustomed to employ the Civil Establishments as a means of providing for the Waifs and Strays of their Families—as a sort of Foundling Hospital where those who had no energy to make their way in the open professions, or whom it was not convenient to purchase one in the Army, might receive a nominal office, but real Pension, for life, at the expense of the Public.

The Dukes of Norfolk, for instance, have provided for their illegitimate children in this manner, generation after generation. There are still several of them in the Public Service, and one of them is the most notorious idler and jobber in it. Another, who shocked his fellow Clerks by continually falling down in epileptic fits, was put into the

[1] P.P., 1854, XXVII.
[2] *Report of the Committee of Inquiry into the Organisation of the Civil Service*, 23 November 1853, P.P., 1854, XXVII.

Treasury a few years ago, and nothing could exceed his astonishment at his being told by me that he was expected to work like his fellow Clerks.[1]

The difficulty of attracting men of the calibre who joined other professions was attributed to several causes: to the system of recruitment based upon patronage; to the employment of most civil servants for very many years, or their whole service, upon copying and other mechanical and routine work; to the system of promoting by seniority which ensured that the 'dull and inefficient' rose side by side with the 'able and energetic'; and to the fragmentary character of the Service in which

Each man's experience, interests, hopes, and fears are limited to the special branch of service in which he is himself engaged. The effect naturally is, to cramp the energies of the whole body, to encourage the growth of narrow views and departmental prejudices, to limit the acquisition of experience, and to repress and almost extinguish the spirit of emulation and competition; besides which, considerable inconvenience results from the want of facilities for transferring strength from an office where the work is becoming slack to one in which it is increasing, and from the consequent necessity of sometimes keeping up particular departments on a scale beyond their actual requirements.

Their prescription for these alleged ills was contained in a single short paragraph:

... the public service should be carried on by the admission into its lower ranks of a carefully selected body of young men, who should be employed from the first upon work suited to their capacities and their education, and should be made constantly to feel that their promotion and future prospects depend entirely on the industry and ability with which they discharge their duties, and that with average abilities and reasonable application they may look forward confidently to a certain provision for their lives, that with superior powers they may rationally hope to attain to the highest prizes in the Service, while if they prove decidedly incompetent, or incurably indolent, they must expect to be removed from it.

Here was distilled the essence of the Northcote–Trevelyan doctrine, the guiding principle for Civil Service reformers during the next seventy-five years. From it they derived their own recommendation to provide for the supply of a thoroughly efficient class

[1] Trevelyan to Delane, 6 February 1854, Brit[ish] Mus[eum], G[ladstone] P[apers] Add. MSS. 44333, fo. 138.

of men by introducing a competitive literary examination on a level with the best university education, open to all, conducted by an independent Board of Examiners. To encourage industry and ability other recommendations were made for separating intellectual and mechanical work, promoting by merit, reporting periodically on conduct and efficiency, and regularly transferring civil servants between different branches of the same department that they might acquire wide experience to fit them for senior posts. Finally to mitigate the evils which resulted from the fragmentary character of the Service, and to help unify it, they proposed that senior posts should be open to civil servants from all departments, and that pensions should be awarded on a uniform and consistent basis according to service and character.

Northcote and Trevelyan were improbable collaborators. Trevelyan was an established and highly experienced administrator with thirteen years service as permanent head of the Treasury. At thirty-five, Northcote was eleven years his junior, and had yet to begin a successful but undistinguished, and now largely forgotten, political career. Stafford Henry Northcote, first Earl of Iddesleigh, was born into an old but neither illustrious nor wealthy Devonshire family, and educated at Eton and Balliol, where he took a first in *Literae Humaniores* and a third in Mathematics, and was remembered by his contemporaries mainly for the grace and neatness of his oarsmanship, 'the perfection of Eton style'. He entered Parliament in 1855 as Conservative member for Dudley, after a long political apprenticeship as Gladstone's private secretary. His capacity for business and his huge industry earned him not only the friendship and respect of his mentor; several Whig ministers recommended him to Prince Albert as a dependable and trustworthy adviser, and in 1850 he was appointed one of the secretaries of the Great Exhibition, quickly gaining the confidence of the Prince and enjoying a considerable success. Earlier, while devilling for Gladstone at the Board of Trade, he had published a pamphlet on the Navigation Laws in which his argument for free trade commanded respect and attention in the country, 'made him conspicuous for the first time, and was of great influence on his career[1].' His resignation from the department after eight years service was regretted by his political and official chiefs; had he

[1] Andrew Lang, *Life, Letters and Diaries of Sir Stafford Northcote, First Earl of Iddesleigh*, i. 77.

stayed he thought it probable that he would be promoted Permanent Secretary within a year or so. By the time he succeeded to the
baronetcy on the death of his father in 1851, he was a rising young
man.

His collaboration with Trevelyan began shortly after, in the
winter of 1852–3. After recovering from a serious illness, and
'afraid of dropping wholly out of sight and out of practice', he
wrote to Gladstone to 'humbly apply for the vacant place on a
Treasury committee to inquire into the organisation of the Board
of Trade about to be commissioned'.[1] Gladstone gave him the
appointment and he began his partnership with Trevelyan. His
contribution, to what Trevelyan later called their masterpiece,
ensured the continuance of their collaboration in the numerous
inquiries which followed, and their joint commission to review the
whole Service followed logically. Trevelyan believed him indispensable, writing to him in May 1853 when there was a danger that
his Parliamentary candidacy might interrupt their work that: 'The
qualifications for this great work are so rare, and you possess them
in so remarkable a degree, that if you were to fail us, I should
despair of its ever being accomplished in my time.'[2]

Northcote's character contrasted sharply with Trevelyan's, but
his personal qualities complemented rather than clashed with those
which his colleague brought to the task of inquiry. Gladstone once
described him to Algernon West as 'pliant, diligent, quick and
acute, and with a temper simply perfect'.[3] 'His eminence was
moral rather than intellectual; his strength was one of balance, not
of brilliance of parts.'[4] He had a disciplined rather than a vivid or
original mind, 'no man . . . was ever less speculative', taking politics
as he found them without deep or novel reasoning. It would be
hard to imagine a more perfect foil for Trevelyan.

Trevelyan's leadership of the campaign for Civil Service reform
in the 1850s, and the recognition of his inspiration of the report
which he wrote with Northcote, have ensured him a permanent
place in nineteenth-century administrative history. Charles Edward
Trevelyan was born in 1807 into 'one of the oldest and best'

[1] Northcote to Gladstone, 18 December 1852, Brit. Mus., G.P. Add. MSS.
44216, fo. 192.
[2] Trevelyan to Northcote, 17 May 1853, Bod[leian], T[revelyan] L[etter]
B[ooks], xxxi, 174.
[3] Horace G. Hutchinson (Ed.), *Private Diaries of Sir Algernon West*, p. 3.
[4] Lang, i. xiii–xiv.

families in England, who had for many centuries lived near Fowey
in Cornwall. He described himself as a Celt, 'belonging to the class
of reformed Cornish Celts, who by long habits of intercourse with
the Anglo-Saxons have learned at last to be practical men'.[1] His
father, George Trevelyan, was archdeacon of Taunton. Both
parents had belonged to the Clapham Sect, an evangelical and
philanthropic group of families who counted Wilberforce and Sir
James Stephen among their number, which had largely directed
the attack on negro slavery. Trevelyan, who was of rigid integrity,
'delighted in reading chapters of the Bible aloud in a deep sonorous
voice'.

After Haileybury, he went into the Indian Civil Service where he
served from 1826 until 1838, displaying at a tender age the
qualities of a tireless, efficient administrator convinced of the
rightness of his own action. Quite soon after his arrival, and while
only twenty-one, he denounced his superior, a powerful and
popular man, for taking bribes. 'A perfect storm was raised against
the accuser', wrote Macaulay, who was in India at the time and
knew Trevelyan well. 'He was almost everywhere abused, and
very generally cut. But with a firmness and ability scarcely ever
seen in any man so young, he brought his proofs forward, and, after
an inquiry of some weeks, fully made out his case.'[2] His superior
was dismissed and Trevelyan congratulated by the Indian Government and the Directors of the East Indian Company 'in the highest
terms', though the Governor-General remarked that: 'That man
is almost always on the right side in every question; and it is well
that he is so, for he gives a most confounded deal of trouble when
he happens to take the wrong one.' Seven years later, at the age of
twenty-eight, Trevelyan married Macaulay's sister; their eldest
son was the statesman and historian, Sir George Otto Trevelyan,
and a grandson, G. M. Trevelyan. Macaulay wrote of him at that
time

He has no small talk. His mind is full of schemes of moral and political
improvement, and his zeal boils over in his talk. His topics, even in
courtship, are steam navigation, the education of the natives, the
equalization of the sugar duties, the substitution of the Roman for the
Arabic alphabet in Oriental languages.[3]

[1] Cecil Woodham-Smith, *The Great Hunger*, p. 54.
[2] Macaulay to Mrs. Cropper, 7 December 1834, G. O. Trevelyan, *Life and
Letters of Lord Macaulay*. [3] Ibid.

He had a 'very sweet' temper, always looked like a gentleman, 'particularly on horseback', and had fervent religious feelings. His face had 'a most characteristic expression of ardour and impetuosity'. In public affairs he was 'rash and uncompromising', his manner 'blunt almost to roughness, and at other times awkward'. Gladstone thought him an upright man, 'truthful and straightforward, clever and able', with a 'great capacity and appetite for work'. He was 'not an unmanageable man, though he is one who requires to be managed', needing a 'strong man over him'.[1]

In 1840 he returned to England and was appointed permanent head of the Treasury by Sir Francis Baring, Chancellor of the Exchequer, who had been impressed by his work in India. Five years later there was famine in Ireland. Trevelyan was thirty-eight, at the height of his powers, immensely conscientious, and with a huge appetite and obsession for work. Within a few months of the appointment of the first Relief Commission he became director and virtual dictator of Irish relief, but his moral rectitude, industry and complacency were not calculated to win popularity in Ireland. One of his Treasury contemporaries said of him that he suffered 'under an inordinate belief in the superiority of his own conscientiousness over that of his superiors'.[2] This great conscientiousness was a weakness: 'Acting from a genuine conviction of doing right, he found it impossible to refrain from interference, official as well as private, when he considered matters were going wrong.' Cecil Woodham-Smith, who has provided a vivid portrait of him in *The Great Hunger*, has written

His mind was powerful, his character admirably scrupulous and upright, his devotion to duty praiseworthy, but he had a remarkable insensitiveness. Since he took action only after conscientiously satisfying himself that what he proposed to do was ethical and justified, he went forward impervious to other considerations, sustained, but also blinded, by his conviction of doing right.

One consequence of this was that Trevelyan was sometimes indiscreet, as occurred in 1854 when his solicitation of the press in support of his campaign for reform gave great offence within the

---

[1] Gladstone to Lowe, 14 August 1869, Brit. Mus., G.P. Add. MSS. 44301; and to Cardwell, 15 September 1869, Brit. Mus., G.P. Add. MSS., Letter Books, 1869.

[2] Quoted by Walter Bagehot in a letter to Elizabeth Barrington's sister, 9 May 1860, in E. I. Barrington, *The Servant of All*.

Civil Service.[1] Another example is quoted by Woodham-Smith, who describes how returning from Ireland at the height of the repeal agitation he reported confidentially to the Prime Minister on the state of the country. He then succumbed to what was, for him, an almost always irresistible temptation to make his views public, and published two letters in the press. The Prime Minister, furious at the publication of the first, rebuked Trevelyan who, unmoved, coolly told Sir James Graham that although he might have been wrong to write to the *Morning Chronicle*, 'I think there cannot be any doubt that now the first portion of the letter has been published it will be better that the second portion should be also'.

Towards the end of the Irish famine he began to turn his attention to the question of administrative reform, a subject which was to absorb his time and energies during his remaining ten years at the Treasury. When he resigned in 1859 to return to India, the seeds of many of his reforms had been sown, some had taken root, and one, the Civil Service Commission was growing steadily. Before the voyage he asked Algernon West to supply him with Blue Books to entertain him on his journey, 'saying that he devoured them all with avidity, and that [West] could not provide him with too many'.[2]

As Governor of Madras he displayed the same uncompromising attitude which had marked his earlier service in India. Within a few months of arrival he publicly criticized the financial proposals submitted to the supreme Government by his former ministerial colleague, James Wilson, now Finance Member to the Governor-General's Council. Wilson's budget had been well received, but the unauthorized publication by Trevelyan of the minutes of the Madras Government stating that additional taxation was unnecessary, together with his own minute which read 'too like a political pamphlet',[3] caused acute embarrassment in India and at home. The storm which broke about Trevelyan's head was abated only by his recall by the British Government.

Wilson had expected trouble from Trevelyan, he confided to his brother-in-law, Walter Bagehot, but never imagined 'that he would proceed to such extremities'.[4] The emotional and bitter

[1] See below, Chapter 3, pp. 59–62.
[2] Algernon West, *Recollections 1832–66*, i. 313.
[3] Walter Bagehot, *The Economist*, 12 May 1860.
[4] Wilson to Bagehot, 4 July 1860, E. I. Barrington, *The Servant of All*.

characterization of Trevelyan which Wilson penned in the heat of
the moment would have been instantly recognizable and
endorsed by others who had suffered similarly at Trevelyan's
hands.

He has so impulsive a mind, so ill balanced, with such an overwhelming
confidence in himself, no matter what the subject might be, equally to
command a squadron, lead an army, or regenerate the civil Government
of a country: with a large smattering upon everything but profound in
nothing; with a dull apprehension but the most dogged obstinacy I ever
saw: and with an inordinate vanity and love of notoriety to be gratified;
without the slightest judgment or discretion or forethought, of calculation of consequences: all these characteristics lead a man so heedlessly
into danger and control him so completely as to leave him hardly a
responsible being.

  Convinced that he was right, it was entirely in character for
Trevelyan to speak out publicly and fearlessly without much
thought of the consequences, but it is interesting to speculate
whether in this instance his motives were entirely uninfluenced by
personal considerations. At the Treasury he had quarrelled on
several occasions with Wilson, most notably over the reorganization of the department when, for once, Trevelyan's own proposals
had been rejected.[1] An earlier quarrel had led to Gladstone's
intercession, but before the proposed interview with the Chancellor
took place, Wilson came and said it had all been settled: he had
spoken strongly to Trevelyan who was thoroughly ashamed of
himself and had promised to behave better in the future. Two
minutes later Trevelyan came and said he had been obliged to
speak very severely to Wilson, who had burst into tears.[2]
  Wilson died soon after Trevelyan's recall from India. Ironically,
his rival now succeeded him as Finance Member, an appointment
which appeared to vindicate Trevelyan's earlier course of action,
although it had been offered first to George Arbuthnot, Trevelyan's
deputy at the Treasury. On his retirement three years later he
returned to England. His last years were marked by the same
vigorous reforming zeal, and he campaigned enthusiastically and
successfully for the abolition of the purchase of army commissions.

[1] See below, Chapter 1, p. 10.
[2] Algernon West, *Recollections 1832–66*, ii. 209.

THE CIVIL SERVICE IN 1854

About 42,000 people were employed in the 'public departments and offices' in 1854, a third as secretaries, under-secretaries, collectors, comptrollers, accountants, and clerks. More still, about 26,000, did more mechanical work, often out-doors, and included postmen, sorters, weighers, stampers, tide-waiters, and the like The remainder were employed as messengers, office-keepers, and servants.[1] Not all of them were employed on a permanent basis, but before the passing of the 1859 Superannuation Act it was difficult to distinguish prolonged temporary service from permanent tenure.

The term 'Civil Service' was not in common use much before the 1850s. It was a 'phrase popularly used for general convenience, and represents the large body of men by whose labours the executive business of the country is carried on', wrote the author of the most comprehensive and accurate of the many handbooks on the Civil Service which appeared after the establishment of the Civil Service Commission.[2] 'Discrepancies and minor distinctions' were innumerable. 'Each office has its specialty, and every department is governed by its own rules and traditions, as its members are remunerated by distinct rates of pay. The term "Civil Service" therefore represents a thing heterogeneous in its nature, embracing posts of every different *status* and widely differing value.' Sir Louis Mallet, Permanent Under-Secretary of State for India, told the Playfair Commission in 1874 that 'under the old system it was not called the "Civil Service" . . . one never talked about going into the Civil Service. When you were asked what you were, you said that you were in a Government Office'.[3] When Trevelyan entered the Treasury in 1840 he was told that 'there was no *Civil Service* but only the *establishment of this or that civil office*'.[4]

[1] Estimates of the size of the Civil Service have varied with the definition of the term 'civil servant'. These are taken from the 1853 return prepared for the *Select Committee on Civil Service Superannuation*, P.P., 1856, IX, Appendix 7.

[2] J. C. Parkinson, *Under Government: An Official Key to the Civil Service of the Crown* (1859, 1st edition). Parkinson was an accountant in the Audit Department; in ten years he published five editions of his book. H. White's, *A Guide to the Civil Service* had run through ten editions by 1869.

[3] 1st Report of the *Civil Service (Playfair) Inquiry Commission*, 1875. P.P., 1875, XXIII, minutes of evidence qu. 4257.

[4] Trevelyan to C. P. Measor, Hon. Sec. to the Committee of the Civil Service College, 27 May 1867, published in *The Civil Service Gazette*, 1 June 1867.

There were almost as many 'services' as there were departments, their diverse organization and administrative practice emphasizing the departmentalism and fragmentation of which Trevelyan and Northcote had complained. Civil Service handbooks and guides were indispensable to those contemplating a career in a department before the introduction of open competition. Parkinson classified situations

> to enable the aspirant for Government employment to ascertain at a glance the respective advantages held out to him by each department of the State, the indispensable qualifications he must himself possess before he is eligible for admission into such department, and the particular channel of patronage through which he may best hope to obtain a nomination.

Patronage meant the control of appointments to public offices, and was usually, but not invariably, exercised by a minister or a board of commissioners or trustees; merit and ability might or might not be considered. The reformers, especially Trevelyan and, later, Lowe and Lingen, rarely used the word in this neutral sense; by patronage they usually meant 'jobbery'. After 1854 the use of the word pejoratively became increasingly common.

A few ministers, principally the First Lord of the Treasury and the Home Secretary, exercised patronage in departments other than their own. With a large number of subordinate departments, employing three-quarters of all those in the Service,[1] the Treasury was in a very special position. Foremost in importance were the Revenue Departments: Customs, Inland Revenue, Woods and Forests, and the Post Office. Although the latter had a minister, who had a cabinet seat for all but three of the years 1854–74, the Treasury nominated to the positions of country postmaster and keeper of receiving office. Another subordinate department, the Office of Works and Public Buildings, also had a minister who was sometimes included in the cabinet, but the patronage of his department belonged to the Treasury, although in 1853 the First Commissioner of Works tried unsuccessfully to claim the right to exercise it.[2]

---

[1] In 1856 of the estimated 42,000 civil servants, 32,898 were employed in the Treasury and its subordinate departments. Tabular statement of numbers in offices under the Treasury, Bod., T.L.B., xxxvi, 91.

[2] The other departments subordinate to the Treasury were: Audit Office; Exchequer; National Debt Office; Paymaster-General's Office; Mint; Paymaster

The nomination to most of the appointments in these and the other subordinate departments was in the gift of the First Lord of the Treasury, but in practice the Patronage Secretary disposed the patronage on his behalf, though the Audit Office clerkships—next to those in the Treasury itself, considered the best at the Treasury's disposal—were usually reserved by the First Lord for himself.[1] A substantial part of the Treasury's patronage was provided by the large Customs' departments where the Treasury appointed to eight different classes of 'in-door' clerkships and eleven different classes of 'out-door' posts. Here and elsewhere, the Treasury surrendered the greater part of its patronage on the introduction of open competition in 1870.[2]

In one or two small offices the patronage was exercised by a minister in another department; the Home Secretary for example nominated to positions in the Factory Inspectors' Office, the Metropolitan Police Courts, the Metropolitan Police, the Prisons Department, and the Royal Observatory, Edinburgh. But most of them enjoyed an independent status, like the Charitable Trusts Commission and the patronage was exercised by the commissioners or trustees themselves.

While patronage was universal, it was adapted to the wishes and requirements of individual departments. Each prescribed its own rules: some required no more than a simple nomination, in others, nomination was followed by a qualifying examination, while a few obliged several nominated candidates to compete for the same vacancy. Other variables included the age of entry, health requirements, and subjects of examination.

Office hours, salaries, discipline, leave, and superannuation were similarly diverse, reflecting the different status and traditions of departments, and the different content and complexity of their

---

[1] *Notes on Treasury Patronage*, 1853, a private and confidential printed pamphlet. Brit. Mus., G.P. Add. MSS. 44579, pt. II, fo. 221. It suggests that the extent of Treasury patronage was not as limited as Edward Hughes argues in 'Civil Service Reform 1853–55', *Public Administration*, xxxii, Spring 1954.

[2] See below, Chapter 4, pp. 92–3.

---

of Civil Services (Ireland); Public Works Loan Commissioners; Queen's and Lord Treasurer's Remembrancer (Scotland); Paymaster of Civil Record Branch; Office of Land Revenue Records; General Register Offices (England and Scotland); Public Record Office; Stationery Office; London Gazette Office; Board of Works (Ireland). This list is compiled from a statement of clerks in offices under the Treasury in 1856, Bod., T.L.B., xxxvi, 91.

work. East-end clerks, those employed in the Customs, Audit Office, Mint, and Merchant Seamen's Office for example, complained that their status, pay and conditions of work were inferior to those enjoyed by clerks employed in offices to the west of Temple Bar. Mobility between departments is a useful index of a unified and integrated Service; in 1854 there was very little, except at the very top where a senior civil servant supported by an influential patron sometimes obtained the headship of another department. More frequently, a minister looked outside the Service when such a post fell vacant and there was no obvious successor within the department. Trevelyan was brought to the Treasury from the Indian Civil Service, Herman Merivale was brought to the Colonial Office from Oxford, where he had been Professor of Political Economy.

Among the civil servants there was little cohesiveness. As individual members, not of a Service or profession, but of a 'fortuitous collection of units without cohesion or corporate character', *esprit de corps* hardly existed. Loyalty was to the department or, more accurately, to the patron to whom one looked for preferment. Nevertheless, here and there, men were beginning to combine on an *ad hoc* basis to seek the redress of common grievances. While these early combinations were mainly of men drawn from the same department, occasionally some of them combined in a wider association, such as the inter-departmental committee which petitioned Parliament in 1852 for the abolition of the superannuation contributions which were deducted from salaries. This campaign, which had begun four years earlier, was provided with a public platform for its views and a forum for debate in the weekly pages of the first Civil Service newspaper, *The Civil Service Gazette*, which appeared for the first time on 1 January 1853. The ultimate success of the campaign several years later provided a practical demonstration for civil servants throughout the Service of the lesson which *The Civil Service Gazette* taught week by week: 'that union is strength and disunion is weakness'.

CIVIL SERVANTS AND MINISTERS

Mid-Victorian cabinets averaged fifteen members, and included most, but not all, ministers with departmental responsibilities. Some were omitted when seats were found for the Lord Chancellor, and one or two others with minimal or nominal duties, such as the

Chancellor of the Duchy of Lancaster, the Lord Privy Seal, or the Paymaster-General. Aberdeen's coalition of 'all the talents' had fifteen ministers in June 1854, but he left out the President of the Board of Trade, the Chief Secretary for Ireland, and the Post-master-General.

It is not easy to generalize about the relations between civil servants and ministers at this time, and to evaluate the contribution which each made to the formulation of policy. The constitutional position was clear: the doctrine of the individual responsibility of ministers meant, as Palmerston had explained earlier to the Queen, that ministers were expected to do their own work. They were 'liable any day and every day to defend themselves in Parliament; in order to do this they must be minutely acquainted with all the details of the business of their office, and the only way of being constantly armed with such information is to conduct and direct those details themselves'.[1] Acceptance of this doctrine had led to the growing disuse of the board as an instrument of government; by 1853 administration by a minister with a clear and undivided responsibility to Parliament was the preferred and normal arrangement.[2]

The tradition of personal involvement and responsibility to which Palmerston subscribed while at the Foreign Office persisted there throughout the 1850s. In 1854, and indeed much later, it was still possible for a Foreign Secretary to see everything which entered and left the office. Arthur Otway, in evidence to a Select Committee, declared that 'it used to make him melancholy to see the heap of trash sent up to the Secretary of State, every paper of which he had to read and put his initials to'.[3] Palmerston's Permanent Under-Secretaries 'were no more than mere clerks and did not interfere in matters of policy', a tradition which Edmund Hammond found unchanged when he was appointed Permanent Under-Secretary in 1854.[4] For many years after, he was 'little more than a superior clerk', did a 'good deal of elementary

[1] A. C. Benson and Viscount Esher, *Letters of Queen Victoria, 1837–1861*, i. 106.
[2] F. M. G. Willson, 'Ministries and Boards: Some Aspects of Administrative Development since 1832', *Public Administration*, xxxiii, Spring 1955.
[3] *Select Committee on Diplomatic and Consular Services, 1870*, P.P., 1871, VII, qu. 1146.
[4] C. K. Webster, 'Lord Palmerston at Work, 1830–1841', *Politica*, i (1934–5), 137.

drafting', and 'at times of pressure even put his hand to copying'.[1]

At the Colonial Office and the Treasury the tradition was quite different: customarily the senior civil servants had played an important part in the formulation of policy. Sir James Stephen and Sir Henry Taylor were both extremely influential in the development of Colonial policy, although there were several notable occasions when the advice of even these two powerful civil servants was rejected by the Colonial Secretary;[2] Trevelyan had been a virtual dictator of famine relief in Ireland in the mid 1840s. Between these two departments on the one hand, and the Foreign Office on the other, there were infinite variations. Where the line was drawn between ministers and civil servants depended upon the tradition and practice of the department, the temperament and ideas of individual civil servants, the status, disposition, and zealousness of ministers, and the volume and complexity of the work. Nevertheless, by the 1850s there is a clearly defined trend away from the individual responsibility of ministers as defined and practised earlier. As the volume of government business grew with the increase in government activity, and the content and administration of legislation became more complex and technical, it was becoming more difficult for the minister to oversee all the business of his department and to decide all policy issues for himself.

The trend away from the Foreign Office 'model' is illustrated by the changing relationship between ministers and civil servants which occurred at the Board of Trade in the administration of railway legislation. Between 1840–6 the political heads of the Board were in close touch with all the details of the railway business. 'Although the officers had had great influence on questions of the highest importance, there had been no class of routine business in which the political heads normally took no part. . . . The Department's decisions were Dalhousie's decisions. A paper which did not bear his instructions for action was so unusual as to call for explanation.'[3] From 1851 onwards, however, the civil servants were dealing with the great majority of cases which came before the Board. While the President and Vice-President continued to take

---

[1] Hammond to Russell, 3 December 1861, P[ublic] R[ecord] O[ffice], Russell Papers, 30/22/28.

[2] H. L. Hall, *The Colonial Office*, pp. 268–9.

[3] Henry Parris, *Government and the Railways in Nineteenth-Century Britain*, p. 132.

responsibility for all the Board's decisions, they were now personally involved in only a small proportion of them. 'Ministerial
responsibility had become a fiction', Parris concludes.[1] The same
tendency is apparent elsewhere, although the change was sometimes more gradual. Cardwell was still able to exercise a personal
supervision of the various divisions of the Colonial Office in the
middle of the 1860s, and to write many of the dispatches himself
when the matters involved a policy-decision;[2] as late as the
eighties, almost everything went to the Colonial Secretary. The
Foreign Secretary was still able to see all incoming and outgoing
dispatches when Hammond left the Foreign Office in 1874,
although by that time the Permanent Under-Secetary had been
recognized as a policy-adviser.[3]

Where the volume of business was growing quickly, or the content of the work was technical, the civil servants appeared to have
had more influence, or to have become influential more quickly.
This tendency is particularly noticeable in those departments
whose responsibilities lay in the field of economic and social
policy. In his study of the Passenger Acts, MacDonagh concludes
that ministers had no permanent and important influence upon the
development of emigrant protection in the first half of the nineteenth century, where the responsibility for policy-making and
advice on policy rested with James Stephen, Elliot and Murdoch
of the administrators, and the emigration officers, the 'field
executives'.[4]

The Privy Council, which during the nineteenth century was
'used as a kind of potting shed for new administrative plants'
accumulated a number of disparate functions in the field of
economic and social policy.[5] The organization of the office was
vague and loose, its component parts often scattered in different
buildings round Whitehall. Fragmentation of structure and
organization, and loose political control, tended to increase the
influence of the permanent civil servants. The Clerk of the Council
had great influence with the Queen and Palmerston; and Chadwick

---
[1] Ibid., p. 209.
[2] G. J. Sellars, 'Edward Cardwell at the Colonial Office', 1864–66, pp. 43–46 (unpublished B. Litt. thesis).
[3] M. A. Anderson, 'Edmund Hammond, Permanent Under-Secretary of State for Foreign Affairs, 1854–73' (unpublished Ph.D. thesis).
[4] O. MacDonagh, *A Pattern of Government Growth 1800–1860*, pp. 330–5.
[5] K. B. Smellie, *One Hundred Years of English Government*, p. 90.

wrote in 1847 of his envy of 'the steady progress which Kay-Shuttleworth had made since 1839 as Secretary of the Education Committee'.[1] The tradition of official initiative was continued by his successor, Ralph Lingen, who exercised great influence over his minister, Lowe, particularly in the introduction of their scheme for 'payment by results'. The medical reformer, Sir John Simon, within two years of his appointment, freed himself from complete subordination to the Privy Council Office. Supported by the Lord President he secured his promotion to Secretary of his own formally and physically independent Medical Department, 'deciding his own programme of action, controlling his own clerical and professional staff and conducting his own local correspondence'.[2] Simon's biographer concludes that

In the technical responsibilities of government, as has been shown for factory affairs, the political chiefs were often unable to lead in the creation and implementation of policy. This was particularly true of public health. After 1858 the influence of the permanent civil servants was greater than it had been under the Presidencies of Hall and Cowper or under the non-responsible Commissioners of Chadwick's Board of Health. Though the responsible politician might rarely serve as a brake he usually became the willing instrument of Simon's policies; and the disruption which the years 1871–76 brought to the sanitary development resulted largely from the dominance of another civil servant. The overloading of departments, a fluctuating and never intense political concern with health, the increasing volume, range and scientific nature of the sanitary work, as Lingen said, made it more difficult than before for lay superiors to check the assertions of the experts and administrators.[3]

Whatever the contribution of individual ministers and civil servants in the decision-making process, it remained true in 1854 as previously, that no more than a handful of the senior members of the permanent staff contributed to the preparation and formulation of policy. The vast majority were engaged in carrying out decisions made by ministers and their two or three advisers, and were remote from the policy-making process. Those nearest the minister often appeared reluctant to share, or incapable of sharing, their responsibility with those beneath them, and in consequence they were often grossly over-worked. Trevelyan worked three

[1] S. E. Finer, *The Life and Times of Sir Edwin Chadwick*, p. 305.
[2] Royston Lambert, *Sir John Simon*, p. 328.   [3] Lambert, pp. 613–14.

hours before breakfast reading papers for which there was insufficient time at the office; three of his senior colleagues, T. C. Brooksbanks, an expert on loans and financial matters, George Arbuthnot, and Edwin Crafer died in office. The reluctance of senior civil servants to delegate or share responsibility was often justified. Many of their junior colleagues, who had advanced slowly through the ranks of the establishment, engaged for most part on work which called for little initiative or judgement were unfitted to assume that responsibility, their minds dulled by years of routine drudgery; and not a few were 'incapable or indolent', having no greater claim to preferment than the length of their service.

Life in a department was comfortable and secure, if generally unexciting. Most clerks, especially those newly recruited, were remote from the real business of the office, where ministers were advised and decisions made. They spent their early years, some their whole career, on routine and humdrum tasks which neither taxed their ability nor fully absorbed their time and energy. Until the invention of carbon paper and the typewriter, no reliable and wholly satisfactory method was known of duplicating papers and documents, and almost all copying was done by hand; letterpresses were in use in one or two departments, but the copies obtained from them were often unsatisfactory and more expensive per folio. Some departments employed temporary copyists and writers for this task, but all had occasion to employ their junior clerks on some copying; indeed routine work of this kind was held to be a necessary and valuable training for higher office.

While the work given to a young clerk might be dull and uninteresting and opportunities for the display of initiative and sound judgement few, contemporary accounts suggest that life in a government department was not without attraction for the able and energetic, as well as the 'incapable or indolent'. Trollope, describing his days as a young clerk at the Post Office, recalled that

There was a comfortable sitting-room upstairs, devoted to the use of some one of our number who in turn was required to remain on the place all night. Hither one or two of us would adjourn after lunch, and play *ecarté* for an hour or two. . . . Here we used to have suppers and card-parties at night—great symposiums with much smoking of tobacco.[1]

Time sometimes weighed heavily on the hands of the Treasury

---

[1] Anthony Trollope, *An Autobiography*, p. 53.

junior clerks. Kempe recalls how occasionally they would be joined at lunch-time by 'equally bored' young Guardsmen from neighbouring barracks and together played cricket in a large room at the top of the office. In the Foreign Office one of the attic rooms was set aside for the 'young gentlemen' of the office. Here in the 'Nursery' they used to pass away their spare time, a 'piano was provided —not by H.M.'s Government, but at their own cost—as well as foils, single-sticks, boxing gloves, and other sources of amusement'.[1] The 'young gentlemen' in the upper rooms used to flirt with the pretty dressmakers who occupied rooms in one of the houses opposite the office; and in summer let down strings of red tape from the top windows and haul up bottles of strawberries sold by fruit-sellers in the street below. Pea-shooting and dousing organ-grinders were other favourite amusements. Hertslet remembered one offending organ-grinder, drowned with water by the young gentlemen, who threw a large stone through the window of an upper room. Such behaviour was not peculiar to the Foreign Office. Edmund Yates recalled a similar incident in the Post Office when there was 'a tremendous row, not unconnected with the peppering, with peas and pellets of saturated blotting paper, of the passers-by'.[2]

The 'young gentlemen' of the Foreign Office had the time, opportunity and inclination for practical jokes. Palmerston, whose nickname was 'Protocol Palmerston' at the Foreign Office, was once called to witness an accidental fire in the Manuscript Library. A young clerk who happened to be passing, put his head round the door and seeing Palmerston called out: 'For God's sake take care of the protocols.' The skeleton of a black cat, accidentally 'walled-up' in the library bookshelves, was put into a red dispatch box and sent up to the Foreign Secretary for his inspection. A dog named 'Pam' was given the run of the old Downing Street Foreign Office, wandering through different rooms at will.

Other details recalled by Hertslet conjure up an almost Dickensian scene. The rooms were lighted by oil lamps and wax candles, the unconsumed ends of which were the housekeeper's perquisite. Coals for the open fires had to be carried up the public staircases. In the old Foreign Office building in Downing Street one man 'had a yoke across his shoulders, and carried up two scuttles at a

[1] Sir Edward Hertslet, *Recollections of the Old Foreign Office*, p. 25.
[2] Edmund Yates, *His Recollections and Experiences*, pp. 97–8.

time'. Each morning 'a roll of bread, round in shape, and slightly sweetened and a decanter of water'—the 'Prison allowance'—was placed in each room by the housekeeper. At Christmas nearly every clerk received a small, double-bladed penknife in a neat little red leather case.

Barnacle junior was not alone in singeing his calves at the parental fire in the Circumlocution Office. At the Admiralty a clerk wore kid gloves in the office for fear that he should dirty his hands with ink; and Algernon West remembered 'the figure of a little chief clerk, always dressed in a black and snuffy suit, who occasionally came to the office in the morning dressed in a great frilled shirt front, and evening clothes, and announced that, as he was going to dine out that evening, he should not be at the office the next day'.[1] Edmund Yates, Trollope's literary successor at the Post Office, conveys the same relaxed, unhurried atmosphere described by Hertslet. Colonel Maberley, the Secretary of the Post Office

used to arrive about eleven o'clock, and announce his arrival by tearing at the bell for his breakfast. This bell brought the head messenger, whose services he arrogated to himself, who, being a venerable-looking and eminently respectable personage, probably well-to-do in the world, was disgusted at having to kneel at the Colonel's feet, and receive the Colonel's dirty boots into his arms with the short adjuration, 'Now, Francis, my straps!' . . . The custom was for certain clerks of recognised status, who had a distinct portion of the official work in their charge, to submit the reports which had been received from the postmasters or district surveyors, on complaints or suggestions of the public, to the Secretary, and receive his instructions as to the course to be pursued, or the style of reply to be sent. This performance we used to call 'taking in papers to the Colonel', and a very curious performance it was.

The Colonel, a big, heavily-built, elderly man, would sit in a big chair, with his handkerchief over his knees and two or three private letters before him. Into a closely neighbouring seat the clerk would drop, placing his array of official documents on the table. Greetings exchanged, the Colonel, reading his private letters, would dig his elbow into the clerk's ribs, saying, 'Well, my good fellow, what have you got there—very important papers, eh?' 'I don't know, sir; some of them are, perhaps—' 'Yes, yes my good fellow; no doubt *you* think they're very important: *I* call them damned twopenny-ha'penny! Now, read, my good fellow, read!' Thus adjured, the clerk would commence reading

[1] Algernon West, *Recollections 1832–66*, i. 71.

C

aloud one of his documents. The Colonel, still half engaged with his private correspondence, would hear enough to make him keep up a running commentary of disparaging grunts, 'Pooh! stuff! upon my soul!' etc. Then the clerk, having come to the end of the manuscript, would stop, waiting for orders; and there would ensue a dead silence, broken by the Colonel, who, having finished his private letters, would look up and say, 'Well, my good fellow, well?' 'That's all sir'. 'And quite enough too. Go on to the next!' 'But what shall I say to this applicant, sir?' 'Say to him to go and be damned, my good fellow!' and on our reading of those instructions we had very frequently to act.[1]

When Yates entered the Post Office in 1847 it was customary to have lunch brought into the office from a neighbouring tavern, but later Colonel Maberley's 'sense of fitness of things was annoyed by encountering strange persons wandering through the lobbies, balancing tin-covered dishes and bearing foaming pewter pots'. Lunching-in was forbidden and the clerks allowed to go out for a quarter of an hour —'a marvellously elastic quarter of an hour'. Before the ban, Yates occasionally lunched off two dozen bottles of stout, but gave up the habit after a new Postmaster-General came across them unexpectedly on a tour of inspection.

Trollope and Yates were not so very exceptional in combining a literary with an official career. The tradition of a 'lyrical profession' was a long and distinguished one; the line included Chaucer, Spenser, Milton, Pepys, and Burns. When Northcote and Trevelyan wrote their report, Matthew Arnold had been an Inspector of Schools for two years; Arthur Hugh Clough was an examiner in the Education Department; Coventry Patmore was an Assistant Keeper in the British Museum; and Henry Taylor, then at the peak of his official career at the Colonial Office, was still revered as an important poet after the success of his verse-drama, *Philip van Artewalde*, twenty years earlier. As the author of the profoundly influential, but much less highly esteemed, *The Statesman*, Taylor had proclaimed himself a man of letters and the sound man of letters as the ideal raw material for the higher ranks of the Civil Service. His essay was the *locus classicus* of the view later espoused by Jowett and Trevelyan, that civil servants should have a general, non-professional education, and an ability to express themselves. In their report, Northcote and Trevelyan stressed the importance of a 'competitive *literary* examination'.

[1] Yates, pp. 97–8.

In 1854 literary ambitions, even a literary career, could still be gratified within Government service, as Thomas Love Peacock and John Stuart Mill at East India House, and Trollope at the Post Office, had done a dozen years earlier. The demands made upon a young man's time and creative energy often allowed ample time and opportunity for writing. Tom Taylor, Secretary of the Local Government Act Office, was one of the most popular and prolific of mid-Victorian dramatists. In the sixties and seventies, the Privy Council Office had a considerable literary reputation. Besides Arthur Helps, who was Clerk of Council, the permanent staff included Henry Reeve, Editor of the *Edinburgh Quarterly*, and the Rev. W. Harness, an author who had been a friend of Byron.

Security and modest financial comfort were attractive to the writer; the short official hours left time for writing, and the flexibility of office procedure and working conditions made it possible to pursue other activities without too much difficulty. When his health began to fail Taylor worked at home for the last twelve years of his official life. 'The civil servant who had a daily pouch sent down to his home in Bournemouth is still remembered as an almost legendary figure in the club talk of the Service.'[1] Above all, in the mid-Victorian age there was the example, encouragement and stimulus to poets, writers, and dramatists from the statesmen themselves, many of whom were, or aspired to be, 'men of letters'. The world of politics and administration provided a congenial environment in which writers moved freely. Breakfast parties at Holland House, Lansdowne House, or Downing Street, united cabinet ministers, peers, poets, and dramatists.

[1] Leo Silberman, Introductory Essay to Henry Taylor's *The Statesman*, p. xlix.

PART ONE

THE TREASURY

1

ORGANIZATION

INTRODUCTION

THE Treasury was the department of departments. While others dealt with particular branches or interests in the Public Service, the Treasury pervaded all, 'the heart of our whole administrative system'.[1] With both controlling and executive functions, it exercised through the Chancellor of the Exchequer the responsibilities of a central financial authority, which Gladstone described as the collection of revenue, the custody of revenue, the initiation of financial legislation, and the control of public expenditure.[2] The latter was peculiarly the function of the departmental Treasury; the collection and custody of revenue were largely executive functions undertaken under its supervision by the Revenue and other subordinate financial departments.

Legislative authority for the power to control the whole of the civil expenditure and the right to 'judge every measure increasing or tending to increase directly or indirectly, the public expenditure' was granted in 1866 when Parliament passed the Exchequer and Audit Act. The claim to do so was very much older. The chief advocate of a more extensive and effective Treasury control of public expenditure in the first half of the nineteenth century was

---

[1] Hamilton to Stansfeld, 21 October 1869, P.R.O., *Hamilton Semi-official Correspondence*, iv.

[2] Memo by Gladstone on 'Commissioners of the Treasury', 20 September 1873, Brit. Mus., G.P. Add. MSS. 44761, fo. 179.

Sir George Harrison, the first Assistant Secretary to the Treasury. Appointed to the new posts of 'assistant secretary' and 'law clerk' in 1805 when the department was extensively reorganized, he held the former position until his retirement twenty-one years later. In his writings, in evidence to Select Committees, and above all through his official conduct, he developed the conception of the Treasury as a supervising and controlling department.[1] Briefly, he argued that the Treasury was 'the first department of the state', and that the Treasury Lords 'are responsible to Parliament and the country as the legitimate and only constitutional advisers of the Crown' in all matters relating to 'the powers and authorities which the Crown, by its ancient constitutional prerogative, might exercise with regard to its revenues'. In this respect, within the limitations of the Common Law, and unless specifically limited by Parliament, the Treasury's discretion was absolute. Claiming that the Treasury was the sole constitutional judge of the propriety and expediency of expenditure, Harrison maintained that it followed that 'the Treasury is a *superintending*, and *directing*, not an *executive* department'.

This conception of the Treasury as a supervising and controlling department he sought to justify by reference to the authority of ancient precedent and usage, and by using the antique and confused law of the prerogative. With these weapons he justified the right of the Treasury to control the whole of the expenditure of the Board of Ordnance, emphasizing the 'difference between the *controlling* functions of the one department, and the *executive* functions of the other'. This novel distinction, derived possibly from the traditional relationship between the Treasury and its subordinate departments, was generalized to justify the extension of Treasury control over all the spending departments. Harrison's conceptual framework challenged the accepted view of each department as a separate entity responsible for its own finance, and provided a basis 'for scrutinizing the entire administration from the point of view of its integration in a single system of finance'.[2]

The need for wider and more efficacious Treasury control of public expenditure was recognized outside the department as well. In 1818 the First Lord of the Treasury, the First Lord of the

---

[1] The account which follows is based mainly upon J. R. Torrance, 'Sir George Harrison and the growth of bureaucracy in the early nineteenth century', *The English Historical Review*, LXXXIII, January 1968.

[2] Torrance, p. 67.

Admiralty, and the Master-General of the Ordnance agreed 'that no department of large expenditure ought ever to be placed beyond the controlling superintendence of the Board of the Treasury'.[1] The previous year a Select Committee on Finance had reported to the House of Commons that it was necessary to bring all financial subjects within the Treasury's purview, and recommended that

It should be made a rule of the Council Office, that every proposition involving any increase of public expense should, according to the nature of the case, either be submitted to a Committee of the Council, consisting of such Members as may be connected with the Treasury Department, or be made by the Council Office the subject of a direct reference to, and report from, the Treasury to that Office before it is presented to His Majesty for his final approbation.[2]

But while the Treasury's right to control expenditure more widely was becoming increasingly recognized, difficulty was experienced in exercising that right effectively. In 1828 another Select Committee reported that 'the ancient and wise control vested by our Financial Policy in the hands of the Treasury over all the departments connected with the Public Expenditure has been a great degree set aside'.[3] Although departments laid their annual estimates before the Treasury, it was unable to control their expenditure subsequently. The Committee called for 'a restoration to the Treasury of its ancient authority . . . in preventing any increase of salary or extra allowance, or any of the emoluments being granted without a Minute expressing the approbation of the Board of the Treasury'.[4] Their recommendation led to no immediate improvement.

Before 1845 none of the departments appear to have applied to the Treasury for authority to exceed a vote included in the estimates. The following year, however, a Treasury Minute obliged them to obtain prior sanction before the surplus on one vote could be transferred to meet a deficiency elsewhere. This was endorsed subsequently by a resolution of the House of Commons; the power to appropriate surpluses on particular votes to cover deficiencies on others in the naval and military departments was conferred

[1] T.M. 13 March 1818, quoted in Alpheus Todd, *On Parliamentary Government*, i. chapter v.
[2] Quoted by G. Arbuthnot before the P[ublic] A[ccounts] C[ommittee], 1862, P.P., 1862, XI, qu. 665.
[3] *2nd Report from Select Committee on Public Income and Expenditure*, 1828, P.P., 1828, V. [4] Ibid.

formally by the Appropriation Act for 1846–7. Further Treasury
Minutes followed explaining in more detail how the power was to
be used and providing for the Treasury's ultimate control in all
cases of unforeseen and unprovided expenditure.

The increase of public business generally made rigorous control
of expenditure by the Treasury more necessary, a Select Committee reported to the House of Commons in 1850. Four years
later it was claimed that there was 'no principle of finance more
important than that of maintaining an efficient control over
departmental expenditure such as can only be exercised by a central
office like the Treasury'. By now it was being urged that the control
of the Treasury should be exercised constantly to prevent additions
to the existing staff of a department, or any increase of salary, extra
allowance or other emolument without its written authority. The
source of all administrative authority for expenditure was the
Treasury, the Secretary of the Audit Office explained.

The right of the Treasury to determine what the several departments
may spend and what they must not spend, though modified occasionally
by certain special acts, is incontestable and rests upon an unbroken
prescription which has accordingly the force of law. The Treasury,
moreover, may exercise this right, provided they do not transgress any
Parliamentary requirements, in any way they please ... the power of
determining by what means the controlling authority of the Crown
over the public expenditure can best be maintained belongs of right to
the Treasury, and the decision of the Treasury as to what expenditure is
or is not sufficiently authorised is final and without appeal.[1]

Macaulay spoke on the eve of the 1866 legislation, but his
explanation to the Public Accounts Committee of the Treasury's
constitutional position with regard to the control of expenditure
may be applied equally to the circumstances of 1854. However, in
later chapters it will be argued that at that time, and throughout
the next twenty years, there were important practical limitations
to the immense authority claimed here for the Treasury, limitations
which were not much disturbed by the statutory powers conferred
upon the Treasury by the Exchequer and Audit Act.

THE TREASURY IN 1854

The site upon which William Kent built the new Treasury in 1737
was inured to conflict: the Cockpit, a familiar landmark in the

[1] Report of P.A.C., 1865, P.P., 1865, X, Appendix I, para. 70.

Whitehall of the sixteenth and seventeenth centuries, had once stood there. Kent's Treasury was the department's main residence in the nineteenth century: the Whitehall Treasury begun by Sir John Soane in 1827 and reconstructed by Sir John Barry twenty years later was used by the department in 1854 merely as an entrance to Kent's building which stood directly behind it. Facing Horse Guards Parade and overlooking the gardens of Downing Street, the situation of the central department of government, at the heart of Whitehall, was well adapted to the limitations of communication and transport in the middle of the nineteenth century. Close by, in the southern part of the Whitehall Treasury, were the offices of the Privy Council and its committees; to the north, the Board of Trade, the Board of Control, and the Home Office, until in 1873 the latter moved to its present site between Downing Street and King Charles Street. Farther along Whitehall was the office of the Paymaster-General; next to it, Admiralty House and the Horse Guards, although a part of each of the two great war departments was housed in Somerset House and Pall Mall respectively. Until its demolition in 1876, No. 14 Downing Street was the home of the Colonial Office; adjacent to it was the Foreign Office which consisted of a block of several very old private houses thrown into one. The occupants of both departments suffered great physical discomfort: at one time workmen had been employed night and day to prevent one room from collapsing; and the basement had to be pumped out once a day, twice in wet weather. 'It is to be hoped the building will fall (for fall I believe it will) at night', a Colonial Secretary exclaimed on one occasion.[1] Before that hope was fulfilled the Foreign Office moved in 1861 to temporary accommodation, and three years later to their new quarters in Scott's building overlooking St. James's Park, where they were joined subsequently by the Home, Colonial and India Offices. Most other departments were to be found in Whitehall or near to it. One or two were situated farther afield: the Customs Office in Thames Street, uncomfortably close to Billingsgate, the Post Office in St. Martin's-le-Grand, while the Board of Inland Revenue shared Somerset House with part of the Admiralty Office.

[1] P.R.O., C.O./323/262. Even Kent's solid building was unable to withstand the vibrations of a mangle operated by the Treasury housekeeper in her laundry: the Revenue Room ceiling collapsed.

Neither the First Lord nor the Chancellor of the Exchequer had rooms in the Treasury, but Downing Street was less than a minute's walk along a passage leading from Kent's building. The working head of the department, the Financial Secretary to the Treasury, was always in residence. 'At the office from 11 till 4; at the House from 4.30 till 12.30' was a routine familiar to other Treasury Secretaries besides Hugh Childers.[1] The Board Room—which until 1856 was used for the twice-weekly formal meetings of the Treasury Board—was later occupied by the Chief Whip, his secretaries, and his assistants, the Junior Lords of the Treasury. No more than eighty other people worked in the building at any one time between 1854–74, of whom between twenty and thirty were messengers and office-keepers. Besides the Treasury, Kent's building housed the office of the Treasury Solicitor.

Treasury civil servants worked a six-day week, with no half-holiday. In 1856 it was laid down that 'the permanent officers will attend so that the business of every department of the Office may be in full operation at 11 o'clock and they will remain in attendance for six hours, or as much longer as may be necessary for the execution of any business which cannot, without inconvenience to the public service, be delayed'.[2] There was ample accommodation, and working conditions were pleasant in the lofty and elegant Georgian rooms, but until the installation of electricity in 1898 the offices were lighted by candles, though gas had replaced oil in the lamps in the passages and lobbies by 1835. Without the telephone, communication between one person and another in different rooms was very formal. The chat with a colleague about a paper, or an informal conference, was rare; almost all communication was in writing. 'In the Treasury, as in every other public office, the officers correspond demi-officially, as it is called, which answers in correspondence, to personal discussion when people meet together.'[3] Memoranda, notes, and all letters and official despatches, were written in long-hand; typewriters were not used in the Treasury until 1889. Official Treasury letters were very formal and went out in the name of 'The Lords Commissioners of Her Majesty's

[1] Spencer Childers, *Life and Correspondence of the Rt. Hon. Hugh C. E. Childers, 1827–1896*, i. 124.

[2] T. M. 4 July 1856, H[er] M[ajesty's] T[reasury], *Departmental Arrangement Book*, iii.

[3] Trevelyan in evidence to the *Select Committee on Miscellaneous Expenditure*, 1848, P.P., 1847–8, XVIII, qus. 1625–6.

Treasury', who had to be mentioned at least once by their full title (generally after 'I am directed by'). In the remainder of the letter they were referred to as 'My Lords', 'Their Lordships', or 'They'. Whatever signature was appended to the letter it was considered improper for another department to distinguish between one Lord and another in an official despatch to the Treasury. A letter from the Controller of the Stationery Office which did so seemed to Robert Lowe, the Chancellor of the Exchequer, 'to be intended to touch on the limits of impertinence'. The formal procedures used in correspondence with other departments, and the insistence upon the preservation of exceedingly full records, meant that there was a great deal of copying and recording work—all of which was done by hand; letter presses which were introduced into some departments in the early seventies found no favour in the Treasury. Shorthand writers were not employed in the department until the late 1880s; and only the senior permanent civil servant, the Assistant Secretary, had a private secretary.

The work of the department centred on the decisions taken formally at the meetings of the Treasury Board on Tuesdays and Fridays. Of the five Lords Commissioners—the First Lord (the Prime Minister), the Chancellor of the Exchequer, and three Juniors Lords, all of whom had seats in Parliament—neither the First Lord nor the Chancellor of the Exchequer was in the habit of attending the meetings of the Board, although the Chancellor was kept informed of all important business presented to it.[1] The Board was served by two Secretaries, the Financial Secretary and the Parliamentary (Patronage) Secretary, both with seats in the House of Commons. The Financial Secretary and the permanent head of the department, the Assistant Secretary, almost always attended, but the Patronage Secretary attended only when he had business to present. The presence of at least one Junior Lord was essential.

The Joint Secretaries, the Assistant Secretary, and five other senior civil servants were together responsible for making policy and taking decisions, dividing the whole work of the department between them, and each preparing business in the form of Minutes

---

[1] The number of Junior Lords was reduced from four to three in 1848 on the recommendation of a Select Committee of the House of Commons. Generally, but not invariably, they sat in Parliament; it was customary to choose a representative for each of the three kingdoms.

for the consideration and decision of the Board. Broadly speaking, the Joint Secretaries were responsible for the business connected with the Revenue Departments, while the Assistant Secretary looked after expenditure generally, everything that concerned establishments and the revision of those establishments, and the alteration of the rules under which expenditure was permitted; he also looked after the business of the Commissariat, and superintended the Treasury establishment, and 'did everything that, for any reason whatever, is not done by anybody else'.[1] The other five senior clerks were the Auditor of the Civil List, who also had charge of all business relating to private and other Bills before Parliament; the Principal Clerk for Colonial Business; the Principal Clerk Assistant, who looked after the smaller matters relating to the Revenue Departments, and the ordinary Irish business; the Law Clerk; and the Clerk of the Parliamentary Accounts, whose responsibilities included everything relating to the Miscellaneous Estimates.

The Board's decisions were carried out by a separate branch of the Treasury, which comprised three divisions staffed by a larger number of more junior clerks. A decision taken by the Board upon the basis of a Minute drawn and submitted by the Principal Clerk for Colonial Business was referred by him to the Registry, and by it to the division which dealt, *inter alia*, with all the correspondence with the Colonial Office. There the Minute was converted into an official letter, which called 'for some little exercise of judgment and good taste', copies made, and records entered into ledgers.

Letters for signature were put up to the Secretaries, who between them reviewed the business of the whole department. Sir Charles Trevelyan's practice was to sign those letters whose subject-matter was familiar to him, or which he thought unobjectionable. When in any doubt, he turned down the corner of the letter and sent it upstairs. This indicated his wish to read the papers. When he had done so he signed the letter if satisfied, or discussed the matter with the person who drew the Minute. A difference of opinion between them was resolved by reference to one of the junior ministers or the Chancellor of the Exchequer.[2]

---

[1] Trevelyan in evidence before the *Select Committee on Miscellaneous Expenditure*, 1848, qu. 1643.

[2] Trevelyan, qu. 1618.

THE REORGANIZATION OF 1856

The reorganization of the department which took place in 1856 was the culmination of a period of prolonged and often bitter argument between Sir Charles Trevelyan, the Assistant Secretary, and the Treasury ministers.[1] From these discussions, and the changes consequent upon them, there emerged for the first time in the nineteenth century a department recognizable as the modern Treasury. Implicit in the reorganization was the desuetude of the Treasury Board as the instrument of decision; long before, however, its meetings had become a mere formality, as authority became concentrated in the hands of the Chancellor of the Exchequer, and responsibility for decision-making passed to the Financial Secretary, advised by the Treasury's senior permanent civil servants. Other changes of greater practical significance were introduced. For the first time in fifty years those responsible for making policy were also charged with supervising its implementation, two hierarchical establishments of the permanent civil servants were created, and an attempt was made to provide a more perfect division of labour between them.

The essence of the reorganization was the abandonment of the functional separation of policy-making and policy-implementation between the Principal Officers and the divisions, which had characterized Treasury organization since 1805. Trevelyan was convinced that their separation was 'in accordance with correct principles of administration'[2]; his complaint was that it had been imperfectly realized in practice: too few clerks had been employed on the work of preparing the business (i.e. Minutes), and too many employed for too long on the work of transcribing the Minutes into official letters and upon copying and record-keeping. To remedy this he then proposed, as he had done previously,[3] that the work of preparing the decisions should be separated from the routine and mechanical work of registration, copying and account work; that more permanent clerks should assist in the preparation of the business, and that other clerks should be specially recruited to do the copying and other mechanical work.

[1] The details of the reorganization are contained in T.M.s 4 July and 1 October 1856, H.M.T., *Departmental Arrangement Book*, iii.
[2] Memorandum 14 May 1856, H.M.T., *Treasury Establishment*.
[3] See his evidence before the *Select Committee on Miscellaneous Expenditure*, 1848, P.P., 1847-8, XVIII, especially questions 1659-1670; and the report of the Treasury committee of inquiry, 2 March 1849, P.R.O., T.1/5533/27830.

While urging a more complete division of the work he never wavered in the belief that the differentiation of policy-making and policy-implementation was administratively essential to the Treasury organization. When, therefore, he learned that Wilson, the Financial Secretary,[1] intended to abandon that principle he reminded him that what he proposed was a return to a system which had broken down under the pressure of the Napoleonic wars. In this important matter, in which Wilson was supported by Cornewall Lewis, the Chancellor of the Exchequer, events were to prove Trevelyan wrong; in two other respects his views prevailed: the senior clerks were provided with more assistance, and clerks were specially recruited to do the copying and other mechanical work.

The reorganization had a threefold purpose: to secure a succession of able officers for the senior posts on the permanent establishment by providing them with a proper training in the higher duties of the department; to ensure that decisions were carried out promptly and accurately; and to prevent the waste of intellectual power and money caused by an imperfect division of labour. With these objects Trevelyan had no quarrel, indeed they accorded perfectly with the ideas he had expressed over the past ten years, but the arrangements through which it was proposed to give effect to them were founded upon an administrative principle which he believed to be unsound. The most important of these arrangements may be set down briefly. It was proposed to divide the whole of the business between six divisions under the immediate control of the Assistant Secretary, the Auditor of the Civil List, and four Principal Officers. Each division was to be responsible for the preparation of the Minutes and their conversion into official letters —in other words, the functions of policy-making and the execution of that policy when approved were to be combined within the same administrative unit. To each division was assigned a number of clerks to assist in the preparation of the Minutes, as Trevelyan had urged. A separate Registry and Copying Department was to be established where clerks specially recruited were to be employed upon copying, recording, registering, and other routine and mechanical work—again as Trevelyan had persistently advocated. And finally, the organization of the department and the procedure

---

[1] James Wilson (1805–60): founded *The Economist* in 1843; Liberal M.P., 1847–59; F.S. to Treasury, 1855–8; Financial Member of the Council of India, 1859–60.

for transacting the business was to be regulated by fixed rules,'for
the exact execution of which, under the general superintendence
of the Assistant Secretary, and when necessary, after reference to
the Secretaries, the Principal Officers will be severally responsible'.[1]
The details of these arrangements, the translation into practice of
the principles affirmed in the Minute of 4 July 1856, and the
subsequent modifications made to the organization of the department, are now examined.

THE TREASURY ESTABLISHMENT

From 1856 the permanent civil servants employed in the Treasury
were divided into two separate establishments, Superior and
Supplementary. The Superior Clerks, employed mainly in the
divisions, although a few juniors acted as private secretaries to the
Treasury ministers, were divided into four classes and paid
the salaries shown in Table I.

TABLE I

Treasury Superior Establishment 1856

4	Principal Officers	£1,000 × £50 to £1,200	
10	1st Class Clerks	£700 × £25 to £900	
16	2nd Class Clerks	£350 × £20 to £600	
7	3rd Class Clerks	£100 × £15 to £250	

In addition there was the Assistant (later Permanent) Secretary,
with a salary of £2,500, and his deputy, the Auditor of the Civil
List, whose maximum salary (until his title was changed in 1867)
was £1,500.[2]

Despite a steady increase in the volume of business during the
next fifteen years, the size of the Superior Establishment was
reduced by over one-third, from thirty-seven to twenty-three; by
1870 it was only half the size of the 1848 establishment. Between
1856 and May 1870 practical experience of the new arrangements
led to a further revision and consolidation of the work done by the

[1] T.M. 4 July 1856, op. cit.
[2] In practice the holder of this office usually received £1,200, the maximum
of a Principal Officer, although often he enjoyed other allowances as well.
George Arbuthnot who was Auditor of the Civil List from 1849 to 1865 had a
special allowance of £350, and also received £400 as auditor of the accounts of
the Ecclesiastical Commissioners.

divisions, which were reduced in number from six to four. With the benefit of hindsight it was possible to say in 1870 (or even with Gladstone in 1860)[1] that too many divisions had been created in 1856, and that there were more First and Second Class Clerks than the business strictly warranted. But the changes which were made in 1856 were so profoundly disruptive of the previous organization that a precise estimate of the requirements of the department was impossible. Nor could subsequent developments in the organization of the department have been reasonably anticipated. The most substantial reduction, the abolition of the entire Third Class, occurred when the department was further reorganized in May 1870. On recruitment to the Treasury a man now entered the Second Class with a salary of £250 rising to £600 by annual increments of £20, the higher salary being justified by the Treasury on the grounds that the new entrant began at once upon more responsible work and was recruited after a more difficult open competitive examination. The Superior Establishment between 1870 and 1874 is shown below in Table II.

TABLE II

Treasury Superior Establishment May 1870–
April 1874

4	Principal Officers	£1,000	× £50	to	£1,200
7	First Class Clerks	£700	× £25	to	£900
12	Second Class Clerks	£250	× £20	to	£600

There was no promotion from the Supplementary to the Superior Establishment. Most of the Supplementary Clerks were employed in the Registry and Copying Department where they provided the necessary ancillary services for the business of the divisions. The number in the department fluctuated from year to year, but at no time exceeded seventeen. Salaries varied widely until 1861, when the clerks were divided into three classes and paid upon scales which began at £100 on entry to the Third Class and rose by fixed annual increments to a maximum of £500 after seven years service in the First Class. The Supplementary Establishment was further re-

[1] Gladstone complained to Hamilton, the Assistant Secretary, that on several occasions since the reorganization it had been found necessary to reduce the size of the establishment and even to reverse 'cardinal arrangements which were then made'. 4 October 1860, P.R.O., *Hamilton Semi-official Correspondence*, i.

organized in 1869 to provide for the additional business thrown upon the Finance Division by the passing of the Exchequer and Audit Act three years earlier. A separate Accounts Branch was set up with a staff of nine Supplementary Clerks, most of whom were attached to the Finance Division where they assisted in the examination of accounts.

At this point it is necessary to describe in a little more detail the nature of the services provided by the Supplementary Establishment in order that the description of the transaction of the business which follows in the next chapter may be more easily understood. At the same time, as all departments had to provide services similar to these, it is convenient to have a point of reference for the discussion of 'routine and mechanical' duties which occurs in later chapters.

Every official letter addressed to the Treasury was delivered to the Registry, where each day about seventy or eighty papers were 'docketed' or endorsed to show in a few words the subject of each, and then registered.[1] In the Paper Room papers 'disposed of' by the divisions on their return from the Secretaries were sorted, attached to past papers on the same subject, and arranged for convenient future reference. In the Copying and Indexing Department documents were copied as required by the divisions or the Secretaries (the official letter for dispatch was written from the draft Minute by the junior Superior Clerks in the divisions); and letters addressed for dispatch and entered into the dispatch books. Careful and accurate indexing was particularly important in the Treasury where the nature of the work called constantly for the production of past papers, and the Supplementary Clerks were warned to take care that 'the indications are given by which the letter is likely to be searched for in after years'; each letter was indexed under at least two heads.[2] Record-keeping was also done in the Copying and Indexing Department, where a copy of each official letter dispatched was entered into an indexed Letter Book; as well, copies were made of all important Minutes and entered into the 'Fair Minute' Book. After 1870 most of the copying was done by writers hired on day or weekly rates supervised by a small number of Supplementary Clerks, who themselves now undertook

[1] This estimate is based upon the number of files opened in each of the years 1854–74, about 23,000. The number of papers received by the Treasury was greater; in 1847 there were 29,914.

[2] T.M. 1 October 1856, op. cit.

D

only the most important or confidential copying and other routine work.

Besides the clerks of the Superior and Supplementary Establishments there was one other permanent post in the Treasury, that of Accountant, to which one of the senior Supplementary Clerks was usually appointed. Temporary clerks were not much used in the Treasury until 1861 when they began to be employed increasingly upon copying work. They were hired mainly from Vachers, the Law Stationers (and for that reason were usually referred to as Vachers's clerks), at weekly rates between £2. 12s. 6d. and £2. 16s.; the number employed at any one time varied with the volume of business, but never exceeded ten. After 1870 the practice was discontinued; temporary clerical assistance was now supplied by a new general class of writers whose services could be hired by the day or week on application to the Civil Service Commissioners who were responsible both for their pay and for their conditions of service.

RECRUITMENT AND PROMOTION

Before July 1855 the Treasury had no precise rules governing the age, health, or character of the candidates nominated to vacancies on the general establishment: it was assumed 'that the persons nominated would not be open to objection in these respects'.[1] The written examination was a simple one, 'decidedly lower' than that used to test candidates for clerkships in the Board of Inland Revenue, a department subordinate to the Treasury. Candidates were examined in the common rules of arithmetic, such as the rule of three, vulgar and decimal fractions, interest and discount, and were required to make an abstract of some official document to test their intelligence and to show that they were able to write and compose correctly. After the establishment of the Civil Service Commission in 1855, and the reorganization of the Treasury a year later, this procedure was abandoned. On the new Superior Establishment appointments were now made only to the Third Class, and candidates who were nominated to compete for a vacancy in it were required to obtain a certificate of qualification from the Civil Service Commissioners upon conditions laid down in the Order in Council of 21 May 1855. Regulations under that Order were prescribed by the Treasury in collaboration with the Civil Service Commissioners shortly before the 1856 reorganiza-

[1] T.M. 13 July 1855, H.M.T., *Departmental Arrangement Book*, iii.

tion: candidates had to be not less than eighteen nor more than twenty-five years old; the general rules relating to health and character which the Civil Service Commissioners had drawn up for other departments were adopted;[1] and the requirement of 'knowledge and ability' was tested by a limited competitive examination conducted by the Civil Service Commissioners.

Usually three candidates were nominated by, or with the approval of, the First Lord of the Treasury to compete for each vacancy. In the written examination candidates were examined in the first three books of Euclid, the History of England, Geography, and translation from a foreign language, besides the traditional tests of orthography, handwriting, arithmetic, and the preparation of an abstract of official papers. Its purpose was 'to ascertain whether the candidate has received a good education and has profited by it—the higher duties of the Treasury being of a nature to call for a superior cultivation and intelligence'.[2] If it was less than a searching and exhaustive test of the talents of young gentlemen of high ability nurtured in Jowett's Balliol, there was an element of competition, and the requirements were immensely superior to those which had been demanded of candidates previously. No important changes were made to the examination regulations until the introduction of open competition in 1870, when the Treasury adopted those prescribed for the Civil Service generally by the Civil Service Commissioners.[3]

Under these conditions some exceedingly able men were recruited to the Superior Establishment, among them three who rose to the rank of Permanent Secretary.[4] Some of the credit for this belongs to Trevelyan's successor, George Alexander Hamilton, who was imbued with the same desire as Trevelyan to encourage the recruitment of bright young men. By 1867 such was his position in the department that on the occurrence of three vacancies on the Superior Establishment he could write in the following terms to the Patronage Secretary:

I venture to express my strong sense of the importance of introducing into the Treasury highly educated and promising young men.

[1] See below, Chapter 3, p. 67.   [2] T.M. 13 July 1855, op. cit.
[3] See below, Chapter 4.
[4] R. E. (later Lord Reginald) Welby, entered the Treasury in 1856, Permanent Secretary, 1885–94; F. (later Sir Francis) Mowatt, entered the Treasury in 1856, Permanent Secretary, 1894–1902; E. W. (later Sir Edward) Hamilton, entered the Treasury in 1870, Permanent Secretary (Financial), 1902–3.

My experience here now for more than 10 years has impressed me very deeply with the importance of this in reference to the public service and interests and to the convenience and safety of Governments to come.

It is to be borne in mind that among the Juniors are the germs of the future Principal Officers who will be the advisers of future Chancellors of the Exchequer and who contribute to the real strength of the Treasury.

Moreover you will find at present men who served their apprenticeship at the Treasury occupying important positions in various departments of the permanent Civil Service and it always ought to be so for there are no means, provided men of ability and industry are appointed to the Treasury, by which the necessary qualifications for the conduct of the business in the permanent service of the State can be so effectually attained as by the experience of this Department.[1]

The appointment of senior Treasury men to important positions in the subordinate departments was not a recent development. There is evidence that the practice had already begun before the end of the eighteenth century.[2] It reappeared whenever the Treasury felt the need to extend or tighten its control of another department. Nine Treasury men were promoted out of the department to key positions in the subordinate departments between 1854 and 1874.[3] Despite this, continuity of service remained a feature of the department. A third of the clerks appointed to Treasury posts in the first half of the nineteenth century remained in the department for over thirty years; 15 per cent, for over forty years.[4] More (17·7 per cent) died in office than were promoted to posts outside the Treasury (15·0 per cent). In the second half of the century there was a marked change. Nearly a half of those appointed after 1850 were promoted to posts in other departments, and only 18·1 per cent stayed for over thirty years; far fewer (9 per cent) died in office. Less than one in five stayed in the department longer than thirty years.[5]

[1] Hamilton to Col. T. E. Taylor, 13 May 1867, P.R.O. *Hamilton Semi-official Correspondence*, iii.

[2] Torrance, 'The Growth of the Bureaucracy', op. cit, pp. 63–4.

[3] They included Chairman of the Board of Inland Revenue, Secretary of the Audit Office, Assistant Comptroller and Auditor-General, and Financial Secretary to the Post Office.

[4] For the continuity of service of the senior officials, see below, Chapter 15, pp. 349–351.

[5] The contrast between the early and late nineteenth century is shown in the detailed figures for two decades. Of the sixteen clerks appointed between 1810 and 1820, one died in office after 32 years; two more were promoted to posts in other

In 1854 Trevelyan had strongly urged the discontinuance of direct entry to the Treasury, believing it better to recruit from among the ablest young men in the subordinate departments. It was not a new idea. During the previous fifty years, outsiders with special qualifications had been brought to newly created positions in the Treasury. The appointment of George Harrison as 'assistant secretary' and 'law clerk' in 1805 was 'the first in a series of moves by which able men were introduced to the top of the Treasury, by-passing the slow-moving and often inefficient hierarchy of the divisions', where promotion was generally governed by seniority.[1]

Trevelyan's purpose in 1854 was different. If adopted, his scheme 'would make the Treasury really a *supervisory* office possessed of a firmer hold of all the branches of business which it had to deal with, would introduce a powerful principle of unity into the Public Service and would give a very beneficial stimulus to exertion in every other department'.[2] But the time was not yet ripe for the creation of such a large Treasury *élite*. After the introduction of open competition in 1870, however, the Treasury 'always got the pick of the successful candidates—generally Firsts or Double Firsts, and sometimes Fellows of their colleges—men of the very highest ability; among them such as Thomas Little Heath and Stephen Spring-Rice, both of them Double Firsts and Fellows of Trinity, Cambridge'.[3] The earlier practice of recruiting from other departments was revived later, and the high proportion of Treasury administrators who had served in other departments became one of the most striking features of the Treasury organization in the twentieth century.[4]

[1] Torrance, pp. 61–4.
[2] Trevelyan to Gladstone, 13 February 1854, Bod., T.L.B., xxxiii, 16–20.
[3] J. A. Kempe, *Reminiscences of an Old Civil Servant*, pp. 35–6.
[4] Writing in 1964, Lord Bridges, a former Permanent Secretary to the Treasury, claimed advantages for the practice which Trevelyan had foreseen a hundred years earlier: 'The bringing together in the Treasury of much varied experience, gained in many departments, gives the officers of the Treasury a wide and synoptic understanding of the problems of Government as a whole', helped to

departments after 11 and 13 years; and thirteen retired or resigned after 6, 9, 12, 17, 18, 31, 39, 39, 41, 43, 45, 45, and 47 years. Of the fifteen clerks appointed between 1880 and 1890, two died in office after 8 and 9 years; three retired after 31, 35, and 37 years; and ten were promoted to posts outside after 2, 12, 12, 14, 18, 22, 22, 23, 23, and 24 years. These figures and those in the text are based on an analysis made by Dr. Henry Roseveare in *British Institutions: The Treasury* (Penguin Books, London 1969).

Trevelyan's plan for 'creaming-off' the brightest young men was inspired partly by the practice which had begun in 1840 of re-recruiting clerks 'extra' to the old general establishment after a competitive examination between candidates who held clerkships in the Audit Office, Customs, Post Office, and the Board of Inland Revenue. By this method it was hoped 'to secure a succession of well qualified clerks for the subordinate branch of the Treasury and to give an additional prospect of promotion to the junior clerks in other offices'.[1] After 1856 vacancies on the new Supplementary Establishment were filled in exactly the same way. A year later the field of selection was enlarged to include all public departments, but in practice candidates were nominated from departments other than those above only once. Recruitment by this novel method was discontinued in 1861 at the direction of Palmerston, the First Lord, and subsequent vacancies on the Supplementary Establishment were filled by persons selected after a competitive examination between candidates nominated by the Treasury.[2] With the introduction of open competition in 1870 appointments were made according to regulations prescribed for the Civil Service generally by the Civil Service Commissioners.

The regulations regarding the age, health, and character of the nominees, which the Treasury prescribed for the Superior Clerks, applied equally to those of the Supplementary Establishment; the test of 'knowledge and ability' was much simpler, however. 'The attainments required in the Supplementary Clerks are quick and legible handwriting, correct English Composition and a familiar acquaintance with Arithmetic and Accounts', the Treasury in-

[1] T.M. 24 March 1840, P.R.O. T.1/6035B/19748.
[2] 'I think it inexpedient to bring the clerks to the Treasury from other offices', Palmerston wrote. 'The best arrangement will be that vacancies among the Supplementary Clerks should be filled up in the same manner in which vacancies in the fixed establishment of the office are filled up. It is better that each Government Office should have its own stream and system of promotion' (Memorandum 25 August 1861, H.M.T., *Departmental Arrangement Book*, iv). It is possible, however, that Palmerston's real reason was a wish to exercise this patronage himself. Earlier he had ordered that all vacancies on the Supplementary Establishment were to be reported to him in order that he might himself take measures to fill them in accordance with the 1857 decision to enlarge the field of selection.

break down any narrow departmentalism, fostered a corporate sense in the higher Civil Service, and made for agreement in dealings between the Treasury and departments. *The Treasury*, chapter xvi.

formed the Civil Service Commissioners who examined the candidates nominated to compete for each vacancy.[1] The requirements were further simplified in 1859, and for the next eleven years the examination was confined to 'quick and good handwriting, correct orthography and arithmetic'. Temporary clerks were examined in the same subjects, for under the Order in Council they, too, were required to obtain a certificate of qualification from the Civil Service Commissioners prior to appointment; in common with most other departments the Treasury usually ignored that requirement.

In the first half of the nineteenth century promotion in the Treasury was governed largely by seniority, although the principle of promotion by merit had been acknowledged in 1776 and reiterated in 1834. When the department was reorganized in 1856, however, it was decided that promotion from class to class within each of the two new establishments was to be made on the grounds of 'superior fitness for the duties to be performed', seniority was to count only in those cases in which the qualifications of the candidates were equal.[2] Supplementary Clerks could not be promoted to the Superior Establishment, nor temporary clerks or writers promoted to either establishment. After some initial difficulty, the principle of promotion by merit was upheld in practice for the next eighteen years. When a vacancy occurred which had to be filled by promotion a meeting was arranged between the Assistant Secretary, the Auditor of the Civil List and the Principal Officers, who then reported to the Financial Secretary who in their opinion was best qualified to perform the duties of the vacant post; in no instance did he reject their recommendation. At different times a First and Second Class Clerk of the Superior Establishment was passed over for promotion though senior in his class; and in 1871 Welby was promoted Principal Officer over the heads of seven men senior to him. When Welby became Permanent Secretary he wanted to promote Stephen Spring-Rice, then junior to J. A. Kempe, to a vacant Principal Clerkship, explaining to the First Lord, W. H. Smith, that he wished to promote not 'the fit man but the fittest'. Smith objected, and the resulting dispute was taken to cabinet where a decision was made in favour of Kempe.[3]

---

[1] T.M. 13 July 1855, op. cit.
[2] T.M. 1 October 1856, op. cit.   [3] Kempe, op. cit., pp. 35–6.

DISTRIBUTION OF THE BUSINESS

The distribution of the business agreed upon in 1856 was based
upon the principle of the mixed division, i.e. all the business
which related to one particular department was combined and
dealt with in the same Treasury division—Supply and Establishments were not distinguished and dealt with separately. Two of the
six divisions were organized functionally: the Third which dealt
with all the legal business; and the Sixth which dealt with most
but not all the financial business. The Assistant Secretary had
charge of the First Division, the Auditor of the Civil List, the
Second, while the four remaining divisions were each put under
the direction of a Principal Officer; the head of the Sixth (or
Finance) Division was also known as the Finance Officer. To each
division was assigned initially a First Class Clerk, two Second Class
Clerks, and one Third Class Clerk, all from the Superior Establishment; the First Class Clerk in the Finance Division was the Estimate Clerk.[1]

TABLE III

Distribution of Treasury Business 1856

First Division (Sir Charles Trevelyan, Assistant Secretary)
War department and military departments; Admiralty and naval departments;
Audit Office; Stationery Office; Public Record Office; Board of Control; Board
of Works (Ireland); Inclosure Commissioners and miscellaneous.

Second Division (George Arbuthnot, Auditor of the Civil List)
Civil List and Household; Woods; Works; Duchies of Cornwall and Lancaster;
Education, Science and Art; currency and banking; municipal corporations and
other local boards; intestate estates; Civil List pensions; and charitable grants,
etc.

Third Division (Wilmot Seton, Principal Officer)
Legal establishments and courts of law; felons effects and forfeitures; sheriffs'
accounts; criminal prosecutions and maintenance of prisoners.

Fourth Division (William Stephenson, Principal Officer)
Revenue Departments (except Woods); Board of Trade (as connected with
Revenue Departments); Receiver General of Isle of Man; Trinity House; and
superannuation.

Fifth Division (Charles Crafer, Principal Officer)
Privy Council Office; Secretaries of State; slave trade and liberated africans;
Chief Secretary for Ireland; Poor Law Offices in Great Britain and Ireland;
General Register Offices of Great Britain and Ireland.

[1] Initially two additional First Class Clerks were assigned to the Finance
Division because of the importance and expected difficulty of the work. One was
soon found to be superfluous and on his resignation from the department his
post was abolished; the other looked after the general business of the division,
but in 1867 was withdrawn when the business of the divisions was re-distributed.

Sixth Division (William Anderson, Principal Officer)
Finance generally; Treasury Chests abroad;[1] Mint; Exchequer; Paymaster-General; Paymaster of Civil Services, Ireland; Queen's and Lord Treasurer's Remembrancer, Scotland, for financial business; Bank of England; National Debt Commissioners; Public Works Loan Commissioners; and ordinary applications from the grants of Parliament, or the Consolidated Fund, or the Treasury Chest Fund.

Although establishments' business was dealt with as part of the ordinary business by each division, the 1856 reorganization provided for an important point of co-ordination by making the Assistant Secretary generally responsible for all establishments matters. 'Papers relating to the revision or regulation of the Public Establishments are to be dealt with in communication with the Officer in charge of the 1st Division, whatever the Division to which they are assigned.' Here was the means to enable the Assistant Secretary to assume an overall responsibility for the Civil Service; by 1874 he had done so and lacked only the title of Official Head of the Civil Service.[2]

The business was distributed between the Assistant Secretary, the Auditor of the Civil List and the four Principal Officers according to their qualifications, previous experience and personal preference. For example, currency and banking was assigned to the Second Division, and not the Finance Division, because George Arbuthnot was an acknowledged authority on that subject.[3] In the next fifteen years a number of changes were made. Primary in importance was the decision made in 1859 to relieve the Assistant-Secretary of his direct responsibility for a division. It was a turning-point in the development of that office. Divested of the detailed, day to day responsibilities of running a division the Assistant Secretary's chief functions became the supervision of the work of the whole department and advising the Treasury ministers.[4]

The decision was inspired by the new Assistant Secretary, George Alexander Hamilton, who on 21 January 1859 gave up the office of Financial Secretary to the Treasury in Derby's Adminis-

[1] Comprised the financial business of the Commissariat, formerly under the personal superintendence of the Assistant Secretary. The name was changed in March 1856.

[2] This is discussed in greater detail below, Chapter 2, pp. 49–1.

[3] Gladstone's extensive semi-official correspondence with Arbuthnot between 1853–65 was concerned mainly with financial matters, particularly currency and banking. For an example see Arbuthnot's memorandum to Gladstone on the question of establishing a National or State Bank, Brit. Mus., G.P. Add. MSS. 44588, fo. 10.

[4] For relations with ministers see below, Chapter 2, pp. 34–43.

tration to become the department's new permanent head in succession to Sir Charles Trevelyan. His translation was not without
precedent: the line between politics and administration could be
crossed and re-crossed with surprising ease before the introduction
of open competition. Endymion's career was not exceptional in
mid-Victorian England:[1] Cornwall Lewis was a civil servant for
fourteen years before he entered Parliament, and Benjamin Hawes
exchanged a political for a Public Service career when he moved
from the ministerial to the official side of the War Department in
1852.

Little is known about Hamilton; he left no private papers, and
his semi-official correspondence and the official Treasury papers
convey little but the capacity for infinite self-effacement. His
public life contrasted sharply with that of his better-known predecessor, the ebullient, temperamental publicist, Sir Charles
Trevelyan. Hamilton moved anonymously, tactfully, and with
great discretion, though not less powerfully on that account.
Mounting no great public campaigns, as Trevelyan had done over
the reform of the Civil Service, his conduct never became the
subject of bitter controversy at Brooks's. And whereas Trevelyan
was rarely out of the public eye—relieving famine in Ireland in the
forties, reforming the Civil Service in the early fifties, India in the
sixties, and the Army subsequently—Hamilton was withdrawn,
avoiding all commitment and controversy that could not be shielded
from the public gaze; in this respect he (and Lingen, his successor)
was much closer to the civil servants of our own day. A similar
regard for anonymity and discretion marked his private life, his
name was never associated with those fashionable politico-literary
gatherings (described by Algernon West and other social observers)
in which many of Hamilton's contemporaries in Parliament and the
Civil Service took such delight.

Hamilton was born at Tyrellus, County Down, the elder son of
the Rev. George Hamilton, whose father had been a baron of the
Exchequer and a nephew of the Bishop of Ossory. Educated at
Arnold's 'temple of industrious peace' and later at Trinity College,
Oxford, Hamilton entered politics in 1835 at the age of thirty-three,
unseating O'Connell at Dublin after a petition, having previously
fought the seat three times without success. A year later he was

[1] Endymion was the hero of Disraeli's novel of the same name, published in
1881.

defeated once more and did not find himself again in Parliament until 1843 when he was returned for Dublin University. Meanwhile, he had been busy forming the Conservative Society for Ireland, the main rallying point for the Conservative Party in Ireland after the Reform Bill, and playing a prominent part in protestant demonstrations. When he renounced politics for the Civil Service at the age of fifty-seven he had held ministerial office briefly, being twice appointed Financial Secretary by Derby, from March to December 1852, and again from March 1858 until he took up his appointment as Assistant Secretary.

He had been permanent head of the Treasury for less than a year when he proposed to Gladstone, the Chancellor of the Exchequer, that he should be relieved of the duties of a head of division. From his short experience he concluded that there was considerable disadvantage in the business of his own division, which included the important and difficult questions relating to the military and naval establishments, being exempt from the double investigation of a Principal Officer and the Assistant Secretary (as happened with the establishments' business of all other divisions)[1] before it was submitted to the Financial Secretary. Encouraged by Gladstone's approval of the principle of his proposal, Hamilton developed his ideas of the position which the Assistant Secretary should occupy in the department on his release from divisional duties. He argued that

the time necessarily occupied in the examination of details by the Assistant Secretary might be more usefully employed in exercising the general supervision and rendering that assistance to the Financial Secretary which the nature of the office would seem to suggest, and which the very onerous duties of the Financial Secretary especially during the sitting of Parliament necessarily requires.[2]

And if the time of the Assistant Secretary were less fettered by details

It would appear a proper part of the functions to prepare business of a general character for the Financial Secretary by conferring personally with Officers of other Departments, and thereby in many cases saving a long inter-departmental correspondence, as well as economising the

[1] The transaction of the business is explained in greater detail in Chapter 2.
[2] Hamilton to Gladstone, 20 December 1859, H.M.T., *Departmental Arrangement Book*, iv.

valuable time of the Financial Secretary, and he might further be of material assistance in aiding him and the Chancellor of the Exchequer generally on questions of finance, and in co-operating with the Estimate Clerk and preparing any information which may be considered useful with a view to their discussion in parliament.

Seven months before, Hamilton had been appointed—largely by his own efforts—as the permanent member of the Treasury super-annuation committee. He now pointed out that he ought to have more time to devote to the work of that committee,[1] and also to serve on the Treasury committees set up from time to time to inquire into the organization and establishment of other depart-ments.[2] The metamorphosis of the office which Hamilton here envisaged would allow him the freedom to undertake, supervise, and direct the most important business of the department; his position in the department would be central, paramount and indispensable. That position was achieved and secured to the office of Permanent Secretary[3] by the time he handed over to Ralph Lingen in 1870. Hamilton's proposal had been 'entirely approved' by Palmerston and Gladstone, and he was free to make of the office what he had envisaged. He also suggested that the First Division should be abolished and its duties distributed among the other five; to this Palmerston and Gladstone agreed as well.

In August 1865 George Arbuthnot died after forty-five years service in the department, and was succeeded as Auditor of the Civil List by William Anderson. The business of the Civil List and Royal Household was now transferred to his (the Finance) divi-sion, and currency and banking from the Second to the Fifth. Despite this redistribution, and the more extensive one made in 1859, the arrangement of the business remained essentially that which had been settled in 1856, but of the six heads of division then appointed only Anderson retained his original position.[4] The distribution of the business no longer reflected the qualifications and experience of each of the Principal Officers, and at the direc-

---

[1] For the formation and work of this committee, see below, Chapter 14.
[2] See below, Chapter 8.
[3] The title was changed in 1867. Hereafter I shall use 'Permanent Secretary' only when referring specifically to the office after that date. On all other occasions, and in discussing the office generally, I shall use 'Assistant Secretary'.
[4] Hamilton had been relieved of his division, Arbuthnot and Seton had died in office, Crafer had retired, and Stephenson had resigned on his appointment as Chairman of the Board of Inland Revenue.

tion of the Financial Secretary, Hugh Childers,[1] a further and
more comprehensive rearrangement was undertaken in July 1866,
with the result that each division became a more cohesive and closely
integrated unit of administration; for example, all the pension
business was now consolidated in the Fourth Division.[2]

This was one of Childers's last acts as Financial Secretary,
Russell's Government having suffered defeat at the hands of
Lowe's Adullamites in the debate on the Reform Bill a few days
previously. On his retirement Childers wrote that 'there is no
prospect of diminished work in the Treasury for some time . . .
with the present amount of business it is impossible to give any
additional duties permanently to any one of the five Principal
Officers'.[3] Yet less than a year later Hamilton was busily persuading the new Financial Secretary, George Ward Hunt,[4] to
reduce the number of divisions from five to four. On the strength
of a proposal made earlier by Childers, Hamilton suggested that
the office of Auditor of the Civil List should be freed from divisional duties to provide further assistance for the Secretaries, and
that its new title should be Auditor of the Civil List and Assistant to
the Secretaries. Further, he proposed that William Law, Principal
Officer of the Third Division, should be appointed to it, Anderson
having resigned from the Treasury on his appointment as
Assistant Comptroller and Auditor-General. At the same time
Hamilton urged upon the Financial Secretary a reduction in the
number of divisions, which was to be accomplished not by
leaving unfilled the vacancy created by Law's promotion, but by
abolishing the Principal Clerkship held by Spencer Shelley and the
division he controlled.[5]

---

[1] Hugh Culling Eardley Childers (1827–96): Liberal M.P. for Pontefract,
1860–86; Financial Secretary to Treasury, August 1865 to July 1866; First Lord
of the Admiralty, 1868–71, where he was responsible for a number of far-
reaching reforms; Chancellor of the Duchy of Lancaster, 1872–3; Secretary of
State for War, 1880–2; Chancellor of the Exchequer, 1882–5; Home Secretary,
1886.
[2] Details of the redistribution are given in T.M. 2 July 1866, P.R.O. T.1/
6665A/19750.
[3] Memo 5 July 1866, P.R.O. T.1/6760A/20269.
[4] George Ward Hunt (1825–77): son of Rev. George Hunt; educated Eton and
Christ Church; bencher of Inner Temple; Conservative M.P. for Northants;
Financial Secretary to Treasury July 1866 to March 1868; Chancellor of the
Exchequer, March to December 1868; First Lord of the Admiralty, 1874–7;
died of gout.
[5] Shelley was to be retired under section 7 of the 1859 Superannuation Act,

Hunt supported the proposal to create the new office of Auditor of the Civil List and Assistant to the Secretaries, but thought at first that appointment to it might be made from outside the office, and that no reduction need be made in the number of divisions and Principal Officers. Against this Hamilton argued that the effect of his own proposal was 'to save the public the salary of one of the Principal Clerks'. The salary which he intended to save was to be Shelley's and no other; in a further letter to Hunt he conceded that the reduction could equally be made by not filling the vacancy created by the appointment of Law to the new office, but declined to recommend it.

I regarded the alterations I proposed as a whole calculated as a whole, to effect greater efficiency and economy but that I am unable to recommend it if only partially adopted.

If therefore you consider it objectionable that Mr Shelley should be allowed to retire with the addition of 3 years, which abolition would give him, I am afraid I must recommend you to revert to the other plan, at least for the present, appointing Mr Law to the new office, without assigning to him any part of his present business—filling up his place as Principal Clerk of the Third Division and leaving the question of reducing the number of the Divisions open for future consideration.[1]

From this exchange it is clear that, for reasons which he did not care to disclose, Hamilton was prepared to forgo a reduction in the number of divisions unless he was able to effect it through Shelley's retirement. He succeeded ultimately in persuading Hunt to agree to his plan; Shelley was retired and his division abolished. Throughout the discussion the determination with which he urged his own scheme, and the tendentious manner in which he presented it to the Financial Secretary suggest that Hamilton was keener to get rid of Shelley than to make a reduction in the number of divisions. He had reason to do so. From time to time, attention will be drawn in subsequent chapters to the nature of the advice tendered by Shelley to Hamilton, and it will be shown that this was frequently unaccept-

[1] Hamilton to Hunt, 20 May 1867, P.R.O. *Hamilton Semi-official Correspondence*, iii.

which provided compensation for those whose retirement was necessary in order to carry out a departmental reorganization. The use of this section is explained in Chapter 14.

able to the Assistant Secretary; later it will be argued that Shelley's ideas about the nature and the exercise of Treasury control were at odds with Hamilton's and those of the department generally. There were also other reasons for getting rid of him: he was the least popular and efficient of the Principal Officers, his colleagues looked upon him disapprovingly—twice they made complaints to Hamilton about his efficiency and ability. On another occasion Hamilton reprimanded him for 'the practice of not infrequently sending down your papers to me unminuted and without a precis', which imposed upon him 'a considerable additional amount of work and delays the other business which passes through my hands'.[1]

William Law was appointed to the new office of Auditor of the Civil List and Assistant to the Secretaries with a salary of £1,500, taking with him some of the legal business which he had dealt with previously as head of the Third Division. He was to

rank next in the office to the Permanent Secretary and take his place in his absence, he shall sign such letters and take charge of such papers and business as from time to time shall be assigned to him by the Secretaries, and deal with such papers in such manner as they shall direct, and generally take such a part in the business of the office as shall be committed to him.[2]

There were now two senior officials largely free from executive duties, whose time and energy was to be increasingly taken up with the tasks of advising and assisting the Treasury ministers, supervising and directing the work of the divisions, especially that part of it which related to establishments, and managing the department.[3]

The process of consolidating and integrating the business which had been begun in 1866 was continued and carried a step farther by redistributing it among four divisions, each supervised by a Principal Officer.[4] To a large extent each division was now responsible for a broad area of administration, and had assigned to it most of the business related or relevant to it—a functional distribution of business was replacing one based primarily upon personality.

[1] Hamilton to Shelley, 7 February 1865, P.R.O. *Hamilton Semi-official Correspondence*, ii.
[2] T.M. 10 May 1867, H.M.T., *Departmental Arrangement Book*, iv.
[3] This arrangement led directly within forty years to the appointment of Joint Permanent Secretaries.
[4] T.M. 21 June 1867, P.R.O. T.1/6760A/20269.

TABLE IV

Distribution of Treasury Business 1867–1874

First (Finance) Division (M. H. Foster, Principal Officer, 1867–71; R. E. Welby, Principal Officer, 1871–74)
Finance generally; banking and currency; Mint; Exchequer and Audit; Pay Office—including the Irish Branch and the Queen's and Lord Treasurer's Remembrancer, Scotland, for financial business; Bank of England; National Debt Commissioners; Public Works Loan Commissioners; ordinary applications for issues from grant of Parliament, or the Consolidated Fund, or the Treasury Chest Fund; the Treasury audit; and the Treasury Chests abroad.
Clerks: One First Class Clerk (Estimate Clerk); one Second Class Clerk; and two Third Class Clerks. Accountant and Assistant Accountant, and a number of Supplementary Clerks employed on accounts.

Second Division (James H. Cole, Principal Officer)
Foreign Office; Colonial Office; War Office; Admiralty; Chelsea Hospital; Land Revenue; Duchies of Cornwall and Lancaster; municipal corporations; and the slave trade.
Clerks: Two First Class Clerks and two Second Class Clerks.

Third Division (Sir William Clerke, Principal Officer)
Home Office (including police); India Office; Privy Council Office; Chief Secretary for Ireland (including constabulary and police); Department of Works; (Ireland); Poor Law Offices (England and Ireland); Channel Isles and Isle of Man; Register General (England and Ireland); Stationery Office; Public Record Office; Inclosure Commission; Education, Science and Art; Scottish business; Board of Trade (not revenue); and miscellaneous.
Clerks: One First Class Clerk; one Second Class Clerk; and two Third Class Clerks.

Fourth Division (C. W. Stronge, Principal Officer)
Revenue departments (except land); Board of Trade as connected with Revenue Departments; superannuation; mail packets; telegraphs; Civil List pensions; charitable grants; and intestate estates.
Clerks: One First Class Clerk; two Second Class Clerks; and one Third Class Clerk.

2

PROCEDURE

THIS chapter outlines Treasury procedure and methods of work; introduces the principal participants in the Treasury's control of establishments, drawing particular attention to the central and dominating position of the Assistant Secretary, whose duties included the surveillance of all establishments' business; and describes the responsibilities and relationships of Treasury ministers and officials.

THE DIVISIONS

When a paper had been 'docketed' and registered, the Registry assigned it to the appropriate division where it was examined by the First Class Clerk who, when he had 'informed himself of the bearings and details of the question, communicates with the Principal Officer of the division, who thereupon either himself prepares or directs the Minute to be made and affixes his initials'.[1] In the Minute a number of short instructions or directions indicated the action to be taken on the paper, but until these had been approved by the Secretaries the Minute could not go forward—at this stage it was merely advice. Sometimes, when the subject of the paper was more difficult or controversial the Principal Officer wrote a memorandum rather than a Minute. This enabled him to develop his views and ideas at greater length, to express any doubts he might have, to raise questions, or draw attention to points of particular importance or difficulty, and to suggest alternative methods of proceeding. Besides the Minute or memorandum, the Principal Officer had to provide the Assistant Secretary with a precis of the paper, which he might prepare himself, or give to the First or Second Class Clerk to do; and had also to forward the 'essential and necessary' previous papers relevant to the subject under discussion. Disregard of this 'proper precaution' was to run 'the risk of an improper decision or one inconsistent with

[1] Hamilton to Gladstone, 20 December 1859, H.M.T., *Departmental Arrangement Book*, iv.

E

opinions previously expressed'.[1] The Assistant Secretary claimed that he was seriously inconvenienced upon three separate occasions in 1865–66 when this procedure was ignored, and as a result made it obligatory for the Principal Officers.

Each Principal Officer was responsible for the discipline of his division. In his absence this duty, and the supervision of the work, fell to the First Class Clerk, whose duties ordinarily included responsibility for the correct and prompt passage of the business through the division, assistance with the preparation of papers for decision by the Secretaries, and minuting the routine and unimportant business. Neither the Second nor the Third Class Clerks were assigned specific duties by Treasury Minute; what they did in the division was decided by each Principal Officer 'as circumstances may require, proper regard being had to their rank and qualifications'.[2] Between them they wrote the official letters for dispatch from the rough Minutes when these were returned to the division from the Secretaries; collected and prepared papers for the consideration of the Principal Officer; and wrote up the 'Fair Minutes'. A legacy from the days of the formal meetings of the Board, the latter's continuance after its demise requires explanation. A 'Fair Minute' was one which in the opinion of the Principal Officer raised a point of principle, or which involved 'an important public or private interest'.[3] All such Minutes he initialled 'F.M.' When the paper had been disposed of, and the order upon it executed, a Minute so initialled was recorded verbatim, together with a precis of the paper, in the division's 'Fair Minute' Book. In

---

[1] T.M. 23 January 1866, H.M.T., *Departmental Arrangement Book*, iv.

[2] T.M. 1 October 1856, op. cit.

[3] The origin of the 'Fair Minutes' is part of the early history of the Treasury Board. In the eighteenth century it was the practice for one of the Secretaries or the Chief Clerk to attend the sittings of the Board to take notes or Minutes of the decisions; these were called the Royal Minutes. Afterwards they were written out fair and read at the next meeting. If they were then approved and confirmed they became the authoritative documents upon which the Letters and Warrants which gave effect to the decisions were prepared. This practice continued until the early nineteenth century, about which time it became customary to bring the Minutes to the Board fully written out for the approval of the Lords. If they approved them they became the authoritative documents upon which the Letters and Warrants were written. In this way the whole process was pushed forward a stage. The 'Fair Minutes' which used to be the practical documents upon which the directions were issued became merely a final record of the proceedings of the Board which was completed at leisure after everything else had been done. (Report of the Treasury Committee of inquiry, 2 March 1849, P.R.O. T.1/5533/27830.)

1870 it was admitted that the system of Treasury record-keeping involved needless duplication. Besides the original paper and the Minute upon it, the copy of the letter written on the Minute was recorded verbatim in ledgers, and important Minutes were written up as 'Fair Minutes'. In the case of all important decisions there was, therefore, a threefold record. In the reorganization of May 1870 the practice of keeping 'Fair Minutes' was discontinued. Subsequently Minutes of general interest, or of sufficient importance as precedents, were printed and bound with an index into yearly books.

The Finance Division differed in some important respects from the other divisions. Unlike other Principal Officers, the Finance Officer was sometimes appointed from outside the department when it was considered that there was nobody with sufficient experience and knowledge of the working of the financial system; M. H. Foster, then Assistant Paymaster-General, was brought in to succeed Anderson in 1867. The need for special qualifications was felt to be essential because the Finance Officer acted as the Chancellor's confidential financial adviser,[1] besides keeping an eye on financial proceedings in the House of Commons for the Financial Secretary.[2] He was also Chief Accountant of the Treasury; beneath him the Accountant was required in all matters to ask for and act under his instructions.

Three First Class Clerks were assigned to the Finance Division at the time of the 1856 reorganization; one acted as Estimate Clerk and sent his papers direct to the Financial Secretary, another looked after the general business of the division, while the services of the third were soon found to be superfluous and his place left unfilled on his resignation from the department. The Second Class Clerk was given more responsible work to do in the Finance Division than elsewhere:[3] he looked after all the business connected with the Treasury Chests abroad, a job originally assigned to one of the First Class Clerks, had responsibility for the audit of all public accounts dealt with at the Treasury; and, subject to the inspection of the First Class Clerk, recorded the progress of the business in the Division Book.

---

[1] Throughout the period 1854–74, but more especially after, this part of the Finance Officer's work became increasingly important. See T.M.s 12 April 1880 and 29 June 1885, H.M.T., *Departmental Arrangement Book*, v.

[2] T.M. 9 April 1867, P.R.O. T.1/6760A/20269.

[3] In the Fourth Division the Second Class Clerk prepared cases for the consideration of the Treasury superannuation committee. See below, Chapter 14.

By arrangement between the Assistant Secretary and the Principal Officers, the clerks of the Superior Establishment—especially those of the Second and Third Classes—were transferred at 'proper intervals' from one division to another to acquire experience of as much of the Treasury business as possible; other opportunities for movement within the department occurred when a promotion took place, or when the business was redistributed.[1] Although they moved fairly frequently, little attempt was made between 1856 and 1870 to associate the Second and Third Class Clerks with the important work of preparing papers for the consideration of the Secretaries. Their training for the higher duties of the office, one of the three main aims of the 1856 reorganization, took place mainly outside the divisions. At any one time, between five and seven Second and Third Class Clerks were employed exclusively as private secretaries: the Financial Secretary, the Parliamentary Secretary, and the Assistant Secretary had one each, and the Chancellor of the Exchequer and the First Lord, one, sometimes two, each.[2] While employed in this capacity the clerks were not attached to divisions, and received in addition to their salaries annual allowances of between £100–300, supplemented on the resignation of their political chiefs by similar amounts as gratuities. Some clerks, Welby, Rivers Wilson, and Delves-Broughton, for instances, spent almost all their early service life as private secretaries. Welby who rose from the Third Class to be Principal Officer of the Finance Division in fifteen years, spent less than four years in the divisions, serving the remainder of the time as private secretary to successive Financial Secretaries. The rapid promotion of some of these private secretaries —Arthur Godley (later Lord Kilbracken) was private secretary to Gladstone at twenty-five, Permanent Secretary at the India Office at thirty-six—caused a good deal of ill-feeling in the early days of entry by examination. Those less fortunate, engaged upon the mundane task of transcribing Minutes in the divisions, had fewer opportunities to reveal their potential and less scope for their talents and initiative.

[1] Besides normal promotions consequent upon death or retirement, the Treasury clerks benefited from the resignation, at different times between 1854 and 1874, of nine senior clerks who left to take up important appointments in other departments.

[2] Apart from those drawn from the ranks of the Treasury, the First Lord had his personal private secretary, e.g. Gladstone's Algernon West, Disraeli's Monty Corry.

The failure to provide a proper training for clerks in the divisions was recognized in the proposals made at the time of the 1870 re-organization. A large measure of responsibility was to be delegated to the First and Second (now junior) Class of Clerks in the divisions: both were to be responsible for the preparation of certain types of decision, relieved entirely of the work of turning the Minutes into official letters, and freed from all copying.[1] But the arrangements for implementing these proposals were ill-conceived. The attempt to delimit the responsibility of the First and Second Class Clerks had the effect of making them and not the Principal Officer responsible for the assignment of the business within the division; for they were to be permitted to sort the papers on their arrival from the Registry and to deal with those which appeared to them to be matters of routine, sending up to the Principal Officer only those papers which in their opinion were too difficult or too important to deal with. The scheme was abandoned after only a few months as a result of pressure from the Principal Officers, who while nominally responsible for the work done in the divisions felt that they had inadequate control of its allocation.

The arrangements introduced in December 1870 were more cautious.[2] In May it had been intended that as many as possible of the Minutes prepared by the Principal Officer or First or Second Class Clerk, as the case might be, should be in the form of written-out letters, which would have eliminated the stage in the procedure where the Minutes were converted into official letters on their return from the Secretaries. The December arrangements provided for a return to the former practice. As before, the Principal Officers, or, under their directions, the First and Second Class Clerks, continued to prepare the Minutes and memoranda to be sent up to the Secretaries. But to save unnecessary work those Minutes which could be written out in full were copied for dispatch without previous transcription into letters. Such Minutes had attached to them the prefix 'write as follows' when they had been approved by the Secretaries. Those Minutes which contained short directions (either by the Principal Officer or the Secretary) for the preparation of a letter were converted into a 'complete draft' by the junior clerks in the division as before. Now, however, they had only to prepare this draft and not the letter for dispatch as well. The latter

[1] T.M. 25 May 1870, H.M.T., *Departmental Arrangement Book*, v.
[2] T.M. 31 December 1870, H.M.T., *Departmental Arrangement Book*, v.

task, and that of copying for record purposes, was assigned to the
writers working under the supervision of the Supplementary
Clerks in the Copying and Indexing Department. As a result the
junior clerks were much less employed in copying than before,
though the task of converting the Minutes into 'complete drafts'
required less an intellectual ability than familiarity with official
procedure. Thus the separation of the intellectual from the routine
work, advocated by Trevelyan twenty-two years before, and one
of the main aims of the 1856 reorganization, proceeded only slowly.
Among the Principal Officers the belief still persisted that junior
clerks needed to be 'familiarised with official forms of transcription' as part of their training for higher duties.[1]

While the junior clerks were still much employed upon routine
work, the status of the First Class Clerks was improved and they
acquired limited authority to prepare business for decision. In the
reorganization of May 1870 they had been relieved of the routine
task of keeping the Division Book, entries in which were now
entrusted to the Second Class Clerk; later they were given the
title of Acting Principal Officer, and in March 1874 authority to
make the final decision on certain carefully defined categories of
divisional business, mainly reports and returns, without reference
to the Secretaries.

THE ASSISTANT SECRETARY

From the Principal Officer the Assistant Secretary received a precis
of the paper, the relevant previous papers, and advice in the form of
a Minute or memorandum. Except when other special arrangements were made,[2] the business of the whole department filtered
through his hands to the Financial Secretary, much of it requiring
little more than an endorsement of the course of action recommended by the Principal Officer; in other cases he prepared a
Minute himself, or wrote a memorandum to the Financial Secretary. As he received advice from the Principal Officers, so in turn
he had to advise the ministers. 'I am bound to give my judgment,
when required, on every subject and to every Government',
Hamilton explained to Gladstone. 'The political officers have a
perfect right to the judgment of the permanent officials and are
perfectly free to adopt or modify or reject their judgment, the
latter are bound to carry out that action, just as if it accorded

---

[1] T.M. 31 December 1870, op. cit.   [2] See below, pp. 51–2.

entirely with their own judgment.'[1] If necessary the Assistant Secretary conferred with the Principal Officer before sending up the papers, but informal meetings were less common than an exchange of memoranda.

The office of Permanent Secretary which Ralph Lingen[2] inherited in 1870 was not that bequeathed to Hamilton by Sir Charles Trevelyan eleven years earlier. It had not only changed in name: the status of the office had been enhanced, and it had acquired greater authority. Above all, the conception of the functions and duties of the office which Hamilton had outlined in his letter to Gladstone in 1859 had been recognized by a Minute of 1867.[3] The office had become the focus for the co-ordination of the whole business of the department, into the Assistant Secretary's hands were gathered the threads of all the departmental business. From this unrivalled position the office drew strength and authority, and from the tenure of it, first Hamilton and then Lingen derived a knowledge and experience of Treasury business which no other Treasury officer could match. To the Financial Secretary the office became an indispensable source of valuable advice and suggestion.

The dominant position achieved by the Assistant Secretary in the discussions which preceded decisions on establishments' matters, and the very great extent to which his judgement and opinions decisively influenced the quality and substance of those decisions, will become apparent in later chapters; for the moment it is sufficient to note that in matters concerning the domestic affairs of the Treasury Hamilton's advice was never rejected. Proposals made to the ministers for the reorganization of the department, the reallocation of the clerks, the transaction and distribution of the business, promotions and transfers, conditions of recruitment—in short, everything connected with the organization of the Treasury except the disposal of the patronage (though even here he attempted to influence the Patronage Secretary)[4] were customarily

---

[1] Hamilton to Gladstone, 9 March 1863, P.R.O. *Hamilton Semi-official Correspondence*, ii.

[2] Ralph Robert Wheeler Lingen (1819–1905): son of Thomas Lingen of an old Herefordshire family; educated Bridgnorth Grammar School, scholar of Trinity College, Oxford, Fellow of Balliol, 1841–4; called to the bar 1847; entered the Education Office 1847, Secretary 1849–70; Permanent Secretary to the Treasury 1870–85; K.C.B. 1878; raised to the peerage as Baron Lingen 1885; Alderman of L.C.C., 1889–92. (See also below, pp. 42–3).

[3] See above, Chapter 1, pp. 23–4.   [4] See above, pp. 15–16.

approved without objection. Opposition was unusual; when it occurred he overcame it. Shelley's removal from the department and the reduction in the number of Principal Officers and divisions despite the doubts and alternative proposal of the Financial Secretary were described above.[1] In 1867 with tireless advocacy he successfully canvassed the candidature of Anderson for the post of Auditor of the Civil List in the face of serious doubts expressed by Gladstone.[2] Two years later he successfully resisted the Financial Secretary's proposal to appoint a Second Class Clerk to the post of Parliamentary Clerk which since 1856 had been held by a clerk of the First Class. Even allowing for the fact that Hamilton was on the verge of retirement and for Stansfeld's irresolute character, his criticism of the Financial Secretary's views was unusually severe and uncompromising; the Financial Secretary was not advised, he was admonished.[3]

Hamilton's views prevailed on two other important occasions. First in 1860 when he resisted Gladstone's proposal to appoint an independent committee of inquiry to report on the organization of the Treasury;[4] and again in 1867, when he obtained approval for the proposal to change the title of his own office and to define more precisely its authority and functions. Although he overcame Gladstone's resistance in 1860, the case argued then by the Chancellor of the Exchequer was a good one, and it may be that then and upon those other occasions described above that Hamilton's views prevailed not so much because they were sound but because they were argued with a fierce determination which left little room for manœuvre or compromise. He was especially prone to present his views tendentiously, and sometimes to deprive the Financial

[1] pp. 25–7.

[2] Gladstone was worried about the accumulation of offices in the hands of one man. Anderson was already Auditor of the Duchy of Cornwall, besides being Principal Officer of the Finance Division. Arbuthnot had been Auditor of the Ecclesiastical Commission, besides Auditor of the Civil List. After a long correspondence between Hamilton and Gladstone, Anderson was appointed Auditor of the Civil List and Auditor of the Ecclesiastical Commission, and retained his two other offices as well. (Hamilton to Gladstone, 2, 4, 7, 10 and 11 August 1865, P.R.O. *Hamilton Semi-official Correspondence*, ii; and Gladstone to Hamilton, 3 and 6 August 1865, Brit. Mus., G.P. Add. MSS., Letter Books, 1865).

[3] Hamilton to Stansfeld, 28 and 31 December 1869, P.R.O. *Hamilton Semi-official Correspondence*, iv; and T. M. 31 December 1869, H.M.T., *Departmental Arrangement Book*, v.

[4] Gladstone to Hamilton, 4 and 11 October 1860; Hamilton to Gladstone, 10 October 1860, P.R.O. *Hamilton Semi-official Correspondence*, i.

Secretary of that balanced judgement and advice which he admitted it was his duty to provide. Through him ran a streak of authoritarianism which he took few pains to conceal. A striking instance of it occurred in 1867 when he asked for the power to appeal to the Chancellor of the Exchequer and the First Lord from the decisions of the Financial Secretary;[1] two years later, although that power had not been granted to him, he did so.[2]

The decision to change the title of the office of Assistant Secretary, to afford formal recognition to the increased authority and enhanced status which it had acquired in practice, and to define its functions more precisely, was the culmination of the process set on foot by Hamilton in 1859, a few months after his appointment. He had been six years in the Treasury when Hugh Childers was appointed Financial Secretary by Palmerston. Childers, one of the ablest administrative reformers to hold office in the second half of the nineteenth century, although Financial Secretary for only a short time, displayed the same zeal for reform and improvement which later characterized his tenure of office at the Admiralty and War Office. He was a business-like administrator, and took to the work of the Treasury 'most vigorously'.[3] Even the indefatigable Gladstone was compelled to remark his 'power of work and willingness to try everything till he is overdone'.[4] As the working head of the Treasury he assumed a personal responsibility for promoting economy and efficiency in the administration of the department (and elsewhere),[5] and consequently was better informed than most of his predecessors about the conduct of the day to day business. Before leaving office on the fall of the Government in July 1866 he placed on record his opinion of the necessity for reorganizing the department. In his view the senior officials had been badly over-worked, particularly the Assistant Secretary, whom he considered had seriously over-taxed his strength. Unlike Gladstone, who at this time was also thinking about the need to reorganize the Treasury, he was not in favour of altering the constitution of the Board to provide further assistance

[1] Hamilton to Disraeli, 25 April 1867; P.R.O. *Hamilton Semi-official Correspondence*, iii.
[2] See below, pp. 46–7; and Chapter 9, pp. 252–4.
[3] Hamilton to Gladstone, 22 August 1865, Brit. Mus., G.P. Add. MSS. 44192, ff. 158–9.
[4] Gladstone to H. Brand, 29 January 1866, Brit. Mus., G.P. Add. MSS., Letter Books 1866–9.   [5] See below, Chapter 5, pp. 132–7.

with the financial work, preferring the existing arrangement under which one of the Junior Lords took a share of the financial business, under the direction of the Financial Secretary, both in Parliament and in the department.[1] 'Where the office requires strengthening is in the assistance to be given to the Assistant Secretary . . . I recommend that the Assistant Secretary be called the Permanent Secretary and a new office of Assistant (permanent) Secretary be constituted.'[2]

The new Government assumed office on 13 July 1866. Disraeli was appointed Chancellor of the Exchequer, and George Ward Hunt, Financial Secretary. On 2 March 1867, in a memorandum to Hunt, Hamilton outlined his proposals for improving the organization of the department based upon those contained in papers left behind by Childers. The most important of these was the suggestion that his position as Assistant Secretary should be defined and the title changed to that of Permanent Secretary. On 6 April, Hunt agreed to this and to the other recommendations that Hamilton had made to him; and in addition, proposed that he, himself, should have a second private secretary. All the recommendations were then submitted by Hunt for the approval of the Chancellor of the Exchequer. Disraeli's reply was characteristically brief: 'I approve of these suggestions as far as the appointment of Mr. Law as Auditor of the Civil List with assistant duties and the appointment of an extra private secretary to the Financial Secretary';[3] no reference was made to the other proposals. As the suggestion to alter the status of his office had not been unequivocally rejected, Hamilton decided to bring the matter before the Chancellor again, but Hunt was away for the week-end and he was obliged, therefore, to contact the Chancellor directly instead of through the Financial Secretary which was the more usual procedure. Explaining this to Disraeli's private secretary, Monty Corry, he stressed the desirability of making the arrangements as soon as possible, and inquired if whether by the qualification that the Chancellor had attached to his approval he intended to exclude the adoption of the recommendations relating to the position of Assistant Secretary.

[1] See below, pp. 50–2.
[2] Memorandum by Childers, 5 July 1866, P.R.O. T.1/6760A/20269.
[3] Quoted in Hamilton's letter to Disraeli, 25 April 1867, P.R.O., *Hamilton Semi-official Correspondence*, iii. A copy of Disraeli's memorandum appears after Hamilton's letter.

In his letter to Disraeli, Hamilton betrayed his anxiety that his position might remain unaltered. Childers had made the suggestion initially, he claimed, without his prior knowledge or influence; and while he did not wish any personal consideration connected with himself to have any influence in determining the future position of the permanent head of the Treasury, he would 'regret with reference to the Public Service if the recommendations of Mr Childers and Mr Hunt in this respect should not be adopted, for I see in the future at least the possibility of a state of things at the Treasury which under some Government which may hereafter be formed [the post] may require all the influence which personal position and character can give to prevent abuses'.[1] If the great powers of the Financial Secretary 'were placed in the hands of an unscrupulous man', Hamilton continued, 'the only effective check would be with the head of the permanent establishment'. It is unlikely that Hamilton seriously believed in the possibility of such a situation arising; if there was a possibility, it is even less likely that it could have been averted or off-set by a strong Permanent Secretary with power and authority to check the excesses of an 'unscrupulous' Financial Secretary. Here Hamilton was seeking the power to appeal against a decision of the Financial Secretary where the advice of the Assistant Secretary had been rejected or disregarded. Should such a situation arise the Assistant Secretary's 'official position and his personal character ought to be such as to give weight to his remonstrance, and if that should prove ineffectual his position should [?]empower him in making a representation to the First Lord and the Chancellor of the Exchequer'.

Whether this extraordinary argument induced the Chancellor to change his mind, or whether there had simply been a misunderstanding about his initial response to the proposals put to him previously, is not certain. It is unlikely that Disraeli felt strongly about the change either way, he was notoriously apathetic about Treasury business, and never showed much interest in the domestic problems of the department.[2] Whatever the reason, by 6 May 1867 he and the First Lord had agreed that the title of the office of Assistant Secretary should be changed and its duties defined. Four days later authority for the change was given in a Minute

---

[1] Hamilton to Disraeli, 25 April 1867, op. cit.
[2] C. Rivers Wilson, *Chapters From My Official Life*, p. 31. While a junior clerk in the Treasury he had served as Disraeli's private secretary.

drafted by Hamilton.[1] The official explanation stated that the functions of the Financial Secretary had greatly increased both in their extent and in their importance, with the result that the work and duties of the Assistant Secretary had become more onerous and responsible. It was decided therefore that 'the office shall now be given a more substantive character than that of Assistant Secretary and they are pleased to direct that its title should be that of "Permanent Secretary" '. The gratification of his other wish—to define the nature of the office he held—Hamilton accomplished in the same Minute; but the definition added nothing new to the responsibilities which he had assumed since 1859.

It will be the duty of the Permanent Secretary to exercise a general supervision over the business of the Office, to keep himself well informed regarding all subjects which come before the Treasury so as to be able at all times to furnish information and advice to the Board and to the Political Secretaries as may be required on all matters before them.

Hitherto it has been widely claimed that the title of Official Head of the Civil Service was conferred with that of Permanent Secretary. No reference to any such title is made in the Minute of 10 May 1867, until recently assumed lost or destroyed.[2] The Permanent Secretary was to have 'particular regard to all increases of Establishments and Salaries in the Public Service', but this was not a new function; since 1856 he had been furnished with all 'papers relating to the revision and regulation of the Public Establishments',[3] and earlier, Trevelyan's responsibilities had included the over-sight of expenditure on civil establishments throughout the Public Service. But it did serve to emphasize the special responsibility for the Civil Service which Hamilton had assumed in practice. Near to retirement he described his ten years 'as the head of the Permanent Civil Service', which was both an indication that the title had not been conferred upon him in 1867 and an acknowledgement of his *de facto* status.[4] Formal recognition of that status was delayed another fifty years.[5] On taking office in

[1] T.M. 10 May 1867, H.M.T., *Departmental Arrangement Book*, iv.

[2] The Minute is reproduced in full, Appendix I.

[3] T.M. 1 October 1856, op. cit.

[4] Hamilton to Gladstone, 25 April 1869, Brit. Mus., G.P. Add. MSS. 44192, fo. 240.

[5] Discussed below in 'A Note on the Title of Official Head of the Civil Service', Appendix II.

1868 Gladstone discussed the change in the title with three or four members of his cabinet. No sufficient reason was seen for reversing the arrangement and 'one or two thought that there was an advantage in the change on account of the more authoritative title which it gives as tending to increase weight in correspondence with other Departments'.[1]

If Hamilton was disappointed with the decisions made in 1867 it can have been only because he had not been explicitly granted the power to appeal from the decisions of the Financial Secretary; but neither had he been denied it explicitly. Determined and tenacious, he had secured for himself the title, status, and authority to which he aspired in 1859. On the eve of his retirement he described the nature of his post to Robert Lowe. He told him that he had presided over the Civil Service for nearly thirteen years,[2] and his experience warranted him in stating that:

The office of Permanent Secretary to the Treasury may be regarded as almost the keystone of the whole Civil Service. Whatever may be the abilities or powers or strength of a Government practically, their facilities and I might almost say their safety in administration will be found to depend, to a very great extent upon the Permanent Secretary of the Treasury. It can scarcely be otherwise in the necessarily complicated system of our Government with its great political changes and the importance and value of the office is not merely in the business which the Permanent Secretary himself actually transacts with political members of the Government but in the business he has to transact with others, and in the direct and indirect influence he exercises throughout the whole public service.[3]

Hamilton received no official recognition of his public services other than a belated admission to the Privy Council. Palmerston had passed him over when the Permanent Under-Secretaries of the Home and Foreign Offices had been made Privy Councillors; and Lord Derby had failed to recall the services he rendered to the Conservative Party between 1836 and 1858. 'I must not allow myself to entertain any feeling of disappointment', he wrote to Col. T. E. Taylor, Derby's Patronage Secretary, in December 1868

[1] Gladstone to Ayrton, 13 August 1869, Brit. Mus., G.P. Add. MSS., Letter Books, 1869.
[2] Hamilton had been permanent head of the Treasury for only eleven years; the figure must therefore be taken to include his two years as Financial Secretary.
[3] Hamilton to Lowe, 21 September 1869, P.R.O., *Hamilton Semi-official Correspondence*, iv.

when on the defeat of the Conservative Government he believed the last opportunity to be sworn a Privy Councillor had passed.[1] He told Taylor that he had been determined that he 'would never suggest anything regarding myself to anyone of my own political friends when in power. They had demands enough upon them without any from me, and any recognition of either present non-political or byegone political services, to have had any great value in my estimation, must have been spontaneous, and not the result of any movement on my part'. To his suprise he was sworn a member of the Privy Council eight months later on the recommendation of Lowe. In February 1870 he retired to Ireland where he was appointed a Commissioner of Church Temporalities, and died at Kingstown eighteen months later at the age of sixty-nine. Gladstone remembered him as 'a man of large heart and large mind; as a most devoted and very able public servant; as one who attracted on every side sentiments of confidence and friendship'.[2]

His successor, Ralph Robert Wheeler Lingen, was brought to the Treasury by Lowe from the Education Office, where together they had been responsible for the introduction of 'payment by results'. A former Fellow of Balliol and close friend of Jowett, Lingen entered the Education Office in 1847 after being called to the bar. Two years later when only thirty he succeeded Kay-Shuttleworth as Permanent Secretary. Experience and disposition made Lingen especially suitable to preside over the Treasury under a Government committed to economy. When at the Education Office it was said of him that he acted on Kay-Shuttleworth's maxim: 'Get it done, let the objectors howl';[3] and that his strength lay not so much in his capacity to make changes as in his ability to negative claims upon the public purse. Fierce and tenacious in the face of public criticism of the policy of 'payment by results' he was said by the *Saturday Review* to be 'quite as powerful as Mr Lowe and a great deal more offensive'.[4] At the Treasury he and the 'Whitehead Torpedo', as Lowe was known throughout the Civil Service, presented an awe-inspiring combination to other departments; together, however, they were not conspicuously more

[1] Hamilton to Taylor, 6 December 1868, P.R.O., *Hamilton Semi-official Correspondence*, iv.

[2] Gladstone to Hamilton's brother, 20 September 1871, Brit. Mus., G.P. Add. MSS., Letter Books, 1871.

[3] Evelyn Abbott and Lewis Campbell, *The Life and Letters of Benjamin Jowett*, i. 185.   [4] 16 April 1864.

successful in 'negativing claims upon the public purse' than were Trevelyan or Hamilton before them.

Lingen was Lowe's choice, Gladstone had favoured recalling Trevelyan to the Service, but Lowe was completely opposed to the idea, thinking 'very meanly', of Trevelyan's judgment.[1] Of the others whom Gladstone consulted, Granville supported Trevelyan, but Sir Alexander Spearman, 'a first-rate Treasury authority',[2] and Cardwell were against him. W. H. Stephenson, now Chairman of the Board of Inland Revenue, was approached unofficially on Hamilton's recommendation and expressed a willingness to return to the Treasury, but Lowe, who had supported his appointment initially, switched to Lingen, and Gladstone deferred to his wishes.[3]

THE JOINT SECRETARIES

The Financial Secretary was the organ and representative of the Treasury in the House of Commons[4] 'responsible for all Treasury action (omitting of course the exercise of the political patronage which belongs to the Patronage Secretary) whether under Minutes sanctioned by himself or where his views may have been overruled by the higher authorities, Cabinet, First Lord or Chancellor of the Exchequer'.[5] Within the department as well, the functions of the Financial and Parliamentary Secretaries were clearly differentiated. The former was the working head of the department and the political officer (under the Chancellor of the Exchequer) responsible for the conduct of the day to day business.[6] The Parliamentary

---

[1] Lowe to Gladstone, 15 August 1869, Brit. Mus., G.P. Add. MSS. 44301, ff. 70–1.

[2] Assistant Secretary to the Treasury, 1836–40.

[3] H. Preston-Thomas in *The Work and Play of a Government Inspector* provides a different but undocumented account. He maintains that Gladstone sought to appoint John Lambert, an inspector of the former Poor Law Board, and his friend and counsellor in the Civil Service, but after a cabinet dispute gave way to Lowe.

[4] Until 1918 ministerial office disqualified an M.P. from sitting in the House of Commons until he had successfully sought re-election by his constituents. Junior ministers were not required to do so, and for the first few weeks after the formation of each new government, the Financial Secretary was the senior Front Bench member.

[5] Gladstone to Childers, 15 August 1865, Brit. Mus., G.P. Add. MSS., Letter Books, 1865; and memo from Northcote to Disraeli 29 June 1866, Brit. Mus., I[ddesleigh] P[apers], Add. MSS. 50015, iii. fo. 135.

[6] T.M. 1 October 1856, op. cit.; and evidence of R. E. Welby before the *Select Committee on Civil Services Expenditure*, 1873, P.P., 1873, VII.

Secretary dealt only with that part of the business which related to appointments in the gift of the Treasury, i.e. appointments in the Treasury itself and those departments subordinate to it; he saw no other papers.

All Treasury papers were supposed to be brought before the Financial Secretary by the Assistant Secretary. In practice arrangements were usually made between them for the convenience of the former whereby those papers of mere routine would be sifted by the Assistant Secretary and (after 1867) by the Assistant to the Secretaries. By arrangement certain other papers would be decided by the Assistant Secretary with reference to the Financial Secretary, though the tendency was 'not to refer too little'.[1] Hamilton's custom was to mark his initials across a paper to signify that the Minute could go on without being sent up to the Financial Secretary. He told one Financial Secretary, James Stansfeld, that he tested the 'propriety of sending on a paper in this manner by putting it to myself whether the decision is such as can be questioned in Parliament. If it is I consider that the judgment of one of the Political Officers of the Government, the Chancellor of the Exchequer or the Financial Secretary should be exercised upon it';[2] and later told Lingen that he referred all papers which involved increased expenditure, or were of a kind which might be noticed in Parliament.[3] Upon this principle almost all establishments papers were seen by the Financial Secretary or the Chancellor of the Exchequer, as well as by the Assistant Secretary. Papers dealing with the Estimates were received by the Financial Secretary direct from the Estimate Clerk.

Normally the Financial Secretary found no difficulty in approving the Minutes written on establishments' papers by his senior advisers, and was content merely to add his initials below those of the Assistant Secretary; very occasionally he might make some slight modification to the Minute before doing so. In certain circumstances, however, he wrote the Minute himself; as, for example, where he cancelled the Minute sent up to him because he disagreed with it—this was very rare indeed. More commonly,

[1] Lingen to J. G. Dodson, 8 August 1873, Bod., M[onk] B[retton] P[apers], box 42.
[2] Hamilton to Stansfeld, 25 October 1869, P.R.O. *Hamilton Semi-official Correspondence*, iv.
[3] Referred to by Lingen in his memorandum to Dodson, 8 August 1873, op. cit.

he wrote the Minute himself when the papers were sent up un-minuted because it was known that he was, or had been, dealing with the matter personally; or where the Principal Officer and the Assistant Secretary had written memoranda but because of the importance of the subject matter, political sensitivity, or plain doubt, had hesitated to draft a Minute. Before endorsing the action recommended to him, or deciding finally for himself, the Financial Secretary frequently discussed the paper with the Assistant Secretary; this communication, like most others in the Treasury, took place more often on paper than informally in conversation. When a decision had been made the Minute or the directions for its preparation, together with all the papers, were sent back to the appropriate division where the Minute was converted into a letter for dispatch.

Some Financial Secretaries, like Frederick Peel,[1] Childers and Northcote, immersed themselves in the day to day administrative work of the department, but William Baxter, according to Lowe, was

a perfect cypher. The whole of the business is done by Lingen and me and I should say by my Secretary to whom people come when they ought to go to Baxter. He has never investigated or worked out a single question of detail or indeed thrown any light on any question whatever. He is personally not unpopular in the office but has neither weight nor influence nor knowledge.[2]

Gladstone described the relationship between a Financial Secretary and a Chancellor of the Exchequer as

one of peculiar intimacy, greater I think in reality (in most cases at least) than between Secretary and Under Secretary of State because the Secretary to the Treasury dispatches great masses of business without referring it to the person holding my office, and it requires much tact and discernment on his part to know when he ought to refer. This though difficult is not unattainable, Peel, for example, I think hardly ever went wrong.[3]

[1] Frederick Peel (1823–1906): son of Sir Robert Peel; born London, educated Harrow and Trinity College, Cambridge; called to the bar 1849; Liberal M.P. 1849; U/S for Colonies, 1851–5; U/S for War, 1855–7; Financial Secretary to the Treasury, 1859–65; K.C.M.G. 1869; member of the Railway and Canal Commission, 1873–1906.
[2] Lowe to Gladstone, 12 August 1872, Brit. Mus., G.P. Add. MSS. 44302, CCXVII.
[3] Gladstone to Childers, 15 August 1865, Brit. Mus., G.P. Add. MSS., Letter Books, 1865.

F

Very little went on to the Chancellor of the Exchequer after having passed the Assistant and Financial Secretaries, 'unless the latter wanted him to see it.' Papers were referred by the Financial Secretary where he was doubtful about the proper decision to make, or where the paper was unusual or particularly important;[1] and also, if it was expected that appeals would be made officially or privately to the Chancellor against a Treasury decision, or where private ministerial pressure was brought to bear upon the Financial Secretary. While the Assistant Secretary might, and often did, advise the Financial Secretary to submit a paper to the Chancellor, or indicate that such a reference was unnecessary, he had no formal power to appeal to the Chancellor against the Financial Secretary's decision or where the two were in disagreement. Nevertheless, there is one recorded instance of such an appeal being made.[2] In July 1869 Hamilton appealed successfully to Lowe against a decision made by Acton Smee Ayrton.[3] On the strength of this precedent, and perhaps also from a liberal interpretation of his powers as a Secretary of the Board under the Minute of 10 May 1867, Hamilton considered thereafter that, in certain circumstances, it was the right and duty of the Permanent Secretary to appeal to the First Lord or the Chancellor of the Exchequer.

To Ayrton's successor, James Stansfeld,[4] he explained the duties of the Financial Secretary, and the nature of the relationship between that office and his own. He wished it to be

clearly understood that while the Financial Secretary is the accredited Political representative of the Board the duty devolving upon the Permanent Secretary, and it is one he should not shrink from discharg-

---

[1] Gladstone to Childers, 15 August 1865, Brit. Mus., G.P. Add. MSS., Letter Books, 1865. See also Gladstone's evidence before the *P.A.C.*, P.P., 1862, XI, qus. 1766-7.

[2] The case is discussed below, Chapter 9, pp. 252-4.

[3] Acton Smee Ayrton (1816-86): son of a barrister; called to the bar and practised in India, 1850-3; Liberal M.P., 1857-74; Financial Secretary to the Treasury, December 1868 to November 1869; First Commissioner of Works, 1869-73; Judge Advocate General, 1873-4.

[4] James Stansfield, jun. (1820-98): born Halifax and brought up as a nonconformist; educated University College, London; called to the bar 1849; Liberal M.P. 1859; Junior Lord of the Admiralty 1863; U/S of State for India, 1866; Third Lord of the Treasury, December 1868 to November 1869; Financial Secretary to the Treasury, November 1869 to March 1871; President of the Poor Law Board 1871, and first President of the new Local Government Board, 1871-4.

ing, of bringing under the notice of the First Lord or the Chancellor of the Exchequer as the case may be, any subject or paper or minute the decision upon which by the Financial Secretary may appear to him to require further consideration.[1]

The power here claimed by Hamilton was handed on to his successor. Explaining the transaction of the business to J. G. Dodson[2] when he took office as Financial Secretary in August 1873, Lingen said that in the case of a difference of opinion between the Secretaries the Permanent Secretary could appeal to the Chancellor.[3] The previous month Gladstone had not challenged Lingen's contention that 'either Secretary should have the power of informing the Chancellor of the Exchequer, and of obtaining his authority independently of their agreeing or differing on the decision of the paper'.[4] Although Lingen had no occasion to exercise this power within the next six months, undoubtedly he thought he had the right to do so.

THE CHANCELLOR OF THE EXCHEQUER

'The relation of the Chancellor of the Exchequer to the Treasury is somewhat anomalous; it does not correspond at all with that of a Secretary of State to his department', Gladstone told the Public Accounts Committee in 1862.[5] The Chancellor was unable to exercise the same personal control of his department because, unlike almost all other departments, much of the current business of the office did not come under his notice at all. In matters of detail he was obliged to rely very much upon his official advisers, 'who knew the precedents and kept up the tradition of the department'.

Apart from those papers which on his own discretion the Financial Secretary referred to the Chancellor, the extent to which the Chancellor engaged in the ordinary business of the department varied with the interest, energy, and disposition of the individual.

[1] Memorandum from Hamilton to Stansfeld, 25 October 1869, P.R.O., *Hamilton Semi-official Correspondence*, iv.

[2] John George Dodson, 1st Baron Monk Bretton (1825–97): born London; educated Eton and Christ Church; called to the bar; Liberal M.P., 1857; Deputy Speaker, 1857–62; Financial Secretary to the Treasury, August 1873 to February 1874; President of the Local Government Board, 1880–2; Chancellor of the Duchy of Lancaster, 1882–4.

[3] Lingen to Dodson, 8 August 1873, Bod., M.B.P., box 42.

[4] Amendment by Lingen to memorandum by Gladstone, 26 July 1873, Bod., M.B.P., box 42.

[5] 3rd Report of the *P.A.C.*, 1862, P.P., 1862, XI, qu. 1640.

Alone of the five men who held the office between 1854–74, Robert Lowe arranged for a part of the routine business to be forwarded to him without having passed first through the hands of the Secretaries. With his accustomed intellectual arrogance, he once told Gladstone that he had initialled every important paper which had passed through the Treasury, and as a result had a 'competent knowledge of the department as a whole and was not driven to form his opinion at second hand.'[1] Also, together with the Permanent Secretary, Ralph Lingen, he assumed a personal responsibility for all questions relating to the introduction of open competition and the application of the 1870 Order in Council.[2] Lowe's practice was unusual, though Goulburn was said to have been a 'cross between Chancellor of the Exchequer and Secretary to the Treasury'.[3] No similar arrangements were made by Lowe's immediate predecessors. Sir George Cornewall Lewis 'preferred a classic, though ready to deal with what came before him'.[4] Disraeli, who 'never cared for Treasury business',[5] as a rule contented himself with laying down principles, and left the general administration and working out of detail almost entirely to his subordinates.[6] On the other hand, Gladstone was 'always ready to deal with questions submitted to him', frequently wrote long Minutes, and was always ready to exchange memoranda with his Financial Secretary and senior advisers when papers were referred to him.[7]

The Chancellor of the Exchequer was concerned more particularly with questions of financial policy, in the formulation of which he had the advice and assistance of the Treasury Finance Officer and his division. A reforming and economizing Chancellor, like Gladstone or Lowe, was

watched with an extreme jealousy in Parliament in regard to whatever expenditure you may recommend on your own responsibility; and all those, on whose toes you will necessarily have trodden, will look out with a preterhuman sharpness for the joints in your own armour. . . . No man wants so much sympathy as the Chancellor of the Exchequer, and . . . no man gets so little. Nor is there any position so lamentable for him as

[1] Lowe to Gladstone, 12 April 1870, Brit. Mus., G.P. Add. MSS. 44301, ff. 142–3.　　[2] See below Chapter 4.
[3] Sir Reginald Welby to Childers, 11 December 1882, quoted in Spencer Childers, *The Life of Rt. Hon. Hugh C. E. Childers*, ii, 148–9.
[4] Ibid.　　　　　　　　　　　　　　　　　[5] Ibid.
[6] G. E. Buckle, *Life of Benjamin Disraeli, Earl of Beaconsfield*, IV. 32.
[7] George Ward Hunt was Chancellor of the Exchequer for only ten months, and it is impossible to obtain any clear impression of his work.

to be defeated in proposing some new charge on the public conceived or adopted by himself. He is like an ancient soldier wounded in the back. Whereas even defeat in resisting raids of the House of Commons on the public purse is honourable, and always turns out well in the end.[1]

Occasionally, a minister appealed personally to the Chancellor against a Treasury decision. As well, suggestions and appeals were made to him on revenue matters from the Revenue Departments; as a rule these came to him directly without passing through the Treasury. As Head of the National Debt Office and Master of the Mint a few questions came to him from the permanent heads of these two offices.

THE FIRST LORD OF THE TREASURY

The time had not long passed when the First Lord had been intimately connected with Treasury business; Peel had presented budgets. But after 1856 the First Lord normally took no part in the formal transaction of Treasury business, unless the office was combined with that of Chancellor of the Exchequer.[2] Occasionally, however, special arrangements were made between the First Lord and the Chancellor of the Exchequer for the reference of certain Treasury papers. On his appointment as First Lord in 1868 Gladstone arranged that Lowe should inform him of 'all subjects involving new expenditure, or guaranteed, or other engagements, which you may think to be sufficiently important, or critical, or novel to recommend it'.[3] From the extensive Treasury patronage the First Lord usually reserved for himself only appointments to the Treasury and Audit Office, and sometimes indicated to the Patronage Secretary what rules he was to follow in filling certain vacancies in the Treasury.[4] Important changes in the organization of the department were always submitted for his approval; for example, the abolition of the First Division in 1859, and the changing of the Assistant Secretary's title in 1867.

[1] Gladstone to Lowe, 26 December 1869, on the latter's taking office as Chancellor of the Exchequer. Brit. Mus., G.P. Add. MSS. 44301, ff. 35–6.
[2] e.g. on Lowe's resignation in August 1873 Gladstone combined the two offices.
[3] Gladstone to Lowe, 26 December 1868, Brit. Mus., G.P. Add. MSS. 44301, ff, 35–6.
[4] For an example, see T.M. 10 November 1857, H.M.T., *Departmental Arrangement Book*, iii.

THE JUNIOR LORDS OF THE TREASURY

The duties of the Junior Lords as members of the Treasury Board diminished with its decline as the instrument for the transaction of Treasury business during the late eighteenth and early nineteenth centuries; by 1854 they were required only to attend meetings and sign letters and warrants. Even these minimal duties disappeared with the reorganization of the department in July 1856. From that time onwards the Board met in a corporate capacity only to signify approval to appointments made by the First Lord to it or to the position of Assistant Secretary, but there was no question of it having authority to dispute or reject his nominations.[1]

After 1856 the Junior Lords were used increasingly as Government Whips in Parliament, but their ties with the Treasury were not completely severed. Since 1831 two of their number had served as members of the Treasury superannuation committee, which considered and reported on all claims made by civil servants for public pensions; one was relieved of this duty when the Assistant Secretary was appointed a permanent member of the committee in 1859.[2] Arrangements were sometimes made, as in 1855, for important papers relating to Scotland to be referred to the 'Scotch Lord' for his opinion. The only other Treasury duty which a Junior Lord might be called upon to perform was service on a Treasury committee appointed to inquire and report on the establishment of one of the departments.[3]

The success of these arrangements prompted Gladstone (and then Disraeli) to experiment further.[4] Between December 1865 and December 1868 the Junior Lord who assisted with the superannuation business was also given authority to minute and initial certain other papers before passing them on to the Secretaries, where his decision was revised 'only in cases of importance or difficulty which seem to require further consideration'.[5] Returning

---

[1] T.M. 10 September 1885, H.M.T., *Departmental Arrangement Book*, v.

[2] See below, Chapter 14.   [3] See below, Chapter 8.

[4] Gladstone was of opinion that the Treasury was under-staffed on the ministerial side, and contemplated reorganizing the Board. For his ideas, see letters to Henry Brand, 16 and 29 January 1866; Brit. Mus., G.P. Add. MSS., Letter Books, 1866–9; letter from Childers, 18 January 1866, Brit. Mus., G.P. Add. MSS. 44128; and letter from Northcote to Disraeli, 1 July 1866, Brit. Mus., I.P. Add. MSS. 50015, fo. 135.

[5] T.M. 18 June 1866, P.R.O. T.1/6665A/19750. Initially the Junior Lord had been given more limited authority, see T.M. 9 January 1866, H.M.T.,

to the Treasury as First Lord in 1868, Gladstone did not undertake the drastic reconstruction of the Treasury Board which he had contemplated two years earlier.[1] Now the only change he made was to appoint a fourth Junior Lord, and select one of the four, James Stansfeld, for a new post of Third Lord with a salary of £2,000 and a private secretary.[2] Lowe, the Chancellor of the Exchequer, then divided the whole of the Treasury business between the Financial Secretary, the Third Lord, and himself; no longer did it all pass (nominally) through the hands of the Financial Secretary. 'It would not be convenient, neither would it be requisite for the information of the Financial Secretary that the papers dealt with by the Third Lord or by the Chancellor of the Exchequer himself should necessarily be submitted before execution to the Financial Secretary', Lowe explained.[3] Of course, it was still open to the Financial Secretary to inform himself upon any paper, and Ayrton took steps to do so, directing that, for his own information and guidance, all Minutes and orders which were not of a formal and routine kind, and which he had not previously seen, were to be forwarded to him as soon as they had been executed. In this way, although he was unable to influence or contribute to the decisions made separately by the Third Lord and the Chancellor of the Exchequer, he was able to apprise himself of all the important business which passed through the department. All the business continued to flow through the Permanent Secretary, but his task of co-ordination was more difficult now that he had to deal with three people.

A few months later Lowe resolved upon a further division of the business, and all papers connected with Scottish affairs were sent in the first instance to the Junior Lord who looked after Scottish business in the House of Commons. Apart from the First Lord and one of the four Junior Lords, each member of the Treasury Board was now assigned a departmental duty. In October 1869

[1] On the resignation of the Government in 1866, Gladstone called in Northcote and explained to him his proposals for reconstructing the Treasury Board; these were conveyed to Disraeli in Northcote's letter 1 July 1866, op. cit.

[2] T.M. 28 December 1868, P.R.O. T.1/6839A/19433.

[3] Memorandum by Lowe, 2 February 1869, P.R.O. *Hamilton Semi-official Correspondence*, iv.

Departmental Arrangement Book, iv. Disraeli merely continued the arrangements made by Gladstone, see T.M. 30 July 1866, P.R.O. T.1/6665A/19750.

Ayrton was appointed First Commissioner of Works, and the resulting changes in the composition of the Board provided Hamilton with the opportunity to protest strongly against the continuation of the arrangements on the grounds that the apportionment of papers between three political officers was impracticable and irreconcilable with the chain of responsibility in the department. He urged, therefore, that all papers should go to the Financial Secretary; and to Lowe he proposed alterations which he thought it desirable to make on Ayrton's resignation. Although this document is missing from both the Treasury papers and Hamilton's correspondence it is almost certain that his proposals were accepted by Lowe, for on Stansfeld's appointment as Financial Secretary the office of Third Lord was abolished. There followed a return to the arrangements introduced in 1865–6, which remained substantially unaltered until the appointment of Lowe to the Home Office in August 1873 when Gladstone combined the offices of First Lord and Chancellor of the Exchequer. To strengthen the parliamentary staff of the department, and to relieve the Financial Secretary of the increased work which would otherwise have fallen upon him, one of the Junior Lords, Lord Frederick Cavendish, was appointed to the new post of Financial Lord to the Treasury with a salary of £1,500 and a private secretary. His functions were similar to those of the Third Lord in 1868–9: he was assigned 'certain duties and the investigation and decision of certain subjects connected with the business of the department',[1] but unlike the 1868 arrangements there was no attempt to define the responsibilities of the Financial Lord more narrowly, nor were any instructions given for the assignment of papers. Lingen was opposed to the reference of papers by himself to anybody but the Financial Secretary, and suggested that any assignment should be made by informal agreement between the two ministers.

[1] T.M. 11 September 1873, H.M.T., *Departmental Arrangement Book*, v.

PART TWO

CONTROL OF ESTABLISHMENTS

3

RECRUITMENT BEFORE 1870

INTRODUCTION

'THE public service should be carried on by the admission into its lower ranks of a carefully selected body of young men', wrote Northcote and Trevelyan in their report. Guided by this 'general principle', they proposed the establishment of a central examination system in which examinations for a given number of vacancies in the Service would be conducted periodically by an independent Board of Examiners, with powers to examine and determine candidates' age, health, and moral fitness, and to test their ability and intellectual qualifications by competitive literary examinations open to all. Successful candidates would be issued with a certificate of qualification and required to serve a period of probationary service.

Sixteen years later, within their own life-time, Northcote and Trevelyan could point to the introduction of most of these proposals, although complete acceptance and implementation was to take another fifty years. It was accomplished very largely by two Orders in Council. The first, introduced by Palmerston's Government in May 1855, provided for the establishment of an independent regulatory body, the Civil Service Commission, whose certificate of qualification ultimately became the condition and proof of appointment to a situation in the Civil Service. The Commission was chosen with great care, the triumvirate—Gladstone, Trevelyan, and Jowett—energetically canvassing names and

Order of Council 1855 - Civil Service Commission - certificate
1870 -

support; Jowett and his friend the Rev. Frederick Temple, principal of Kneller Hall, were Gladstone's and Trevelyan's first choices, but both declined. Ultimately, Sir Edward Ryan, Assistant Comptroller-General of the Exchequer, a former Chief Justice of Bengal, and a friend of Macaulay's, was appointed chairman. The other two members were J. G. Shaw Lefevre, Clerk to the House of Lords, who had commented enthusiastically upon the report when consulted by Trevelyan prior to its publication,[1] and Edward Romilly, Chairman of the Audit Board.

The Commissioners soon began to loosen the departments' grip of recruitment, but did not succeed in breaking it until the introduction of open competitive examinations in 1870, when Gladstone's Government brought forward the second of the two great Orders in Council. Until this time the Treasury's influence upon the development of recruitment had been minimal, limited to tacit approval and occasional support for the Civil Service Commissioners' cautious assault upon the jealously guarded departmental autonomies. But with the introduction of open competition the Treasury assumed the initiative, and began to exercise a close and detailed control over the whole recruitment process, the Civil Service Commissioners now relegated to a subordinate and largely executive position. The explanation of this abrupt change of attitude is not simply that the Treasury was given final authority over the whole process in the 1870 Order in Council, whereas in the earlier one it had power only to approve the appointment by the Civil Service Commissioners of a secretary and assistant examiners. To a large extent what was written into each of them accurately expressed the intentions at the time of the prime movers in the campaign for reform, given the prevailing attitude towards reform within the Service and outside.

THE CAMPAIGN FOR REFORM

A few months before Trevelyan and Northcote undertook Gladstone's commission to inquire into the British Civil Service, Trevelyan was engaged with Macaulay, his brother-in-law, in a new and successful attempt to liberalize the Indian Civil Service on the occasion of the renewal of the East India Company's charter. Sir Charles Wood, who as Chancellor of the Exchequer

[1] Lefevre to Trevelyan, 23 January 1854, Brit. Mus., G.P. Add. MSS. 44333, fo. 30.

at the time of the Irish famine had been greatly influenced by Trevelyan, was now Secretary of State for India and bent upon abolishing the East India Company's civil patronage; Robert Lowe, an enthusiastic advocate of open competition, was his Parliamentary Under-Secretary. Trevelyan was at the very centre of the agitation, explaining and persuading influential people and committees of the merits of open competitive examinations, and mobilizing support for the campaign; it was he who recruited Jowett to the cause.

By the time the Northcote–Trevelyan Report was completed, Wood's India Bill had passed the Commons, but, largely as a result of a formidable pressure group mobilized by Jowett, had been amended to throw open appointments in the Indian Civil Service to all candidates, whether or not they had been trained at Hailey-bury. The campaign for reform of the British Civil Service which followed the publication of the report in February 1854 proceeded *pari passu*; indeed the reformers were confident that Aberdeen's Government could be persuaded to introduce similar legislation to that which applied to India. Trevelyan and Macaulay saw the introduction of open competition into the I.C.S. in 1854 mainly as a victory in the campaign, then well under way, for the reform of the British Civil Service. The Northcote–Trevelyan Report was profoundly influenced by proposals made for the reform of the I.C.S. When they proposed the introduction of open competitive examinations and the establishment of an independent Board of Examiners, it was with the knowledge that these and other pro-posals had already been accepted for India.

Reform in both Services, largely predicated upon competition, literary ability, and reward for industry and merit,[1] was at the same time influenced by the reform movement in the universities. In the 1840s Oxford began to feel pressure for reform from out-side. The middle classes elated by the passage of the first Reform Bill and the repeal of the Corn Laws began to take notice of pro-posals that would open Oxford and Cambridge to more than the handful for whom they had been reserved. 'Principles of liberalism, utilitarianism, science and specialisation were in the air.'[2] The device of competitive examinations employed by the Chinese

---

[1] The inspiration of these concepts was Bentham's *Constitutional Code*, Mill's writings, and Henry Taylor's *The Statesman*.
[2] M. Richter, *The Politics of Conscience*, p. 62.

centuries before, was rediscovered, and a few Oxford colleges, notably Oriel and Balliol, began to use the method systematically in the first half of the nineteenth century.[1] Balliol threw its scholarships open to competition in 1828, and enjoyed greater success in Schools and elections to Fellowships at All Souls than Christ Church, more than twice its size.

In 1853-4 the movements for the reform of the universities and the two Civil Services, which until then had proceeded separately, converged as four of the leading protagonists—Gladstone, Northcote, Trevelyan, and Jowett—drew closer together, inspired not by a single objective, but by agreement on broad principles which applied equally to all three movements. Their motives for acting in concert while not identical were not irreconcilable. Trevelyan supported the educationalists largely because they provided him with greater strength and additional arguments for opening up the Indian and British Civil Services. Jowett was drawn into this struggle because he quickly perceived the advantage for his own educational reforms in the universities. 'I cannot conceive a greater boon which could be conferred on the University than a share in the Indian appointments.' It would provide an 'answer to the dreary question which a college tutor so often hears "what line of life shall I choose, with no calling to take orders and no taste for the Bar, and no connections who are able to put me forward in life?" '.[2] Gladstone, besides backing Trevelyan's efforts at administrative reform from within the Treasury, had been converted to the reform of Oxford by the report of the 1850 Commission of Inquiry and charged by Aberdeen in 1853 with the task of framing a Bill. While drafting it, he was brought into frequent and close contact with Jowett who prepared an alternative version for submission to cabinet. Meanwhile, Northcote had been collaborating closely with Trevelyan on the departmental inquiries and the review of the British Civil Service.

[1] France had experimented with competitive examinations in 1776 in recruiting the teaching staff of the Faculty of Arts of the University of Paris. Just after the Revolution, teachers in the State secondary schools and in the universities were recruited similarly. But on the eve of the Third Republic direct selection was still the normal means of access to the public service, although auditors in the *Conseil d'Etat* had been recruited by competitive examinations since 1849. R. Gregoire argues in *The French Civil Service*, p. 54, that France only gradually and imperfectly followed the English example, but see below, p. 60, Trevelyan's request for details of the French *Concours*.

[2] R. Symonds, *The British and their Successors*, p. 44.

The convergence of the three movements dates from July 1853 when Trevelyan visited Jowett at Balliol and explained to him what Wood's India Bill meant for the future of Haileybury. At once Jowett wrote to Gladstone urging upon him the advantages of opening the Indian Civil Service to university graduates, and emphasizing the stimulus it would give to university education. The Rev. Dr. Charles Vaughan, Headmaster of Harrow, who was with Jowett at the time of Trevelyan's visit, strongly objected to the proposed constitution of Haileybury outlined in the Bill and was persuaded to write formally to Trevelyan. Jowett sent a copy of this letter to Gladstone, Sir Charles Wood, and to Dr. Henry Liddell, Headmaster of Westminster. While Gladstone took up the question raised in Vaughan's letter with Aberdeen, Trevelyan suggested to Jowett that he should see Earl Granville, another member of Aberdeen's cabinet. In the meantime, Liddell in agreement with his Harrow colleague, had passed his copy of Vaughan's letter to Granville, together with a covering letter expressing his own opinion. As the Bill had already passed the Commons, Granville who sat in the Lords, had been singled out for particular pressure, and it was he who subsequently moved the amendment of the Bill. The Secretary of State for India had already been won over, largely by Jowett whose letter to Gladstone, subsequently passed to Wood, stressed the advantages of open competition to the Indian Civil Service. Such arguments were calculated to appeal to Wood who had declared his intention of sending to India such a service 'as the world had never seen'. Thus was the 'amendment of Wood's Bill . . . floated by an Oxford reformer into the broad stream of educational reform'.[1] Thereafter, the reform of education in the universities was indissolubly linked with the reform of the Civil Service.

Jowett and Trevelyan now pressed the advantage they had won in the Lords. Jowett quickly drafted an outline scheme covering age, qualifications, subjects of competition, and other questions which were discretionary with the Secretary of State and sent it to Wood, who then appointed a committee to advise him. Trevelyan's lobbying secured the chairmanship for his brother-in-law and a place for Jowett.[2] The outline scheme was expanded and developed

[1] R. J. Moore, *Sir Charles Wood's Indian Policy*, p. 90.
[2] The other members were Lord Ashburton, Dr. Melvill, Principal of Haileybury College, and J. Shaw Lefevre.

in the committee's report which Macaulay wrote himself. It has
since become famous as the classic statement of the case for competitive literary examinations and a Civil Service of educated men
with no particular specialist knowledge or training.

We believe that men who have been engaged up to one or two and twenty
in studies which have no immediate connections with the business of
any profession and of which the effect is merely to open, to invigorate
and to enrich the mind, will generally be found in the business of every
profession, superior to men who have at eighteen or nineteen devoted
themselves to the special studies of their calling. . . .
He should have received the best, the most liberal, the most finished
education that his native country affords. Such an education has been
proved by experience to be the best preparation for every calling which
requires the exercise of the higher powers of the mind.[1]

'Trevelyan was much pleased with the report', and he and Jowett
were confident that their campaign for opening the British Civil
Service, now well under way, would be attended by a similar
success. 'The end of the wedge has been inserted', *The Civil Service
Gazette* commented. 'The introduction of competition, as a test of
appointment to the Civil Service of India, has forced on the discussion of its application to the Civil Service at home.'[2]

But the reformers, particularly Sir Charles Trevelyan, seriously
under-estimated the strength of the interests opposed to the large-
scale reform of recruitment in 1854–5, and were altogether too
sanguine about the prospects of introducing open competition
immediately into the British Civil Service. Flushed with the success of their persistent and persuasive lobbying and propaganda
to open the I.C.S., Trevelyan and Jowett, with Gladstone's
support and Northcote's assistance,[3] began early in 1854 to prepare the ground for the publication of the report. Between them
they had a wide range of influential contacts in government, administration, education, and journalism. A few of these were now
carefully chosen to test the probable reaction to the report and

[1] Quoted in N. C. Roy, *The Civil Service in India*, pp. 35–6.
[2] Leading article, 2 July 1853.
[3] Northcote's main contribution was an article published in 1854, 'Suggestions respecting the conditions under which University Education may be made
more available for Clerks in Government Offices'. Besides, he commented on
opinions received on the report, and on the draft of the Order in Council. He was
very firm about the need for open competition, and wrote several times to
Gladstone urging him not to settle for less.

Jowett's practical application of it. Copies were circulated privately to Ralph Lingen, Secretary of the Board of Education, Shaw Lefevre, Clerk to the House of Lords, John Wood, Chairman of the Board of Inland Revenue, Capt. H. H. O'Brien, editor of the *Quarterly*, and to a number of leading educationalists. Lefevre and Wood were warmly enthusiastic, while Lingen, 'not a man to give in without good reason', was a welcome convert.[1] O'Brien's response was much less favourable, and Trevelyan took pains to answer his detailed criticisms of the proposed examination scheme. Twenty copies of the paper and Trevelyan's comments upon it were then circulated privately.

Trevelyan was indefatigable, discussing tactics daily with Gladstone and Jowett, canvassing support, commenting on opinions from those consulted privately, and personally directing the operation of the campaign from the Treasury. He talked personally to Sidney Herbert and Sir James Stephen, and found time to 'walk across the park' with John Wood, who 'made himself acquainted with all the objections commonly made to the plan [and] employed himself in answering them'.[2] The mobilization of support in Oxford was left largely to Jowett and Dr. Jeune, the Master of Pembroke, but even here Trevelyan suggested that 'an effort should be made to get the University to speak out *as such*. Possibly the unreformed Hebdomadal Board might not be unwilling to show that they are not indifferent to a measure of real improvement; and if they were to do so *their* support would imply a great deal'.[3] In Cambridge, encouraged by Trevelyan, the Regius Professor of Greek was canvassing support on a similar scale, while Dr. Jelf at King's College, London, was likewise engaged.

Trevelyan was in constant touch with Delane, editor of *The Times*, feeding him letters and editorial material. Two weeks before publication, the report and Jowett's application of it were discussed in a leading article. Trevelyan later estimated that three-quarters of the press—among them the *Morning Advertiser*, the most popular daily paper—supported him. After the report had been presented to Parliament in February 1854, copies were sent to the headmas-

---

[1] Lingen to Northcote, 21 January 1854, Brit. Mus., G.P. Add. MSS. 44333, fo. 118.

[2] Trevelyan to Gladstone, 2 March 1854, Brit. Mus., G.P. Add. MSS. 44333, fo. 241.

[3] Trevelyan to Dr. Jeune, 20 March 1854, Brit. Mus., G.P. Add. MSS. 44333, fo. 279.

ters of public schools and to Mechanics' Institutes. Trevelyan
readily perceived the need for a broadly based appeal: 'The classes
interested in the maintenance of Patronage are so powerful that
unless we can get our Plan read and understood by the rest of the
Community I shall begin to fear for its success.'[1]

Skilful, experienced, and determined propagandists, Trevelyan
and Jowett never hesitated to indicate precisely to their supporters
what contribution they could make, and the manner in which they
should make it. They never doubted for a moment that they were
leading the movement, and issued instructions to their supporters,
regardless of their status or seniority. Gladstone received his orders
just as anybody else did.

We all think it desirable that you should write at once to Lord Clarendon
and request him to ascertain to what extent the system of appointment
by *Concours* (Competing Examination) exists in the several Departments of French administration—what the details of its application are
—and what are the effects with which it is considered to have been
attended. We have reason to believe that much interesting and important
information would be obtained by such a reference.[2]

One of the most influential opponents of open competition was
Lord John Russell, who had voted against it in cabinet. Gladstone
spent some time subsequently trying to win him over, but even
personal pleading, of 'incomparable trenchancy and force',[3]
proved unavailing. Jowett then wrote to the Dean of Hereford,
whom he had met briefly once before, to urge him to write to his
patron, Lord John Russell, in the hope that he might be influenced
by his protégé's views on the educational benefits of open
competition to the lower classes. Jowett wasted no words in conveying to the Dean exactly what he wanted him to do.

Will you allow me to point out to you how I think you may be of
essential service at the present time. It is by writing a few pages showing
the bearing of the measure on the education of the lower classes. To
put the proposal in a definite form the most effective mode of doing it
appears to me to be by a letter to Lord John Russell on the Organization
of the Civil Service with reference to its bearing on the education of the
lower classes. I do not think it would matter that the pamphlet should

---

[1] Trevelyan to Gladstone, 1 March 1854, Brit. Mus., G.P. Add. MSS.
44333, fo. 226.
[2] Trevelyan to Gladstone, 9 March 1854, Brit. Mus., G.P. Add. MSS. 44333,
fo. 251.   [3] Morley, *Life of Gladstone*, i. 380.

be long or elaborate—a few words from you speedily put out might, I think, make the difference of the ministry carrying out the scheme effectually or shrinking from what they are half committed to already. . . . If you should kindly adopt my suggestion, would you touch on the importance of a competing and not merely negative examination.[1]

Trevelyan was much less optimistic of persuading Lord John Russell by this means, and thought that the Dean's support could be used more effectively in another direction. The next day, asked by Jowett to 'back' his request with a few lines, he wrote confidentially to the Dean.

In its bearing on education this is *your* subject and a public expression of your approbation, however short, at the present time will be of great assistance to the Government—but if your observations are cast in the form of a letter, I would suggest that it should be addressed to the Earl of Aberdeen and not to Lord John Russell—for Lord John, although he is as honourable and public minded a man as ever lived, is too deeply imbued with the traditional habits of Parliamentary management to be favourable to the plan, although willing to give it a fair trial. If, therefore, you wrote to him, *he might give you an answer we should not like.*[2]

The intensity of the campaigning, the agitation in the press, and the flow of propaganda from the Treasury was occasionally embarrassing for Gladstone and some of his cabinet colleagues. Twice he called a halt to Trevelyan's press-priming activities. On another occasion he rebuked him for circulating a confidential Treasury memorandum to Jowett and two or three other supporters. Arbuthnot, second in command at the Treasury, was particularly critical of Trevelyan's activities, complaining to Gladstone about his letters to the press and the articles inspired by him, and alleging on one occasion that a private campaign letter had been printed at the Government press and circulated under Trevelyan's name from the Treasury.

Arbuthnot was not alone in his opposition to the report and to Trevelyan's dubiously ethical conduct. After its publication a growing volume of criticism was heard from within the Service, in Parliament and the country at large. *The Civil Service Gazette* spoke for many serving officers when it drew attention to the elitist

[1] Jowett to Dean of Hereford, 5 February 1854, Brit. Mus., G.P. Add. MSS. 44333, fo. 142.
[2] Trevelyan to Dean of Hereford, 6 February 1854, Brit. Mus. G.P., Add. MSS. fo. 143. My italics.

G

principle of the recruitment scheme and criticized the academical
nature of the literary competitive examinations. The report aimed
at 'vastly too much'. It 'will have a *prima facie* object of benefiting
the Universities, instead of conferring a boon upon the Service and
effecting a public good in the more efficient administration of
public business'.[1]

Not all those consulted privately had agreed with the report or
Jowett's application of it. Sir James Stephen, whom Trevelyan
had earlier counted an ally, now spoke out against open competition and the plan to separate intellectual from mechanical work.
His paper, specially commissioned by Gladstone, followed closely
upon a discussion of the report in the House of Lords in March
1854 during which Lord Monteagle criticized its discussion by the
press before presentation to Parliament, and asked for information
on the instructions given to Northcote and Trevelyan and what
evidence they had called. He alleged that the report was *'partial
and ex parte'*, a criticism voiced by others who spoke in the debate.[2]

The euphoria of the first three months of 1854, which followed
the cabinet decision[3] and the knowledge that the principle of open
competition was to be applied without dilution to every class of
first appointment,[4] and which inspired Northcote to declare privately to Trevelyan that Gladstone would 'come out with a trium-
phant demolition of all that has been said against the scheme',[5]
now gave way to a growing realization of the strength of the opposing forces. Macaulay went to Brooks's and 'found everybody
open-mouthed . . . against Trevelyan's plans about the Civil
Service. He has been too sanguine. The pear is not ripe. I always
thought so. The time will come, but it is not come yet. I am afraid
that he will be much mortified'.[6]

Gladstone did not, could not, silence the critics, among them the

[1] Leading article, 23 February 1854. Other leading articles attacking the
report appeared on 4, 11, and 18 March 1854.
[2] Parl. Debs., H. L. CXXXI, 13 March 1854, cols. 640–55.
[3] The cabinet decision was taken on 26 January 1854. Gladstone noted eight
in favour, five against; Palmerston left before the vote and had not spoken
decidedly, but was later opposed. All the Whig leaders voted against. Cornewall
Lewis later told Trevelyan that 'the self-denial of the Government in abandoning
its Patronage—for which it has always been suspected and blamed—surprises
and staggers People'.
[4] Trevelyan to Northcote, 28 January 1854, Bod., T.L.B., xxxii. 265–8.
[5] 10 March 1854, Brit. Mus., G.P. Add. MSS. 44333, fo. 283.
[6] 4 March 1854, quoted in G.O. Trevelyan, *Life and Letters of Lord Macaulay*,
iv. 158.

Queen, Palmerston, and several other cabinet colleagues, and many in the Service and Parliament resented the 'injustice done by that Report to the civil servants of the country'. The ambitious Bill promised in the speech from the throne in January 1854, was abandoned; the Government had decided not to introduce a measure that Session, Gladstone told the Commons in May. The decision to abandon the 'ill-digested plan for throwing the Civil Service of the country open to all sorts and conditions of men on the sole test of a literary examination', was welcomed by *The Civil Service Gazette*.[1] Since the appearance of the report, the paper had taken

much trouble to expose the fallacy of the principles upon which this reform was based, and the total impracticality and useless expense of a system of selection involving the national maintenance of wandering bands of University Tutors, and a recognition of the inherent right of every free-born Briton periodically to compel the country, at its own expense, to fathom the depths of his ignorance.[2]

Proposals for immediate, thorough-going reform gave way to those of a more cautious and limited nature intended to achieve the same object more gradually. In the winter of 1854–5 Trevelyan prepared successive drafts of the Order in Council which he submitted to Gladstone, Northcote, his Treasury colleague W. H. Stephenson, and, later, Sir George Cornewall Lewis,[3] Gladstone's successor at the Treasury. Pains were taken to reconcile the needs of reform with the necessity to preserve the authority of individual ministers to prescribe their own recruitment regulations. The earlier proposals were watered down: the Civil Service Commissioners were invested with very limited authority, nothing was said about competition.

The Order in Council was a compromise between the scheme outlined in the report and Jowett's letter, and the opinions of the 'best authorities' in the country elicited by the Government after the abandonment of the Bill. Heads of departments and other distinguished administrators were asked formally by the Treasury in June 1854 for their opinion of the report, and for their view of the defects of the present system and of the remedies to be applied to them. No one 'who would generally be considered an

---

[1] Leading article, 13 May 1854.   [2] Leading article, 6 January 1855.
[3] Lewis was opposed to the introduction of open competition, and before his arrival at the Treasury had spoken against it. But he favoured a minimum standard of examination and supported a scheme of limited competition.

authority has been omitted to be asked his opinion', Trevelyan assured Gladstone.[1] Their comments were collected and printed as *Papers on the Reorganization of the Civil Service*.[2] There was broad agreement that Northcote's and Trevelyan's strictures on the quality and competence of serving officers were undeserved and exaggerated.[3] Opinion was sharply divided on the question of the abolition of patronage, but most opposed the introduction of open competitive examinations. A central examination system with an independent body of examiners was not so stoutly resisted, although there was a general desire to retain the power of nomination and final selection in the hands of departments. Given the strength of the departmental interests opposed to the report and the examination scheme, competition among a small number of selected candidates was about the limit of practicable reform.

Gladstone, bowing before the storm of criticism aroused by the report, had settled for this some time before he resigned in February 1855. When he handed over to Cornewall Lewis, the preparation of the Order in Council was virtually complete, and the negotiations concerning the appointment of Commissioners were well advanced. Palmerston's Government inherited a measure prepared by Trevelyan and his fellow reformers to accommodate the views of those, like Lewis, who had criticized the scheme for open competitive examinations. The decision to bring it forward on 21 May 1855 may have been precipitated by the revelation of administrative mismanagement associated with the Crimean War, and the formation of the Administrative Reform Association on 5 May 1855, but the intention to do so and the substance of the reform was uninfluenced by either.

Members of Parliament were far less reconciled than the Government to the prospect of diminished patronage and to the need to submit their nominees to the impartial scrutiny of an independent Commission. When the Order in Council was laid before the House it was voted down, although the result did not affect the Government's decision to proceed with reform. Layard's motion deploring the sacrifice of merit and efficiency to party and family, debated a month later, was heavily defeated by 361 votes to 48;

---

[1] Trevelyan to Gladstone, 24 October 1854, Brit. Mus., G.P. Add. MSS. 44334, fo. 117.   [2] P.P., 1854–5, XX.

[3] For a discussion of the views of those supporting and opposing reform, see Edward Hughes, 'Civil Service Reform, 1853–55', *Public Administration*, xxxii, Spring 1954, pp. 17–51.

and Vincent Scully's motion in July, welcoming the Order and praying for an open public examination, was narrowly lost.

Content now to see time and the working of the Civil Service Commission achieve the end which he had once hoped to accomplish with a single stroke, Trevelyan was not dissatisfied with the reform introduced by the 1855 Order in Council. In the month following its promulgation he wrote to Jowett that he was 'quite satisfied with the progress we are making. The institution established by the Order in Council will, I think, develop naturally, without any new violent effort, into all we desire[1].' But even he must have been surprised by the vigour and determination with which the Commissioners began their work. Within a year they had rejected as incompetent nearly a third of the candidates sent up for examination. 'Not a few members of Parliament had such favourites thrown back upon their hands and were angry. . . . Great pressure was brought upon the Board by members and high officers, to allow favourite dunces to pass, but in vain.'[2] In view of this, and M.P.s' earlier hostility towards the examination system, the Commissioners must have been surprised by the welcome given by the House of Commons to the report on their first year's work, which was approved on a resolution by 108–87. Earlier, the Commissioners had demonstrated their impartiality by failing one of Palmerston's nominees. When the Prime Minister learned of it, he sent to the Commission for his candidate's papers, but was told firmly that the papers could not be removed from the office, although they were available for inspection there. Palmerston acceded to their ruling and did not pursue the matter further. It was a clear warning of the Commissioners' determination to subordinate the claims of party, influence, and family to considerations of merit and efficiency.

THE TREASURY AND THE CIVIL SERVICE COMMISSION

Between 1855 and 1870 the Treasury was (in Gladstone's phrase) 'the *point d'appui* of the Civil Service Commissioners', upholding and supporting their decisions when called upon to do so, but for the most part careful to avoid interfering in their work, or in the

---

[1] 6 June 1855, Bod., T.L.B., xxxv, 235–6; and see letters to Gladstone 14 July 1855, Brit. Mus., G.P. Add. MSS. 44334, and Edward Romilly, 27 December 1855, Bod., T.L.B., xxxvi. 41–2.

[2] D. B. Eaton, *Civil Service in Great Britain*, p. 39.

recruitment process generally. Support was provided in three ways. By the willingness with which it accepted and adopted their recommendations, the Treasury served as exemplar for other departments. Secondly, it consistently refused to interfere with decisions, or to act as a court of appeal from them. Thirdly, by enforcing that requirement of the 1859 Superannuation Act which made it necessary for persons appointed after 19 April 1859 to hold a certificate issued by the Civil Service Commissioners in order to qualify for a pension, the Treasury provided the means whereby departments could be more readily brought within the terms of the 1855 Order in Council.

Before 1855 departments prescribed their own conditions of entry. Some, like the Treasury, War Office, and Admiralty, required in addition to his nomination that a candidate should pass a qualifying examination, while others, such as the Foreign Office, Colonial Office, and Board of Trade, required only a simple nomination. Not only were there different rules of admission in different offices, they differed also from branch to branch within the same office. Thus a youth was eligible for a junior clerkship in the Inland Revenue as soon as he was sixteen, but was ineligible for a junior clerkship in the excise branch of the same office until he was nineteen.

The setting up of the Civil Service Commission in May 1855 marked the beginning of the end of this departmental recruitment. Under the Order in Council the three Commissioners had power to examine 'all such young men as may be proposed to be appointed to any junior situation in any Department of the Civil Service' in respect of their age, health, moral character, and knowledge and ability, according to rules agreed separately with each department. Thus a young man wishing to enter the Civil Service had not only to obtain nomination to a vacancy in a particular department, but also to submit himself to tests conducted by the Civil Service Commissioners, obtain their certificate of qualification, and serve six months' probation in the same department.

Prudently the Civil Service Commissioners disclaimed initially any intention of inducing departments to introduce uniform regulations.[1] Once established, however, they repeatedly and insistently canvassed the benefits of uniformity in their annual reports and in correspondence with departments. Despite their

[1] 1st Report of CSC, 4 March 1856, P.P., 1856, XXII.

inability to coerce reluctant or recalcitrant ministers, they were surprisingly successful. By 1870 they had established strict requirements of health, moral fitness, and, to a lesser degree, of age, which were universally applicable throughout the Service. To a more limited extent they were also able to introduce a measure of uniformity into the tests of knowledge and ability prescribed separately by each department, but they were much less successful in persuading them to adopt some form of competitive examination in those tests. Here their position was far weaker: no reference was made to competition in the Order in Council, and departments were free to make appointments without any element of it. In spite of this, the Commissioners urged continually in their reports that limited competitive examinations should be introduced into all departments. By 1860 they were in use in a few of the most important,[1] though a year later the Commissioners observed that there were still many to which the system had not been applied. It was beyond their 'province to suggest when and in what manner and by what means the system of limited competition for clerkships should be extended so as to embrace the clerkships in all public offices', they pointed out to the Treasury.[2]

Very few open competitions were held before 1870. A Select Committee of the House of Commons, appointed in 1860 to inquire into the method of selecting persons for first appointments, supported the principle, but reported against its immediate introduction on the familiar ground that to do so before greater experience of its application might endanger its ultimate and assured success.[3] Instead they recommended that all departments should adopt a system of limited competition. To prevent abuse they further proposed that the number of competitors examined by the Commissioners should never be less than a fixed proportion of the number of vacancies offered for competition, five to one where a single vacancy was competed for, and three to one where several vacancies were offered for competition at the same time. To ensure that only those candidates who could achieve a minimum standard would compete for the vacancy, the Committee urged that all candidates should be required to show in a preliminary test

[1] Among them the Treasury, Foreign Office, Colonial Office, Home Office, War Office, Admiralty, Board of Trade, and Poor Law Board.
[2] CSC to Treasury, 18 March 1861, P.R.O., T.1/6302B/8169.
[3] *Report of the Select Committee on Civil Service Appointments*, 1860, P.P., 1860, IX.

examination that they were qualified for the situation. In many previous instances there had been no element of real competition, departments had nominated three candidates to compete for a vacancy of whom two would have no chance of attaining the minimum standard to qualify for the Civil Service Commissioners' certificate. This method had been perfected in the pre-1854 Treasury, where one Patronage Secretary (W. G. Hayter) is alleged to have retained specially for the purpose two lads known as the 'Treasury idiots'.

The Committee's proposals were welcomed by the Civil Service Commissioners, although in the absence of Government initiative they were themselves powerless to 'originate any measures for giving practical effect to them'.[1] As a result little was accomplished in the next ten years. Apart from the Treasury and its subordinate departments, only the War Office and the India Office introduced a preliminary test examination; the remainder ignored the recommendation. Little more than lip-service was paid to the Select Committee's other recommendation: in only 3 per cent of the limited competitions held between 1862 and 1868 were five candidates nominated to compete where a single vacancy was offered; in those competitions for more than one vacancy (half the number of the former) the proportion of three or more candidates to each vacancy was observed in no more than 27 per cent.[2]

Two years after it had withheld approval from the Order in Council, the House of Commons resolved unanimously that experience of the new system pointed in favour of the principle of competition, and recommended that it ought to be extended.[3] In this they were joined by *The Times* and other daily newspapers, but *The Civil Service Gazette*, echoing the views of many serving officers, remained unconvinced. The scepticism and suspicion with which it had greeted the Order, hardened into opposition towards the Commissioners and the principle of literary competitive examinations. The more it saw 'of the development of this Chinese scheme for filling the Civil Service of the country with pedants and mere book-worms, the more [it was] convinced of its absurdity'.[4] Vigorously opposed to all forms of patronage, it

---

[1] 6th Report CSC, 1860, P.P., 1861, XIX.
[2] See Appendix III, table 1.   [3] Parl. Debs. H.C., Vol. 146, col. 1468.
[4] Leading article, 22 September 1855. See also, 12 June 1858, 21 May 1859, 20 October 1860, 10 and 24 November 1860.

professed to see in the introduction of limited competition advocated by the Civil Service Commissioners an extension rather than a limitation of ministerial influence: the patron could bestow three favours for every one nomination given previously. Open competition was more objectionable still, *The Civil Service Gazette* argued. While its supporters claimed it was more democratic, it was in fact aristocratic, for only those who had been educated at a university had any real chance of succeeding in a competitive literary examination. In support of this, it pointed to the results of an open competition for posts in the Indian Civil Service, where eighteen of the twenty places offered to the sixty-five competitors were filled by university men from Oxford, Cambridge, and Trinity College, Dublin.[1]

It was important for the Civil Service Commissioners to be able to point to the Treasury's compliance with the requirements of the Order in Council, and to its acknowledgement of the Commissioners' responsibilities under it. In prevailing upon the Treasury to raise the standard of the examination for its Superior Clerkships they observed that

The position held by the Treasury among the Civil Establishments of the Crown, its direct authority over some and its influence over others, impress upon us the conviction that we shall enter with far greater prospect upon the reconsideration [of the examination schemes in other departments] if we are able to bring under the notice of those with whom we may communicate a liberal and judicious scheme of examination sanctioned by your Lordships.[2]

Shortly after, the Commissioners published in their annual report details of a revised scheme of examination agreed with the Treasury.

The Treasury reacted promptly to the Commissioners' appeal to departments to enlarge the field of competition by nominating a proportionate number of candidates to compete for several appointments offered at the same examination. 'The Secretary of the Treasury, acting in entire unison with our views on this point, has carried them into effect with earnestness and completeness, and with very satisfactory results', the Commissioners were able to report in 1858.[3] More important still, in March 1861 the Treasury

[1] Leading article, 21 May 1859.
[2] CSC to Treasury, 11 January 1856, H.M.T., *Departmental Arrangement Book*, iii.   [3] 4th Report CSC, 1858, P.P., 1859, VIII, Appendix ii.

informed them of its intention to introduce the preliminary test examination and other proposals made by the Select Committee into the department itself and those subordinate to it. The alacrity of the Treasury's response was noted in the Commissioners' next report, where it was revealed that 622 candidates had been nominated for situations in the Treasury and its subordinate departments in the previous year, of whom 540 had been tested in the preliminary examination and 45 per cent rejected as unfit to compete for a vacancy.

Not only was the Treasury willing to comply with the general recommendations made by the Civil Service Commissioners, it was also anxious to avoid weakening their authority by appearing to reject decisions by them which affected it alone. For example, as part of the decision to abandon the practice of recruiting to Supplementary Clerkships from subordinate departments, the Treasury raised the upper age limit from twenty-five to thirty. The Civil Service Commissioners opposed this decision on the grounds that it would alter a rule which had been operative since 1855; and that men recruited at a later age, retiring later in order to qualify for a full pension, would be less valuable towards the end of their service. Hamilton, who had drafted the Minute, argued in favour of raising the age limit, but Gladstone felt 'strongly that the Treasury is the *point d'appui* of the Civil Service Commissioners and that our overruling them in our own case must greatly weaken their authority'.[1] The Minute was cancelled and the former age limit restored. On another occasion a temporary clerk nominated by the Treasury to a Supplementary Clerkship was refused a certificate by the Civil Service Commissioners because of his unfitness for the post. Supporting their decision, Hamilton wrote to the Parliamentary Secretary that 'it is essential that the Civil Service Commissioners should see and feel that there is no disposition on the part of the Treasury to allow the decisions of the CSC to be questioned'.[2]

The Treasury's anxiety to avoid questioning their decisions was not confined to those which affected it alone. An appeal by the War Office against the Commissioners' refusal of a certificate to a

---

[1] Memorandum from Gladstone to Frederick Peel, 14 November 1861, Brit. Mus., G.P. Add. MSS., Letter Books, 1861–2.

[2] Memorandum from Hamilton to Glyn, 19 February 1869, P.R.O. T.1/6944B/21427.

temporary clerk was disallowed by the Treasury on the grounds that it had no power to interfere. More important still, it announced that it would not in future act as a court of appeal from their decisions. This was an important turning-point in the development of the Civil Service Commission struggling to establish itself as the focus of Civil Service recruitment. It meant that their decision on the award of a certificate was not subject to appeal; their discretion was absolute. In the case of the War Office temporary clerk the Treasury's self-restraint was remarkable. Each official consulted agreed that the Civil Service Commissioners' decision was harsh, and wished to temper its severity by suggesting an 'exceptional mode of dealing with the case'.[1] But none could be found consistent with the more powerful desire to uphold the Commissioners' ruling. The Treasury's helplessness in this instance led Arbuthnot to remark to Hamilton that 'there ought to be a safety valve, permitting some relaxation of the strict rules of the CSC in special cases under Treasury sanction and approved by the Commission'.[2] Eight years later, in the seventh clause of the 1870 Order in Council, the Treasury reserved the right to dispense wholly or partly with the Civil Service Commissioners' examination when such dispensation was 'for the Public Interest'.

While the Treasury's ready acceptance of the Commissioners' decisions in its own case, and its refusal to act as a court of appeal from those made in others, helped to enhance the Commissioners' status *vis à vis* the departments, and to bolster their limited authority, the Commissioners still possessed no means of coercing those departments which refused to send up candidates for examination. Before 1859 the requirements of the 1855 Order in Council could be avoided or disregarded with an impunity which threatened the total frustration of their tentative and modest efforts to introduce a uniform system of examination throughout the Service. Recalcitrant departments could not be brought to heel because the Civil Service Commissioners had no power under the Order to enforce the requirement that each person appointed to the Civil Service should be examined by them and issued with a certificate of qualification. All this was changed by the effect of section seven-

[1] Memorandum from Hamilton to Arbuthnot, (?) March/April 1862, P.R.O., T.1/6381A/15932. See also memoranda by Arbuthnot and Stephenson.

[2] Memorandum from Arbuthnot to Hamilton, 5 April 1862, P.R.O. T.1/6381A/15932.

teen of the Superannuation Act of 1859, which made it necessary for all those who joined the Service after 19 April 1859 to obtain a certificate of qualification from the Civil Service Commissioners in order to establish a *prima facie* claim to a pension. Thus indirectly the Commissioners were enabled to take a firmer grip on recruitment.

There is no evidence to suggest that section seventeen was other than an attempt to define more precisely those entitled to the benefits of the 1859 Act; its indirect effect upon recruitment may or may not have been foreseen (and hence provided for) by the Treasury in drafting the Bill. If it was foreseen it is unlikely that the Civil Service Commissioners were informed of it, for they and not the Treasury drew attention to the effect of the section upon recruitment. The Commissioners wrote to the Treasury in December 1859 that

The provision in question will have a beneficial operation . . . it has the effect of bringing practically under the operation of the Order in Council certain descriptions of situations which, though clearly subject to its provisions, had for one reason or another not been recognised by the heads of Departments to which they belonged as so subject. The Order will thus be more completely carried out and the interests of the public service will, it may be hoped, be thereby advanced.[1]

The effect of section seventeen was soon demonstrated. The Civil Service Commissioners were asked by some departments to issue a certificate to satisfy its requirement without reference to the 1855 Order in Council. This they refused to do, maintaining that the Superannuation Act recognized the obligation created by the Order in Council but did not authorize the issue of a certificate of qualification on conditions other than those contemplated by that Order.[2] As the department responsible for the award of superannuation allowances the Treasury was inevitably drawn into the discussions which took place between the Commissioners and the departments. On each occasion it provided consistent and unequivocal support for the Commissioners' ruling. Answering the Home Office in 1864 the Treasury stated that although the Superannuation Act provided an additional reason for obtaining a certi-

---

[1] 31 December 1859, 6th Report CSC, 1860, P.P., 1861, XIX, Appendix ii, correspondence.

[2] CSC to Admiralty, 29 March 1864, Appendix to 10th Report CSC, 1864, P.P., 1865, XVI.

ficate 'it does not appear to my Lords to weaken in any way the force of the Order in its obligatory character with regard to all persons admitted into the Public Service, whether entitled to claim superannuation or not'.[1] Similar judgements were made by the Treasury in other instances, each rooted in and consequential to an acceptance of the interpretation made initially by the Commissioners. While the Treasury was willing to lend its weight and authority to uphold that interpretation on those occasions when its validity was challenged by the departments, it never attempted to prescribe the conditions upon which certificates of qualification might be issued.

[1] 29 March 1864, 10th Report CSC, op. cit.

4

OPEN COMPETITION

THE INTRODUCTION OF OPEN COMPETITION

ROBERT LOWE was appointed Chancellor of the Exchequer in Gladstone's first Administration which took office in December 1868. A year later he wrote to him:

As I have so often tried in vain will you bring the question of the Civil Service before the Cabinet to-day. Something must be decided. We cannot keep matters in this discreditable state of abeyance. If the cabinet will not entertain the idea of open competition might we not at any rate require a larger number of competitors for each vacancy? five or seven or ten?[1]

What induced Lowe to concern himself at this particular time with the introduction of open competition has never been satisfactorily explained. As the political head of the Treasury, and in view of the personal responsibility for Civil Service recruitment which he assumed throughout his tenure of office, his motives are important. It is appropriate, therefore, to begin by explaining why open competition was introduced in 1870, to attempt to relate Lowe's conduct to the circumstances obtaining at that time, and to assess the factors which influenced it.

The introduction of open competition was not the inevitable culmination of a gradual evolutionary process in which experiments were made with an ever-widening element of competition. As 1870 drew nearer the element of competition began to shrink.[2] In the year preceding the introduction of open competition fewer than one in two hundred appointments were made after an open competitive examination; 94·5 per cent were made without competition of any kind. The dominion of 'party and family' which Layard had deplored in 1855 still flourished. Even the staunchest advocates of open competition welcomed the continuance of patronage where it touched them most nearly. Sir Stafford North-

---

[1] Lowe to Gladstone, 10 November 1869, Brit. Mus., G.P. Add. MSS. 44301, fo. 104.
[2] See below, Appendix III, table 1 (c).

cote, hard put to it to place his seven sons, had been promised a clerkship for one of them in the Colonial Office, but on the resignation of the minister it had been cancelled. In March 1867 he appealed anxiously to Disraeli, Chancellor of the Exchequer, to find a place for his son in the Civil Service.[1] Another who benefited from his party and family connections was George Kekewich, who entered the Service in March 1868.[2] His father, an M.P., asked Northcote, who was at that time President of the Board of Trade, and to whom he was related by marriage, to obtain an appointment in the Service for his son. Northcote interceded on Kekewich's behalf with the Duke of Marlborough, newly appointed Lord President of the Council, and wrote to Kekewich that if he called at the Privy Council Office and asked for an interview, the Duke of Marlborough would appoint him to an Examinership in the Education Department. Kekewich called at the office, where he was interviewed by both the Lord President and the Secretary to the Education Department, Ralph Lingen. Both interviews were of 'exceedingly short duration', and no inquiry was made of his knowledge of education or the system then in operation.[3]

Between 1 January 1862 and 30 June 1868, there were 858 limited competitions, but in only ninety-seven had the recommended proportion of qualified candidates to offered vacancies been maintained.[4] Reviewing the situation in 1868 the Civil Service Commissioners said that 'the conditions which the Select Committee [of 1860] regarded as indispensable have been very imperfectly realised in the practice of the nominating departments.'[5] Over 70 per cent of the certificates issued by them between 1855 and 1867–8 were awarded without competition, and open competition had been applied to only twenty-eight situations on twelve separate occasions by no more than six departments.[6]

---

[1] Northcote to Disraeli, 10 March 1867, Brit. Mus., I.P. Add. MSS. 50015, fo. 191.

[2] Sir George William Kekewich (1841–1921): Permanent Secretary to the Education Department and later the Board of Education.

[3] Sir George Kekewich, *The Education Department and After*, pp. 5–7.

[4] See below, Appendix III, tables 1 (a) and (b).

[5] 13th Report CSC, 1867, P.P., 1867–8, XXII.

[6] During this time the CSC issued 9,826 certificates of qualification for appointments to clerkships, supplementary clerkships and other clerical positions; twenty-eight of these were awarded after open competitive examinations, 2,765 after limited competitive examinations, and 7,033 without competition of any kind.

Still less was the introduction of open competition in 1870 the result of a campaign for reform such as that which preceded the establishment of the Civil Service Commission. It is reasonable to suppose that in the three years 1867-9 there would be some evidence or indication of the discussion of the question of open competition and of the continuance (if not the actual formulation) of a climate of opinion favourable towards its adoption. But an examination of contemporary sources—Parliamentary debates, newspapers, and periodical literature—does not support the view that at this time the educated middle classes (who had most to gain for their sons from a system of open competition) were drawing public attention to the subject of Civil Service recruitment as they had done ten years earlier.[1] While *The Times* affirmed its support for the principle of open competition, it did not press for its immediate introduction; and although letters appeared in its columns discussing the organization of the Civil Service and suggesting proposals for its reform, none made even passing reference to the subject of open competition. Ninety-seven magazines, journals, and periodicals were in general circulation in this country and the United States in the three years 1867-9, but only three published between them four articles dealing with some aspect of the British Civil Service; none argued for the introduction of open competition.[2]

---

[1] A tentative but tendentious account of some of the factors which contributed to the introduction of open competition is given by Emmeline Cohen in *The Growth of the British Civil Service*, pp. 120-1. Sir Charles Trevelyan's evidence before the Playfair Commission of 1874 (which, based upon his recollection of events which had taken place twenty years before, would not seem to be an entirely reliable source), is misrepresented, and his description of middle-class support for the competitive system (limited competition) in 1856-7 is applied to the circumstances of the period 1860-70. It is by no means certain that in 1856-7 they would have been willing also to support the introduction of open competition; and there is no evidence at all that a lobby similar to that which Trevelyan claims was formed in 1856-7 for the preservation of limited competition was formed in 1860-70. About middle-class attitudes towards competition, open or limited, in the sixties Trevelyan tells us nothing. Miss Cohen claims also that between 1860-70 there occurred a gradual change in the attitude of periodicals towards Civil Service reform and recruitment by open competition. Her evidence is provided by three literary articles, the first two of which published in 1860 and 1864 are attacks upon the principle and the adoption of open competitive examinations. This 'attitude' it is contended, is reversed by a third article, praising reforms already implemented and drawing attention to remaining imperfections.

[2] 'Internal Organisation of the Civil Service' (anonymous), *Cornhill Magazine*, XIX, March 1869; Horace Mann, 'Some statistics relating to the Civil Service',

M.P.s were less interested in open competition and administrative reform than they had been ten years earlier when the Civil Service Commissioners began to produce the first statistical proof of the unfitness of many candidates. After the appointment of the Select Committee in 1860 interest gradually waned. The matter was discussed only once more, in 1863, when Palmerston declared himself contented with existing arrangements and against open competition. There is no record of any question on open competition being asked in the House of Commons between 1867 and 1869, although the subject was discussed once, on a private member's motion to throw open to competition all appointments in the Civil and Diplomatic Services.[1] Speeches by Lowe and Gladstone resisting the introduction of open competition until a thorough reorganization of the Civil Service had taken place were sufficient to secure for the Government an overwhelming majority of 281 votes to 30. Gladstone promised only 'to see whether we are or are not disposed to act upon the principle'. Discussions were begun in cabinet in June 1869.

Although *The Civil Service Gazette* had moved from the position of outright opposition to open competition, which it had taken up in the fifties, towards support for the principle, in no sense did it lead a campaign for its introduction, as it had done on so many other similar issues. In a sober leading article it welcomed Fawcett's motion, but thought he had misjudged the temper of the House in forcing a division at a time when more important matters were awaiting the decision of Parliament. In the early months of 1870 it ran several leading articles supporting the introduction of open competition, but by now the cabinet decision had been taken.[2] Similarly, the advocacy of open competition by *The Civilian*, which began publication on 27 November 1869, came too late to influence Lowe, the cabinet or public opinion before the decision was made.[3]

There was some public agitation for the reform of the Civil Service, though not upon the same scale as that which had preceded

[1] Parl. Debs., H.C. CXCV, 9 April 1869, cols. 480–97.
[2] 8 and 15 January 1870, 25 February 1870, 5 March 1870 and 31 May 1870.
[3] 27 November 1869, 26 March 1870 and 2 and 9 April 1870.

Journal of the Statistical Society, XXXI, 1868, and 'On the cost and organisation of the Civil Service', *Journal of the Statistical Society*, XXXII, March 1869; and 'Women in the Civil Service' (anonymous), *Victoria Magazine*, XII, 1868.

H

the introduction of the 1855 Order in Council, or that which followed the disclosure of the administrative mismanagement of the Crimean campaigns. Considerable anxiety was expressed about the increase in the number of civil servants, the rise in the civil estimates, and the discontent within the Service about pay and conditions, but proposals for dealing with these problems did not include the improvement of recruitment procedures. Edwin Chadwick's pleas for the introduction of open competition which appeared in the *Journal of the Statistical Society* in 1858, 1859, and 1863 had no literary counterpart in the middle or late sixties. Satisfaction with the existing system of recruitment, if not overtly expressed, was implicitly affirmed in the adherence to established procedures. Experience of systems other than that of simple nomination was much less extensive in the period 1860–70 than was commonly believed at that time. Henry Fawcett, the member for Brighton, was not challenged or corrected when he said in the Commons in 1869 that 'it might be said that there now existed a system of qualified competition, as when an appointment was vacant it was usual for two or three persons to be nominated'.[1] In the same year less than six in a hundred civil service appointments were made after a limited competitive examination. Taking its cue from the Civil Service Commissioners, *The Times* described the situation more accurately when on 9 November 1868 it said that 'open competition for the civil service can scarcely be said to exist at all, whilst limited competition is strictly limited'. Since Lord Stanley's experiment at the India Office in 1858 no major department had recruited by the open competitive method.[2] The subsequent examples of the Probate Court Registry, the University of London, or even the Civil Service Commissioners themselves (all of which were open competitions for Supplementary Clerkships), were hardly likely to induce the War Office, the Admiralty, or the Secretaries of State, to change their minds, or to inspire confidence generally in the superiority of recruitment by open competition.[3]

[1] Parl. Debs., H.C. CXCV, 9 April 1869, cols. 480–97.
[2] 339 candidates presented themselves for 8 writerships.
[3] The open competition for 4 copying clerkships in the Probate Court Registry was held in 1866 and attracted 52 candidates; that for the Supplementary Clerkship offered by the University of London in 1868 attracted 86 candidates; while the 11 Supplementary Clerkships offered at five separate examinations by the Civil Service Commission attracted 237 candidates.

Perhaps it has been too readily assumed that the introduction of open competition in 1870 was the creature of middle-class agitation, part of the more general reform movement that had been given a powerful impulse by the extension of the franchise three years earlier. But there is no obvious and immediate connection between Lowe's action and the state of public opinion. If the middle classes were impatient and dissatisfied with the existing system of recruitment to the Civil Service their attitude achieved no apparent manifestation.[1] Had Palmerston's Government not already decided to introduce in May 1855 the draft Order inherited from Aberdeen, public dissatisfaction with the administration of the Crimean war would have obliged him to make some improvement in recruitment methods. In 1870 were was no similar pressure upon the Government, no equivalent to the Northcote–Trevelyan Report or the vigorous campaigning of the Administrative Reform Association; six months before Lowe wrote to Gladstone, no more than thirty M.P.'s voted for the immediate introduction of open competition. Ministerial action in 1869 was not inevitable, nor were the cabinet agreed upon the desirability of adopting open competition. Lowe did not lead a movement as Trevelyan had done before him, his agitation was partly due to his conviction of the necessity and desirability of introducing open competition into the whole Service,[2] and partly the result of impatience with the procrastination of his ministerial colleagues during the summer and autumn of 1869. His impatience was justified, for while the Civil Service Commissioners had introduced a substantial measure of

---

[1] Middle-class dissatisfaction may have been expressed privately through the lobbying of M.P.s. After 1867 more of the middle class could turn to their local M.P.s to secure places for their sons in the Civil Service, or to press for the introduction of open competition. Although little is yet known of the nature of the private correspondence received by M.P.s at this time, on the face of it it seems likely that there was very little such pressure. There was no hint of it in the Commons debate, and not one recorded parliamentary question. If M.P.s had been pressed the pressure exerted was clearly not intolerable, for only 30 out of 311 M.P.s who voted in the debate voted for the immediate introduction of open competition.

[2] Lowe maintained his conviction was of long standing. In the Commons he said that: 'I do not think that anyone who has ever taken the trouble to consider what I have said on this subject will suppose that I am in any way an enemy to competition. Since I have been in Parliament I have always done everything in my power to promote it. Indeed, I had the happiness to take my share in founding the system of Indian competition in 1854, when I was Secretary to the Board of Control.' Parl. Debs., H.C. CXCV, 9 April 1869, cols. 480–97.

uniformity into the examination regulations, there was no visible
sign of a gradual movement towards open competition such as
Trevelyan and Jowett had envisaged. It is against this general
background that the cabinet deliberations of 1869 must be set.

The decision by which open competition was finally introduced
owed much to Gladstone's shrewdness and Lowe's tenacity and
single-mindedness—a formidable combination. Cabinet agreement
was based upon what Morley has called Gladstone's 'ingenious
suggestion' that only those branches of the Civil Service were to be
thrown open where the minister agreed. The question was taken up
by the cabinet for the first time on 5 June 1869, when it was decided
to set up a cabinet committee on competitive examinations and
the division of labour.[1] Seven ministers were appointed to it:
Clarendon and Bright who were opposed to the principle of open
competition, Lowe, Goschen, Kimberley, de Grey, and Childers
who were in favour of it.[2] In a printed confidential memorandum
of 29 June 1869 the committee proposed the application of open
competition to all Superior and Supplementary Clerkships in the
Civil Service,[3] to which provisional approval was given at a
cabinet meeting on 31 July 1869. Gladstone's notes of that meeting
indicate that discussion arose on the memorandum, and that it was
agreed to circulate it again.[4] It seems probable that other cabinet
ministers besides Clarendon and Bright were opposed to the principle, among them almost certainly Bruce and Fortescue.[5] On 9
August 1869 the memorandum was discussed again in cabinet,
the strength of the opposition was undiminished and agreement
impossible. At this juncture Gladstone made his 'ingenious suggestion' in an attempt to salvage some part of the principle.[6]
At first Lowe was not in favour of the limited application of the
principle, anticipating that if it were left to individual ministers

---

[1] Cabinet Minute 5 June 1869, Brit. Mus., G.P. Add. MSS. 44637, fo. 63.

[2] Lowe's estimate of the division of opinion at November 1869.

[3] Brit. Mus., G.P. Add. MSS. 44610, fo. 111. A copy of this memo is re-
produced in Edward Hughes, 'Postscript to the Civil Service Reforms of 1855',
Public Administration, xxxiii, Autumn 1955, pp. 304–5. Its significance and
Hughes's interpretation of it is discussed below, Chapter 5, pp. 137–9.

[4] Cabinet Minute, 31 July 1869, Brit. Mus., G.P. Add. MSS. 44637, fo. 97.

[5] Bruce proved as obdurate as Clarendon, and while Home Secretary held
out against the considerable pressure brought to bear by Lowe. Fortescue, Chief
Secretary for Ireland, tried later to renounce open competition for the Irish
Offices.

[6] Cabinet Minute, 9 August 1869, Brit. Mus., G.P. Add. MSS. 44637, fo. 100.

nothing further would be done. 'Could you not prevail on the Cabinet to leave the matter in our hands with the understanding that we do not go for perfectly open competition?', he asked Gladstone before the meeting of the cabinet on 10 November 1869.[1] What he had in mind was to throw open all Superior Clerkships and to restrict the Supplementary Clerkships to a large but limited competition. The acceptability of his suggestion was not tested, as discussion of Civil Service recruitment was postponed until the next meeting of the cabinet on 7 December 1869.[2] In the meantime the more Lowe thought about Gladstone's suggestion the more he saw the force of it; by 22 November 1869 he was prepared to push it as hard as he could.[3] On that date he proposed to Gladstone that the Treasury and all its subordinate departments should be put under open competition at once; he thought that 'Cardwell and Childers are ready to do the same and Goschen and de Grey', and that Bruce would not object. This, he continued, 'would be quite enough for a start and we might leave Clarendon, Bright, and any other obstructives alone. I think to force the plan on unwilling heads of departments where there are so many ready to adopt it would be a waste of time and temper'. Gladstone agreed, but suggested that the right to withdraw from the scheme or to modify it in particular cases should be preserved intact.[4] The cabinet approved the scheme on 7 December 1869, and gave Lowe permission to circularize the departments for their views.[5]

The initiative which Lowe seized on behalf of the Treasury on 10 November 1869 was held by it for the next four years. On the day following the cabinet meeting of 7 December 1869 preparations were put in hand at the Treasury to give effect to the decisions then made. The cabinet had discussed not only the question of open competition but had also considered because of the 'heavy and growing increase in the charge of superannuation . . . the expediency of effecting a substantial reduction in the number

[1] Lowe to Gladstone, 10 November 1869, Brit. Mus., G.P. Add. MSS. 44301, fo. 104.
[2] Cabinet Minute, 10 November 1869, Brit. Mus., G.P. Add. MSS. 44637, fo. 113.
[3] Lowe to Gladstone, 22 November 1869, Brit. Mus., G.P. Add. MSS. 44301. fo. 106.
[4] Gladstone to Lowe, 23 November 1869, Brit. Mus., G.P. Add. MSS., Letter Books, 1869.
[5] Cabinet Minute, 7 December 1869, Brit. Mus., G.P. Add. MSS. 44637, fo. 115.

of permanent civil employments'.[1] Gladstone and Lowe had given an undertaking to consider how far these two principles could be applied to the Treasury and its subordinate departments. They had promised also to inform other departments of their intention and 'to ascertain how far they may be disposed to co-operate in establishing in their several offices a system founded upon [the two] principles'. All this was stated in a Treasury Minute of 8 December 1869, copies of which were sent to all departments. The accompanying letter made clear Lowe's intention to retain the initiative he had won in cabinet. Departments were asked to prepare their schemes in consultation with the Treasury, not the Civil Service Commissioners.

I have to request on the part of their Lordships that you will give your consideration to the subject and that you will be good enough to let me know for their Lordships information how far you may be disposed to render your co-operation in establishing in your Department a system founded upon the principles set forth in this Minute. And in the event of the proposition being favourably entertained by you, that you will make known to this Department your views as to the best mode of applying those principles and as to the preparation of a scheme appropriate to your Department.[2]

Replies to the circular were received at the Treasury in the early months of 1870. With the exception of the Home and Foreign Offices they were almost all favourable to the introduction of open competition, but many ministers entered reservations similar to that of Cardwell at the War Office who thought 'that for highly confidential situations some qualities which lie outside the province of examination are indispensable . . . [and hoped] that in framing a general scheme this consideration will not be overlooked [in order] to ensure the maintenance of a high tone of honour by the selection of persons likely to maintain it'.[3] On behalf of Lord Clarendon, Hammond opposed the introduction of open competition into the Foreign Office maintaining 'that from the peculiar nature of the work in which the Foreign Office is engaged, it would be highly inexpedient as regards the efficiency of the Department

---

[1] T.M. 8 December 1869, P.R.O. T.1/6971A/7615.

[2] The original of this letter which appears immediately after the Minute of 8 December 1869 in the same file, is undated. It is probable that copies of it were not circulated before 14 December 1869, on which date the last signature, that of the Patronage Secretary, G. G. Glyn, is appended to the Minute.

[3] War Office to Treasury, 27 January 1870, P.R.O. T.1/6971A/1879.

and not conduce to economy to apply to it the system sketched out in the enclosures in [the Treasury] letter'.[1] Later he added 'that a competitive examination open to all comers would not be a test of the general intelligence, the habits of subordination and the moral character, that are essential to the well-working of a Department like the Foreign Office'.[2] With an improbable but splendid irony the case pleaded here by the Foreign Office rested upon suggestions made privately by Gladstone to his friend and colleague Clarendon, who had sent the draft of his reply to Lowe's circular to Gladstone for his comments. His friendship and admiration for Clarendon notwithstanding, Gladstone's conduct in this instance was dubiously ethical—he, of course, had no such doubts, and found no difficulty in reconciling his action with his advocacy of open competition.[3] 'Desirous to give full effect to the decision of the cabinet that our several autonomies should be respected', he was able with a 'good conscience' to suggest to Clarendon that he should plead the special nature of the department as the reason for its exception.[4] On another point connected with the same subject he advised Clarendon not to appeal to the Treasury's opinion when 'your own will suffice'. This treating with the 'enemy' would have had a special bitterness for Lowe had he known about it, for Gladstone's brief was used later by the Foreign Office to resist Lowe's demands for the adoption of the principle of open competition there.

The Home Office reacted similarly to Lowe's circular. After careful consideration, Bruce, the Secretary of State, wrote to the Treasury that in his opinion

it would not be desirable that the Home Office should be included in such a proposed arrangement. Much of the business done at the Home Office is of such a character that great trustworthiness is required in those through whose hands it passes and any betrayal of confidence might prove very detrimental to the Public Service.[5]

---

[1] Foreign Office to Treasury 2 January 1870, P.R.O. T.1/6971A/145.
[2] Foreign Office to Treasury 17 February 1870, op. cit.
[3] Gladstone had a high regard for Clarendon. 'A statesman of many gifts, a most lovable and genial man', he noted in his diary. He told Morley that of the sixty men or so who had been his colleagues in cabinet 'Clarendon was the very easiest and most attractive'. Quoted in Morley's *Life of Gladstone*, ii. 25.
[4] Gladstone to Clarendon 31 December 1869, Brit. Mus., G.P. Add. MSS. Letter Books 1869–70.
[5] Home Office to Treasury 19 February 1870, P.R.O. T.1/6971A/3696.

Respecting the discretion reserved to each minister under the terms of the cabinet agreement, the Treasury made no attempt at this stage to influence Bruce or Clarendon to accept the principle of open competition.

At least two other replies expressed disapproval of the principle of open competition. The Paymaster-General was against it on the grounds that 'it could not fail especially after a few years to make the establishment, the duties of which are of a uniform character throughout, a mixture of persons of very various social positions'; and, that it would be a security risk.[1] In the Exchequer and Audit Department it was said that the duties required 'qualities of trust and integrity which can not be tested by examination'.[2] But these two departments were subordinate to the Treasury and Lowe had already answered for them in cabinet; both names appeared in the schedule of those departments which had adopted open competition when the Order in Council was promulgated in June 1870.

Apart from the members of the Government, at least one M.P., Sinclair Aytoun, was aware of the steps taken by the Treasury to communicate with the departments after the cabinet meeting of December 1869, but his question to Gladstone elicited only the admission of the existence and circulation of the Treasury Minute of 7 December. More encouraging news was given to the House in a debate on the motion, again introduced by Fawcett,[3] that all appointments in the civil and diplomatic services should be thrown open to competition. Speaking for the Government, Gladstone assured the House 'that we have not waited for the appearance of his Motion on the Paper to spur us on to make progress towards the fulfilment of our engagement with him'.[4] However, as legislative authority was not needed for the introduction of open competition the Government was not obliged to reveal its plans. Earlier in the nineteenth century the practice of introducing important Civil Service reforms by Order in Council rather than Statute had become customary, had been followed in 1855 when

[1] Paymaster-General to Treasury February 1870, P.R.O. T.1/6971A.
[2] Exchequer and Audit Department to Treasury February 1870, P.R.O. T.1/6971A.
[3] Henry Fawcett, Liberal M.P. for Brighton, was Professor of Political Economy at Cambridge. In the sixties and seventies he became known as the 'M.P. for India', pressing for the Indianization of the I.C.S. in order to save money on the Indian budget and to lessen the outflow of currency from India.
[4] Parl. Debs., H.C. CXCIX, 25 February 1870, col. 814.

the Civil Service Commission was established, and was now employed again. On this occasion Parliament was hardly involved at all, either in the preliminary stages of initiation, or later when the principle of open competition was introduced to departments and schemes drafted.

The cabinet approved the Order on 25 May 1870. Nothing is known of the preliminary discussions which preceded that decision, yet it is clear from its provisions, and from Lowe's and Lingen's identification with open competition, initially and after the issue of the Order, that the drafting must have been done by them or under their direction. When the Order was promulgated on 4 June 1870, Parliament, the press and a majority of civil servants welcomed the system of open competition which it introduced. *The Civil Service Gazette*, however, felt 'no particular enthusiasm for the system of open competition, and we do not believe that it will be attended with such glorious consequences as some of its votaries seem to anticipate'.[1] Feeling the interests of its readers threatened by the Order in Council and the possibility that appointments would be made to senior posts from outside the Service, its brief espousal of open competition was abruptly ended and it took up an increasingly critical attitude towards the new measure. By August 1872 concern for the interests of the serving officer had forced upon it an extreme position: open competition was 'erroneous in principle and unsatisfactory in practice'; it served

only to gauge probable merit. Competitive examination can at best but raise a mere presumption of efficiency; it is ridiculous to place it upon a higher level than proved merit; and yet this is what has been most stringently done, and men of proved ability and official fitness have suffered, because, forsooth, they have been beaten, as any one might have foreseen, in a competitive examination by lads fresh from school.[2]

THE ORDER IN COUNCIL OF 4 JUNE 1870

The order can be divided into two parts: first, that part which restated with certain modifications, the regulations laid down in the 1855 Order, but which included also new provisions dealing with open competitive examinations. The second part dealt with situations for which no certificate of qualification was required.

The provisions made in the earlier Order for testing candidates' qualifications were slightly modified. The Civil Service Com-

[1] Leading article, 11 June 1870.   [2] Ibid., 3 August 1872.

missioners argued that the difference was one of language and not intention, but it can not be denied that the greater stringency and precision of the terms used in the 1870 Order made it easier to carry that intention into effect without the difficulties of interpretation to which the earlier one had given rise.[1] In this respect the language of the 1870 Order admitted of but one interpretation: that any person engaged in any capacity (unless excepted under clauses seven and eight) was obliged to submit to examination by the Civil Service Commissioners and to receive a certificate of qualification before appointment to the Civil Service. Another important modification was that the rules relating to age, health, character, and knowledge, which previously had been agreed between the Civil Service Commissioners and the individual departments, were now to be subject to Treasury approval.

From 31 August 1870 appointments to those situations which departments had agreed to recruit by open competition were to be made

> by means of competitive examinations according to regulations to be from time to time framed by the said Civil Service Commissioners, and approved by the Commissioners of H.M. Treasury, open to all persons (of the requisite age, health, character, and other qualifications prescribed in the said regulations) who may be desirous of attending the same.

Here, and in all other aspects of open competition, it was impossible for the Civil Service Commissioners, alone or in concert with the department concerned, to move a step without first consulting the Treasury and obtaining its approval. Besides the drafting of examination regulations, Treasury approval was required for the scales of examination fees, the announcement of open competitions, and the number of situations offered for competition.

Under the earlier Order a minister could appoint to any situation for which there were no prescribed limits of age 'a person of mature age, having acquired special qualifications for the appointment in other pursuits', without sending him for examination before the Civil Service Commissioners, and without obtaining a certificate of qualification for him. In the new Order the scope of this discretionary power was drastically curtailed. Such appointments could now be made only if the qualifications in respect of knowledge and ability which were thought requisite for the situa-

---

[1] See 17th Report, CSC, 1871–2, P.P., 1872, XIX.

tion were wholly or partly professional 'or otherwise peculiar, and not ordinarily to be acquired in the Civil Service', and were thought to be so not only by the department but by the Treasury too. Furthermore, it was necessary for the department concerned 'representing the particular interests involved', and the Lords Commissioners of the Treasury 'representing the general interests of the Service' to agree that the examination should be dispensed with wholly or partly in each particular case. In addition the appointee was now required to obtain a certificate of qualification from the Civil Service Commissioners who were not obliged to award it unless he produced satisfactory evidence that he possessed the requisite knowledge and ability and was qualified in respect of age, health, and character. Thus a minister's discretion to dispense with examination in a particular case became subject to the approval of the Treasury, and the adequacy of the candidate's qualifications a matter for the judgement of the Civil Service Commissioners. The examination of the Civil Service Commissioners could also be dispensed with wholly or partly 'either for the purpose of facilitating transfers from the Redundant List, or for other reasons', if the minister and the Treasury agreed that it was in the public interest to do so.

Situations placed within Schedule B annexed to the Order were exempt from the operation of all other parts of it, and candidates were not required to obtain a certificate of qualification from the Commissioners. There were three categories of exemption: first, those appointments which were held directly from the Crown, or which the Treasury declared to be 'professional' or 'special' under the fourth clause of the Superannuation Act 1859.[1] The second category included those appointments which 'were so slightly and remotely connected with the Civil Service that on the one hand the holder of them had no claim for superannuation allowance, and on the other there appeared to be no necessity for that guarantee of efficiency which a certificate of qualification supplied'.[2] This category included all the office cleaners, porters, and domestic servants. Lastly, there were those appointments which were filled normally by promotion within the department. No situation could be added, withdrawn or restored to Schedule B without the Treasury's consent.

[1] These situations are discussed below, pp. 323–4.
[2] 17th Report, CSC, 1871–2, P.P., 1872, XIX.

What emerges most clearly from the comparison of the two Orders is the further diminution of the discretionary power which remained to each minister under the 1855 Order. Even more striking than this—and in part an explanation of it—is the scope of the Treasury's newly assumed powers. From a position where it lacked any formal authority to participate in, or influence, the selection of candidates for the Civil Service, the Treasury in 1870 made itself responsible for the oversight of the whole process. Entry by qualifying examination alone, the regulation of open competitive examinations, the award of certificates without examination, and the exemption of situations from the Order, all became subject to the approval of the Treasury. It had given itself the power, its influence was potentially enormous. How this power was used in practice to regulate the direction and the pace of development is now examined.

THE APPLICATION OF THE ORDER IN COUNCIL

The Government's attitude towards the introduction and application of open competition was one of non-interference. A decision binding upon all departments was avoided, it was explained to the House of Commons, because it was believed that in the initial and experimental stage the principle would be better served and the system work more satisfactorily if each minister decided whether to adopt it, and, where he did so, of its application to particular situations.[1] To this policy Lowe had pledged his support in November 1869 when it became apparent that it was the largest measure of reform acceptable to a majority of the cabinet. But once open competition had been accepted in principle, once he had secured the commitment of the cabinet to the scheme outlined in the 1870 Order, he implicitly repudiated the compromise solution. Under his and Lingen's direction, the Treasury now proceeded to act upon the conflicting assumption that the immediate and universal adoption of open competition, and its uniform and consistent application to the greatest number of situations, was essential.[2] Departments which had already accepted the principle were restrained by the Treasury from placing certain situations,

[1] Gladstone, in reply to a question in the House of Commons, Parl. Debs., H.C. CCI, 13 June 1870, cols. 1943–4.

[2] Memo from Lowe to Lingen 9 October 1870, P.R.O. T.1/7021A/22006; memo by Lowe February 1871, P.R.O., T.1/7121B/18378; memo by Lowe 15 April 1871, P.R.O. T.1/7139B/19509.

which might properly be made subject to open competition, within Schedule B; and by influence, persuasion, and other indirect pressures the Treasury endeavoured to secure the adoption of the principle in those departments which had opposed it.

In discharging these self-imposed tasks Lowe 'had a great deal of trouble and a very hard battle to fight. The Home Office and the Foreign Office are against me and very few really for me'.[1] In a moment of truth he confessed to Gladstone that 'you and I have rather forced it upon them and that nothing but their inability to deal with the Order in Council from its complex form and matter has enabled me to hold my ground'.[2] The departments neither understood the Order nor liked it.[3] Because of this Lingen thought that there was 'no choice but to concede a great deal that relates to the past at starting'.[4] To Lowe he confided that 'we would do ourselves very differently from what is proposed to us if we changed places with our correspondents'.[5] Lowe was reluctant to concede anything. To avoid impairing the uniformity with which the principle was applied he preferred a department to withdraw from the scheme altogether rather than to introduce its own special conditions. But even he was obliged to warn Gladstone of the danger of a reaction to the principle six months after its introduction. Fortescue wished to be released from the promise he had given to bring all the Irish Offices under open competition; Monsell at the Post Office had brought only the clerks in the Secretary's Office under it; and both the Home Office and the Foreign Office continued to stand firm against its adoption.[6] 'Pray help me in this matter', Lowe wrote to Gladstone, 'or I foresee that a great deal of work will be lost if I meet with a check now.'[7] He urged him to use his influence to prevent Fortescue from raising the matter in cabinet, fearing that 'an adverse decision might do incalculable mischief'; and at the same time to 'put as much pressure as may be needed on Granville and Bruce for if not I think there is a very fair chance of reaction'. The danger passed; Fortescue was restrained and persuaded to give effect to the policy to which he stood committed, but Granville (who had succeeded Clarendon as Foreign Secretary) and Bruce remained

---

[1] Lowe to Gladstone 12 January 1871, Brit. Mus., G.P. Add. MSS 44301, fo. 178.   [2] Ibid.
[3] Memo from Lingen to Lowe 16 August 1872, P.R.O. T.1/7258B/19279.
[4] Ibid.   [5] Ibid.   [6] Lowe to Gladstone 12 January 1871, op. cit.
[7] Ibid.

obdurate. Gladstone had the impression from talking with Granville that he did not intend to resist the adoption of open competition, but was told that any immediate reversal of Clarendon's 'decided and notorious judgment' would be invidious. Writing privately to him Gladstone warned that if appointment by nomination were retained in the Foreign Office there was the danger of the House of Commons putting down an address to the Crown. Gladstone promised Lowe to write also to Bruce if that became necessary, but although the attitude of the two Secretaries became more conciliatory, neither gave way.[1] Only Lowe's translation to the Home Office in September 1873 ended the resistance of that department to the introduction of open competition. After that date, of the major departments only the Foreign Office continued to hold out against it.

In those departments where the principle of open competition was adopted generally, particular situations could not be exempted from its application without Treasury approval; it was also required before situations could be placed within Schedule B where they were exempted from any part of the 1870 Order. To obtain Treasury approval the head of a department had to show that the qualifications required for a particular situation could not be tested better and more easily under conditions of open competition, or where it was inappropriate, limited competition. In some instances departments attempted to restrict the application of open competition by an excessive and unjustifiable use of the provisions of Schedule B. The most common argument was that the situation was one of confidence; that the duties from time to time entailed work of a secret and confidential nature.[2] Lingen pointed out the danger of admitting such a plea: 'On this principle competition will run the risk of being recognised in the abstract only.'[3] Holding that the more strictly confidential situations ought to be accessible only through promotion within the department, he considered that 'a department is ipso facto ill-

---

[1] On 9 January 1871 Algernon West drew Gladstone's attention to a letter from Lowe complaining of the determination of the Home and Foreign Secretaries not to apply the principle to their Departments. Brit. Mus., G.P. Add. MSS. 44341, fo. 55.

[2] Another reason sometimes advanced by departments was that the status and tenure of a civil servant admitted under open competition was in some way different from that of one admitted without competition.

[3] Memo from Lingen to Lowe 20 November 1870, P.R.O. T.1/7025A/22423.

organised which is obliged to put at once an unchecked trust in the holders of its junior situations'. Writing to Lowe he advised him: 'you must, I think, generally fight for the principle that the Civil Service Commissioners can judge character and that the Public Departments must in all cases accept their judgment of it'.[1] Lowe's reply, pungent and impatient, was characteristic of his attitude towards those who wished to escape the application of open competition: 'I cannot listen to the suggestion that successful candidates are less likely to be honest than selected persons.'[2]

Lowe's insistent pressure upon those departments which had accepted the principle of open competition to apply it to as many situations as possible was backed up by a very powerful and persuasive sanction. Situations placed within Schedule B carried no pension entitlement unless they were declared by the Treasury to be 'professional' or 'special' within the meaning of clause four of the Superannuation Act, 1859. Shortly after the passing of that Act the Treasury listed those situations to which it applied, adding to them subsequently only after searching inquiry. The necessity to satisfy the Treasury in this respect meant that exemption was more difficult to obtain and less tempting because of the attendant risk that pension entitlement might be refused.

The intensity of the Treasury's efforts to secure the widest possible application of open competition was not apparent to the public. Critics saw only delay and procrastination and sought eagerly for signs that the principle was being subverted. In the House of Commons and elsewhere it was alleged that the Treasury's power to exempt situations under clause eight was being used to restrict the application of open competition, particularly in the lower ranks of the Civil Service; and that the introduction of open competition had been deliberately delayed. *The Times* was asked by one of its readers why 'an immense amount of patronage of the most valuable kind has been clutched back by the Treasury under the 8th Clause' and the situations of second-class assistants of Excise, of out-door officers of the Customs, and of clerks in the Census Office had been removed from Schedule A.[3] Commenting upon the paucity of vacancies for open competition in November 1870 *The Times* said that Excise clerkships had not been made

[1] Ibid.
[2] Memo by Lowe 26 November 1870, P.R.O. T.1/7025A/22423.
[3] 11 November 1870.

subject to open competition because of 'exigencies of the Public Service' as represented by the Patronage Secretary to the Treasury.[1] In explanation *The Times* said that appointments in the Excise and Census Offices which ought to have been filled by open competition after 31 August 1870 had been exempted from that system until Christmas 1870, by which time the Treasury would have fulfilled the promises of vacancies in the Civil Service previously made to party members. On one of its faces the Treasury was all for open competition and on the other all for reducing examination to the utmost of its power, it concluded.

If these allegations came to the notice of the Treasury they were ignored; here they warrant some explanation. In view of Lowe's and Lingen's unconcealed enthusiasm for the introduction of open competition and their insistent, at times importunate, efforts to bring within its scope as many departments and situations as possible, it is inconceivable that they were engaged concurrently upon a deep-seated scheme to retain in their own hands the patronage of subordinate departments such as the Customs, Excise, and Census. Lingen believed that open competition could be applied in the lower ranks of the Service more safely and more usefully than in the higher; more safely because the necessary qualifications were few, simple and easily tested, and more usefully because lower appointments were the most numerous and could be 'jobbed' with greater impunity than others.[2] The decision to 'clutch back' some of the Treasury patronage was a political decision forced upon Lowe by Gladstone and George Glyn, the Liberal Chief Whip. Glyn, a close friend of Gladstone, was opposed to open competition and had been distressed that his patronage had been '*entirely swept away*'. Learning of the cabinet decision of 7 December 1869 and Lowe's intention to circularize the departments, he wrote immediately to Gladstone imploring him to save 'my fall' by requiring the principle of open competition to be generally adopted and not partly agreed to before the Treasury patronage was wholly surrendered.[3] Gladstone did not save his fall but

---

[1] Leading article in *The Times*, 26 November 1870.
[2] Memo from Lingen to Lowe 30 December 1870, P.R.O. T.1./7025A/22423.
[3] Glyn to Gladstone 7 December 1869, Brit. Mus., G.P. Add. MSS. 44347, fo. 355. Patronage in the Civil Service was not entirely swept away by the 1870 Order. But what remained at the disposal of the Patronage Secretary falls outside the bounds of this study. For example, in 1885 rather more than 20,000 posts were in his gift. In addition to some 17,000 sub-postmasterships, they

softened it by agreeing to the withdrawal from Schedule A of the Census Office clerkships in September 1870,[1] and the Customs House officers and Excisemen in the following month.[2] Glyn, Gladstone explained to Lowe,

is the person who is called upon, alone among us all, to encounter a serious difficulty in putting an end to the system of parliamentary patronage. He has naturally and I think properly looked to these small appointments as likely to afford him his assistance in softening a system of denial and repulse.[3]

There are at least two reasons which absolve the Treasury from blame for the delay in the commencement of open competition. First, the examination regulations for open competition were not finally settled between the Civil Service Commissioners and the Treasury until the end of October 1870. Although departments had been asked to comment upon a draft in July, some delay during the 'dead season' was not unusual. Second, by January 1871 the Treasury's classification of all Civil Service appointments—a pre-requisite of the commencement of open competition —remained incomplete, few departments having replied to the request for a return of establishment sent out in the beginning of August 1870.

Getting the departments to apply the principle of open competition once they had accepted it was difficult: more difficult still was the Treasury's task of introducing the principle into those few departments which had chosen to remain outside the scheme. Lowe was aware of his inability to coerce unwilling departments. Writing in 1871 to the Office of the House of Commons, a small and specialized department with only a handful of clerks, he

[1] Gladstone to Lowe 10 September 1870, Brit. Mus., G.P. Add. MSS., Letter Books, 1870–1.
[2] Gladstone to Lowe, 12 October 1870, Brit. Mus., G.P. Add. MSS., Letter Books, 1870–1.
[3] Gladstone to Lowe 10 September 1870, op. cit.

included such miscellaneous offices as those of preventive men in the Customs' Waterguard Service, Customs' House boatmen, housekeepers, messengers and cleaners in Revenue Offices and the National Gallery. Also, the Patronage Secretary continued to exert a great deal of influence in the choice of Lord Lieutenants, the Colonial Office supplied him with a small quota of Colonial Governorships, and the Foreign Office with the occasional consulship. See H. J. Hanham, 'Political Patronage at the Treasury, 1870–1912,' *The Historical Journal*, Vol. 3, No. 1, pp. 75–84.

I

deplored the 'dominion of patronage' which existed there and pointed to the favourable experience which had been obtained of the competitive system elsewhere. Yet he was forced to admit that 'my Lords have no power in this matter except to remonstrate'.[1] But the Treasury's remonstrances and deprecatory gestures were effective, if imponderable, sources of pressure, for they could not be ignored without explanation nor disregarded without justification.

A more effective means of pressure was tested for the first time in 1872 when the British Museum, which had refused to adopt open competition, applied for an increase of establishment. Lingen thought that if it were considered good policy to have a fight about the introduction of open competition 'this is not an unfavourable field'.[2] Lowe agreed to fight, and the Trustees were informed that the Treasury was unwilling to agree to an increase of the establishment until open competition was further considered. Pressure of a different kind was brought to bear upon the Home Office and the Foreign Office: the former were promised a pay increase when open competition was introduced, and the latter threatened that it would be withheld until it was. Later, the British Museum, still unyielding, was also refused a pay increase. Lingen hesitated to insist upon open competition as the *sine qua non* of a rise but Lowe, as ever, was unbending.

The Home Office and the Foreign Office were the most important departments which contracted out of open competition, and their continued exclusion drew criticism from the House of Commons.[3] No steps were taken officially by the Treasury to raise the subject with Bruce, the Home Secretary, between February 1870 when the Treasury learned of his intention to remain outside the scheme and January 1871 when the return of establishment was received in the Treasury. The latter was accom-

---

[1] Letter drafted by Lowe 30 August 1871, P.R.O. T.1/7088B/13559.

[2] Memo from Lingen to Lowe 2 July 1872, P.R.O. T.1/7257C/19163.

[3] There were very few exceptions, none of them were important or large departments, e.g. the Lunacy Commissioners whose clerks were not added to Schedule A until 12 January 1872; the Friendly Societies Registry which continued to recruit to its two clerical situations without an open competitive examination until 18 February 1876, and the Office of the Comptroller of Bankruptcy, where the junior clerks were not added to Schedule A until 27 January 1873. More significant than these exceptions was that of the Ecclesiastical Commission where the junior clerks on the Superior and Supplementary Establishments were not recruited by open competition until 1 April 1873.

panied by details of certain changes which Bruce proposed to make to the establishment, the most important of which was the proposal to recruit the Supplementary Clerks of the Home Office and its subordinate departments by open competition.[1] Lowe reacted characteristically, not by welcoming the proposal but by deploring the continued exclusion of the clerks of the Superior Establishment from open competition. To Lingen he expressed his regret that 'the Home Office should in the matter of competition place itself in antagonism to the rest of the Civil Service and thus take up a position which will expose it to much obloquy and which it will be found impossible long to maintain', and instructed him to prepare a letter conveying the sense of this criticism to the Secretary of State.[2]

Bruce was warned that his action might invite much adverse criticism and urged to reconsider his decision; if he did so the Treasury promised to revise the pay of junior clerks on the Superior Establishment. To the comments made by the Treasury upon his proposals Bruce agreed in principle, but added that he 'would be glad to have the parts about competition omitted'.[3] If this were done he was willing to offer himself 'to persuasion in camera with the Chancellor of the Exchequer'.[4] Subsequent events point to Lowe having been unsuccessful. In November 1871 the Supplementary Clerkships were added to Schedule A as proposed, but clerkships on the Superior Establishment were excluded from open competition until 1873. On 9 September of that year they were gazetted as Schedule A situations, immediately following Lowe's resignation from the Treasury and his arrival at the Home Office. Having waited three years to bring the Home Office under open competition, he delayed not a moment before communicating his intention to the Treasury when that decision rested with him alone.

The Foreign Office clung tenaciously to the belief that the work of other departments was not comparable to its own. Because of this the task of persuading the Secretary of State to adopt open competition was especially difficult. Foreign Office work, it was

[1] Departments subordinate to the Home Office were the Office of the Director of Convict Prisons, the Office of the Public Courts of the Metropolis, and the Offices of the Inspectors of Factories, Salmon Fisheries, and Burial Grounds.
[2] Memo by Lowe February 1871, P.R.O. T.1/7121B/18378.
[3] Quoted in memo by Lingen 7 and 10 March 1871, P.R.O. T.1/7121B/18378.
[4] Ibid.

said, was often of a secret and confidential nature which could not be entrusted to persons whose antecedents and integrity were not known personally to the head of the department.[1] While this argument was valid for some of the posts in some of the branches of the Foreign Office, it did not apply to them all, as Lord Granville admitted in 1872. For a while the Treasury chose not to dispute this, confident that open competition could not be indefinitely resisted in the Foreign Office.

Greater deference was shown to the Foreign Secretary than had been accorded Bruce. References by the Treasury to the application of open competition were more moderate in tone and altogether less insistent than those made to the Home Office in similar circumstances. When the Foreign Secretary was informed that 'my Lords look forward to a day when these appointments may be added to such as are offered for public competition', it was with the assurance that the Treasury had no wish to press such considerations against his judgment. In May 1872 it seemed that this hope might soon be fulfilled. Granville, who had supported the introduction of open competition into the Colonial Office, had succeeded Clarendon as Secretary of State, and he now wrote offering to throw open posts in the Chief Clerk's Department. Having secured the admission that the special reasons which had induced Clarendon to object to the introduction of open competition did not apply to those employed exclusively there, the Treasury pressed for its extension to the Treaty and Librarian's Departments, which as regards pay and promotion were analogous. Resisting this argument, Granville claimed that the clerks in these two departments had access to 'some of the most secret and confidential transactions of the department in the performance of their daily duties'. Advised by Lingen, Lowe now insisted that, before any improvement was made to their salaries and those of the clerks in the Chief Clerk's Department then under review at the Treasury, an inquiry should be held to determine whether they should be recruited by open competition. Granville refused to enter into such an agreement and the proposed inquiry was never made.

Following the disclosure of financial irregularities at the Post Office a short while after, Gladstone re-shuffled his cabinet, moving Lowe to the Home Office and assuming the office of

[1] Letters to the Treasury 2 January and 17 February 1870, P.R.O. T.1/6971A/ 145.

Chancellor himself. Doubly burdened, and with a Government weakened by its defeat on the Irish University Bill, he had little time to pursue the question of open competition with Granville. The moment had passed, for the remainder of the nineteenth century circumstances were never again so propitious. Open competition was not finally introduced into the Foreign Office until the end of the First World War.

CONTROL OF EXAMINATIONS

The Treasury's control of open competition under the Order in Council meant no more than the power to approve proposals put up by the Civil Service Commissioners. In practice the limits of Treasury action were extended much farther, as Lowe and Lingen, bent upon making examination regulations uniform throughout the Service, took the reins of control into their own hands. Their ideas and beliefs, rather than those of the Civil Service Commissioners, largely determined the substance and quality of the regulations, and they alone interpreted them and ruled in difficult cases. The Treasury's arrogation of authority to initiate proposals as well as to approve them, and to direct the Commissioners in addition to advising them, was neither disputed nor (apparently) resented by the Civil Service Commissioners. Between the two departments the closest co-operation prevailed, replacing the earlier relationship which had been governed by the Treasury's desire to keep the Commissioners at arm's length.

Three separate schemes of open competitive examinations were introduced, Regulations I, II and III, providing for an establishment similar to that which had been introduced into the Treasury on 25 May 1870. Before a candidate was permitted to enter for an open competition under Regulations I and II, he had to take a preliminary test examination to satisfy the Civil Service Commissioners of his competence in handwriting, orthography, and simple arithmetic; candidates for Regulation I were also tested in English composition. Regulation I was designed to test the qualifications of clerks who were to be employed exclusively upon intellectual work. Before the date of the examination a candidate could name any or all of the subjects shown in Table I, but no marks were awarded in any subject unless he showed a 'competent knowledge' of it. Candidates were placed in order of merit according to the total number of marks awarded.

The competitive examinations held under Regulation II, designed to test the qualifications of those who would be primarily engaged upon mechanical and routine work, were less exacting. Candidates could offer any or all of the subjects shown in Table II, and were placed in order of merit according to the total number of marks awarded.

TABLE I

Examination Subjects for Open Competitions, 1870–1874
Regulation I

	Marks
English Composition, including precis	500
History of England—including that of the Laws and Constitution	500
English Language and Literature	500
Language, Literature, and History of Greece	750
Rome	750
France	375
Germany	375
Italy	375
Mathematics (pure and mixed)	1,250
Natural Science: that is (i) Chemistry, including Heat; (ii) Electricity and Magnetism; (iii) Geology; and Mineralogy; (iv) Zoology; (v) Botany	1,000*
Moral Sciences: that is, Logic, Mental and Moral Philosophy	500
Jurisprudence	375
Political Economy	375
Additional Subjects	500

* The total 1,000 marks could be obtained by adequate proficiency in any two or more of the five branches.

TABLE II

Examination Subjects for Open Competitions, 1870–1874
Regulation II

Handwriting	400
Orthography	400
Arithmetic	400
Copying MS (to test accuracy)	200
Indexing and docketing	200
Digesting returns into Summaries	200
English Composition	200
Geography	200
English History	200
Book-keeping	200

Writers were selected by open competition under Regulation

III, and supplied by the Civil Service Commissioners to the departments as the need arose.

Before open competitive examinations could begin, the Treasury had to agree with each department a classification of its situations under Regulation I or II. In negotiating with them, the Treasury applied and adhered to two principles—uniformity and economy. Those departments which submitted proposals inconsistent with either were required to modify them. The Colonial Office, Lowe said 'write as if they were to have an examination for themselves alone. This cannot be and it would be better that they should withdraw altogether than introduce a sectarian element into the Catholicity of our plan';[1] and he criticized the Office of the Secretary for Ireland for a 'disposition which ought to be resisted . . . to put too many in the 1st Class'.[2] The Board of Inland Revenue's suggestion that there should be an intermediate class between Regulations I and II, because the qualifications required in certain of their clerks were higher than those needed for Regulation II but lower than for Regulation I, was also rejected by Lowe; they should be recruited, he said, under Regulation I and an alteration made in the system of promotion. Questions arising from the preparation of the classification were discussed at meetings arranged by the Treasury at the request of the departments, and were attended by the Permanent Secretary to the Treasury, the Secretary of the Civil Service Commissioners, and a senior official of the department concerned. No records of these informal and private discussions exist, and it is impossible, therefore, to estimate the degree to which the Treasury influenced the final classification. Given the determination of Lowe and Lingen to secure uniformity and economy, and the presence of the latter, the Treasury voice was probably dominant and decisive.

By 31 August 1870, the official date for the commencement of open competition, the classification of situations was still incomplete, departmental heads having been slow to comment upon the draft of the proposed examination regulations. By the end of the following month no more than a handful of replies had been received, few of which contained the required information. In consequence, although they were not to blame, the Civil Service Commissioners became the target for much criticism. To avoid

[1] Memo from Lowe to Lingen 9 October 1870, P.R.O. T.1/7021A/22006.
[2] Ibid.

further blame they now asked the Treasury to approve a modified version of the original draft of the examination regulations without further delay. Before doing so Lowe and Lingen examined the draft carefully, making several amendments to it, the most important of which concerned examination subjects. Their comments illustrate three characteristics of the Treasury's control of recruitment after 1870: Lowe's and Lingen's close, personal control of recruitment details; their preoccupation with uniformity; and the subordination of the Civil Service Commissioners. At the request of several departments the Civil Service Commissioners had added to the condition that none of the subjects of examination were to be obligatory the qualification 'except those specially required by the several departments'. Submitted for approval, the Treasury instructed the Commissioners to withdraw it, Lingen observing that 'success is meant to attend on the greatest number of marks and marks are meant to be so arranged as to favour no particular course of education, but to ensure that the winners are well educated'.[1] Departments were to be permitted, however, to require candidates successful in the open competitive examination to pass in prescribed special subjects before entry. Some months later, in April 1871, the Commissioners wrote to the Treasury for permission to ask each minister in what special subjects he wished the successful candidates for his department to be tested; but even this went too far in Lowe's judgement.

I think the Commissioners ought not to send circulars to ask the Department to suggest special subjects in which they wish the successful candidates to be tested. Such requests should be left to come from the Departments and ought not to be prompted or encouraged. We shall end at this rate by breaking down the principle of uniform examination and depriving the success in competition of the greater part of its value.[2]

Further revision of the examination regulations did not take place until March 1872 when the Civil Service Commissioners proposed to place in 'a general code those which are intended to affect equally all competitions held under the 5th clause of the Order in Council of 4th June 1870 and issuing separately the special rules governing each kind of competition'.[3] The Treasury agreed to

[1] T.M. 10 October 1870 drafted by Lingen, P.R.O. T.1/7021A/22006.
[2] Memo by Lowe 15 April 1871, P.R.O. T.1/7139B/19509.
[3] CSC to Treasury 28 March 1872, P.R.O. T.1/7221B/15464.

this, but not before each code had suffered amendment by both Lowe and Lingen. Once again the process of amendment is revealing. On several occasions the Commissioners had raised with the Treasury the question of allowing the number of candidates selected at each competitive examination to exceed the number of vacancies available at the conclusion of the examination, but the Treasury had always stood firm against this. 'It is contrary to every principle of an examination held for a limited number of prizes, and it opens the door to all sorts of pressure', the meritocratic Lingen had written to Lowe previously. The latter, ever anxious to preserve the integrity of the system he and Lingen had introduced, now objected strongly to allowing a candidate who had done less well than others to obtain an appointment which fell vacant only after the results of the examination had been declared and the most successful candidates had filled the existing vacancies. He seized the opportunity to settle the matter, and as he confided to Lingen 'to put it as far as possible beyond the reach of further negotiation with the Civil Service Commission'.[1] This he accomplished quite neatly by insisting upon the transfer of the clause from the Special Code of regulations, which varied from one competition to another, to the fixed General Code which applied to them all.

Unusual or difficult questions of interpretation or administration of the examination regulations were submitted by the Civil Service Commissioners to the Treasury. Where the existing regulations were silent the Treasury formulated a rule for their guidance. In July 1871 the question was raised whether candidates successful at previous examinations should be allowed to compete again. Lowe's *obiter dicta* was that 'no successful candidate should be allowed to stand again if he has got a place, it is manifestly against the public policy to encourage a roving discontented spirit among the members of the Civil Service'.[2] Subsequently his ruling acquired regulatory force, being published as an official notice in the *London Gazette*. Later, it was invoked on several occasions by the Civil Service Commissioners to refuse permission to successful candidates to compete at further examinations. Rules such as this were generally made after consideration of the cir-

---

[1] Rivers Wilson (Lowe's private secretary) to Lingen 5 April 1872, P.R.O. T.1/7221B/15464.
[2] Memo by Lowe 26 July 1871, P.R.O. T.1/7221B/15464.

cumstances of a particular case, others as a result of proposals made to the Treasury by the Civil Service Commissioners.

So far reference has been made only to the control of open competitive examinations, but not all departments had adopted the principle of open competition, and in them recruitment was governed by other parts of the Order in Council. Unless a situation was placed within Schedule B and thus totally exempted from its operation, the application of these parts ensured that appointments were made by way of qualifying examination with or without some element of competition according to the wish of the department. The Treasury made no serious attempt to influence the departments in the exercise of this choice; nor was it much concerned with the conditions of recruitment. Although it had only a shared authority (it approved proposals agreed upon between the departments and the Civil Service Commissioners) no doubt it could have taken more positive steps than it did to control the conditions under which candidates were recruited by qualifying examinations. But neither Lowe nor Lingen, pre-occupied with the introduction of open competition, seemed disposed to do so. From time to time they raised objections to proposals put up to them, but did not insist upon them.

THE COMMENCEMENT OF OPEN COMPETITIVE EXAMINATIONS

Each open competition gave rise to three inter-related questions: when the examination was to take place, how many vacancies were to be offered, and the number of competitors who were to be declared successful. In each instance the decision was made by the Treasury and implemented by the Civil Service Commissioners. Sometimes instructions were issued to the Commissioners, for example, the dates of the first and second open competitions; at other times the Treasury decided only after receiving a proposal from the Commissioners.

Open competition was due to begin on 31 August 1870. Three factors made this impossible. First, the Civil Service Commissioners and the Treasury had not prepared and agreed upon the examination regulations. Secondly, the Treasury had not completed the classification of situations under Regulations I and II. Lastly, there were insufficient vacancies to offer for competition. The first two of these factors have been explained above; the third led the Treasury on 29 November 1870 to instruct the Civil Service Commissioners to postpone open competitions for the time being. The scarcity of vacancies was the direct result of the reorganization of establishments contemplated or actually taking place in accordance with the principle laid down in the Treasury Minute of 8 December 1869. Reductions in the numbers of clerks, particularly those on the Superior Establishments, had led to some redundancy, and the Treasury's policy was now to use its powers under clause seven of the 1870 Order to persuade departments with vacancies to fill them from the Redundant List. Because of this it was not until January 1871 that the Civil Service Commissioners were permitted to announce the first preliminary test examination for open competitions under Regulations I and II. Another month passed before Lowe and Lingen informed the Commissioners that the first open competition under Regulation II might now take place; that they could offer twenty vacancies; and that no more than that number of candidates was to be declared successful. An open competition under Regulation I was not held until January 1872, there being fewer vacancies than for Regulation II. Upon this occasion the proposal came from the Civil Service Commissioners, but it was the Treasury which decided that it was desirable 'in the first open competition under the Scheme No. I to restrict the number of actual vacancies'.[1] As before, the risk of having to hold another examination soon afterwards was preferred to that of having on hand selected candidates for whom no appointments could be found. Other competitions under Regulations I and II followed, the Treasury deciding in each instance the number of vacancies to be offered and the number of competitors who were to be declared successful.

DISPENSATION

The Treasury could have used its dispensing power to restrict the application of open competition; in fact *The Times* alleged that the intention of clause seven was to provide it with the means to do just that. More bluntly, *The Civil Service Gazette* warned the Government that it must not use the section for 'jobbery'.[2] But it was not easy for a department to obtain the agreement of the Treasury to its use for that purpose. Lowe was 'very much

[1] Treasury to CSC 23 November 1871, P.R.O. T.1/7221B/15464.
[2] Leading article, 23 July 1870.

disinclined to exercise the dispensing power . . . except when the circumstances are very special and exceptional'.[1] Besides, an additional safeguard was provided by the Civil Service Commissioners' right to refuse to issue their certificate, even when the Treasury had agreed, if they considered that the candidate did not possess the requisite qualifications for the situation.[2]

In any case clause seven was used less for the purpose of dispensing with examination on first appointment than to facilitate the transfer of redundant clerks. To help those departments which had undertaken large-scale reorganizations, particularly the Admiralty, the War Office, and the Customs, where the first and largest reductions were made, the Treasury tried to arrange for the transfer of redundant clerks to other departments with vacancies. Between 1870–3 'about half-a-dozen attempts were made'.[3] In 1872 the Education Office was prevailed upon to fill nine new posts with clerks transferred from the Admiralty and Customs; and in the same year the Mint was persuaded to accept three redundant clerks from the Customs. Most departments were understandably reluctant to accept redundant clerks who were often the least efficient or most elderly officers, and whose recruitment under the diverse departmental conditions which prevailed before 1870 gave no guarantee of even a minimum level of competence. Nor was their transfer welcomed by the other clerks who saw them as a threat to their own prospects of promotion, although this objection was partly met by the Treasury's rule that redundant clerks entered at the bottom of an establishment, but with their previous rate of pay. On one occasion, the Treasury offered sixteen redundant Admiralty and War Office clerks to the Exchequer and Audit Office. Those from the War Office refused to move, but the Admiralty clerks, all with eight or nine years' seniority, were transferred and began at the bottom of the department. An attempt to transfer four more to the same office was strongly resisted by Sir William Dunbar, the Comptroller and Auditor-General, on the ground that as former Customs' officers they had not passed an examination equivalent to that which was sat by a junior examiner

---

[1] Private letter from Rivers Wilson (Lowe's private secretary) to War Office 21 February 1872, P.R.O. T.1/7182B/7138.

[2] This right was exercised in quite a few cases, see 18th Report CSC, 1872–3, P.P., 1874 XVI.

[3] Lingen in evidence to the *Select Committee on Civil Services Expenditure*, 1873, qu. 2908.

in the Audit Office. His protest was supported by the Civil Service Commissioners, who refused to issue certificates of qualification to the four clerks.[1]

Before 1870 transfer was exceedingly rare, although there was some movement of clerks between departments, particularly those belonging to the Supplementary Class. From time to time they were offered and accepted better appointments in other departments. Some chose to move uninvited to obtain better conditions of service or improved prospects of promotion, but before they could do so they had to be nominated by the head of the department which they wished to enter, obtain permission to compete from their own head of department, and then to compete successfully in an examination where this was competitive and not merely qualifying. The hazards and complexity of this procedure, together with the Treasury rule that those who moved at their own volition were entitled only to the minimum of the scale fixed for the new post, tended to inhibit voluntary movement between departments.

Among clerks of the Superior Establishments there was little movement before 1870. A career begun in one department rarely ended in another, although there was some mobility at the very top among the permanent secretaries and their deputies, and a few senior men were regularly promoted out of the Treasury to other departments.[2] Secondment was rarer still. An accountant lent to the Foreign Office in 1861 was recalled by the Admiralty before he had time to complete his assignment. The acrimonious correspondence which ensued, involving both the Treasury and the Civil Service Commissioners, provided an infelicitous precedent for arrangements of a similar kind.

CONCLUSION

Within fifteen years of their appointment, and largely unaided, the Civil Service Commissioners had loosened the departments' grip of recruitment. But while they had succeeded in establishing strict

[1] Quoted in a leading article in *The Civil Service Gazette*, 31 May 1873. Between 1870 and 1874, 276 appointments were made under clause seven, of which about a half were to clerical posts. From the return it is impossible to distinguish between those who were transferred from the redundant list, and those who were appointed without examination, genuinely or otherwise, because the qualifications for the post were deemed to be professional or special. P.P., 1882, XXXVII.   [2] See above, Chapter 1, p. 16.

and uniform conditions of health, moral fitness, and, to a lesser extent, age of entry, it seemed improbable in the late sixties that, without further Government action and support, they would become the central recruiting agency envisaged by Trevelyan and Northcote in their report. The Commissioners had been very much less successful in persuading departments to adopt some form of competitive examination; indeed they appeared to be losing ground won earlier. Stanley's experiment with open competition at the India Office in 1858 had not been followed by any other major department. Limited competitions were held infrequently, and competition was strictly limited. The proportion of qualified candidates to vacancies was rarely that recommended by the 1860 Select Committee. In 1867–8 it was only 11 per cent, and had never risen above 14 per cent in the previous five years. In the same year nine out of ten appointments in the Civil Service were made without competition of any kind.

During this time the Treasury had little influence upon the development of recruitment. Its self-appointed role was that which Gladstone described accurately as the *point d'appui* of the Civil Service Commissioners. In this capacity it upheld and supported their decisions when required to do so, but for the most part scrupulously refrained from interfering with their work, exercising no direct influence upon recruitment outside its own subordinate departments. All this was changed in 1869 when Lowe began to press for the introduction of open competition. Ineluctably the Treasury was drawn into the very centre of the recruitment process, and for the next five years controlled every part of it.[1] From a position where it lacked any formal authority to participate in or influence the selection of candidates, the Treasury made itself responsible under the 1870 Order in Council for the oversight of the whole process: entry by qualifying examination alone, the regulation of open competitive examinations, the award of certificates without examination, and the exemption of situations from the

[1] In 1871 the Treasury even entered the field of probation which until that time it had been quite content to leave to the departments and the CSC. Despite the opposition of Lingen and the CSC, Lowe with his customary obstinacy, pushed through an Order in Council amending the probation provisions of the earlier one. His reasons for doing so are not altogether clear; the effect was to make the six months probationary period obligatory, thereby removing from the CSC the means of ensuring that satisfactory proof of fitness was furnished by the candidate, i.e. the power to withhold the certificate, which was now issued immediately after appointment.

operation of the Order all became subject to the Treasury's approval.

This vast and comprehensive power of approval was used by Lowe and Lingen for the avowed purpose of securing the immediate and universal adoption of the principle of open competition, and its uniform and consistent application to the greatest number of situations. Ignoring the cabinet agreement that each minister should be free to adopt or reject the principle of open competition, by influence, cajolery, and other indirect pressures, and, where necessary, by threats, salary 'bribes' and the enforcement of sanctions, they restrained those departments which had already accepted open competition from excluding certain situations from its operation, and endeavoured to secure the adoption of the principle in other departments which opposed it. To a large extent they were successful; by 1874 the only important exception to the universal adoption of the principle was the Foreign Office.

Because of the reduction in the number of situations after 1868 and the transfer of redundant clerks to vacancies in other departments,[1] only nine open competitions were held under Regulations I and II in the period 1870–74.[2] It could not be claimed, therefore, that by 1874 open competition was firmly established, that the superiority of candidates chosen by this method had been convincingly and amply demonstrated. But by this time the principle had been secured, to reverse it would have been as difficult as its establishment.[3] Whatever the deficiencies in the details of the scheme drawn up by the Treasury and the Civil Service Commissioners, whatever the doubts entertained by some ministers, it had been established that recruitment to clerical and administrative appointments in the Civil Service should be by open competition. While the division of the Service into two separate classes was

---

[1] The cabinet decision of December 1869 was reinforced by the recommendations of the *Select Committee on Civil Services Expenditure* in 1873 that there should be a reduction in the number of Civil Service appointments, and that redundant clerks should be transferred to vacancies in other departments. The Treasury acted on both recommendations. P.P., 1873, VII.

[2] For details of these see Appendix III, table 2.

[3] W. L. Burn in The *Age of Equipoise*, p. 114 comments that: 'The storms which blew up in 1871 and 1872 over the appointment of Sir Robert Collier to the Judicial Committee of the Privy Council and the presentation of the Revd. Mr. Harley to the living of Ewelme, although deliberately inflated for political purposes, did reflect the suspicions of a country almost pathologically afraid of jobbery.'

strongly attacked by the Playfair Commission in 1874, there was no attempt to overthrow the principle.[1]

Their preoccupation with uniformity, which occasionally assumed the proportions of an obsession, led Lowe and Lingen perforce to control the open competitive examinations. They were not content with approving and rejecting proposals which came up to them from the Civil Service Commissioners, time and again they took the initiative themselves, directing the Commissioners as well as advising them. The substance and quality of the examination regulations was decided very largely within the Treasury, their interpretation entirely so. Furthermore, the Treasury decided when open competitions were to be held, how many vacancies were to be offered, and the number of candidates who were to be declared successful at each examination.

Lowe, of whom Gladstone said that he did not 'get up all things' but allowed himself a choice, 'as if politics were a flower garden and we might choose among the beds',[2] 'got up' recruitment. He saw the subject of open competition in that 'burning, almost scorching light' which Gladstone once told him was a difficulty and a danger to him. In the preservation of the principle of open competition undiluted these qualities and those of tenacity and single-mindedness served his purpose splendidly. He was proof against the blandishments of his colleagues, caring little for the irritation and resentment which his manner and methods aroused. By temperament he was unsuited to a patient wooing of Clarendon, Granville, Bruce and other 'obstructives' who perhaps could have been persuaded but not coerced. But he was especially well-

[1] Some writers have interpreted the terms of reference and the report of the Playfair Commission as reactionary. See, for example, R. Moses, *The Civil Service of Great Britain*, Chapter VI which he calls 'The Decade of Scepticism'. Northcote who appointed the Commission intended that it should look at the working of open competition under the 1870 Order, but that he continued to support the principle there can be no doubt from his correspondence with Lyon Playfair. In his second letter of 27 January 1875 he viewed with 'alarm' the Commission's proposal to recruit to staff appointments from outside the Service. That proposal and the suggestion that heads of departments should select candidates to fill vacancies from among those who had passed the open competitive examinations were received with a certain amount of suspicion within the Service and in the press. They may be fairly criticized as reactionary, but Moses exaggerates when he claims that 'the creation of a list of candidates for division I, from which heads of departments were to choose, was a return to patronage'.

[2] Gladstone to Lowe 13 August 1873, Brit. Mus., G.P. Add. MSS. 44302, ff. 144–5.

endowed to deal with those who having accepted open competition in principle attempted to avoid its application by claiming exemption under Schedule B. In resisting such attempts his obstinacy, ruthlessness, and disregard for considerations other than his own enabled him to undertake a course of action—such as the refusal to extend the benefit of pension entitlement under clause four of the Superannuation Act 1859 to certain Schedule B situations—from which others might have shrunk. Without so determined a Chancellor at the Treasury it seems likely that many departments exercising the freedom of choice agreed in cabinet would not have been brought under open competition at all, while others (like the Irish Offices and the Post Office) would have secured their release from a previous commitment. It was perhaps fortunate that Gladstone's restraining hand was laid upon his rash, intemperate colleague, but without the latter's determination there is reason to doubt whether Gladstone's conviction was strong enough to allow him in the circumstances which obtained in 1869–70 to fly directly in the face of colleagues and trusted friends. His conduct in the exchange with Clarendon revealed the limitation of his support for open competition, for in helping the 'obstructives' to avoid it he appeared to exceed the demands upon him even of friendship.[1] Lowe (with Lingen's assistance) is perhaps entitled to more credit than has so far been accorded him; Gladstone, rather less. His achievement was considerable, for Parliament with a few exceptions had shown little enthusiasm for the immediate adoption of the principle in 1869–70; there had been no great movement for Civil Service reform such as that which had erupted between 1853–6; and cabinet approval had been won only by Gladstone's 'ingenious suggestion'. Few were on Lowe's side; he and Gladstone had 'rather forced it upon them'.

[1] Besides the exchange of letters with Clarendon, Gladstone frequently reiterated the right of each cabinet member to choose open competition or not; on several occasions he reminded Lowe that this 'right' must be preserved intact. Then there is the odd episode when he reminded Lowe that he had not been asked to agree to any scheme for the recruitment of Treasury clerks; Lowe must have been surprised by this, for he and Gladstone had already pledged the department to open competition in the cabinet meeting.

K

5

DIVISION OF LABOUR

THE ORIGIN OF
THE TWO-TIERED ESTABLISHMENT

BEFORE 1848 a formal division of labour between different classes of clerks was virtually unknown in the Civil Service. Young men were not specially recruited to do what Trevelyan later called intellectual work, nor a separate class specially recruited and employed upon what he called mechanical duties; both kinds of work were done by the same class of clerks, the more junior of them employed mainly upon mechanical work, while the senior clerks contributed mainly to the preparation and formulation of policy or supervised work done by the juniors.[1] This one-tiered establishment was common to most departments, though there were variations of nomenclature, conditions of service and organization. Its *raison d'être* was the firmly held belief that a new recruit could become familiar with departmental procedure and business only by being employed initially upon routine and mechanical work. Moreover, it was argued that such a training was indispensable preparation for higher office.[2] Besides this argument, in departments which had relatively small establishments, the scope for a division of work, other than between junior and senior clerks of the same class, was more limited and the need for it less obvious.

Belief in the superiority of the one-tiered establishment was not seriously challenged until 1848, when in response to Parliament's demand for a reduction in the cost of civil administration a Select Committee was appointed to advise what further economies were desirable, and to consider the existing methods of preparing and presenting the Estimates of the civil departments. Sir Charles

---

[1] 'Intellectual' is used here and throughout this chapter as convenient shorthand to distinguish that kind of work which in the Treasury after 1856 was done mainly by the Principal Officers and the 1st Class Clerks, from the more 'mechanical', meaning by this term duties similar to those of the Treasury Supplementary Clerks and the unestablished copyists and writers. See above, Chapter 1, pp. 13–14 and Chapter 2, pp. 29–34.

[2] Evidence before the *Select Committee on Miscellaneous Expenditure*, 1848, P.P., 1847–8, XVIII.

Trevelyan, Assistant Secretary to the Treasury, called before it to give evidence on behalf of his department, took advantage of the opportunity to express publicly his criticisms of the Treasury Establishment, alleging that the tasks of recording and communicating decisions were mechanical and dulled the intelligence of the better type of recruit. He proposed that these and similar mechanical duties should be distinguished from those with a greater intellectual content, and that the clerks on the establishment should be entrusted only with those of the latter kind, while the mechanical and routine duties should be the sole responsibility of a class of writers or copyists such as those employed by commercial law stationers.

These views, contrary to those customarily advanced to justify the one-tiered establishment, drew little support or sympathy from other witnesses, most of whom argued much more convincingly for the continuance of the existing system. Sir Alexander Spearman, a former Assistant Secretary to the Treasury, disagreeing with the plan to employ large numbers of copyists, argued that Trevelyan had underrated the importance of the work of record and communication, which, he said, required a knowledge of procedures and forms which could be obtained only by long experience, itself a valuable and indispensable preparation for the work which the clerks would be called upon to perform in higher positions later in their official life. Another witness, a Treasury Chief Clerk, declared the work of drafting and summarizing papers to be unsuitable for mere copying clerks; while Sir Francis Baring, a former Chancellor of the Exchequer, to whom Trevelyan owed his appointment, did not believe that a great part of the work done by the junior clerks of the establishment could be given to copyists. The uniformity and weight of opinion opposed to Trevelyan could not be ignored, and it was hardly surprising that the committee pronounced unfavourably upon his scheme.

Trevelyan's strategy was neither subtle nor shrewd. As happened so often in his public career he had fought the right battle at the wrong place, at the wrong time and with the wrong weapons. At that time his critics could not be convinced intellectually by abstract argument, they had to be shown that what he alleged was true, and that what he proposed would work in practice. This he now proceeded to do, working from within the Treasury. With two Junior Lords of the Treasury he was appointed to a committee to inquire into the establishment of the department. Guided and inspired by Trevelyan they reported in favour of a more extensive division of labour, but Sir Charles Wood, the Chancellor of the Exchequer, influenced by George Arbuthnot, Trevelyan's second in command, cut it down to a 'half and half measure', approving only a partial separation of the intellectual and mechanical work. While the Chancellor agreed with Trevelyan that 'the Clerks on the general Establishment should be less employed in copying',[1] and a number of 'Extra Clerks' introduced into the department for employment solely upon the copying and other mechanical work, nevertheless he believed that it was still necessary for them to master 'those details of the business of the Office, which however distasteful, are essential to the efficient performance of their duties'.[2]

Elsewhere Trevelyan enjoyed greater success. He now began upon the series of departmental inquiries which culminated in the report which he wrote with Northcote in 1853. Following the Select Committee's report to the House of Commons in 1848, he assisted in the revision of the Home Office and was then invited by the Colonial Secretary to serve on a committee to inquire into the organization of the Colonial Office. In the report Trevelyan called

for a decided change of system based upon the principle of establishing by degrees, a clear distinction between those kinds of labour which call for the exercise of the higher intellectual faculties, and those in which good penmanship and common attention to exactness and regularity, are all that is required, [and recommended] a distinction between a class of Clerks below the Senior to be engaged exclusively upon the intellectual work of the Department . . . and to employ under the Superintendent of Copyists as many persons, to be paid at existing rates, as may be required to do the whole of the copying and other merely manual work of the Department.[3]

Trevelyan's recommendations were accepted and implemented; later he claimed that the report established the 'first model for the construction of a Public Office on the principle of making a proper distinction between intellectual and mechanical labour.'[4]

Despite these changes, and those made earlier in the Treasury,

[1] Report of the Treasury committee of inquiry, 2 March 1849, P.R.O., T.1/5533/27830.   [2] T.M. 27 March 1849, P.R.O. T.1/5533/27830.
[3] Report of the inquiry into the Colonial Office, 15 December 1849, P.P., 1854, XXVII.
[4] Trevelyan to Gladstone, 15 September 1853, Bod., T.L.B., xxxii. 59–64.

the establishments of both departments remained essentially one-tiered, for the copyists were unestablished. A two-tiered establishment founded upon a complete separation of function between two permanent established classes of clerks was not created until Trevelyan and Northcote began work in 1853 upon their 'masterpiece', the inquiry into the organization of the Board of Trade.[1] To the President they recommended that all the mechanical work should be transferred to a copying department and that a fixed number of copyists (later called Supplementary Clerks) should be employed upon it. He agreed to this, and to their suggestion that the copyists should be recruited by an examination similar to that with which the Treasury tested the qualifications of its own permanent 'extra clerks'. In addition the copyists were to receive all the benefits of established service: annual salaries (upon a scale £80 × £5 to £180, with provision for further advancement in cases of unusual merit), superannuation, annual paid leave, and so on; but they were to be kept entirely separate from the Superior Establishment, with no claim to promotion to it.[2] The result of their inquiry, Trevelyan told Gladstone, was that the Board of Trade had been recast on a good model, 'with a considerable pecuniary saving, a great increase of efficiency, and so far as we know, to everybody's satisfaction'.[3]

This two-tiered establishment, with both a Superior and a Supplementary Establishment, became the model for other offices which Trevelyan and Northcote investigated subsequently: the Department of Science and Art, the Poor Law Board, the Privy Council Office, the Colonial Emigration and Land Office, the Copyhold Enclosure and Tithe Commission, the Board of Ordnance, the Office of Works, the Post Office, the Audit Office, and the Board of Control.[4] In each, mainly as a result of their

[1] So described by Trevelyan to Gladstone, ibid.

[2] Report of the committee of inquiry into the organization of the Board of Trade by C. E. Trevelyan, Sir Stafford Northcote, and James Booth (Secretary of the Board of Trade), 20 March 1853, P.P., 1854, XXVII.

[3] Trevelyan to Gladstone, 15 September 1853, op. cit.

[4] Reports from the Committees of Inquiry into Public Offices and Papers connected therewith, P.P., 1854, XXVII. The report on the Office of Works was not made until after Trevelyan and Northcote had reported on the organization of the Civil Service. The reports of the inquiries into the Post Office, the Audit Office, and the Board of Control are not among the printed Parliamentary Papers; that they were also investigated is clear from Trevelyan's letters to Gladstone, 15 September 1853, op. cit., and 18 December 1853, Bod., T.L.B., xxxii. 169–70.

recommendations, the intellectual and mechanical duties were separated and a second establishment, now called the Supplementary Establishment (and the clerks, Supplementary Clerks), was introduced upon exactly the same conditions as it had been in the Board of Trade. Gladstone, Chancellor of the Exchequer in Aberdeen's Administration, explained that these inquiries had been established

for the purpose of consolidating redundant offices, supplying additional assistance where it is required, getting rid of obsolete processes, and introducing more simple and compendious modes of transacting business, establishing a proper distinction between intellectual and mechanical labour, and generally so revising and readjusting the public establishments as to place them on the footing best calculated for the efficient discharge of their important functions according to the actual circumstances of the present time.[1]

As a result of their inquiries into these and other offices,[2] Trevelyan and Northcote were asked by Gladstone on 12 April 1853 to inquire into the organization of the whole Civil Service. In the report which they presented to him on 23 November 1853 they drew attention to the necessity for separating intellectual and mechanical labour in the public departments and made this comment on their efforts to achieve it in the preceding eighteen months:

We consider that a great step has been taken by the appointment in several offices of a class of Supplementary Clerks, receiving uniform salaries in each department, and capable therefore of being transferred, without inconvenience from one to another, according as the demand for their services may be greater or less at any particular time, and we expect that the moveable character of this class of officers, and the superior standard of examination which we have proposed for the higher class, will together have the effect of marking the distinction between [the Superior and Supplementary Establishments] in a proper manner.[3]

Soon after the publication of the report Trevelyan and Northcote

---

[1] T.M. 12 April 1853, P.P., 1854–5, XXX.

[2] They looked at a number of Irish Offices as well. Excluding these, Trevelyan was a member of each committee, and Northcote served on all except those which inquired into the Treasury and Colonial Office in 1849. Sometimes they were assisted in the inquiry by the permanent head of the department, other times they worked alone.

[3] *Report of the Committee of Inquiry into the Organisation of the Civil Service*, 23 November 1853, P.P., 1854, XXVII.

explained in more detail the importance of establishing and maintaining a proper distinction between intellectual and mechanical work.[1] At the same time, however, they emphasized that they were not proposing that the principle should be universally adopted, whether it was applicable or not. Work should be divided only in those departments where there was a great deal of copying and figure work and 'well defined Sections of intellectual work'.[2] Anticipating other objections, they also warned that care had to be taken to ensure that those clerks who would be called upon to perform higher duties 'obtained a sufficient acquaintance with the details of the machinery of the departments', and explained that what they proposed did not exclude such training; although the clerks were to be employed upon intellectual work from the beginning, they were to do a certain amount of mechanical work as well.

Thus in the six years 1848–54 the traditional pattern of establishment had been significantly changed. In more than a dozen departments the one-tiered establishment had been replaced by a two-tiered structure in which the work was divided between a Superior Establishment (the old established clerks) and a new Supplementary Establishment; two years later a second tier was introduced into both the Treasury and the Home Office. But having been primarily responsible for these first attempts at specialization, both Trevelyan and Northcote on behalf of the Treasury now disclaimed responsibility for maintaining the distinction between intellectual and mechanical labour in those departments where it had been introduced at their instigation. In their *Report on the Organisation of the Civil Service* they said:

The proper maintenance of such distinction depends more upon the discretion and management of the chiefs of office and those immediately below them, than upon any general regulation that could be made by a central authority.

How ineffective and inadequate the chiefs of office and their subordinates were in discharging that obligation became apparent in the next six years.

[1] Memo by Trevelyan, 28 February 1854; memo by Northcote on *The Division of Labour in Public Offices between Intellectual and Mechanical Work*, undated, P.P., 1854–5, XX.
[2] Trevelyan to Spring-Rice, 10 March 1854, Brit. Mus., G.P. Add. MSS. 44333, fo. 262.

THE TWO-TIERED SYSTEM 1854–1860

Trevelyan and Northcote held office in the Treasury for almost the whole of the period 1854–60, Trevelyan as Assistant Secretary until his resignation in January 1859, and Northcote as Financial Secretary for the six months thereafter. Not unexpectedly, the official attitude of the department towards the principle of the division of labour was both favourable and consistent. Departmental policy is summarized in this Minute written in June 1859:

My Lords are fully convinced that there is nothing which contributes more effectively to the good working of an Office than a proper distribution of labour among persons employed in it, and they are satisfied that the work ought so far as possible be so divided as to separate the higher from the simpler and more mechanical duties.[1]

But it was a policy to which the Treasury subscribed in principle only, adhering rigidly to the view expressed earlier by Trevelyan and Northcote that it should be left to the departments to implement and maintain the separation of functions which had been recommended to them—that it was for them to ensure that the distinction between intellectual and mechanical duties was upheld and the identities of the two separate establishments maintained without any central guidance or control. In practice the departments found it difficult to do this, none more so than the Board of Trade, where the difficulties encountered by all were experienced most acutely.

The main difficulty arose from the substantial and continuing growth in the volume of business dealt with. At the same time the attractiveness of the conditions of service enjoyed by the Supplementary Clerks led to the recruitment of men whose intelligence and qualifications were superior to those required for merely mechanical and routine work. As the pressure of intellectual work became too great for the Superior Clerks to deal with alone, clerks of the Supplementary Establishment were put to work alongside them, and temporary (unestablished) clerks were engaged to deal with the routine business. With a steady accumulation of new duties the pressure of work continued to build up, and it became increasingly advantageous to recruit to the Supplementary Establishment men whose abilities and qualifications fitted them for more responsible work than that which they were intended to do

[1] T.M., 10 June 1859, P.R.O. T.1/6206B/15985.

originally. In this way the separation of functions became blurred and the line between the two establishments, to which Trevelyan and Northcote had attached so much importance, indistinct, the Supplementary Clerks being employed wherever they could be most usefully used in the department. The result was precisely that foreseen by Trevelyan and Northcote: growing discontent among the Supplementary Clerks, who while employed upon similar work to the Superior Clerks were denied similar pay and prospects of promotion.

Soon the volume of work became too great even for the two establishments combined and redeployed, and an appeal was made to the Treasury in 1857 for additions to both establishments and a pay rise for the Supplementary Clerks. Despite the Treasury's agreement to both requests, in the next two years the Board of Trade was obliged to continue to impose important and responsible duties upon the Supplementary Clerks—in March 1859 only seven out of thirty-two were employed upon copying and other mechanical work. With an almost daily addition to its duties the department found it impossible to maintain a strict separation of function in the manner intended by Trevelyan and Northcote, and in 1859 asked the Treasury to agree to the removal of the formal distinction between the two establishments. In its place the Board of Trade suggested that all first appointments should be made to the junior class of the Supplementary Establishment, and that entry to the Superior Establishment should be discontinued, apart from the promotion to it of the more able of those recruited to the Supplementary Establishment; those incapable of doing the work of a Superior Clerk were to remain in the Supplementary Class.

This proposal struck at the roots of the principles laid down by Trevelyan and Northcote and reaffirmed by the Treasury in the previous five years. Unless the Treasury was now prepared to abandon them also it had to suggest to the Board of Trade, and those other departments which were experiencing similar difficulties, a satisfactory method of translating principle into practice. Northcote clearly had no intention of discarding them. In a memorandum to George Hamilton, Trevelyan's successor as Assistant Secretary, he wrote:

I feel the strongest doubts as to the expediency of the changes proposed by the Board of Trade. In our Reports of 1853–54, Sir C. Trevelyan and

I attached great weight to the proper division of intellectual and mechanical labour, and I see no reason to doubt that the principles we laid
down were sound. There is, however, much difficulty in giving effect
to them. . . . The letter before us shows this difficulty in a very forcible
light. But the way in which the Board of Trade propose to deal with the
difficulty is most objectionable. They propose virtually to get rid of all
distinction between Supplementary Clerks and [Superior] Clerks . . .
I should therefore be disposed on this ground to dissent from their
recommendation, or at all events to require a full investigation before
assenting to it.[1]

Replying to the Board of Trade, Northcote felt it necessary to
comment upon the proposed change 'because any considerable
alteration in the position of the Supplementary Clerks attached to
one department must affect that of the corresponding class in other
departments'. It was, he wrote, 'a step in the wrong direction, and
that if any change at all is to be made in the position of the Supplementary Clerks, it should rather be one which would mark more
clearly the difference between their duties and official position,
and those of the Superior Clerks',[2] but he admitted that a division
of labour was difficult to achieve in practice. A solution for which
he now showed some enthusiasm, and one to which he was to
return a year later, was that of dividing the work between the
Superior Establishment and a number of unestablished writers on
a weekly engagement, the Supplementary Establishment being
allowed to die out. However, the Board of Trade preferred 'to see
the question thus dealt with as a whole rather than have this
Department dealt with separately', and suggested a postponement
of decision in the hope that the Treasury would devise a solution
applicable to all departments.

The decision to appoint a committee to inquire into 'the nature
and working of the arrangements at present adopted in various
offices for getting the simpler portions of their work done' represented the earliest Treasury attempt to deal with an establishments' problem upon a wider basis than that of an individual
department. Because of the variation in recruitment procedures,
conditions of service and methods of working, it had hitherto been
impracticable to think of a decision or solution being applied to a

[1] Memo from Northcote to Hamilton, 12 April 1859, P.R.O. T.1/6202B/
14918.
[2] Treasury to Board of Trade, 12 May 1859, P.R.O. T.1/6202B/14918.

number of departments or the whole Service. These local differences, combined with departmental traditions and ministerial autonomy, necessitated for the most part a separate solution to each problem. But now that several departments had introduced (separately) a class of clerks recruited by the same method, engaged upon similar conditions of service, and ostensibly employed upon the same kind of work, the Treasury could begin to think of dealing with problems relating to them on a much wider and more uniform basis. An awareness of this is apparent in the reply to the Office of Works' request for authority to increase the rates of pay of their Supplementary Clerks: 'It will be impossible to maintain the scale of pay of Supplementary Clerks in other Offices if clerks performing similar duties in the Office of Works are paid at higher rates', the Treasury wrote.[1]

In the Minute setting up the committee of inquiry Northcote referred to the need for a uniform settlement of the difficulties faced by all those departments employing Supplementary Clerks.

The subject is one which has of late years repeatedly engaged the attention of this Board, and has more than once been discussed by the Committees which from time to time have been appointed for the revision of particular Establishments. But the time appears now to have arrived when it requires to be treated as a whole [and] my Lords consider it desirable that these matters should be settled upon an uniform basis and they think it the more important that this settlement should take place at once.[2]

Two weeks later he left the Treasury on the resignation of Derby's Government—Trevelyan had resigned six months earlier. Knowing nothing of Northcote's intention to appoint a committee of inquiry the Board of Trade still awaited a reply to its letter of 8 June 1859.[3] On 17 September the Treasury was reminded of this, but by now the Board of Trade's earlier letter had been lost and the Treasury was obliged to ask for a copy of it. When it arrived the whole question of Supplementary Establishments was taken up *de novo*.

The new committee of inquiry appointed by the Treasury on 9 February 1860 comprised four members: Northcote (now out of

[1] Treasury to Office of Works, 8 January 1856, P.R.O. T.1/6041A/20465.
[2] T.M. 10 June 1859, P.R.O. T.1/6206B/15985.
[3] Northcote had in fact appointed the committee, Arbuthnot, Lingen, and Horace Mann, Registrar of the CSC, but it never met.

office); Horace Mann, the Registrar of the Civil Service Commission; Major Graham, the Registrar-General; and Ralph Lingen, Secretary to the Board of Education. Besides the letters from the Board of Trade (in the latest of which the President had declined to submit the Estimates until the Treasury replied to the letter of 17 September), the Treasury had also received a letter from the junior clerks of its own Supplementary Establishment 'praying for an increased rate of salary'. The observations now made by the Treasury Board upon the situation in its own and other departments employing Supplementary Clerks emphasized more strongly even than Northcote the desirability of a uniform settlement.

Considerable difficulty occurs to their Lordships in dealing with these and similar applications which occasionally are addressed to them from different offices, owing to the want of uniformity which exists in the classification of supplemental clerks, in the nature of the work assigned to them, and in the scale of their remuneration

It appears very desirable, therefore, to establish some fixed principle and some general system applicable as far as possible to the whole of this important branch of the Civil Service.[1]

When the committee reported to the Treasury later the same year it noted that the character of the Supplementary Establishments which had been introduced into several departments had changed in almost every particular.

Instead of one uniform body of public servants, receiving salaries commencing at £80 p.a. and advancing by an annual increment of £5 to £180 with a further increase in cases of particular merit, to £250 we have now a number of Establishments attached to different Offices, each of which differs from all the rest, both in respect of the rate of pay and in the classification and prospects of the Clerks. In some of them the rate of pay rises to £300 and in the Treasury apparently to £500 a year, and in other cases the Supplementary Clerks are becoming Junior Established Classes from which promotion to the higher ranks of the office may be expected.[2]

Uniform salaries were an essential feature of the system devised originally by Trevelyan and Northcote, permitting transfer between departments without alteration of salary or prospects of promotion. But by 1860 no two of the departments which had

---

[1] T.M. 9 February 1860, P.R.O. T.1/6206B/15985.
[2] *Report of the Committee of Inquiry into the Supplementary Clerks in the Civil Service*, 1 June 1860, P.R.O. T.1/6250A/9059.

introduced Supplementary Clerks between 1848–53 had uniform
rates of pay for this class. Most had found it impossible to carry on
without extra clerical assistance. In addition to 362 Supplementary
Clerks, they were now employing almost as many temporary clerks
at an annual cost of £37,870.[1] In most cases the Supplementary
Establishments had been unable to undertake all the work which
it was intended that they should do—not because there were too
few Supplementary Clerks, but rather because too many of them
were employed upon other (higher) work in the department. As a
result, temporary clerks, copyists, and writers were hired to do
much of the copying and other mechanical work.

This system has some convenience [the committee commented] but it
also has some disadvantages. The [writers and copyists] can be taken on
as they are wanted, and dispensed with at the shortest notice. They have
no claim to Superannuation, and no right to promotion. There is,
however, a less security for the character and efficiency of the men
thus obtained than there is for that of the Established Clerks. If the
men are engaged, as is frequently the case, through the intervention of a
Law Stationer, a large proportion of the sums paid to them (generally
about one-third) is taken by the Stationer as his profit. If they are engaged directly by the Heads of Departments and are not called upon to
pass the Examination of the Civil Service Commission, a door is opened
for the appointment, through favour, of men who have failed in other
employments, and who fall back upon the Civil Service as a last resource.
It is certain that in both of these cases the Government must suffer—
in the former case by paying a larger price for the services of the Clerk
than he would himself accept for them, and in the latter case by obtaining inferior men.[2]

What the committee described in their report was the almost
total failure to maintain the division of work between the Superior
and Supplementary Establishments in the manner intended by
Trevelyan and Northcote. They suggested, therefore, the abolition
of the Supplementary Establishment and a return to the old

---

[1] In addition to those offices where they had been introduced by Trevelyan
and Northcote, Supplementary Clerks were to be found in the Admiralty Court,
British Museum, Customs, House of Commons Office, Board of Inland Revenue,
and Office of Woods. However, the committee did not distinguish very clearly
between Supplementary Clerks held on a second establishment as in the
Trevelyan-Northcote offices, and those in which clerks 'extra' to the main
establishment had acquired a permanent status by length of service.
[2] The average payment to a Law Stationer for the services of one of his
clerks was 1s. per hour, of which the clerk received 8d.

one-tiered establishment, dividing the work between it and a class of unestablished, temporary clerks hired from a central agency. They proposed that

the distinction between Established and Supplementary Clerks in the several departments be abandoned, and that no more appointments be made to the Supplementary Classes, and that they be allowed gradually to die out, unless it be thought desirable and found possible to transfer any portion of the men at once to the Department of which we are about to speak.

Further propose that a Central Copying Agency be established under the control of a Superintending Officer to which the several Public Departments may make application from time to time for as many writers as may be required. This Establishment comprise two classes, the lower consisting of youths employed at weekly wages, and on a temporary footing with no claim to superannuation, and the higher of men employed in an established capacity, at moderate rates of salary and with the same right to superannuation as other Government Officers.

The abandonment of the two-tier system did not mean that the committee had also abandoned the principle of the division of labour. On the contrary, their proposal for a Central Copying Agency was intended to make it easier to achieve it in practice by relieving the departments of responsibility for mechanical work. Within each department there would be only one establishment— the Superior Establishment—whose clerks would be primarily responsible for the intellectual work, while the mechanical work would be done by copyists hired daily or weekly from the Central Copying Agency. By separating the copyists from the establishment it would be more difficult for the departments to employ them upon higher work, and for the copyists to establish claims to a permanent tenure—both of which factors had contributed to the breakdown of the division of work between the Superior and Supplementary Establishments.

In the Treasury the report was considered first by George Arbuthnot, the Auditor of the Civil List. Sceptical of the committee's scheme to set up a Central Copying Agency, he doubted

whether a class of men copyists would be so well trained under [it], as they are by apprenticeship to Law Stationers, and whether the various requirements of public departments for, in some cases, copyists, in others men of secondary class from the higher establishments, and in others (as the War Office and the Admiralty, and on past occasions the

Audit Office) for strictly extra assistance, could be met by the proposed scheme.[1]

Hamilton was broadly in agreement with Arbuthnot, doubting the expediency of the committee's plan on the ground that Law Stationers' writers were cheaper and more convenient. 'But it is a large opinion upon which it will be desirable to have the views of the Principal Offices of State', he wrote to Peel, the Financial Secretary.[2] These, received early in February 1861, were uniformly hostile to the proposed abandonment of the Supplementary Establishment and the substitution of a Central Copying Agency. Although the departments chose to emphasize the difficulties and disadvantages attendant upon the creation of such a body, for example the problem of equating the demand for copyists with their supply, their hostility may well have been inspired as much, if not more, by the fear that the employment of centrally controlled copyists would restrict their freedom under the present system to disregard the distinction drawn originally between intellectual and mechanical work, and to deploy their clerical labour as they thought best. If care was taken to recruit copyists of ability and intelligence a department was able, when necessary, to employ them upon work other than mere copying; similarly with the Supplementary Clerks.

A decision upon the report was not made until some months later, September 1861, by which time the subject could be shelved no longer for the Home Office was pressing for a decision upon an application made in March of the previous year for an increase to the salaries of their Supplementary Clerks, which at that time the Treasury had referred to the committee of inquiry. Writing now to the Financial Secretary Hamilton said: 'As nothing is likely to come of that report it is proper to come to a decision.'[3] Subsequently the Home Office was informed 'that it is not the intention of this Board to adopt any general scheme for the regulation of Extra and Supplemental Clerks in the Civil Service founded upon the Report of the Committee of 1860'.[4] Any other decision can scarcely have been contemplated. With the strength

[1] Memo by George Arbuthnot, 25 June 1860, P.R.O. T.1/6250A/9059.
[2] Memo from Hamilton to F. Peel, 4 December 1860, P.R.O. T.1/6250A/9059.
[3] Memo from Hamilton to F. Peel, 23 September 1861, P.R.O. T.1/6309A/11602.
[4] Treasury to Home Office, 23 September 1861, P.R.O. T.1/6309A/11602.

of departmental and Treasury opinion opposed to it the adoption of the report, or even part of it, was impracticable at that time.

THE PATTERN UNALTERED 1860–1865

The decision not to act upon the report brought to an end the period of inquiry and re-thinking about the organization of the departmental establishments which Northcote had initiated in April 1859. From it the departments emerged with the pattern of their establishments undisturbed, those employing Supplementary Clerks continued to use them in the manner described by the committee in their report.

Trevelyan's and Northcote's departure from the Treasury in 1859 brought no change of attitude towards the division of labour and the two-tiered establishment. Hamilton, who succeeded Trevelyan, and Arbuthnot, his chief lieutenant, had rejected the recommendations made by the committee of inquiry and affirmed their belief in the policy to which the department had been committed earlier. If Northcote now no longer believed it practicable to divide the work between a Superior and Supplementary Establishment, Hamilton had no such doubts. The old orthodoxy—the division of labour between two established classes—was very much in his mind when writing to Arbuthnot in January 1862: 'My theory would be to have classified Supplemental Clerks as we now have here [in the Treasury] for the class of business which is inferior to the proper business of Established Clerks.'[1]

While between 1860 and 1865 no fundamental change occurred in the Treasury's attitude, it was modified to provide for the continuance of the two-tiered system in its existing form. Provision had to be made for copying, writing, and other routine work which Trevelyan and Northcote had intended should be done solely by the Supplementary Clerks. As the volume of government business continued to grow, (particularly in the Board of Trade), the need for more clerical assistance became greater. To meet it Hamilton now officially recognized and approved the practice of employing copyists and writers in the Treasury and other departments with Supplementary Establishments. But while he did so, he made it clear that the Treasury believed that the need for additional clerical assistance could be supplied in only one way:

[1] Memo from Hamilton to Arbuthnot, 25 January 1862, P.R.O. T.1/6333A/ 18167.

'Mere copying is better done and cheaper done through such means as Vachers.'[1] The introduction of these clerks meant that in some departments the line which Trevelyan and Northcote had insisted was necessary to maintain the principle of the division of labour was now drawn more between them and the two established classes, than between the latter.

Several departments, principally the War Office, Admiralty and Foreign Office, had escaped scrutiny by Trevelyan and Northcote in the fifties, and continued after 1860, as before, without a second tier, dividing the work between a single class of established clerks and a number of unestablished temporary clerks. In practice there was not very much difference between these departments and those with Supplementary Establishments, for the two-tiered system tended to function in very much the same way.

In the War Office and Admiralty the intellectual and the more important mechanical work was done by the clerks of a single establishment, the greater part of the mechanical work and almost all the copying by a larger number of unestablished temporary clerks. The reason for this pattern of establishment was a practical one. The work of both departments, and that of the Foreign Office too, fluctuated in time of war or emergency, and additional clerical assistance was often required very quickly but over a short period of time; for example, in 1859, and again a year later, large numbers of temporary clerks were taken on at short notice to meet the increased business in the Admiralty consequent upon the formation of a Naval Reserve and the additions which were made to the Fleet.

The Civil Service Commissioners were required to examine candidates for temporary as well as established appointments. Most departments hired temporary clerks and copyists without certification, but the War Office almost always sent up candidates to be tested. Their temporary clerks enjoyed no greater permanency of tenure, although in practice some of them were employed for a very long time. A few were recruited into the establishment, for (unlike writers and copyists in the two-tiered departments), those who were qualified and recommended by their superior officers could compete for vacancies. Thus while there was a division of work, the line between the established clerks responsible mainly for the intellectual work, and the unestablished temporary clerks

[1] Ibid.

L

responsible mainly for the mechanical work was not intended to inhibit movement between the two, as happened in the two-tiered departments. This was generally true of the Admiralty as well.

Hamilton believed that the two-tiered system could be introduced into the War Office and Admiralty as it had been into other major departments, but confessed to Arbuthnot that there was only a remote prospect of convincing either of them that it was superior to their own organization; nor was he very hopeful of persuading them that copying was better and more cheaply done by Vachers's clerks than by their temporary clerks.[1] Beliefs and hopes notwithstanding, the Treasury was obliged to recognize the one-tiered system and, by agreeing to add to the number of temporary clerks and to the promotion of some of them into the establishment, to afford assistance for its continued viability.

While the departments remained wedded to their one-tiered systems, the Treasury could do very little. Ministerial discretion in such a matter was absolute, a directive or instruction out of the question. Suggestion and persuasion was the limit of Treasury action. Even here the Treasury preferred to await an opportunity to comment upon a proposal put up to it than to take the initiative and risk the charge of improper interference. An opportunity to comment upon the War Office's pattern of establishment occurred in 1862. The Secretary of State had recently received a report from an internal committee of inquiry recommending that the employment of temporary clerks should be discontinued when their services were required permanently. Acting upon this, he now sought Treasury approval for the appointment of twenty-one temporary clerks to the establishment, and the formation of a Supplementary Establishment from the remaining twenty-nine.

In the Treasury reply, Arbuthnot pointed out the inconsistency of the War Office's proposals: that the nomenclature and pay of the Supplementary Class was accepted but not what this logically entailed—the creation of a two-tiered establishment with a permanent class of clerks subordinate to the (Superior) Establishment.[2] The Supplementary Establishment would be little more than a 'catchment area' for those temporary clerks who failed to obtain promotion to the 'Superior' Establishment, but whose services it

---

[1] Memo from Hamilton to Arbuthnot, 25 January 1862, op. cit.

[2] To avoid confusion with the proposed class of Supplementary Clerks, the Established Clerks are referred to here and below as 'Superior'.

was felt desirable to retain. As an alternative, the Treasury suggested the introduction of a permanent Supplementary Establishment, recruited separately and with conditions of service distinct from those of either the 'Superior' Establishment or the temporary clerks, but this proved unacceptable to the War Office who preferred to retain their one-tiered establishment. In their view a new Supplementary Establishment was to be merely an appendage to that system, it was not intended that it should change it. The War Office now withdrew their proposal for a new class of clerks, and asked the Treasury merely to approve the increase in establishment. Earlier, to the Secretary of State's annoyance, the Treasury had deferred consideration of it until the War Office had had time to reflect upon the proposal for a Supplementary Establishment. Further delay while the proposal was pressed again upon him would have achieved little. Without the risk of conflict the Treasury could not have brought greater pressure to bear than it did; at no time did the War Office appear sympathetic to the notion of a two-tiered system, nor give any indication that it was prepared even to discuss the possibility of substituting it for the existing system.

With the acknowledgment that copyists and writers were indispensable to the two-tiered system, there was after 1860 a closer correspondence between Treasury policy and departmental practice than at any time since 1848–54; but Treasury policy had changed to accord with departmental practice, the latter had not changed at all. The situation described by the 1860 committee of inquiry, in which few Supplementary Clerks were employed upon routine and mechanical work in the manner envisaged by Trevelyan and Northcote, continued unaltered. Treasury approval of Vachers's clerks made it easier to fill the gap left by the employment of Supplementary Clerks on higher work, although the ease with which they could be engaged facilitated, even encouraged, the employment of still more Supplementary Clerks upon higher work. But viability in the two-tiered system was purchased dearly, because worked in this way it was prone to two recurring difficulties. As more and more Supplementary Clerks were employed upon higher work, there was a greater probability of their dissatisfaction with a situation whereby they were called upon to do work comparable to that of the Superior Clerks but were denied similar rates of pay and prospects of promotion. Secondly, the longer the departments held on to able and experienced copyists and writers, the more permanent became their *de facto* status in the department, and attempts were made to secure *de jure* recognition in the form of annual salaries on a sliding scale, pensions, and other benefits of established service—even promotion to the Supplementary and Superior Establishments.

These difficulties could be mitigated, though not eradicated, by acceding from time to time to the demands of the Supplementary Clerks and the copyists for pay increases. Almost all departments which employed Supplementary Clerks submitted applications to the Treasury; one of the first was made by the Treasury's own Supplementary Clerks in February 1858. The Supplementary Clerks in the Board of Trade had their salaries raised in 1857, and those in the Poor Law Board in the following year. In the latter department, the Office of Woods, and elsewhere, the annual increment was raised from £5 to £10; by 1861 only the Supplementary Clerks in the Privy Council Office remained on the scale originally introduced by Trevelyan and Northcote. In the same year the salaries of the Supplementary Clerks in the Treasury and the Home Office were further revised. These pay increases, while gratifying to the Supplementary Clerks, did not disturb the root cause of their dissatisfaction, but if its eradication was desirable, it was not vital to the continuance of the two-tiered system; for the moment discontent among the Supplementary Clerks could be held in check by periodic adjustments to their salaries. In the Board of Trade, however, the condition of the whole establishment was much more serious, and could not be alleviated by such temporary expedients; by 1863 it was ready for yet another overhaul.

The report which Hamilton, Arbuthnot, and the Secretary of the Board of Trade submitted to the Treasury early in July of that year criticized the failure on previous occasions (1853, 1857, and 1859) 'to accommodate the Establishment of the Department to its growing requirements', and attributed to this omission much of the dissatisfaction complained of in the department at that time.[1] Although the volume of work had grown rapidly in the previous six years, the number of Superior Clerks (28) had remained the same as that agreed in 1857. The extra business had been met wholly by increasing the size of the Supplementary Establishment

---

[1] Report of the Treasury committee of inquiry into the Board of Trade Establishment, 4 July 1863, P.R.O. T.1/6433B/13012.

from thirty-seven to fifty-two. 'The greater proportion of the latter were, in fact, employed upon the same description of business as the [Superior] Clerks,' said the committee, 'and the evil has gone on increasing with the additional business which every year has since brought to the Department.' This has led to 'some confusion and blending of classes of officers whose functions were intended to be kept distinct'. To remedy it the committee proposed to abolish the Supplementary Establishment, and to divide the whole work of the department between established and temporary clerks, as in the War Office and the Admiralty. Trevelyan's and Northcote's two-tiered system was to be abandoned and replaced by one in which the work was divided between a one-tiered establishment and a number of unestablished temporary clerks. Their duties were to be

strictly confined to the performance of work of routine or mechanical nature; that the limit defining the business of the temporary clerks should be distinctly drawn and rigidly maintained, and that it should be clearly explained to each temporary clerk on his first entering the Office that he is not on the Establishment, that his engagement, notwithstanding his Civil Service certificate, and the prospect which the limited class affords, is temporary, and that it may at any time be terminated on a weekly engagement.

These proposals, which after some minor modifications were accepted by both departments, did not represent a fundamental revision of the Treasury's attitude towards the pattern of establishment in the Civil Service as a whole. Hamilton and Arbuthnot regarded the situation which they found at the Board of Trade as exceptional, demanding, and justifying exceptional measures to deal with it. That this was so is clear from a correspondence the following year with the Foreign Office. There the work was divided simply between junior and senior clerks held on the same, single establishment, although a few 'extra clerks' had been taken on to help with the routine work, but without claim to promotion. Anxious to improve the salaries of some of these unestablished clerks, the Foreign Office made discreet inquiries at the Treasury about its probable official reaction to a concrete proposal.

The significance of this unusual approach will be more readily understood if something is said briefly of relations between the two departments, which were unlike those between the Treasury and any other department. To a large extent they were governed by the Foreign Office's reluctance to acknowledge, or tacitly to affirm by its actions, that the obligation to seek prior Treasury approval for additional expenditure implied subordination to another department. The traditional Foreign Office view was that its own work and responsibilities, different in kind and of greater importance than those of other departments, entitled it to special consideration; this argument had been used to resist the introduction of open competition.[1] It was employed again when the department declined to give evidence to the Select Committee on Civil Services Expenditure in 1873. On that occasion, as so often, the Foreign Office claimed that it was *sui generis*, 'that the business and classification of this office are so different from those of other departments, that they are unable to afford any information or to offer any observations which could be of use to the Commission'.

While the Treasury did not admit the Foreign Office's claim to equality of status, it frequently deferred to the Foreign Secretary's judgement as to no other minister's. This was partly an acknowledgement of his cabinet and party seniority—occasionally, like Russell, the Foreign Secretary had been, or was destined to be, Prime Minister—and partly to avoid giving cause for offence to a department hypersensitive about its status *vis-à-vis* the Treasury.

On this particular occasion the Foreign Office was unwilling to risk the embarrassment of an official rebuff or refusal from the Treasury. If it asked officially only for what it had confirmed privately that the Treasury would agree to, the question of openly acknowledging an authority superior to its own need not arise. Thus, before submitting the official application, Edmund Hammond, Permanent Under-Secretary at the Foreign Office, talked privately with Hamilton about the question of pay rises and told him 'that Lord Russell is unwilling to make a proposition regarding the officers of his Department if likely to be rejected by the Treasury'.[2] Instead, he had been instructed to submit it to the Treasury in 'demi-official shape'.

Some of the proposed increases were too large, Hamilton advised his minister, but he was more concerned to draw his attention to the Treasury's opportunity to propose a revision of the conditions

---

[1] See above, Chapter 4, pp. 82–3 and 95–6.
[2] Quoted in Hamilton's memo to Frederick Peel, 8 June 1864, P.R.O. T.1/6519B/17518.

upon which the 'extra clerks' were then employed in the different branches of the Foreign Office. He suggested to him that the Foreign Secretary should be urged to place in a Supplementary Establishment, upon conditions of service similar to those enjoyed by the Treasury Supplementary Clerks, not only the 'extra clerks' employed in the two branches proposed by Hammond, but those in all the others as well. With the Financial Secretary's approval Hamilton then wrote semi-officially to Hammond[1] setting out the details of the proposed Supplementary Establishment in order that he could suggest to Lord Russell 'what the Treasury might be disposed to accede to'.[2] Russell's agreement to what in effect constituted the creation of a second classified and permanent establishment was given some six months later, in December 1864. His official application, proposing a classification of the clerks and salaries identical with those of the Treasury, differed in only one minor respect from that suggested originally by Hamilton to Hammond.

To represent the decision taken in the previous year to abolish the Board of Trade's two-tiered system as a change in the Treasury's general policy it would be necessary to explain away the determination of Hamilton, supported by his Financial Secretary, to press upon the Foreign Office the introduction of a Supplementary Establishment upon the principles laid down by Trevelyan and Northcote in 1848–54. If as a matter of policy the introduction and maintenance of the principle of dividing work between two permanent establishments had been repudiated by the 1863 decision, Hamilton would scarcely have contemplated initiating a discussion with the Foreign Office about the classification of their 'extra clerks' in a Supplementary Establishment—the question of a pay rise could have been resolved without any such reference. And even if it was felt desirable to discuss the future position of the 'extra clerks' it might be expected, if the 1863 decision had represented the future trend of Treasury policy, that Hamilton would have proposed some alternative, such as their replacement by temporary clerks or copyists, similar to those sanctioned for the Board of Trade, leaving the one-tiered establishment undisturbed.

[1] Hamilton to Hammond, 12 December 1864, P.R.O. *Hamilton Semi-official Correspondence*, ii.
[2] Memo from Hamilton to Peel, 8 June 1864, op. cit.

TREASURY POLICY 1865–1869

Five years after the report of the 1860 committee of inquiry the question of dividing labour in a two-tiered system was raised again. Shortly after taking office as Financial Secretary, Hugh Childers was confronted with an application for a pay increase from the Supplementary Clerks of the Emigration Office. Turning his attention to the more general question of the pattern of departmental establishment throughout the Service, he discussed with Hamilton the possibility of assimilating the various systems adopted by those departments employing Supplementary Clerks and unestablished writers and copyists. By the time the next pay claim arrived (from the Home Office Supplementary Clerks) his thinking had crystallized: he resolved to abolish the Supplementary Establishment throughout the Service and to divide each department into two classes, Established Clerks and writers, the latter performing the purely mechanical work of writing. In essence that was what Northcote and the 1860 committee had proposed, and the system used in the War Office, Admiralty, Board of Trade, and a few other departments.

Asked for his opinion, Hamilton reminded Childers that 'it is peculiarly my duty with reference to the constitution of the office I hold, to keep in view the organization of the Civil Service generally'.[1] Uniformity such as that contemplated by Childers was to his mind 'very questionable'. 'I think we could not lay it down as anything like a general rule that Departments in the Civil Service should be divided into the classes of Established Clerks and writers.' To do so would be both expensive and inconvenient, he claimed, for it had been shown in the Treasury that the cheapest and most convenient method of having mere writing done was to employ Vachers's clerks by the hour. In support of this view he submitted a memorandum by the Superintendent of the Treasury Supplementary Establishment who argued that there was 'an intermediate description of work requiring higher qualifications which according to my experience is performed better not by temporary clerks but by Supplementary Clerks than either by writers on the one hand or Established Clerks on the other'.[2] The 1853 Committee on the Organization of the Civil Service

---

[1] Memo from Hamilton to Childers, undated, P.R.O. T.1/6599B/18966.
[2] Memo by L. Jones, undated, P.R.O. T.1/6599B/18966.

had come to the same conclusion, and Hamilton now referred Childers to that part of the report where Trevelyan and Northcote had written:

Copying is not the only work of a mechanical, or nearly mechanical character which is performed in the public offices. A great deal of work of various kinds, such as registering, posting accounts, keeping diaries, and so forth, may very well be done by supplementary clerks of an inferior class under the direction of a small number of superiors.

but omitted to add that Trevelyan and Northcote had envisaged that the introduction of a permanent Supplementary Establishment would make the employment of temporary clerks, copyists, writers, etc., unnecessary.[1] Believing what Trevelyan and Northcote had written to be still true, Hamilton set out in a long memorandum what he thought the 'proper organisation of the Civil Service' should be.[2]

1. Established Clerks: Classes, numbers and salaries dependent upon the nature and proper distribution of the business. Promotion on merit from the lowest to the highest. No advancement on admission into the Establishment except by original appointment to the lowest class, within age limit and with a Civil Service Certificate.
2. Supplementary Clerks: Where necessary, for systematic and confidential work of the more mechanical kind such as precis, indexing, registering, arranged probably into two classes. The maximum salary of the first class being sufficient as a permanent and ultimate object to the description of person, say £250 or £300 p.a. Admission by Civil Service Certificate, annual increments; superannuation.
3. Either Writers or Law Stationers' Clerks: Where the demand varies and law stationers' clerks can be had I prefer them to writers, because they are cheaper and there is no claim or tendency to claim to become connected with the office. If it is desirable from circumstances to have them connected with the office, then I incline to think they should be Supplementary Clerks.

In ordinary circumstances even the most experienced Treasury ministers found it hard to resist the advice of their senior officials; when they were not presented with a viable alternative, it was

[1] In June 1859 Northcote wrote: 'It appears, however, that the employment of these [Supplementary] Clerks has not had the effect of enabling the Departments in which they serve to dispense with the assistance of Law Stationers and other persons hired by the hour, the day or the week.' T.M. 10 June 1859, P.R.O. T.1/6206B/15985.
[2] Memo from Hamilton to Childers, undated, P.R.O. T.1/6599B/18996.

virtually impossible. Hamilton was, of course, especially prone
to tendentiousness, and in this instance (as so often) he did not
offer the Financial Secretary a balanced judgement arrived at after
a careful consideration of the alternatives, but gave him instead his
personal belief, argued with all the passion and determination he
could muster. A minister with more experience than Childers
would have hesitated to reject the advice of his senior official
when the alternative was a course of action for which he had found
no support and very little consideration. Forced to reconsider his
own proposal Childers returned Hamilton's memorandum to him
having written upon it:

I concur, if it is clearly understood that [Supplementary] clerks are
only employed as an exception in a few specialised departments such as
the Treasury and the Sects. of State. As a general principle the class
should I think be discouraged.[1]

He remained convinced, however, of the desirability of unifying
Treasury decisions on establishment matters and explained:

What I am anxious to do is to impress upon the [Treasury] divisions
the necessity of keeping in view the general principle both as to the
difference between established clerks and writers and as to as uniform
classification as practicable, e.g., that the maxima and minima of the
lower classes should be uniform, irrespective of numbers and of the
existence of more or less higher classes.

Childers provided no guidance as to the manner in which his
general principle of 'discouraging' the employment of Supplementary Clerks was to be implemented; nor did Hamilton seek any. In
practice nothing was done to discourage their employment without
first receiving a dispatch referring to the Supplementary Establishment, to have taken more positive steps to discourage the employment of these clerks, for example by way of a general Minute or
circular, would have been contrary to Treasury practice, and likely
to provoke complaints of unwarranted interference in departments'
domestic affairs. As a result the new policy led to the abolition of
the Supplementary Establishment in only one department, the
Poor Law Board, while in the Board of Trade the decision to
abolish the Supplementary Establishment taken in 1863 was reaffirmed. In both cases Hamilton's support for Childers's ruling

---

[1] Comments written by Childers on Hamilton's undated memorandum, ibid.

was unequivocal, despite the force with which he had argued against it earlier. When the Poor Law Board attempted to introduce a new class of Extra Clerks he warned Childers's successor that it was a reversion to the old system of Supplementary Clerks 'which it has been the policy to get rid of generally [and] which the Poor Law Board and the Treasury in June 1866 proposed to abolish in June 1866 and actually abolished'.[1]

Still more new duties had been assigned to the Board of Trade between 1863 and 1866, and before the Treasury would agree to a further increase of the establishment it insisted upon yet another committee to consider 'the whole question of the organisation of the Department with a view to the best distribution of the business and efficient working of the office'.[2] It was discovered that the recommendation made by the 1863 committee of inquiry, that the status and functions of the copyists and the established clerks should be sharply differentiated, had not been wholly observed: in some branches the copyists had been employed on more responsible work than the Superior Clerks. In acknowledgment of the Board of Trade's wish to make the best use of copyists' abilities, the committee now recommended that those with the capacity for higher work should be eligible to compete for vacancies on the Superior Establishment, while those whose capacity was limited to 'steadiness and accuracy' were to be rewarded with higher pay. The earlier decision to abolish the Supplementary Establishment was thus implicitly reaffirmed, while at the same time an attempt was made to maintain more easily and effectively the distinction between established and non-established clerks by providing an official route of entry into the Superior Establishment for the abler copyists.

Those departments which Childers had decided should be excepted from the general rule discouraging the employment of Supplementary Clerks, namely, the Treasury, Foreign Office, Colonial Office, and Home Office, continued after 1865 to employ Supplementary Clerks in the same manner and with the same consequences as they had done previously. The difficulties to which the working of the two-tiered system gave rise continued unabated, and the discontent of the Supplementary Clerks was

[1] Memo from Hamilton to Sclater-Booth (?)October 1866, P.R.O. T.1/6821B/17977.
[2] Treasury to the Board of Trade, 16 August 1866, P.R.O. T.1/6671A/20139.

alleviated as before by the periodic adjustment of their salaries. Just four years after their last demand the Supplementary Clerks of the Home Office urged their minister to apply to the Treasury for another increase. After some delay the Treasury finally agreed to a new scale 'upon the understanding that it must be accepted as a final settlement'. Childers, who earlier had expressed the wish that the 'maxima and minima of the lower classes should be uniform, irrespective of numbers and the existence of more or less higher classes', now directed that the new scales should 'be adopted in all future cases of a similar nature'.[1] When the Colonial Office submitted a pay claim two years later, in 1867, the Treasury took the opportunity to assimilate their scales with those approved for the Home Office, with the result that the classification and salaries of Supplementary Clerks in the four 'first-class' departments were now substantially the same.[2] Despite this uniformity, Trevelyan's and Northcote's hope that these clerks would be transferred 'without inconvenience from one [department] to another, according as the demand for their services may be greater or less at any particular time', remained unfulfilled.[3] By this time the Supplementary Clerks had become firmly entrenched in their separate departments, many of them holding positions of great responsibility, and their transfer from one office to another was a very remote possibility, favoured neither by the clerks, the departments, nor the Treasury.

Before leaving the Treasury in July 1866, Childers was instrumental in introducing a new class of writers into the Customs Department; shortly afterwards the Admiralty adopted a similar system. The significance of these two experiments was their anticipation of the general writer class introduced into the whole Service in 1870. In both departments writers were substituted for temporary clerks, and later for several of the established clerks as well. The agreement of the Customs that up to a quarter of their established clerks could be replaced by writers was striking confirmation of Trevelyan's evidence to the 1848 Select Committee that many established civil servants were employed upon mundane tasks. Conditions of service were much the same in the two departments:

[1] Quoted by Rivers Wilson in a memo, March 1867, P.R.O. T.1/6721B/15009.
[2] See below, Chapter 9, p. 246.
[3] *Report of the Committee of Inquiry into the Organisation of the Civil Service*, 23 November 1853, op. cit.
</body>

in the Admiralty they were paid between 6s. 6d. and 9s. 6d. per day according to length of service, but had no claim to promotion to the establishment or to superannuation; while in the Customs they were paid slightly less, 5s. 6d. to 8s. 6d. per day, and after five years service were entitled to a month's pay as gratuity on their discharge, but like the Admiralty writers they had no claim to establishment. Both departments admitted that in practice writers and junior established clerks did much the same kind of work.[1]

THE INTRODUCTION OF OPEN COMPETITION
1870-1874

It has been claimed that the introduction of open competition in 1870 implied the abandonment of a 'two-tier structure' and the departure from the Trevelyan–Northcote principle of separating the intellectual from the mechanical work; also that the requirements of many of the major departments necessitated a 'three- if not a four-tiered structure, to which effect was given in 1870'.[2] This conclusion is derived from a cabinet committee memorandum of June 1869 which stated that the Civil Service was to consist of four divisions: (*a*) first class; (*b*) second class permanent; (*c*) writers, non-permanent; and (*d*) attendants.[3] But the classification of the Civil Service which was adopted here is by no means exhaustive, although it has clearly been regarded as such by later readers. At least two other important and clearly distinguishable classes of civil servants were omitted: the professional class (e.g. solicitor, accountant, draughtsman), and the technical class and inspectorate (e.g. Hydrographer in the Admiralty, Inspector of Schools)—neither fall within the four classes listed by the cabinet committee.

Trevelyan and Northcote were aware that their original two-tier classification was not comprehensive. The attendant class, which was almost as numerous in 1853 as in 1869, might equally have been included by them as a third tier: it was not because they were concerned with that part of the Civil Service engaged primarily upon

[1] Replies of the Customs and Admiralty to a questionnaire circulated by the *Civil Service Inquiry Commission* in June 1874. 1st Report 1875, P.P., 1875, XXIII.
[2] Edward Hughes, 'Postscript to the Civil Service Reforms of 1855', *Public Administration*, xxxiii, Autumn 1955, 299.
[3] Brit. Mus., G.P. Add. MSS. 44347, fo. 355.

clerical work. It is misleading, therefore, to compare Trevelyan's two-tier classification with the four-tier proposed by the cabinet committee in 1869 and to deduce from it conclusions as to the recognition of the principle of the division of labour and the changing pattern of establishment in the Civil Service. A valid comparison can be made only if the fourth class, the attendants, is ignored in the cabinet classification. A second, and more important, factor must then be considered. 'Established' (i.e. permanent) must be distinguished from 'un-established' (i.e. non-permanent) service. In their *Report on the Organisation of the Civil Service* in 1853, and in the reports of the committees of inquiry on which they sat between 1848–54, Trevelyan and Northcote proposed the creation of two-tiered systems in which the work of the department was divided into 'intellectual' and 'mechanical' *within the establishment*; that is to say, both tiers (or classes of clerks) were to be established.[1] A comparison between Trevelyan's and Northcote's two-tiered structure, whose elements were wholly permanent, and that of the cabinet memorandum which (ignoring the attendant class) comprised both permanent and non-permanent tiers is meaningful only if this crucial distinction is made clear. When the two are compared it can be seen at once that the cabinet memorandum provided for a division of work between two established classes and an unestablished class of writers—Trevelyan's and Northcote's two-tiered system as it had worked in practice after 1856.

The cabinet memorandum did not, therefore, herald the introduction of a 'three- or four-tier structure'—all four classes existed before 1869. Nor was it a manifesto presaging a great change in the pattern of establishment—it was descriptive rather than prescriptive. All that was changed as a result of it was the Treasury's support for the general rule made by Childers three years earlier, which in any case had led to the abandonment of the Supplementary Class in only the Poor Law Board.[2] The Treasury remained

---

[1] The failure to appreciate this distinction and the circumstances in which the Supplementary Establishments were introduced into the Civil Service has led to some confusion among writers on the history of the Civil Service. On the assumption that Supplementary Clerks were unestablished Emmeline Cohen in *The Growth of the British Civil Service 1780–1939* concludes that Northcote and Trevelyan advocated unestablished clerks for copying and other mechanical work; while Hughes, loc. cit., p. 129, claims that the Board of Trade was *obliged* to employ 'supplementary clerks'.

[2] Significantly, although his decision was now implicitly reversed by the

committed to that pattern of establishment advocated by Hamilton in his memorandum to Childers; and those departments with Supplementary Establishments were encouraged to maintain them. Treasury policy after 1870 is summarized in this letter by Lingen:[1]

The organisation at which my Lords think it desirable to aim is, the number of senior and principal clerks should be no greater than is sufficient to place each of them in separate charge of a convenient portion of the official business under the Secretary of State. When the smallest number of senior and principal clerks has been settled my Lords think that the number of second and third class clerks of the Superior Establishment should not altogether be more than double of the number of senior and principal clerks. These relative numbers become feasible if such second and third class clerks are relieved of mechanical work (fair copying, registration, etc.) and are confined to the duty of assisting the senior clerks in the minuting of answers on the simpler cases and preparing the material for minutes on the rest.

Fair copying, registration, statistics and accounts are the work of a Supplementary Establishment of which the greater part should be Registered writers, working under a small number of established clerks of a Supplementary Class.

The registered writers to whom Lingen referred here had been introduced on Lowe's initiative to replace the Law Stationers' clerks. Like them they were to be employed only upon mechanical work, and rigidly separated from the establishment. The need for a 'clear space' between 'the end of the establishments and the com-

---

[1] Treasury to the Home Office, 25 February 1871, P.R.O. T.1/7121B/18378. The same view had been expressed in a letter to the Board of Trade in November 1870. See also Welby's evidence to the *Select Committee on Civil Services Expenditure 1873*, qus. 27–8.

---

cabinet memorandum and the regulations for open competition drawn up later by the Treasury and the CSC, neither the Poor Law Board nor the Board of Trade on the one hand, nor the Treasury and the Government on the other, pressed for the re-introduction of the Supplementary Class. Similarly, where departments had employed only established clerks (the 'first class' of the cabinet memorandum) and temporary clerks or writers (the 'writers non-permanent'), for example the War Office and Admiralty, nothing was done after 1869 to introduce a class of Supplementary Clerks (the 'second class permanent'). They remained one-tiered establishments employing in addition a number of unestablished writers now obtained from the register kept by the CSC. A few departments, e.g. the Board of Inland Revenue, the Local Government Board, and some branches of the G.P.O., divided the work between a one-tiered establishment in which the clerks were all of the Supplementary Class recruited under Regulation II, and writers supplied by the CSC.

mencement of the writers'[1] was more urgent now that departments
had surrendered their patronage because the ease with which they
could obtain writers from the Civil Service Commissioners'
Register would put into their hands 'an unlimited license to
create things equivalent to clerkships, which would be more or
less at their own disposal'.[2] Unless something was done to prevent
writers from becoming established, it would be like 'putting down
patronage with one hand and setting it up with the other'. Lowe
acted promptly but peremptorily, without consulting the departments and with his customary disregard for considerations other
than his own. By Order in Council temporary service was made
strictly temporary by the abolition of progressive wages, sick-
leave and holidays, and by forbidding appointment to the establishment.[3] Complaints to the press and Parliament that many
writers had suffered hardship as a result of Lowe's Order quickly
followed and led to the appointment of a Select Committee in
1873.[4] It reported against his new regulations, which as a result
were modified. Holidays and sick-leave were restored to the writers,
they were allowed special rates of pay for special work, and their
claims to establishment recognized where they could prove a
well-founded expectation.

The principle of dividing the intellectual from the mechanical
work was not abandoned in 1869 or 1870—indeed it was explicitly
recognized in the cabinet memorandum. Echoing Trevelyan and
Northcote the line between the 'first' and 'second' classes was to be
sharply drawn: there was to be no promotion between the two.
Herein lay the importance of the memorandum, providing the
first recognition by government, as distinct from the Treasury, of
the principle of division of labour and of a pattern of establishment
for the Civil Service as a whole. But official recognition did not
guarantee that the principle would be strictly applied or upheld.
The situation in the departments changed little after 1869. In 1873
the Select Committee on Civil Services Expenditure criticized
the excessive number of civil servants, which it ascribed partly to
the lightness of the work of many permanent officers, and partly
to the waste of time which resulted from the employment of all

[1] Memo by Lingen, 11 March 1871, P.R.O. T.1/7143B/19698.
[2] Robert Lowe in evidence before the *Select Committee on Civil Services
Expenditure*, 1873, P.P., 1873, VII, 661.
[3] 19 August 1871.
[4] *Select Committee on Civil Service Writers*, 1873, P.P., 1873, XI.

educated men on merely mechanical work. Two years later the Playfair Commission noted the tendency for departments to employ as many writers as possible because they were cheap and could be obtained by a simple requisition to the Civil Service Commissioners.[1] When the departments were hard pressed they employed them on any work for which the established clerks had not time, with the result 'that Clerks on the Superior Establishment, Supplementary Clerks, Temporary Clerks engaged on weekly wages . . . and even Civil Service Writers are too frequently employed side by side on the same work'.[2]

CONCLUSION

After his inopportune and precipitate attempt in the late forties to win public approval for the principle of the division of labour before a Select Committee of the House of Commons, Trevelyan conducted a campaign of sustained brilliance within the administration where he was stronger, more influential, and his weaknesses as a publicist, especially his irritating omniscience, were less damaging to his cause. With Northcote he perfected the unofficial inquiry and report procedure—the Treasury's most successful device for controlling establishments.[3] Between 1848 and 1856 together they examined the organization of more than a dozen departments and induced each of them to accept and introduce the principles they had formulated for dividing the intellectual from the mechanical work, and to add a second tier of permanent, established clerks specially recruited for the latter work. Subsequent argument was concerned less with the advantages of dividing work than with the best way to give practical effect to it—an argument which was continued before the Civil Service Inquiry Commission in 1874–5, whose main recommendation—the creation of a Higher and Lower Division—was intended to secure a more perfect division of labour throughout the Service.

But from their inception the two-tiered establishments rarely functioned as Trevelyan and Northcote had intended. Almost with their introduction the Supplementary Clerks were employed in some departments upon higher work making it necessary to engage

[1] In 1873 the CSC had 2,420 writers on their register, of whom 1,100 were at work and 200 unemployed.
[2] 1st Report of the *Civil Service Inquiry Commission*, 1875, op. cit.
[3] See below, Chapter 8.

M

unestablished copyists and writers to fill their place. Thus in
neither these, nor the one-tiered establishments where the work
was divided (ostensibly) between the established clerks and unestablished temporary clerks, was the division of labour strictly
maintained in practice; and in both only a few senior clerks
advised ministers and contributed to the preparation and formulation of policy.

For most of the period 1854–74 the Treasury subscribed to a
modified form of Trevelyan's and Northcote's two-tiered establishment, holding that the most efficient and economical (as well as the
most practicable), division of work was between Superior, Supplementary, and Vachers's clerks or writers. But it was for each
department acting independently, without Treasury guidance
or control to preserve the distinction between intellectual and
mechanical work, and the separate identities of the two establishments. Eschewing direct intervention, the Treasury's influence was
limited to what it could get the departments to accept in principle
and maintain in practice: the Home Office and the Foreign Office
could be persuaded to introduce a Supplementary Establishment,
the War Office could not; it could impress upon those departments
which had adopted the two-tiered system the importance of
maintaining the line between the Superior and Supplementary
Establishments, and between them and the unestablished copyists
and writers, but it was unable in practice to prevent the distinction
between the classes becoming blurred. The preservation of the
division of labour was the responsibility of the departments alone.
Understandably, they often employed the best of the many able
and industrious men attracted by the conditions of service of the
Supplementary Establishment upon higher work than Trevelyan
and Northcote had intended, but they did so with little regard
to the inevitable dissatisfaction which such employment caused,
and which the two Treasury men had anticipated. Supplementary
Clerks (and even writers) employed upon the same work as the
more junior members of the Superior Establishment pressed for
higher salaries and promotion to it. While their dissatisfaction
could be temporarily alleviated by the periodic adjustment of
salaries, its source remained, despite the Treasury's reiteration of
the need to preserve the distinction between the two establishments. Among writers and other unestablished clerks discontent
was inaudible while to the diligent and able the promise was held

out of obtaining an appointment to the Supplementary Establishment or, where there was a single tier, to the Superior Establishment.

The three separate schemes of open competitive examinations introduced in 1870 reflected and reinforced the general pattern of establishment which had emerged during the previous two decades. Subsequently it would have been as difficult to overthrow the principle of dividing work, which underpinned the pattern of establishment, as it would to renounce open competition. If as yet there was little agreement among departments on the most practical and effective way of implementing the principle, and if many of them were unable or unwilling in practice to adhere strictly to the lines drawn between different classes of clerks, as the evidence to the Playfair Commission bears witness, neither before it, nor its successors, was the case argued against the validity of the principle as it had been so convincingly in 1848. It was now generally accepted that the work could and should be divided, distinguishing that which had an intellectual content from that which was mainly mechanical and routine.[1] The difficult, and seemingly intractable problem, of how the departments should be organized to give effect to the principle, remained, to be taken up and dealt with exhaustively, but not conclusively, by each of the great Civil Service inquiries which followed in the next fifty years.[2]

---

[1] The validity of the principle was, however, denied by the *Select Committee on Civil Services Expenditure* which reported in 1873. Little attention was paid to this and other generally reactionary recommendations, and there followed soon after the decision to set up a commission under Lyon Playfair to inquire into the condition of the Civil Service.

[2] *Civil Service (Playfair) Inquiry Commission*, P.P., 1875, XXIII. *Royal (Ridley) Commission on Civil Establishments*, P.P., 1887, XIX; 1888, XXVII; 1889, XXI; and 1890, XXVII. *Royal (MacDonnell) Commission on the Civil Service*, P.P., 1912–13, XV; 1913, XVIII; and 1914, XVI.

6

INCREASES TO ESTABLISHMENT

BEFORE a department could increase its establishment it had to apply officially in writing to the Treasury for approval, giving details of the number and class of clerks required, stating whether their engagement was to be permanent or temporary, and explaining why they were needed. The Treasury then had to satisfy itself that an increase was necessary, and that that proposed was appropriate. As Sir Stafford Northcote explained to the War Office on one occasion:

If the Treasury are to be responsible for the financial results of any arrangement, they must be allowed to inquire into the details of the arrangement, in order to ascertain whether its advantages are worth the cost it will entail, whether those advantages could be attained at a cheaper rate, and whether the arrangement which is proposed is likely to affect the arrangements already in existence.[1]

TREASURY DISCUSSION

There were different degrees of 'Treasury satisfaction'. At one extreme the Treasury had to be positively satisfied that a clear case of necessity had been proved by the department; at the other, it applied a simple test of non-objection. If the examination of the application gave rise to certain doubts or anxieties in the mind of a Principal Officer or the Assistant Secretary, or revealed some point of special difficulty, then the Treasury had to be positively satisfied of the necessity for the increase before approving it. In the following case the Principal Officer having examined the application felt doubtful about the size of the increase and also drew attention to the effect which it would have upon the proportion between different classes of clerks within the establishment.

In 1867 the Admiralty applied for Treasury authority to appoint another 2nd Class Clerk and two more 3rd Class Clerks in the Department of the Accountant-General to meet the increased

---

[1] Semi-official letter to Sir Benjamin Hawes (War Office), 2 May 1859, Brit. Mus., I.P. Add. MSS. 50046.

business caused by the transfer from the Audit Office of the Pay-master-General's expenditure for the Effective and Non-effective services of the Navy.[1] The Navy's Accountant-General wrote a supporting letter setting out the nature of the extra duties and explaining the necessity for an increase to his establishment. The application was dealt with by James Cole, Principal Officer of the Treasury's 2nd Division, who at once wrote to the Audit Office to inquire of the Secretary—a former Treasury colleague—'the real number of clerks employed on this service', and was told that the Audit Office had employed only two, though at that time the work had not included the effective payments as well.[2] Cole urged Hamilton to agree to the 2nd Class Clerk in addition to the two 3rd Class Clerks, because as a member of a recent committee which had inquired into the Admiralty establishment he had seen that 'the prospects of promotion in the Accountant-General's Department are so miserable'. He was convinced also that 'con-sidering the fight made by the Admiralty throughout the whole question and the time that has elapsed in the discussion . . . they must have satisfied themselves that the increase is absolutely required'. Nevertheless, he counselled caution as 'it is easier to add than to subtract in matters relating to official numbers and we might on the strength of the Audit Office consent to a 2nd Class Clerk and a 3rd Class Clerk and ask them to make the best of it'.

With this advice from Cole, Hamilton now wrote to Hunt, the Financial Secretary: 'I think we had better sanction what the Accountant-General requires, viz. one Second Class Clerk and two Third Class Clerks, a considerable addition must necessarily be thrown upon that Department of the Admiralty by the examina-tion of Vouchers relating to the effective and non-effective expen-diture at the Admiralty under the new Audit system'.[3] Cole's point

[1] The Admiralty had a large number of separate departments, some of which were in Whitehall and some at Somerset House. Besides the Department of the Accountant-General there was the Department of the Secretary, the Department of the Storekeeper-General, the Department of the Comptroller of Victualling and Transport (two separate departments until 1857), the Department of the Director-General of Medical Services, and (from 1860) the Department of the Director of Works. They were known collectively as the Departments of the Principal Officers. When an application was made by the Admiralty (through the Secretary's Department) for an increase to the establishment of one of these departments, it was usual for the Principal Officer to send a supporting memo-randum.

[2] Memo from Cole to Hamilton, 16 October 1867, P.R.O. T.1/6722B/15241.

[3] Memo from Hamilton to Hunt, 17 October 1867, P.R.O. T.1/6722B/15241.

about the 3rd Class Clerks' unfavourable promotion opportunities was reiterated, Hamilton commenting that 'the addition of even one 2nd Class Clerk if otherwise justifiable has the advantage of mitigating the complaints as regards promotion'.[1] On 28 October 1867 Hunt drafted the Minute authorizing the addition requested by the Admiralty.

The basis of the Treasury's positive satisfaction with the case argued by a department is revealed more clearly in the next example, which illustrates at the same time the way in which the ground was sometimes prepared semi-officially before submission, and the Treasury's reaction to this procedure. In December 1866 the Colonial Secretary, Lord Carnarvon, instructed his Permanent Under-Secretary, Sir Frederick Rogers, to approach the Treasury semi-officially to find out whether if an official application was made proposing the appointment of a Legal Adviser the Treasury would agree to it. Rogers went round to the Treasury and discussed the proposal informally with Hamilton who later asked Buckland, a 1st Class Clerk in the 2nd Division, to prepare a memorandum on the question. On 5 December 1866 Buckland advised him that there appeared to be a case for appointing a Legal Adviser. Six days later Hamilton wrote to Hunt, the Financial Secretary: 'Sir F. Rogers is at present legal adviser and Under-Secretary—I need not say that he is a most efficient public officer and has no desire to shrink from work—but I consider the double business quite too much for him.'[2]

Encouraged by Hamilton's private assurance to Rogers that 'we should agree to the appointment of a Legal Adviser', the Colonial Office submitted an official application on 17 December 1866. James Cole, Principal Officer of the 2nd Division, examined it first and commented: 'There is ample reason shown for the appointment of a Legal Adviser in this letter.'[3] Ten days later Hunt informed the Chancellor of the Exchequer, Disraeli, that 'the application for the Colonial Office to add to the Establishment a Legal Adviser has now taken an official shape. Mr Hamilton and I have gone into the question and are satisfied that there is ample reason for this addition. If you see no reason to the contrary I

[1] There were in the Department of the Accountant-General at that time 108 Third Class Clerks and 39 Second Class Clerks.
[2] Memo from Hamilton to Hunt, 11 December 1866, P.R.O. T.1/6666A/19184.
[3] Memo by Cole, 20 December 1866, P.R.O. T.1/6666A/19184.

propose to assent at once'.[1] Disraeli scribbled 'approved' on Hunt's memorandum. The draft of the Minute authorizing the appointment, which Hamilton had prepared on 23 December 1866 in anticipation of this reply, was signed by Hunt, converted into an official letter, copied and dispatched.

Reference to the Chancellor was unusual where there had been no disagreement, or the likelihood of disagreement, between the Treasury and the department—here it was probably felt to be necessary because of the creation of a new post and the establishment of a precedent which might be quoted by other departments. (In fact, a similar application for the appointment of a Legal Adviser was made by the Home Office three years later.) The Financial Secretary consulted the Chancellor on certain other occasions, for example, when the latter had been a party to any preliminary private discussion with the departmental minister, or when the Treasury officials or Financial Secretary were of opinion that the application involved some important point of principle.

To enable those dealing with the application to form a better judgement of the necessity for the increase, use was sometimes made of expert opinion and knowledge available in the Treasury or outside. While examining a Foreign Office application for an increase of two 3rd Class Clerks in the Chief Clerk's Department, Cole consulted Vine, a Treasury Officer of Accounts who had previously been engaged upon an inquiry into the Accounts Branch of the Chief Clerk's Department. Vine informed him that there was a big difference between the Foreign Office accounts and those of other departments due to the large number of sub-heads, and did not think that the work could be done by the existing staff in normal office hours. The substance of this was incorporated in a memorandum which Cole wrote on 13 November 1871, together with his own verdict that 'some increase of Establishment must be allowed if the Accounts are to be sent into the Audit Office in proper time'.[2] The application was then passed up to the Permanent Secretary, Ralph Lingen, who on 22 November 1871, wrote this about it:

Assuming the statement to be correct, as no doubt it is, regarding the pressure upon the Chief Clerk and his staff, there are but two ways of meeting it, viz. to increase the number of officers or to reduce their

[1] Memo from Hunt to Disraeli, 28 December 1866, P.R.O. T.1/6666A/19184.
[2] Memo by Cole, 13 November 1871, P.R.O. T.1/7126A/18726.

work by arranging it better. I have seen Mr Vine who thinks nothing can be done in the latter way and that the increase asked for is only reasonable. Assent.[1]

The Financial Secretary concurred, writing on the following day: 'A case in my opinion has certainly been made out for additional assistance in this Department and the appointment of two junior clerks should at once be sanctioned.'[2]

In each of the cases discussed so far, 'Treasury satisfaction' was eventually expressed positively and unequivocally. But it was not always so. Departments had not necessarily to rely upon such a positive degree of 'Treasury satisfaction'. The application could succeed without it, given the presumption that the applicant department had satisfied itself of the necessity for the increase, and provided that the Treasury found nothing in the application to which it could object, or which gave cause for anxiety or doubt. This was a test of 'non-objection'—a different degree of 'Treasury satisfaction'. The Treasury was satisfied not because 'ample reason' had been shown (though it might have been too) but because there was nothing in the application to which it could reasonably object. For example, writing to the Financial Secretary about an Admiralty proposal to appoint an Assistant Accountant-General and a 2nd Class Clerk, and to convert the Deputy Accountant-General into a second Assistant Accountant-General Hamilton said: 'I am not prepared to say that the change is not desirable. Indeed I think the additional Supervision over the work of 157 clerks may probably be advisable. But the reasons the Admiralty give for so large an increase of expense and raising the Deputy from £900 to £1,000 at the same time with the appointment of a second officer with the same salary of £1,000 are not very strong.'[3] The increase was approved.

A practice which has been referred to already—and one by no means peculiar to this branch of establishments' business—was that of obtaining Treasury agreement semi-officially before submitting an official application. It was quite common and 'most useful, for the heads or representatives of other Departments which had serious changes of establishment or augmentation to recommend, to *see* the Chancellor of the Exchequer or representa-

---

[1] Memo by Lingen, 22 November 1871, P.R.O. T.1/7126A/18726.
[2] Memo by W. E. Baxter, 23 November 1871, P.R.O. T.1/7126A/18726.
[3] Memo from Hamilton to Hunt, 5 February 1868, P.R.O. T.1/6772A/2143.

tive of the Treasury and to avoid writing until the subject was
nearly matured'.[1] For a department it had distinct advantages: it
avoided the embarrassment of official Treasury refusal and reduced
the possibility of open conflict as a result of Treasury objections.
Also, it was both easier for the department to explain verbally in a
tête à tête why the increase was necessary and to convince the
Treasury of it; and more difficult for the Treasury when face to
face with the permanent head of a department or a minister to
resist a demand. When the Treasury was approached in this way
a note referring to the private agreement was made on the file.
Besides this, the Treasury always insisted that the department
submitted to it a formal application in order that it should possess
a full written record of the decision taken. The Treasury's official
answer to the application was also a safeguard for the department
when required by the Audit Office and (after 1866) the Comptroller and Auditor-General to produce Treasury authority for an
additional item of expenditure. An example of an increase privately agreed between the Treasury and the Home Office occurred
in 1869 when Hamilton was informed by the Chancellor's private
secretary, Rivers Wilson, that 'the Chancellor of the Exchequer
has privately assented to a recommendation which the Home
Office is about to make officially for the appointment of a lawyer
to be attached to the Home Office as Law Clerk at a salary of
£1,000 p.a.'[2] A month later the Treasury received the official
application. It made no mention of the private agreement; out-
wardly it appeared to be an ordinary application, containing the
request for the increase and a detailed explanation of the circumstances which made it necessary.

Many applications were approved without any apparent discussion between Treasury officials, or between them and their
ministers. The file on each contained simply the letter from the
department and the brief instruction written by a Principal Officer
or one of the Secretaries: 'give sanction accordingly' or 'signify
concurrence'. There are no other papers and from this it may
reasonably be inferred that these applications provoked little or
no discussion within the Treasury. What is known about the

[1] Gladstone to Monsell (Post Office), 1 March 1873, Brit. Mus., G.P. Add.
MSS. 44542.
[2] Memo from Rivers Wilson to Hamilton, 23 August 1869, P.R.O. T.1/
6943A/21356.

transaction of business supports this. Normally Principal Officers communicated with the Secretaries by memorandum. Sometimes, however, a particular application was discussed verbally and a note to that effect made on the file, occasionally containing details of what had been said or agreed to. The reason for this was the desire to have as complete a record as possible of how and why a particular decision had been made. Even though Treasury approval was sometimes given to a proposal before an application was made, the Treasury always insisted not only upon an official letter being submitted with details of the increase and a full explanation of its necessity, but was careful to note upon the file that the decision had been made in this way.

It is highly improbable, therefore, that an application was approved following private agreement between the Treasury and the department without some written indication of this on the file. Of course this does not rule out absolutely the possibility that on occasions an application was discussed between the senior Treasury officials without that discussion being recorded on the file. In a small department like the Treasury where the senior people knew each other well, it would be most surprising if this did not happen from time to time. But what does seem certain is that when such discussions took place, and remained unrecorded, they did not give rise to the expression of serious doubts or anxieties about the application.

What emerges from this is that some applications could succeed upon the initial approval given to them by the Principal Officer or the Assistant Secretary, provided of course that the Financial Secretary did not disagree when the application was passed up to him. In these cases the necessity for the increase was so patently obvious to the Principal Officer examining it that discussion with his colleagues was felt to be unnecessary. From his knowledge and experience of the department the case made out by it appeared to him to be reasonable; and having examined the application he had found that it involved no point of principle, that it raised no difficulty, to which he wished to draw the attention of his colleagues or the minister.

DEMUR

When a Department asks for an increase of Establishment . . . the

Treasury demurs—as it is its duty unless satisfied as to the necessity for such increase. (G. A. Hamilton).[1]

To some applications the Treasury demurred in an official reply; what it did thereafter depended upon the department's response to the demur. But first demur must be defined and its use described. Derived from the Latin *morari* to delay, demur was used for the first time in the sense of hesitating or pausing in uncertainty in the early part of the nineteenth century; after 1827 another meaning ascribed to it was 'to object to'. These two uses of the word, current in the third quarter of the nineteenth century, almost exactly describe the Treasury's response to certain applications which came before it: in demurring the Treasury hesitated to give its assent to an increase until the uncertainty or difficulty which it felt about a part or the whole of it had been removed or dispelled by further representation from the department. The action taken by the Treasury on these applications is distinguishable from that taken on those discussed above in that the uncertainties and difficulties which were expressed there did not become the subject of an official Treasury communication with the department; they were resolved within the Treasury.

A demur was not intended to terminate the negotiations begun by a department, but to evoke a response. Its purpose was not to refuse an increase, but to elicit further information about it. As Northcote explained to Sir Benjamin Hawes (War Office), it was necessary to put 'to you some questions to bring out more fully the advantages of the arrangement you propose, and our ultimate decision would probably depend upon your answers'.[2] The use of a demur is best explained by an actual example, which although not typical—the Treasury was obliged to demur more frequently than usual because of the remarkable intransigence of the Admiralty— has the advantage of revealing in the course of a single application a number of the reasons which inspired its use, and its effect upon the department.

On 20 January 1858 the Admiralty asked for another 1st Class Clerk and two more 2nd Class Clerks to help superintend the large number of junior clerks in the Department of the Comptroller of

[1] Hamilton to Gladstone, 10 October 1860, P.R.O. *Hamilton Semi-Official Correspondence*, i.

[2] Semi-official letter to Sir Benjamin Hawes, 2 May 1859, Brit. Mus., I.P. Add. MSS. 50046.

Victualling and Transport Services, explaining that the Crimean War and the abolition of the Transport Board had greatly increased the work there. The Treasury demurred, and asked:

Whether the large proportion of clerks of the higher classes in the proposed Establishment to those of the lower classes, as compared with other offices of the Admiralty Establishment is required by the nature of the duties which devolve upon the Department of the Comptroller of Victualling and Transport.[1]

In their reply the Admiralty merely reiterated the necessity for the increase without providing any of the additional information called for.[2] The Treasury demurred again.

My Lords do not consider the division of the duties of the Establishment (which is the only ground herein alleged for the proposed classification) to be of itself sufficient to justify the constitution of a second clerkship of the highest grade in the Department in question; nor are they prepared to exercise the discretion confided in them by the Legislature without satisfying themselves from the circumstances of the case that the intended measure is consistent with the principles upon which the Establishments of Public Departments are generally regulated.[3]

Ignoring the Treasury's hint of the kind of information which would satisfy it, the Admiralty repeated in a further letter that the increase was 'absolutely necessary'. The Treasury demurred a third time, pointing out that they had not refused previously to give their consent to the arrangements proposed by the Admiralty but had *'stated reasons for hesitating to authorize the proceeding'*, and expressed their sense of what was implied by the responsibility imposed upon them in reference to additions to authorized establishments.[4] 'It is necessary', the letter concluded, 'that they shall be furnished with a more full explanation of the grounds of the proposal before they can form an opinion of it.'

This was now provided, together with a table showing details of the increased business of the Victualling Branch between 1853 and 1858. Satisfied at last with the case argued by the Admiralty, but anxious to make the most economical arrangement, the Treasury suggested the re-employment of three officers made redundant by reductions in other Admiralty departments. How-

---

[1] Letter to the Admiralty, 27 January 1858, P.R.O. T.1/6120A/7050.

[2] Letter to the Treasury, 29 January 1858, P.R.O. T.1/6120A/7050.

[3] Letter to the Admiralty, 17 February 1858, P.R.O. T.1/6120A/7050.

[4] Ibid, 1 April 1858, P.R.O. T.1/6120A/7050. The italics in the quotation are mine.

ever, as one of these had already been absorbed, while the other two, the Admiralty claimed, were unfitted for office, authority was finally given for three new appointments.

This example shows how the demur was used to interpose a period of delay between application and authorization to oblige a department to make out a case for an increase and to justify the size and nature of it when the Treasury was not satisfied that either or both requirements had been fulfilled in the initial application. In answer to a request from the Audit Office for an increase to the establishment the Treasury replied:

My Lords are not at present satisfied that a necessity exists for a revision of the establishments recently fixed after a careful inquiry conducted by officers of the Treasury. Many of the new duties enumerated in the letter of the Commissioners [of Audit] do not appear to be of a difficult or extensive description, and other duties referred to by the Commissioners are not of a permanent nature.[1]

In cases like these where the Treasury was not satisfied, it usually asked for a further explanation or for specific items of information. When it demurred it said to the department in effect: 'There is probably a case to be made out for an increase: you have not done it, explain further.' Even where the department was the Foreign Office, the increase 'indispensably necessary', and the Foreign Secretary did 'not doubt that the Lords of the Treasury will concur', more information was required. In this instance the Treasury felt unable to decide whether an extra clerk was needed until it knew more about the nature of the increase in business.

My Lords desire to be informed whether the pressure of public business which is considered to require an appointment to be made to the vacant Junior Clerkship in the Foreign Office is not of a temporary character and may not be met by engaging temporary assistance without adding to the Establishment.[2]

The Treasury had always to bear in mind the effect of an increase upon departmental promotion. An alteration in the number of one class could change the ratio of senior to junior appointments and hence the opportunities for promotion available to those in the junior classes. Maintaining fairly constant ratios between different classes was especially difficult in the Admiralty where there were a large number of separate departments each with their own line of

[1] Letter to the Audit Office, 18 June 1863, P.R.O. T.1/6457B/17759.
[2] Letter to the Foreign Office, 29 August 1870, P.R.O. T.1/7017A/21461.

promotion. To avoid unrest and dissatisfaction among the clerks the Treasury attempted the almost impossible task of maintaining the same ratio of senior to junior appointments in each of them.[1]

When a department omitted details of the size and nature of the increase, the Treasury invariably demurred. Even where it admitted that some increase was necessary, it demurred in the absence of a specific proposal. To Arthur Helps at the Privy Council Office Hamilton wrote in 1865:

My Lords do not gather from the communication what is the mode of relief the Lord President would recommend for meeting the pressure of business in his Department, and whether any permanent addition to the existing Establishment is proposed . . . [but] will consider any arrangement for rendering the Department more capable of dealing with the emergencies which arise from time to time . . . provided it involves no material departure from the constitution of the Office as adopted upon the recommendation of the Committee of Inquiry of 1853.[2]

The Treasury demurred likewise to an Admiralty request for approval in the 1860 Estimates of a sum of £6,600 for temporary clerical assistance, and asked for 'information as regards the manner in which it is proposed to meet the probable pressure on the Civil Establishments arising from increased Naval Expenditure by the employment of Temporary Clerks'.[3] And in answer to a request from the Charity Commissioners for authority to employ six Temporary Clerks 'to prepare certain returns' the Treasury demurred, saying that 'before considering their application for additional clerks my Lords are desirous of learning what would be the nature, extent and probable cost of the work'.[4] In a case such as this, where the department was not proposing to add to the permanent establishment, the Treasury usually pressed for an estimate of the probable duration of the emergency, or the temporary increase of business.

When it was satisfied that a case had been made out for an increase, the Treasury sometimes objected to the way in which it was to be made. In 1859 the Treasury admitted the need for a special accountant in the Accounts Branch of the War Office, but demurred to the suggestion that one of the temporary clerks should

---

[1] For a discussion of this see below, Chapter 12.

[2] Letter to the Privy Council Office, 28 January 1866, P.R.O. T.1/6597B/18892.

[3] Letter to the Admiralty, 2 February 1860, P.R.O. T.1/6241A/2304.

[4] Letter to the Charity Commission, 11 May 1861, P.R.O., T.1/6261A/14296.

be appointed with the salary and position of an established 1st Class Clerk. Here the Treasury was worried about the precedent of appointing a temporary clerk to the highest class on the establishment 'unless thay can be satisfied that such an appointment is indispensably necessary to accomplish the end in view'.[1] Sometimes the Treasury went even further, suggesting alternative ways in which the need for additional assistance could be met.

Occasionally a demur was used to interpose a longer period of delay between application and authorization to enable a Treasury committee of inquiry to report on the whole establishment, or a particular part of it. The Treasury twice demurred to a Foreign Office proposal to provide the Chief Clerk with additional assistance on the ground that a prior investigation by the Public Accounts Commissioners (the two Treasury Officers of Accounts) was necessary 'to inquire and report whether so much of the Chief Clerk's work as consists of Accounts does not admit of simplification and reduction. With this information the Treasury will be better able to judge what sort of assistance and how much, if any, is required'.[2]

RESPONSE TO THE DEMUR

Departments replied to a demur by official letter. Some of their replies were, by and large, conciliatory and helpful, providing with more or less detail the explanations, assurances or specific information called for by the Treasury; others consisted mainly of a restatement of the original proposition, accompanied usually by an expression of the urgency or extreme necessity of the increase, but little by way of further explanation or additional information though this had been called for by the Treasury.

When the department provided the information or further explanation asked for, the increase was almost always authorized without much further discussion in the Treasury, or subsequent communication with the department, apart from the official letter granting the increase. Those responsible for the final decision in the Treasury, the Assistant Secretary and/or the Financial Secretary, were now satisfied that an increase was necessary and that the size and nature of it was justified. Less positively, they might be satisfied

---

[1] Letter to the War Office, 1859, P.R.O. T.1/6180B/5106.
[2] Memo from Lingen to James Stansfeld, 6 November 1870, P.R.O. T.1/7017A/21461.

not so much that the department had made out a case for an increase but that it would be inexpedient to demur to the increase any longer. The two examples which follow indicate the kind of informative reply which the Treasury received.

In 1858 the Treasury called upon the Admiralty to explain more fully why they needed two extra 3rd Class Clerks in the Legal and Manning Branch, when the previous year they had told the Treasury that following a report of an internal committee of inquiry they hoped 'to propose further arrangements with the view of promoting economy and the efficiency of the Office'. Replying to this the Admiralty pointed out that

at the date of [that] letter, 14th March 1857, the business of the Coast Guard had not yet been transferred to this Office. . . . The Coast Guard Force has been entirely reorganised and its control, management, and discipline placed under this Board. These duties involve a very heavy correspondence exceeding the amount which was originally contemplated and for which no provision whatever has been made as regards the clerical staff of this office. Enrolment of Naval Coast Volunteers and the development of this force together with the continuous service system has also added largely to the correspondence of this Office. This correspondence is largely conducted in the Legal and Manning Branches.[1]

This reasonable and easily verifiable explanation of the change in circumstances at the Admiralty between March 1857 and June 1858 satisfied the Treasury of the necessity for an increase of the size and nature requested, and without further discussion authority was immediately given for two additional 3rd Class Clerks.

In the next example the Treasury was not wholly satisfied by the Home Office's response to its request for a more detailed explanation of the need for the continued employment of a temporary clerk in the Roads Department. They pleaded 'absolute necessity' on the grounds of the heavy correspondence which arose from the proceedings of the Turnpike Act Continuance Committee in 1869; the increased number of Trusts expiring annually; and several very detailed returns ordered by the House of Commons and by the departmental ministers during the Parliamentary Session, over and above the ordinary work of the department. It was also argued that the work of the Roads Department could not be continued satisfactorily without the temporary clerks' help. Before demurring,

[1] Letter to the Treasury, 3 July 1858, P.R.O. T.1/6128A/11789.

Lingen had had doubts about the proposal and had written to the Financial Secretary after the receipt of the initial application: 'This Temporary Clerk is long lived—two years already. Refuse and suggest a writer at 6/6 per day.'[1] But Stansfeld while confessing to similar doubts instructed the Principal Officer merely to ask for more information. When this arrived neither Lingen's nor Stansfeld's doubts were completely dispelled, but authority was given for the appointment for another year nevertheless.

Unhelpful replies, which were at least as numerous as those which were informative and conciliatory, were examined more critically. Discussion within the Treasury, and between it and the department, was more searching and prolonged. The Financial Secretary played a more active part, often his participation was decisive, and the Chancellor of the Exchequer was drawn into the difficult or contentious cases, either by his Treasury advisers, or by the personal intervention of his cabinet colleagues in the departments concerned. Both were subjected to more intense political pressure through semi-official and private letters and personal conversation, frequently causing their advisers to revise or even reverse their carefully considered judgements.

The case now described is perhaps the most revealing of any yet given in illustration. Not only does it lay bare the process by which a decision was reached, it provides a senior Treasury official's view of the nature of 'Treasury satisfaction'.

In demurring to an Admiralty application in 1861, the Treasury admitted the need for additional assistance in the Accountant-General's Department, but suggested that instead of reviving the office of Deputy Accountant-General the Admiralty should appoint the two Chief Clerks as Assistants. The Admiralty rejected this and asked the Treasury to reconsider the original proposal.

My Lords [of the Admiralty] had satisfied themselves that additional assistance in superintending the duties of the Accountant-General's Department was required by that Officer, and they proposed the appointment for that reason . . . the suggestion made by the Treasury does not really give any additional superintendence, but merely a change of title to these officers with an addition of £50 p.a. to their salaries.[2]

[1] Memo from Lingen to James Stansfeld, 8 April 1870. P.R.O. T.1/7028A/22564.

[2] Letter to the Treasury, 4 March 1861, P.R.O. T.1/6296A/3881.

N

George Arbuthnot, Principal Officer of the Second Division, was far from satisfied with this.

I do not think that this letter gives any real answer to ours, and it is evident from the tone of it that the Board of Admiralty *resent* any proposal for a modification of suggestions made by them.

There is no apparent ground for giving the Accountant-General of the Navy more assistance than that which is given to the Accountant-General of the War Office, who has a larger Establishment to superintend. I believe that Sir R. Bromley [Accountant-General of the Navy] would be satisfied with the arrangement which is proposed. Long before this application came from the Admiralty, he told Anderson and myself, after our report on the WO Accounts, that the same assistance which we had recommended for that Department ought to be given to him, but I have not seen him since.[1]

An 'angry correspondence' ensued, but after Hamilton had met two of the Admiralty ministers both departments agreed to withdraw letters and 'friendly relations' were restored.[2] Two days later, on 17 March 1861, Sir Richard Bromley, the Navy's Accountant-General, wrote privately to Arbuthnot that

the business requires additional *controlling* power—assistance to be given to my two Chief Clerks ... does not meet the object in view. The labour of controlling—considering, signing bills and performing duties of a very high order, many of which need to be done by Commissioners of the Navy, cannot be lowered with safety to the 1st Class Clerks ... and although the proportion of 1st and 2nd Class Clerks to the 3rd Class, as you state, is less in my Department than in others, I assure you that it would be a waste of money to increase that proportion, as the 3rd Class have quite sufficient chance of promotion already. ...

It is in the controlling powers in which the deficiency exists, *for the interests of the public service*, if the relief of a zealous overcrowded public officer is not to be taken into account. ... A Deputy ... would be required to know the duties of both sections and be the complete representative of myself or whoever might hold office.[3]

Arbuthnot brought this note at once to the attention of the Financial Secretary, Frederick Peel. While remaining unconvinced of

[1] Memo by George Arbuthnot, 7 March 1861, P.R.O. T.1/6296A/3881.
[2] Memo from Hamilton to Frederick Peel, 15 March 1861, P.R.O. T.1/6296A/3881.
[3] Semi-official letter from Sir Richard Bromley to Arbuthnot, 17 March 1861, P.R.O. T.1/6296A/3881.

the need for a Deputy Accountant-General, Arbuthnot was now willing to bow to Bromley's judgement.

> I confess I think that, in general principle, one head of an Office, with subordinate superintendence of separate divisions, seems the preferable arrangement; but there are peculiarities of detail in every office which those who work it are alone qualified to judge of. I think therefore that the opinion of Sir R. Bromley is entitled to consideration ... If you think that we may yield, we might perhaps say that we have made private inquiry on the subject and incorporate the substance of Sir R. Bromley's note in our Minute.[1]

The Financial Secretary agreed, and Arbuthnot drafted a Minute authorizing the appointment of a Deputy Accountant-General with a salary of £900 rising after five years to £1,000. He could not resist pointing out to the Admiralty his continuing belief in the principle 'that subordinate control is generally best maintained by constituting heads of Departments to act under the direction of one Chief', and referred to the adoption of this system in the War Office 'where it is apparently working with success'.[2]

After a bitter dispute the Admiralty had obtained Treasury authority for their increase. Much of the ill-feeling which had been engendered could have been avoided, and the increase approved more quickly, if the Admiralty had answered the Treasury demur in the sense and tone of Sir Richard Bromley's private note— at least this is what Arbuthnot thought. But what he says about the need for the demur, and the department's response to it, is more significant.

> It is to be regretted that the Admiralty instead of writing us an angry letter, would not condescend to say as much as Sir R. Bromley says in his note, for when questions are submitted to the Treasury we ought to have the means of forming a mature judgment upon them, and the reasons for our decisions should be on record. Still it would be a pity that a deserving public officer should be left without proper assistance on a mere question of etiquette between two Departments.[3]

In this next case the Treasury officials seemed to have satisfied themselves that no increase was necessary, but their 'mature judgment' was overborne by the persistence of the department and the

[1] Memo from Arbuthnot to Frederick Peel, 21 March 1861, P.R.O. T.1/6296A/3881.
[2] Draft of letter to the Admiralty, 23 March 1861, P.R.O. T.1/6296A/3881.
[3] Memo from Arbuthnot to Frederick Peel, 21 March 1861, op. cit.

intervention of the Financial Secretary and the Chancellor, and they were obliged to give way for political reasons.

The Audit Office asked the Treasury to approve a substantial increase to their establishment. Hamilton, who dealt with the application, thought it was unnecessary, but sent the papers for a second opinion to William Anderson, the Principal Officer of the Finance Division, who had sat with him on a recent Treasury committee which had looked at the Audit Office establishment. Later they met to consider whether a decision could be reached on the application without another committee of inquiry, but agreed that Anderson should first conduct his own private investigation. In the meantime, anticipating (rightly) that a rejection might lead to trouble with the Audit Office,[1] Hamilton informed the Chancellor of the Exchequer (Gladstone) of the situation, writing to him that 'as the Commissioners are disposed to complain, we had better, before we come to any decision inform ourselves *fully* as to the additional business—and this Mr. Anderson has undertaken'.[2] Gladstone replied that he expected to hear shortly from Edwin Romilly, one of the Audit Commissioners, on the subject of the increase, and promised to let Hamilton know what was decided. At that meeting Romilly complained of the attitude of Treasury permanent officers (principally Hamilton and Anderson) towards the Audit Office 'as evidenced in their recent revisions of the Department'.[3] Afterwards Gladstone sent a memorandum of the conversation to Hamilton, who on 9 March 1863 replied to the charges laid against himself and Anderson in a long letter to Gladstone.[4]

It is not certain whether during the next three and a half months Gladstone discussed the matter again with Romilly, or replied to Hamilton's letter. But on 18 June 1863 the Audit Office were informed that the Treasury were not satisfied that there was any necessity for an increase. Hamilton's original opinion must have been confirmed by the results of Anderson's private inquiry, as

[1] The report of the committee of inquiry had led to a dispute between the Audit Office and the Treasury which was settled finally by Gladstone. This must have been very much in Hamilton's mind at this time.

[2] Memo from Hamilton to Gladstone, 27 February 1863, P.R.O. T.1/6457B/17759.

[3] Heading to semi-official letter from Hamilton to Gladstone, 9 March 1863, P.R.O. *Hamilton Semi-Official Correspondence*, ii.

[4] Hamilton to Gladstone, 9 March 1863, op. cit.

reference was made in the letter to the new duties not being difficult or extensive and to the other work not being of a permanent nature. That Romilly had been prepared for this decision by his conversation with Gladstone seems unlikely, for the Treasury now received an intemperately worded reply in which the conduct of Hamilton and Anderson was again commented upon unfavourably. Passing the file to the Financial Secretary (Peel) to deal with, Hamilton commented: 'The Commissioners of Audit have unjustly attributed to us the indisposition to consider fairly the case', and felt sure that 'no way will be made towards a satisfactory settlement until it is known that Mr. Gladstone or yourself have undertaken the settlement without reference to Mr. Anderson or myself.'[1]

It seems clear that Hamilton, who had taken part in the recent Audit Office inquiry, and Anderson who in addition to his participation in that investigation had conducted a further one privately, were convinced that an increase was not justified. After thorough examination, and with extensive and recent knowledge of the department's organization and functioning, their 'mature judgement' was that the Audit Office had failed to make out a satisfactory case, and that, therefore, the increase should be refused. Urged by Hamilton, the Financial Secretary now examined the re-submitted application for himself and concluded that 'the Board of Audit makes out a case for some increase to their Establishment'.[2] Asked for his opinion, Hamilton fully concurred: 'I do not think we can refuse them some increase in consideration of the case which they make out of additional duties since 1860.'[3] His judgement of the necessity for the increase was now contrary to that of five months earlier—yet the Audit Office had furnished no new evidence. Undoubtedly he had been disturbed by the personal allegations made by the Audit Commissioners, for he had taken the unusual step of passing the file to Peel without first commenting upon it, 'a somewhat derogatory course',[4] he admitted, and one which 'may seem humiliating to Anderson and myself'.[5] He was

---

[1] Memo from Hamilton to Frederick Peel, 26 July 1863, P.R.O. T.1/6457B/17759.
[2] Memo from Frederick Peel to Hamilton, 14 November 1863, P.R.O. T.1/6457B/17759.
[3] Memo from Hamilton to Frederick Peel, 17 November 1863, P.R.O. T.1/6457B/17759.
[4] Ibid, 26 July 1863, P.R.O. T.1/6457B/17759.
[5] Hamilton to Gladstone, 9 March 1863, op. cit.

worried too by the ill-feeling which the demur had provoked. 'There is much inconvenience and detriment to the public service as well as discredit in the present hostile relations supposed to exist between the Treasury and the Audit Office' he wrote to Peel and to Gladstone.[1] Wishing to avoid the exacerbation of an embarrassing and difficult situation, he was probably relieved that Peel had recommended approval, and glad to be able to acquiesce in that decision. Earlier he had written to Gladstone: 'If you think that any concession will tend to remove the misapprehension and feeling which Mr. Romilly's letter exhibits I am sure Mr. Anderson and myself will acquiesce, most cheerfully, in any decision you may come to.'[2]

Hamilton and Anderson had decided that administratively there was no justification for the increase, but their judgement was outweighed by more important political factors. Romilly was determined; in addition to the direct pressure which he brought to bear upon Gladstone, he had intimated to the Prime Minister his intention of resigning if he were denied the increase. This threat constituted an extreme example of the political pressure to which the Treasury was sometimes subjected by a minister, though for Romilly it was a logical step, the culmination of two years' dissatisfaction with the Treasury's attitude towards his department.

What is of particular importance here is Hamilton's recognition of the subordination of his judgement (and that of all other Treasury officials) to that of the Treasury ministers. In his letter to Gladstone he had written:

The Acts of the Treasury are not the acts of its *permanent* but of its *political* officers. For those acts the political officers, and they alone, are responsible to Parliament and the Public. . . . The political officers I need not say, have a perfect right to the judgment of the permanent officers, and are perfectly free to adopt, modify or reject their judgment; and when action is taken by the political officers adverse to the judgment of the permanent officers, the latter are bound to carry out that action, just as if it accorded entirely with their own judgment.[3]

In other words, 'Treasury satisfaction' of the necessity for an increase could sometimes be determined solely by political expediency because the 'satisfaction' of the permanent officials was always

---

[1] Memo from Hamilton to Frederick Peel, 26 July 1863, op. cit. Hamilton to Gladstone, 9 March 1863, op. cit.

[2] Hamilton to Gladstone, 9 March 1863, op. cit.   [3] Ibid.

subordinate to that of the Treasury ministers. And when the
'satisfaction' of the permanent officials conflicted with political
expediency, the latter usually prevailed. This was an important
practical limitation to the power of the Treasury to control increases to establishment.

A somewhat similar struggle took place between the Treasury
and the War Office in 1859, although in this instance the dissatisfaction of the Treasury was overcome by the intervention of the
Secretary of State. The Treasury held that a number of War Office
proposals could not be decided safely without further explanation
because certain principles were involved which had recently
been discussed 'by the highest authorities in the House of Commons', and 'the Government and the Treasury ought to be very
careful in not allowing any change which would infringe upon these
principles'.[1] The demur succeeded only in goading the War Office
to repeat more strongly what had been said in the initial application.

General Peel [Secretary of State for War] is of opinion that the Public
Service imperatively demands that the changes proposed . . . should be
sanctioned at once—as not only necessary for the better administration
of this Branch of the Military Business of the country but with no less
important object of securing the utmost possible economy in the expenditure for which the Secretary of State is responsible to Parliament.[2]

No more enlightened by this emotional appeal, the Treasury
demurred a second time on 10 March 1859. The Secretary of State
was asked for a further explanation concerning two of the four
proposals which he had made; the third was considered advantageous and expedient (though the War Office had provided no additional information) and the Treasury now 'required only to be
informed of the particulars of the Establishment proposed'.
Consideration of the fourth, was deferred pending inquiry into the
business of the Accounts Branch, the Treasury declining 'to
entertain the proposal to add another clerk to the higher classes of
the Office, even if for some reason that step would be advantageous'.[3] Such an unequivocal refusal was rare.

The War Office now decided to be more co-operative, and in

[1] Memo from Hamilton to Northcote (probably early February) 1859,
P.R.O. T.1/6196A/13254.
[2] Letter to the Treasury, 9 March 1859, P.R.O. T.1/6196A/13254.
[3] Letter to the War Office, 10 March 1859, P.R.O. T.1/6196A/13254.

letters of 15 March 1859 set out in some detail the information requested by the Treasury in its second demur. But in the meantime General Peel, not waiting for the Treasury reply to his latest communication, had written privately to his cabinet colleague, the Chancellor of the Exchequer.

We have now at the War Office a Treasury letter stating that all the changes proposed by me in my Department must be deferred until the Committee to be moved for to-morrow by Captain Vivian [M.P.] have reported.[1] I beg to present to you that it is absolutely necessary that some of these changes should be effected immediately and that great inconvenience is experienced from the delay that has already occurred. There is no expense beyond what is at present incurred and I should think it a matter with which the Treasury has very little to do. I have sent an official reply to the letter and should be very much obliged when it comes before you by giving your sanction to my proposals.[2]

His intervention proved timely and decisive. Despite the Treasury's very firm objection to the fourth proposal, approval was given to them all in a letter of 12 May 1859. Undoubtedly the Secretary of State's private appeal to Disraeli was instrumental in overcoming the continuing objection of the Treasury to the fourth proposal. But neither in the official letters nor in his own private note did General Peel produce any information to dispel the doubts harboured in the Treasury about the propriety of authorizing these additions before the Parliamentary Committee had reported. The Treasury's continuing unease permeated the authorizing letter, where to safeguard itself from possible future criticism reference was made to the principles enunciated in the House of Commons debate. In essence it came to this: the Secretary of State had pleaded officially and privately: 'absolute necessity' and 'inconvenience of delay'; the Treasury had not been satisfied that a case had been made out, but was obliged to give way.

Less satisfaction even than this was obtained on two Home Office applications for the continued employment of an Irish barrister in connection with the Fenian movement in Ireland. The response to the Treasury's demur stated merely 'that the Secretary of State considers that Mr. Anderson's services should be

---

[1] Peel was exaggerating. This had been the tenor of the Treasury's first demur of 7 March, but three days later, replying to Peel's official reply of 9 March, the Treasury had conceded one of the proposals, had asked for further information on two others, and had deferred decision on only one.

[2] Undated letter from General Peel to Disraeli, P.R.O. T.1/6196A/13254.

retained for a time as they are indispensable at present'.[1] 'I suppose
we can do no more', Hamilton noted on 14 May 1868.[2] Earlier the
Financial Secretary had spoken to Gathorne-Hardy, the Home
Secretary, but had learned nothing more from him than that 'the
public service requires this appointment to be acceded to'.[3]
It is impossible to conclude that the explanations provided by the
Home Office enabled the Treasury to judge the necessity for the
appointment, but the case was somewhat unusual for Anderson
was engaged upon secret service work for the Home Office and
presumably the nature of it and its probable duration could not be
disclosed even to the Treasury.[4] Six months later when the Home
Office applied for a further extension of the appointment, Hamilton, even more sceptical of the necessity for the appointment than
he had been previously, urged the Financial Secretary, George
Sclater-Booth, to see the Home Secretary again. 'Mr Anderson has
been attached to the Home Office at a salary of £600 a year now
for a year... I should like to know what he does for this!',
he wrote, and reminded him that he had seen Hardy in May 'but
Fenianism has evaporated since then'.[5] Sclater-Booth left the
Treasury before he was able to see Hardy, but the case was settled
(though Hamilton can scarcely have been satisfied) after Ayrton,
his successor, had received a private note from the new Home
Secretary, Henry Austin Bruce, who stated that he had 'taken
some time to inquire into the present state of the Fenian movement
in America and Ireland and also into the value of Mr Anderson's
services. And I regret to say that there never was more need of
vigilance than at the present moment, and that in my opinion Mr
Anderson's services cannot be dispensed with'.[6]

REJECTION

Few applications were rejected: few enough to cast serious doubt
upon the reliability of untested theories about the nature of Trea-

[1] Letter to the Treasury, 12 May 1868, P.R.O. T.1/6821A/17942.
[2] Memo by Hamilton, 14 May 1868, P.R.O. T.1/6821A/17942.
[3] Memo from Sclater-Booth to Hamilton, 4 May 1868, P.R.O. T.1/6821A/
17942.
[4] Anderson was Head of the Secret Service, and the Home Office had difficulty
in getting him established without revealing the nature of his work. They
managed eventually to get him appointed Secretary of the Prison Commission.
[5] Undated memo from Hamilton to Sclater-Booth, P.R.O. T.1/6821A/17942.
[6] Bruce to Ayrton, 2 January 1869, P.R.O. T.1/6821A/17942.

sury control in the second half of the nineteenth century, at least so far as that control was concerned with expenditure on establishments. Much has been written about Treasury caprice and the autocratic way in which it exercised control; there is little sign of it here. If, as Gladstone maintained at this time, candle-ends saving was the mark of a good Financial Secretary, then there were none measured by the yardstick of approval withheld from applications for increases. Clearly the Treasury possessed the necessary constitutional authority to exercise control in this way, there appeared to be no limit to the extent to which it could do so—nothing in fact to prevent it from refusing an increase when this was thought to be prudent and necessary. But in practice the Treasury rarely sought to use its power in this way; and when it attempted to do so the department and not the Treasury usually prevailed. Where the Treasury objected to an increase, or was not satisfied that it was necessary, it was unable or unwilling to sustain its objection when opposed by an uncompromising and determined department. Provided that a department was prepared to swear that an increase was 'absolutely necessary' and to do battle with the Treasury, if need be, at ministerial level, approval could be obtained despite the most strongly held objection.[1] Most departments appeared willing to accept this condition as the price they had to pay for their increases.

THE EFFICACY OF THE TREASURY'S CONTROL

The obligation to seek the prior approval of the Treasury before any increase could be made meant that a department had to satisfy the Treasury that it was desirable and necessary. The Treasury's satisfaction was the 'mature judgement' of its permanent officials who interpreted and appraised the explanation and any information supplied in support of the application in the light of their own knowledge and experience of the department concerned.

Unless there was something to which the Treasury could object in principle, or which was likely to cause particular difficulty,

---

[1] Dr. Lambert in his massively documented life of Sir John Simon provides unintentional but striking support for this view. Having described several successful attempts by Simon to secure additional staff for his office despite very strong Treasury objection, Lambert observes: 'It seemed as though by relying on a few pretexts and on Lowe's sympathy, the Treasury could be forced to come to terms with any proposition from the Medical Department.' Royston Lambert, *Sir John Simon*, pp. 449–53.

or which raised a serious doubt, there was a *prima facie* case for approving the increase. The presumption was that the head of a department knew best what assistance he required and that he must be taken to have satisfied himself that the increase was necessary. Doubts or difficulties which arose in the course of the examination were discussed between the Financial Secretary and the permanent officials. Sometimes these were resolved without further communication with the department, on other occasions the Treasury demurred, asking it for further information.

Looked at objectively there is no doubt that departments did not always provide sufficient or adequate information in their initial application to enable an independent judgement to be made. But to look at them in this way serves no useful purpose, for the Treasury had no objective standards of 'necessity' or 'desirability' against which each application was measured, though it did have certain principles which it tried to uphold. They can be looked at meaningfully only through the eyes of the Principal Officers and the Secretaries. The allocation of Treasury business on a departmental basis ensured that a Principal Officer dealt with all the business connected with a particular department, supply and establishments' questions. Such a close association with the whole range of a department's work enabled him to form a shrewd idea of what establishments were necessary to keep it functioning efficiently. Given his knowledge and experience of the department and of the circumstances which had given rise to the request, an application supported by only a brief explanation might appear entirely adequate, and the increase so reasonable and obviously necessary that it required nothing more than the direction 'signify approval'.

But the Treasury's control was weakened in practice by the failure of the demur to fulfil the purpose for which it was intended. It was by no means wholly successful in eliciting adequate additional information from the departments to enable the Treasury to make a 'mature judgement' upon the necessity and desirability of an increase. Admittedly some departments responded by providing the Treasury with such information, but more still were able to obtain their increases without doing so. When this happened the demur failed: increases were ultimately approved without that data which the Treasury thought indispensable for the formulation of a 'mature judgement', favourable or unfavourable to a department. Such attempts to make an independent assessment were continually frustrated by the persistent official, semi-official and private entreaties made by the departments when their judgement was challenged. Less often, the demur was used to convey an unfavourable or adverse judgement: to inform a department that it had not made out a satisfactory case. But in no instance was the Treasury able to sustain an unfavourable judgement where the department chose to dispute it.

To control the size of establishments effectively, the Treasury needed a sanction which it could both impose and sustain: one which the departments would acknowledge and accept. That is to say, the departments had to recognize the Treasury's authority to refuse an increase and be prepared in certain circumstances to accept it. There is some doubt whether the departments were prepared to acknowledge that the Treasury had such authority[1]— a doubt which the Treasury seemed to share;[2] but very little doubt that the departments were not prepared to accept a refusal from the Treasury. Unable to enforce their decisions the basis of the Treasury's control was considerably weakened, because the departments were aware that in the last resort they could get what they wanted.

It is customary to talk of the Treasury backed by the authority of the Chancellor of the Exchequer,[3] but between 1854 and 1874 there is little evidence that this authority was used to overcome the intransigence of the departments, to sustain the objections of the Treasury to particular departmental proposals. There is much more to show that when he was called in either by the Financial Secretary or the senior Treasury officials, or by reason of an appeal made by a cabinet colleague, the Chancellor of the Exchequer had a marked preference for conciliation and appeasement, often to the disappointment and embarrassment of his Treasury subordinates who were obliged to revise and, sometimes, reverse their judgements. But it is not really so surprising that a Chancellor should prefer in these matters, in which the sums involved were small and which the head of each department could

---

[1] *Vide* the Home Office in 1860, P.R.O. T.1/6258A/13006; and the War Office and Admiralty in 1871–2, P.R.O. T.1/7251A/18607.

[2] Ibid; and below, pp. 169–170.

[3] Even more so perhaps in the nineteenth century than today. In his evidence to the *Royal Commission on Civil Establishments* in 1888, R. E. (later Lord) Welby, then Permanent Secretary of the Treasury, said: 'This financial control is really the control of the Chancellor of the Exchequer, exercised through the subordinate or Departmental Treasury acting as his advisory staff.'

with some justification claim to judge better than the Treasury, rather to accommodate the wishes of a colleague than to run the risk of a deterioration in relations with him and the prospect of the issue being raised in cabinet.

The failure of the demur to fulfil the purpose for which it was intended is to be found then principally in the conciliatory attitude adopted by the Treasury towards the departments. To avoid offending a department the Treasury was prepared to lean over backwards to concede what the department had requested, even where the department had failed to satisfy it of the necessity for the increase. It did so because generally it preferred to be guided rather by expediency than principle—where the two conflicted it was seldom prepared to subordinate the former to the latter. Often this gave rise to a paradoxical situation in which the Treasury objected to an increase because an important point of principle was involved, but eventually 'yielded', agreeing to the increase without having obtained satisfaction upon that point. The motive for this action was the Treasury's constant anxiety to preserve good relations with the departments, to avoid the kind of clashes which occurred with the Admiralty in 1861 and the Audit Office two years later. At times this anxiety to preserve good relations was the prime motivation of the control which the Treasury exercised; this was particularly true of the War Office case in 1859 and that of the Audit Office in 1863 where, it will be remembered, Hamilton's distress led him to write:

There is much inconvenience and detriment to the public service as well as discredit in the present hostile relations supposed to exist between the Treasury and the Audit Office.

Also, the Treasury's attitude towards the departments was essentially conciliatory because, in private, the senior Treasury people acknowledged important practical limitations to the extent of the department's authority to control increases. These derived partly from the nature of the Civil Service at that time and the relationship between one department and another, but more particularly from an awareness of, and a great respect for, ministerial independence and autonomy. In private the Treasury was acutely sensitive to the minister's position *vis-à-vis* the Treasury. This was manifested in a number of different ways: the acknowledgement that the minister was a better judge of departmental organization—'I do not think we can tell the Secretary of State how he is to manage the details of his Department', wrote Cole on one occasion;[1] the admission that the minister could not be refused what he really required to keep up the work of his department; but above all, the civility, sobriety, and moderation with which the Treasury conducted its correspondence with the departments.

Further, the Treasury's attitude towards the departments was influenced by their own behaviour towards the Treasury, and in some respects was a response or even anticipatory to it. It is hardly to be supposed that a cabinet minister would be willing to accept an unfavourable decision made by Treasury officials or junior ministers, upon a matter which affected the organization of his department, without frequently attempting to use what influence he had with his cabinet colleagues in the Treasury; or that the officials in other departments were always prepared to accept unfavourable decisions without sometimes attempting to bring pressure to bear upon their opposite numbers in the Treasury. It would be equally unrealistic to assume that the expectation of such pressure, as well as its use, had no effect upon the way in which the Treasury exercised its control.

The attitude of the departments towards the Treasury cannot be fully comprehended without taking into account the nature of the Civil Service at this time. Departments were traditionally independent and autonomous, resentful of any interference in the details of their establishments. Treasury control of increases represented interference, acceptable when it led to the exercise of a favourable judgement, disputed when it led to an unfavourable one. Reluctant to accept a refusal, departments not only disputed the judgement but questioned the Treasury's authority to control establishments and its competence to decide the requirements of the department better than the minister himself. Sometimes the demur evoked little more than exasperation and resentment at being called upon to explain further. To some departments the fact that the minister had satisfied himself of the necessity of an increase was sufficient evidence, and as much as the Treasury had a right to expect.

It is perhaps more realistic to judge the effectiveness of the Treasury's control within these limitations: to look at those occa-

[1] Memo from Cole to Hamilton, 17 February 1866, P.R.O. T.1/6646B/17284.

sions when departments gave their reasons for an increase without any prompting from the Treasury. This was no small achievement, for they did not relish having to justify their actions and decisions to another department. The requirement that increases could be obtained only by seeking prior approval was generally well observed, and was of course a precondition of more effective control in the future. More significantly, by insisting upon the condition that a satisfactory case had to be made out for an increase, the Treasury demonstrated to the departments that increases were not to be had lightly; even where it was unsuccessful in obtaining satisfaction it caused the department to resubmit its application. When the Treasury demurred an increase was never obtained easily, even if it was always obtained in the end. Departments were obliged to fight for their increases; that they did so was taken to be some indication of the necessity for them: 'Considering the fight made by the Admiralty throughout the whole question and the time that has elapsed in the discussion ... they must have satisfied themselves that the increase is absolutely required.'[1]

Approval was granted reluctantly. Even where the Treasury was obliged to retreat from a position of outright objection, it managed to convey in the authorizing letter an air of concession not lightly granted. The language of approval was guarded and cautious, convoluted periphrases almost concealing the reluctant consent. The meticulous use of language to convey the right nuance is illustrated by the care with which Arbuthnot drafted a reply to an Admiralty application in 1860. He began it:

My Lords are not disposed to question the necessity for a considerable increase of the Establishment of the Departments of the Accountant-General, the Storekeeper-General, and the Comptroller of Victualling proportioned to the permanent increase of the business.[2]

The complete draft was approved by both the Financial Secretary and Hamilton. Subsequently, however, Hamilton had second thoughts about certain parts of it, but not that quoted above, and cancelled the official letter before it could be dispatched. Arbuthnot was directed to prepare another draft in the light of comments which Hamilton had now scribbled on the first.

Re-reading his original draft Arbuthnot must have considered

[1] Ibid, 16 October 1867, P.R.O. T.1/6722B/15241.
[2] Draft of letter written by Arbuthnot, 30 July 1860, P.R.O. T.1/6273B/18620.

the language of certain parts of it altogether too immoderate for he now substituted for the passage quoted above one in which approval was given more guardedly:

that my Lords are ready to admit that the increase of business which has occurred of late years in the Naval Departments so far as may be ascertained to be of a permanent character, would justify a considerable addition to the permanent Establishments of the Departments.[1]

Thus the Treasury were now disposed to question the necessity for the increase and to make their consent dependent upon it. But Arbuthnot remained unhappy with the admission that it 'would justify a considerable addition to the permanent Establishment of the Department', struck it out and substituted:

would appear to call for an adequate addition to the permanent Establishment of clerks in the Department.[2]

The effect of this intention to create an atmosphere of reluctance, where increases were sanctioned as concessions grudgingly bestowed, may well have been that departments refrained from submitting applications to the Treasury unless they were convinced that they were absolutely necessary; this is discussed further in Chapter Fifteen.

Whatever the outcome of a particular application the Treasury's reasons for a decision were carefully recorded. 'For the justification of the government of the day and for the information of our successors' the Treasury was able to show precisely how it had discharged the responsibility laid upon it.[3] When the Treasury gave way but retained its objection the circumstances in which it did so were explicitly stated:

My Lords retain the objection which they expressed to the creation of a second Assistant Under-Secretary of State and although they do not think it necessary to insist upon this objection against the recorded expression of Lord Granville's preference for the arrangement, they desire to place their objection on record, in order that if proposals should be hereafter made either in the Colonial Office for varying the arrangements by which each of its Assistant Under-Secretaries is to

---

[1] Draft of a letter written by Arbuthnot, 27 August 1860, P.R.O. T.1/6273B/18620.   [2] Ibid.
[3] Northcote to Sir Benjamin Hawes (War Office), 12 May 1859, Brit. Mus. I.P. Add. MSS. 50046.

receive £1,200 p.a. or in any other office my Lords stand no wise committed to the present arrangement apart from the reduction in expense which accompanies it.[1]

In some respects the manner in which it discharged its responsibility resembled an elaborate game, the rules of which were well known to both contestants but never openly discussed between them, as the following example illustrates. In 1871 the Local Government Act Office wrote asking for authority to continue the employment of a clerk who had been engaged without prior approval; Lingen, the Permanent Secretary, refused. The Home Secretary, who had an overall responsibility for the working of the Local Government Act Office, then spoke to Lowe, the Chancellor of the Exchequer. What was said between them is not known, but soon after Lowe wrote to Lingen 'that when the Secretary of State upon whom the responsibility for the work rests urges so strongly the necessity of employing a particular engineer with special qualifications the Treasury can hardly, with propriety, refuse assent', and directed that a letter of consent should be substituted for the previous letter of refusal. Lingen, furious at the proposed reversal of a Treasury decision, replied:

I regret extremely this decision. The ground taken is simply financial. I hope that you will at least make the HO put on record a further appeal and not require this letter to be withdrawn. The extra expenditure I believe to be absolutely unnecessary, and therefore unjustified.

I do not think that the Treasury should lightly give up such a position or at least not without the conventional honours of war expressed by a further skirmish.[2]

Lingen's pride was salvaged: Lowe wrote privately to the Home Secretary 'that if a further appeal is made the Treasury will assent', and the Treasury was not made to suffer the indignity of having to withdraw a letter in addition to reversing a decision.[3]

AUTHORIZATION

When the decision to approve an increase was finally made, authority for it was conveyed to the department in a formal letter.

[1] Letter to the Colonial Office, 29 March 1870, drafted by Lingen, P.R.O. T.1/7030A/22645.
[2] Memo from Lingen to Lowe, 6 April 1871, P.R.O. T.1/7142A/19621.
[3] Undated memo from Rivers Wilson to Lingen, P.R.O. T.1/7142A/19621.

Ordinarily it was given unconditionally and without reference to any control which the Treasury may have exercised through the use of the demur. Sometimes, however, it was dependent upon the fulfilment of certain conditions which had not been discussed previously with the department; less positively, the Treasury occasionally suggested a course of action which the minister might adopt in the future, and wrote this into the authorization.

The Treasury relied wholly upon the goodwill of the department in the fulfilment of such conditions. Apart from the memory of the permanent officials, the Treasury had no administrative machinery for checking the filling of vacancies, the expiration of temporary appointments, the abolition of offices, and other conditions prescribed in the authorization. Unless the Treasury reminded the department, conditions blithely accepted were forgotten, overlooked or simply ignored. Clerks appointed temporarily were retained for long periods of time; offices which were to be left vacant on the retirement or death of the incumbents were filled; and clerks were appointed to offices earmarked for abolition. Only those conditions which related to salary and promotion were at all well observed, those which attempted to limit the future size and shape of the establishments were largely nugatory.

That departments were prepared to accept without challenge conditions which purported to bind their future action suggests either that they thought them reasonable or that they could be avoided. While there is no evidence to support the first contention, at least one minister, himself a former Chancellor of the Exchequer, disputed the Treasury's authority to limit the scope of his action by virtue of a condition which had been imposed upon his predecessor.[1] Most conditions were avoided, and perhaps departments were not unmindful of this possibility when accepting them without challenge. Moreover, it was apparent that the Treasury could hardly refuse to authorize the filling of a vacancy or agree to the continuation of a temporary appointment if the minister urged it strongly enough. A Foreign Office clerk appointed initially

---

[1] Usually the conditions upon which the Treasury was willing to approve a particular increase were discussed between it and the department. Where conditional sanction to an increase provoked a response from the department it has been considered as part of the demurring process, although the Treasury might not have intended it to have had that effect. Where conditional approval of an increase was accepted by the department without further communication or discussion with the Treasury it has been dealt with here.

for twelve months in 1862 remained in the department until at least February 1868. During this time the Treasury agreed to several requests for extensions of six and twelve months, on each occasion making its assent conditional upon the termination of the employment at the end of the extended period.

7

REDUCTIONS IN ESTABLISHMENT

PRIOR approval was not the only means by which the Treasury
controlled the size and composition of departmental establishments. By encouraging departments to make reductions it tried
to keep the numbers of both permanent and temporary appointments as low as possible. But it was much less well equipped for
this task than for dealing with increases. While it could refuse an
increase, it had no similar authority (short of Parliament's refusal
to grant supply) to enforce reductions where these were resisted, or
where departments expressed themselves unable to do so. In this
respect the Treasury's position *vis-à-vis* the departments was much
weaker, the consequence of its dependence upon their willingness
to propose a reduction or to agree to one suggested by itself.
Where its own disposition towards economy was not shared by the
department it could sometimes be induced, but the limits of such
action were narrow, prescribed by the Treasury's powers of persuasion and its persistence. Unresponsive departments left the
Treasury powerless to do anything but remonstrate.

Giving evidence to the Select Committee on Civil Services
Expenditure in 1873, both Gladstone and Lowe were pressed hard
about the Treasury's power to enforce reductions, but both denied
that it had any such power, short of raising the matter in cabinet.
Asked whether the Treasury exercised any practical control of a
reduction of an existing establishment, Gladstone replied: 'The
Treasury makes a remonstrance, and gives good reasons for it, and
it very often works out in the end to what we want, but it is a
moral suasion, it is not that we have any power to enforce it.'[1]
The weakness of the Treasury's position was exposed in an exchange between Lowe and the chairman:[2]

Chairman: The Treasury, as a Department, could not at present call
upon any department to say "In our opinion you have too

[1] *Select Committee on Civil Services Expenditure*, 1873, qu. 4583.
[2] qus. 4577–8.

many officers, and when vacancies occur we shall object to their being filled up, because we think them superfluous"?

Lowe: We could say so of course; and we would object; but our objection would not prevent the vacancies being filled up if the Secretary of State thought it was necessary to fill them up.

Chairman: Then departmentally, with reference to all existing officers, the departments are practically independent and autonomous in their action?

Lowe: Certainly.

The years 1854–74 bear Gladstone's financial *imprimatur*. As Chancellor and then Prime Minister he was uniquely placed to direct or supervise the financial administration of the country for all but six of them, while his influence was felt at the Treasury throughout. 'He held it to be his special duty in his office not simply to abolish sinecures, but to watch for every opportunity of cutting down all unnecessary appointments', wrote John Morley.[1] Here, we are concerned to indicate what opportunities there were for 'cutting down all unnecessary appointments' and to show how the Treasury did this. The period is divided by Gladstone's accession to the premiership. From 1854 until the formation of his first Administration the political and administrative climate was unsympathetic, sometimes hostile, to retrenchment, the Treasury struggling virtually single-handed to secure reductions. After he became Prime Minister it became easier, though never easy, for the Treasury to secure reductions from departments whose ministers had pledged support for a concerted policy in a government committed to economy and the retrenchment of expenditure.

1854–1868

'Economy is the first and greatest article in my financial creed', Gladstone wrote to his brother Robertson in 1859, but he was given little opportunity to practise it in the unfavourable political climate which obtained until at least 1864.[2] During the Crimean War the establishments of many departments, especially those of the War Office, Admiralty and Foreign Office, had grown rapidly. When it ended the Treasury looked, not unnaturally, for a return to normal peace-time levels, and especially to a reduction in the number of temporary clerks. This expectation remained largely

---

[1] John Morley, *Life of Gladstone*, i. 697.   [2] Ibid., p. 696.

unfulfilled. Hard on the heels of the Crimean War followed in swift succession, the Indian Mutiny, the China expedition and war, and the French invasion scare and fortifications crisis, all of which made Palmerston, and almost all Gladstone's other cabinet colleagues, reluctant to embark upon the retrenchment of naval and military expenditure. Without their co-operation his task was difficult. The weakness of his own and the Treasury's position was exposed in a memorandum which he wrote on the 1860 Budget: 'In the great departments of expenditure it is only by the Ministers individually concerned that any plans of reduction can be satisfactorily devised, proposed or executed.'[1] Throughout the whole of Palmerston's administration, the subject of expenditure was bitterly disputed in cabinet. The estimates were normally settled at 'sword's point; and the anti-economist host was led on by the Prime Minister'.[2] Not until the winter of 1862–3, after the Liberal Party's memorial to Palmerston urging economy, did circumstances become more favourable. In November Gladstone wrote to his wife:

I am very fully occupied till dinner-time, but not over-worked or anything like it. My heart is also lighter about my prospects for the Session. For I believe the members of the Government are at last possessed with the belief that some retrenchment is wanted.[3]

Meanwhile the Treasury did what it could, maintaining a continuous pressure upon the War Office and, to a lesser extent, the Admiralty too, to reduce their swollen war-time establishments. But it did so only indirectly, waiting first for the opportunity provided by the receipt of an official dispatch before raising the question with the department. Even then, and in sharp contrast to the practice after 1868, the Treasury rarely ventured to assert that a particular reduction could and ought to be undertaken.

To begin with, the Treasury enjoyed an encouraging success. Early in 1856, in answer to a War Office letter, it referred 'to the practicability of reducing some of the offices immediately subordinate to the Secretary of State for War'.[4] The suggestion was well received, towards the end of the year the Secretary of State proposed the abolition of six senior posts and the creation of three

[1] Quoted in Francis W. Hirst, *Gladstone as Financier and Economist*, p. 241.
[2] Spencer Childers, *Life and Correspondence of the Rt. Hon. Hugh C. E. Childers, 1827–1896*, i. 125–6.   [3] Morley, p. 248.
[4] Letter to the War Office, 22 January 1856, P.R.O. T.1/6049/20946.

new offices in their place, with an annual net saving of £4,150. With regard to the less important posts he hoped 'that the time is not far distant when further and extensive reductions may be made . . . to the numbers and cost of the Establishment'.[1]

The Treasury next turned its attention to the War Office temporary clerks to whose request for an increase of salary Trevelyan replied:

My Lords deem it right to take this opportunity of again calling attention to the public importance of early arrangements being made for reducing the temporary appointments which were made during the war in the different offices connected with the Military Administration and they will be glad to receive a communication from the Secretary of State for War showing the steps which have been or are proposed to be taken for this purpose.[2]

A month later the Treasury learned that inquiries had been set on foot in the departments of the Military Secretary, the Q.M. General, and the Adjutant-General. Not content with the promise which this seemed to hold of further reductions, the Treasury pointed out that inquiries should be made as well in other departments, such as that of the Secretary, and in the subordinate outstations at Woolwich and elsewhere. With more firmness than it had displayed hitherto, the Treasury went on to say that 'it may be hoped that the Temporary Establishments employed in consequence of the late war may soon be entirely discontinued, and the permanent Establishments may be reduced and consolidated in a manner which will be conducive to both efficiency and economy'.[3] To this the War Office replied that only twenty-seven temporary clerks were employed in the out-stations, and that none of them could be dispensed with at that time without detriment to the efficiency of the service. In such circumstances the Treasury could do little else but bow to the minister's judgement. Further pressure was more likely to irritate the Secretary of State for War (whose 'susceptibilities' it took great care not to 'wound') than to induce him to propose a reduction.

The situation looked more promising in the Secretary's Department, where, the Treasury were told, 'extensive measures' were being taken to reduce the number of temporary clerks. But these

---

[1] Letter to the Treasury, 30 December 1856, P.R.O. T.1/6049/20946.
[2] Letter to the War Office, 25 March 1857, P.R.O. T.1/6072B/12370.
[3] Ibid, May 1857, P.R.O. T.1/6072B/12370.

were halted abruptly on the outbreak of the Indian Mutiny in 1857, and the War Office had once again to ask the Treasury to agree to increase both the permanent and temporary establishments. Despite this set-back, the Treasury derived some comfort from the Permanent Secretary's promise of further reductions—by 31 March 1858 he hoped to have got rid of sixty temporary clerks—and from the assurance that 'searching investigations' were being made into the state of the business and the organization of those departments of the War Office whose establishments were increased. The weakness of the Treasury's position, not only here but on other occasions with other departments, was revealed by the admission to the War Office that 'this is a matter in which my Lords can only rely upon the desire of the Secretary of State to keep the expense of his Establishment as low as the official performance of the Service will allow'.[1]

By November of the following year the War Office's promise was still unredeemed, and without first awaiting the receipt of a War Office dispatch, Trevelyan now took the unusual step of writing officially to the Permanent Secretary asking him to bring the subject of the reduction of the number of temporary clerks to the notice of his minister. Reminding him of the promise which had been made the previous year he hoped that

it has since that time been found practicable not only to avoid making any additional appointments of Temporary Clerks, but to effect a further reduction of those who were then employed. . . . My Lords would be glad to be in possession of full information as to the extent to which the temporary establishment has been reduced, and of General Peel's views how far further steps may be taken in the same direction and whether the diminution of the number of clerks may not be extended to some branches of the permanent Establishment.[2]

Five fewer clerks were now employed on the permanent Establishment, the Treasury were told, but 188 additional temporary clerks had been taken on at the time of the Indian Mutiny. Forty-eight more permanent clerks were needed, to be partly offset by a reduction of about ninety in the number of temporary clerks. The reductions promised in 1856–7 receded further into the distance, and were not finally secured until the implementation of

---

[1] P.R.O. T.1/6103B/19882.
[2] Treasury to the War Office, 27 November 1858, P.R.O. T.1/6155A/19493.

the report made by a Treasury committee which inquired into the War Office in 1864–5.[1] In the meantime the Treasury's task became one of containment and limitation in the face of further War Office demands.

The Treasury enjoyed even less success in its exchanges with the Admiralty. Although a large number of temporary clerks were discharged after the end of the Crimean War, this and the dismissal of seventeen more from the Department of the Comptroller of Victualling and Transport Services in January 1858 were the only examples of Admiralty reductions made in response to Treasury initiatives. For the most part there were only increases—some of them huge. The formation of a Naval Reserve and the additions made to the Fleet between 1859 and 1861 necessitated the employment of large numbers of temporary clerks in almost all the Admiralty departments. In successive years Supplementary Estimates of £3,000 and £6,600 were laid before Parliament. The number of temporary clerks in the Secretary's Department rose from two in 1858–9 to 439 the following year, and by 1860–1 the number employed there was just short of a thousand. Similar increases were made in other Admiralty departments: nearly a hundred temporary clerks were added to the Department of the Surveyor in 1859–60, by the following year 363 were employed there; in the Department of the Accountant-General the estimate for temporary clerical assistance rose from £1,675 in 1858–9 to £4,582 in 1860–1. As the political crisis subsided the number of temporary clerks was gradually run down, but without, it seems, any pressure from the Treasury. By 1866 the Department of the Secretary employed only twelve temporary clerks, and the other departments, sixty-four between them.

In a similar manner to that just described, the Treasury encouraged the civil departments to reduce the size of their establishments, continually emphasizing the desirability of reducing establishments and reiterating the need to keep expenditure on salaries to a minimum. But reluctant to assume the initiative from fear that such action would be represented as interference with departmental autonomy, and without the backing of a concerted cabinet policy, little was achieved, although, following the repeal of the *ad valorem* duties in 1860, the Customs' establishments were reduced from 600 to 400.

[1] See below, Chapter 8, pp. 210–211.

RETRENCHMENT 1868–1874

By December 1868, when Gladstone returned to the Treasury, this time as First Lord, and Robert Lowe had received the office of Chancellor of the Exchequer in his new Administration, the process of reducing the establishments of the War Office and Admiralty was well under way, having derived considerable impetus from the energy and zeal with which Hugh Childers pursued economy and administrative reform when Financial Secretary to the Treasury two years earlier. His predecessor, Frederick Peel, had initiated a full-scale Treasury inquiry into the whole of the War Office establishments in 1864. The first four reports which appeared in the next twelve months, enthusiastically greeted by Childers, led to substantial reductions in almost every department, at Whitehall, Woolwich, and elsewhere. A year later the committee which inquired into the Admiralty's organization, upon which the Treasury had been represented by a Principal Officer, had recommended the abolition of a number of junior clerkships on the permanent establishment, and the substitution for some of them of writers employed on day rates of pay.

The Treasury was guided by the same principle in the civil departments, but before its commitment to a general policy of reducing establishments there was first an attempt to limit the number of new appointments throughout the Service by bringing back or retaining those clerks declared redundant in departmental reorganizations. A Redundant List was begun in the Admiralty early in 1869 by Childers, now First Lord. No new appointments or promotions were made in any of the Admiralty departments until the suitability of those on the Redundant List had been considered. Soon after the introduction of this scheme the Secretary to the Admiralty suggested to the Treasury that a general Redundant List should be set up for the whole Civil Service. The Treasury agreed and began at once to compile a list of names of all those clerks discharged from the War Office, Admiralty, Customs, and elsewhere, intending that when vacancies occurred anywhere in the Service they should be filled as far as possible with clerks drawn from the List, all of whom had been discharged subject to recall. In practice the Treasury was rarely able to arrange this. The success of the scheme depended entirely upon the support given to it by the departments, and upon their willingness to accept redundant clerks. Some departments were understandably reluctant to accept men declared redundant by others—before 1870 the qualities looked for and tested by each department were very different; and it was probable that those declared redundant would be less efficient or more elderly than those retained. While in May 1869 the Home Secretary was willing to fill a vacancy with a clerk nominated by the Treasury from the Redundant List, two months later the Foreign Office successfully resisted considerable Treasury pressure to fill a vacant junior clerkship by the same method.

The formulation of the Treasury's general policy for reducing establishments began with Lowe's Minute of 8 December 1869. It referred to the agreement reached in cabinet a short while before to throw open to competition all first appointments to permanent clerkships in the Civil Service, and at the same time 'with a view to check the heavy and growing increase in the charge for superannuation, [the Government] have also considered the expediency of effecting a substantial reduction in the number of permanent civil employments'.[1] No comparable decision had been taken between 1854 and 1868. Nor was there any counterpart then for the action now taken by the Treasury to bring the subject to the attention of all departments, military and civil, and to secure their collaboration in making reductions throughout the Service. Gladstone and Lowe had told the cabinet that they would consider how far the two principles of open competition and the reduction of permanent clerkships could be applied to the Treasury and its subordinate departments, and that they would communicate with other departments 'to ascertain how far they may be disposed to co-operate in establishing in their several offices a system founded upon the principles stated'.[2] Lowe now circularized his ministerial colleagues, inviting them to consider the subject and suggesting that they should then get in touch with the Treasury.

The proposal to reduce establishments generally and to substitute a new class of writers for some of the permanent clerks, details of which were given in the Treasury circular, was well received,[3] although no department responded quite so enthusiasti-

---

[1] T.M. 8 December 1869, *Treasury Minutes and Circulars 1831–1879* (*Second Division*). [2] Ibid.
[3] Departmental views on the introduction of open competition were discussed in Chapter 4.

cally as the Admiralty, where the policy had been adopted in 1866. They 'entirely approve of the Treasury suggestion as to the employment of writers, etc., but consider that it may be carried much further. A large proportion of clerkships and similar offices need not be held by gentlemen in the permanent Civil Service.'[1]

The general agreement of the departments that a reduction in the size of their establishments was desirable and practicable was a pre-condition of the implementation of the policy implicit in the Minute of 8 December 1869—without it the task of the Treasury would have been much more difficult, perhaps impossible. For even now it could not enforce reductions where the minister was unwilling, or professed himself unable to do so. Opposition came only from the Foreign Office (where the introduction of open competition had been resisted also) and the Registrar-General's department. Clarendon, the Foreign Secretary, was

convinced that it would be impossible to reduce the number of clerks (40) without seriously impairing the efficiency of the Office; for the business which those clerks are called upon to perform could neither properly nor satisfactorily be confided to the class of persons who could be engaged as copying clerks at a daily rate of pay . . . that the small saving, if any, which would result from a substitution of copyists for junior clerks would be dearly purchased by disturbance of a system which there is no just ground for complaint and which has proved to work satisfactorily and the substitution of a new system of which would for any good be uncertain but which would infallibly tend to disorganise the Office.[2]

The Registrar-General said simply that it was impossible to reduce the number of his permanent clerks.

The full extent of the Treasury's commitment to a policy of reduction was revealed by Lingen in a letter to the Board of Trade in November 1870:

The views entertained by this Board respecting the organisation of the Public Departments point to a reduction in the numbers of all officers entitled to a pension, especially of those among them receiving the higher rate of pay, by means of such division of work as leaves nearly all that part of it which does not involve the giving of advice or direction to be performed by writers under a few [Supplementary] clerks.[3]

---

[1] Admiralty to Treasury, 26 January 1870, P.R.O. T.1/6961A/1880.
[2] Foreign Office to Treasury, 2 January 1870, P.R.O. T.1/6971A/145.
[3] Treasury to Board of Trade, 17 November 1870, P.R.O. T.1/7091A/21862.

To implement this policy the Treasury was not content merely to rely upon the support of those departments which had reacted favourably to the circular, it now provided the means and the incentive for all of them to undertake the reduction of their establishments. 'In all cases where [they] provide for largely reducing their Establishments as vacancies occur by the introduction of writers, my Lords will be ready to consider such a revision of salaries in the reduced classes of the Establishment as the change may require.'[1] No similar offer had been made in the period 1854–68. 'The principle is a good one of diminishing offices and increasing work and pay', Hamilton had written in 1868, and it was now adopted and applied to the establishments of all those departments where reductions were made.[2]

A further incentive was the Treasury's willingness to facilitate reductions by offering favourable terms of retirement in special cases, and by arranging transfers under clause seven of the Order in Council.[3] Empowered by the 1859 Superannuation Act to award special pensions on the abolition of office, it was now prepared to add a number of years to the period of completed service of all those who retired compulsorily or voluntarily. Those who entered the Civil Service after 5 August 1829, and had served between ten and fifteen years, could claim five extra years; those with service between fifteen and twenty, seven years, and so on. These terms were offered to the Admiralty in February 1869, the War Office in April 1870, and the Colonial Office in February of the following year. The same offer was made later to those who retired on abolition in the Home Office, Foreign Office, Board of Trade, Treasury and elsewhere.

The selection of particular offices for abolition was made by the departments, the Treasury had no part in it, as Hamilton carefully explained to his minister:

It is a matter entirely at the discretion and on the responsibility of the Head of a Department . . . to select the parties whom they oblige to retire or rather whose offices they abolish on reduction of Establishment. Various considerations may operate. The paramount one ought to be the efficiency of the public service in the Department and that consideration generally would lead to retaining the most efficient and discharging the

[1] Treasury circular, August 1870, P.R.O. T.1/7021A/22006.
[2] Memo by Hamilton, 2 June 1868, P.R.O. T.1/6788B/9458.
[3] Treasury circular, August 1870, op. cit.

most inefficient. At the same time all the circumstances ought to be
taken into account. In the Admiralty there is a number of ABC divisions
each with special subjects. There may be 2 efficient men in A and 2 less
efficient in B but for the special knowledge and experience required it
may be more for the public interest to discharge 1 in A and 1 in B than
2 in B. I am assuming of course that there is no favouritism and good
reason. But what can the Treasury know of these details? It is for the
proper exercise of the judgment of the Head of the Department and why
should we be mixed up in it.[1]

The substitution of writers for permanent clerks begun by the
Admiralty in 1866 continued without interruption, leading eventually to a comprehensive reorganization of all the establishments and
further extensive reductions in the numbers of permanent clerks.
Before this, however, several individual reductions were proposed
to the Treasury, of which the most important was the reduction in
the number of Naval Lords from four to three in December 1868,
followed in February by the abolition of the offices of Comptroller
and Deputy Comptroller of the Coast Guard and the retirement
of the greater part of their staff.

The Admiralty reorganization began in June 1869 with the
Accountant-General's Department, where the permanent establishment was reduced by twenty-three clerks at an estimated annual
saving of some £3,600 to £5,000. All the remaining departments
were dealt with together by an Admiralty committee of inquiry
in January of the following year. In the three years from 1 April
1868, eighty-four clerical and administrative posts were abolished,
a 20 per cent reduction in the overall size of the Admiralty establishments. The net saving on salaries during this time was £85,868
9s. 2d., but the greater part of it was accounted for by the abolition
of jobs in the dockyards. The gradual reduction of the Admiralty
establishments and the substitution of writers for established
clerks, is shown below in Table I.

At the War Office Cardwell was pledged to administrative as well
as military reforms. By separating the mechanical from the intellectual work, reducing the numbers of both the established and
temporary clerks, and substituting writers for some of the former,
he proposed to cut the size of the civil establishment from 728 to
560 and eventually to save £58,500 p.a. No fewer than 156 of the

---

[1] Memo from Hamilton to James Stansfeld, 22 February 1869, P.R.O.
T.1/6907B/17186.

established clerks were to be declared redundant, among them sixteen 1st Class Clerks. Such large reductions could not be made quickly by the normal method of leaving vacancies unfilled: either the clerks chose to retire, or they had to be retired compulsorily. The War Office chose the former method, and with Lowe's approval Cardwell invited those of them who wished to do so to retire immediately on the same terms that the Treasury had offered

TABLE I

Admiralty Civil Establishments, 1868–1873[1]

	1868–9	1869–70	1870–1	1871–2	1872–3
Clerks earning more than £1,000	26	21	20	20	20
Clerks earning less than £1,000	447	427	389	375	368
Writers	113	107	128	144	149
Total employed	586	555	537	539	537
Total cost	£186,292	£167,213	£156,773	£161,907	£168,417

the Admiralty. Even with this incentive it was not easy to induce retirement among clerks who feared 'to relinquish the dismal certainty of their present prospects in order to search late in life for a new career'.[2] Repeatedly the Treasury was asked to extend the limited period during which the special terms were on offer, in the hope that more clerks might come forward. These requests from Cardwell, and his inability to reduce his establishment more quickly, drew criticism from the Treasury, where there was much irritation and impatience with him because he had 'shrunk from clearing off by compulsory abolition'.[3] Lowe was exasperated by the delay, and incensed that the War Office were treating the special terms as a right instead of a concession limited in time, allowed them by the Treasury exercising its discretionary powers under the 1859 Superannuation Act. With his usual acerbity, but not unfairly in this instance, Lowe commented:

It is for the heads of Departments to consider whether the advantage of a [reorganisation] is counter-balanced by the hardship it inflicts. I cannot agree that they are to make these changes, reduce their esti-

[1] *Comparison of Civil Establishments, Admiralty, 1868–69 to 1872–73*, P.P., 1872, XXXIX.
[2] Memo by Lansdowne (member of the Treasury Superannuation Committee) to Lowe, 4 March 1872, P.R.O. T.1/7120A/18249.
[3] Memo by Lansdowne to Baxter, 20 April 1871, P.R.O. T.1/7120A/18249.

mates and get credit for smaller establishments and then expect us to
redress the hardships by straining Acts of Parliament and making bad
precedents. There has been a great deal too much of this already.[1]

Despite his difficulties, Cardwell had made some progress
towards the achievement of his target by 1871. Seventy-five
permanent posts had been abolished, and a further forty-nine
earmarked for abolition when they became vacant. Together with
the reductions of labourers, artisans, and artificers employed in
the manufacturing departments, R.O.F.s, etc., the net saving on
salaries between 1868 and 1871 totalled £55,234 14*s.* 8*d.*[2]

Substantial economies were made in the civil departments, but,
while undoubtedly these helped to keep down expenditure, the
general trend throughout the years of Gladstone's first Administration was a rising one.[3] When he left office, Parliament was asked
to vote 16 per cent more for salaries than it had been in the year
he took office, the result of an increase in the number of civil
servants rather than a rise in the general level of salaries.

TABLE II

*Estimates of Expenditure on the Salaries and
Expenses of Civil Departments, 1867–1875*

	Total	Increase/ Decrease	% Increase/ Decrease
1867–8	£1,703,230	+£123,174	+7·8
1868	£1,661,179	−£42,051	−2·5
1869	£1,733,681	+£72,502	+4·4
1870	£1,712,960	−£20,721	−1·2
1871	£1,852,536	+£139,576	+8·1
1872	£1,803,008	−£49,528	−2·7
1873	£2,003,383	+£200,375	+11·1
1874	£1,933,356	−£70,027	−3·5
1875	£2,489,379	+£556,023	+28·8

Contrary to his earlier experience in the Palmerston Government, Gladstone found on taking office that almost all his colleagues, if not quite as single-minded as himself and Lowe, were
at least ready to make proposals to the Treasury for reducing the
size and expense of their establishments. Granville, the new
Colonial Secretary, at once instituted an inquiry into the organization of the department 'in order to ascertain what alteration could

---

[1] Memo by Lowe, 4 March 1872, P.R.O. T.1/7120A/18249.
[2] P.P., 1871, XXXVII.
[3] See below, Appendix V, Table 3.

at once or eventually be made to reduce its expense or increase its efficiency'.[1] After re-allocating the duties of the General Department he was able to reduce the expenditure on salaries by about £800 p.a.; later, three clerks were compulsorily retired at a net annual saving (i.e. the difference between their salary and their retirement allowance) of £850, and several vacancies were left unfilled. Between 1868–71 the cost of the permanent establishment was reduced from £26,675 to £24,210, and that of the Copying Department from £2,288 to £2,060.[2] Granville's successor, the Earl of Kimberley, was able to make greater reductions still. On the understanding that the Treasury were prepared to offer special terms of retirement, he began in March 1872 upon an extensive reorganization, and scheduled nine of the twenty-seven clerkships on the Superior Establishment for abolition.

Six posts were abolished in the Board of Trade where a net saving of £1,077 p.a. was claimed. In the Foreign Office, despite earlier protestations that no reductions were possible, two permanent clerks in the Foreign Department were retired, saving £490 p.a.,

---

[1] Colonial Office to Treasury, 28 June 1869, P.R.O. T.1/7030A/22645.

[2] The Treasury drew Granville's attention to the large increase of the cost of the department during the last thirty years. Expenditure had increased by nearly £10,000 p.a. despite the fact that the Office had been relieved of the duties of the Secretary of War, and that twelve colonies had obtained self-government and only five more added to its responsibility. Yet the establishment had grown from thirty-six to fifty-six, 'a great increase where a great reduction might have been expected'. On the face of it this growth bears a striking resemblance to the growth of the number of Admiralty officials between 1914–28 at a time when the number of ships in commission and the number of officers and men decreased by two-thirds and one-third respectively. Observation of the latter phenomenon (and of the growth of the CO during a period of imperial decline) led Professor Parkinson to propound his famous law: 'Work expands so as to fill the time available for its completion.' However, in the Colonial Office case in the seventies there was some doubt about the validity of the conclusions drawn by Lowe from the information supplied to him. Hamilton warned him of this, but Lowe did not heed him. In terms instantly recognizable to all those who have ever sought to disarm Treasury criticism, however justified, the Colonial Secretary began his rebuttal by claiming that comparisons between past and present expenditure were misleading; whether the business was well and economically done could be decided only by an examination of what was going on in 1870. Several of the points made by Lowe were corrected: the increase to the establishment had been nine and not twenty; twelve and not five colonies had been added to the Empire; the work done by the CO as War Secretariat in 1840 cost only £10–20, its detachment therefore did not reduce the work of the Office. Between 1840–70 the Establishment had increased by less than one-fifth, the expenditure of the department by less than one-third, but the work had increased by more than a half. In 1840–1, 17,986 letters had been received and dispatched, in 1869–70, 28,098.

P

while in the Slave Trade Department (amalgamated with the Consular Department in January 1872) six permanent clerks and a temporary clerk were retired, the annual saving being £2,757 19s. 9d. Reductions made in the Treasury were as great as those made by any other major department: eight of the twenty-seven Superior Clerkships were abolished in the reorganization of May 1870. Few were made at the Home Office, however, where the Treasury's refusal to discuss the probable scale of retirement allowance 'before it has been decided whether any, and if any, what reductions can be effected in the permanent Establishment', and its refusal to accept *in toto* the Home Secretary's proposals for reorganizing the department, led to the withdrawal of four reductions promised earlier.

To enable the Treasury to assess the financial effects of the reductions made in the first three years of the Gladstone Administration, departments were asked in 1871 to submit a return showing which clerks had been retired, the amount of compensation paid to those whose offices had been abolished, and details of any new appointments which had been made during the same period. 257 clerical and administrative posts had been abolished in the civil departments at a net saving of £21,633 3s. 1d. With the reductions made in the Admiralty and War departments, the total net saving for the three years amounted to £162,736 6s. 11d.

Today such returns are commonplace, a matter of routine administrative procedure, but in the third quarter of the nineteenth century, apart from those called for by Parliament, they were exceedingly rare. The precedent established in 1871 was an important one in the development of Treasury control, for it was noted earlier that the efficacy of the Treasury's control of the size of the establishment was seriously diminished by the lack of just such an administrative procedure for checking upon the filling of vacancies scheduled for abolition.[1] Improvements in the process by which departments were held accountable to the Treasury, such as this and that described immediately below, were a reflection of more

---

[1] See above, Chapter 6, p. 174. Under an Act of William IV departments were required to submit an annual return to Parliament showing every increase and diminution of establishment, together with any increase or decrease in salaries, emoluments, and retirement allowances. The usefulness of this data serially is vitiated by uncertainty whether the figures include temporary as well as permanent posts, and by the failure to distinguish between those clerks who retired through old age and those whose offices were abolished.

important changes in auditing and accounting methods, which beginning with the setting up of the Public Accounts Committee in 1861 and the appointment of the Comptroller and Auditor-General five years later, greatly strengthened Parliament's control of the Executive.

The need to improve the accountability of departments to the Treasury made itself felt in another direction at roughly the same time. Quite soon after the introduction of the policy of reducing establishments the question was raised whether departments could employ writers without obtaining the Treasury's prior approval, provided that the sum inserted in the Estimates for that purpose was not exceeded. An answer was required fairly quickly because it became apparent after correspondence with the Comptroller and Auditor-General that departments could obtain writers or temporary clerks without Treasury approval, concealing their employment by charging their wages in the Estimates to the general fund provided for 'Contingencies' or 'Incidental Expenditure'. Expenditure incurred under either of these two heads did not require the production of special Treasury authority, and was passed by the Comptroller and Auditor-General without question. Here was a loop-hole which had to be closed, for with the general substitution of writers for established clerks the opportunity existed for their employment on a scale large enough to offset the economies resulting from the reductions. In October 1871 the Treasury took steps to ensure that in future any instance of the unauthorized or irregular employment of writers was brought to its attention. Lingen instructed the Estimate Clerk 'to see that in all estimates for Establishment the estimate for extra clerical assistance under whatever name appears at least as a separate item, if it would be inconvenient to make it in all cases a separate sub-head'.[1] An additional safeguard was to be provided by the Comptroller and Auditor-General's audit. Lingen preferred to give instructions to him rather than to issue a circular to all departments 'which always breeds questions'; 'we shall deal better with each case in detail upon the Auditor's Report', he explained to Lowe.[2] Regulations for the employment of writers, their rates of pay and conditions of service, had been prescribed in an Order in

[1] Memo from Lingen to S. A. Blackwood, 18 October 1871, P.R.O. T.1/7143B/19698.
[2] Memo from Lingen to Lowe, 19 October 1871, P.R.O. T.1/7143B/19698.

Council of 19 August 1871, and the Comptroller and Auditor-General was now instructed by Lingen to see that from 1 November 1871 nothing at variance with that Order was passed without question in the public accounts.

In those Offices where a vote is taken for extra clerical assistance (under whatever name) my Lords do not desire the discretion of the Heads of such Offices to be questioned as to the numbers of writers whom they employ, within the limit of their Vote. But in all cases where the cost of such extra assistance is charged to a merely general head of 'Incidentals' or the like my Lords wish reference to be made to the Board for information before allowing the charge, whether, and to what extent my Lords have agreed to the employment of such extra assistance. In no case unless excepted by Clause IV of the said Order in Council[1] are payments for such extra assistance to be passed without question, in the public accounts, if they appear to have been made (a) in excess of the scales warranted by the Order, or (b) to writers who have not been registered by the CSC.[2]

Another difficulty which came to light with the implementation of the Treasury's policy arose from the special terms of superannuation offered to those clerks who retired, or were retired, to facilitate the reduction of the establishment. It was soon realized that reductions made in this way did not always lead to greater economy. If the pension and compensation allowance paid on the abolition of office was nearly equal to the salary which had been paid prior to retirement there might be very little saving; when the extra sum for the employment of writers was added there might be none at all, or even an increase in expenditure. Lowe drew attention to this unforeseen consequence in April 1871, and gave instructions that the Treasury was not to answer proposals for departmental reorganizations which involved the abolition of office with compensation until they had been examined and reported on, not only by the appropriate Treasury Division, but also by the Superannuation Committee, which at that time consisted of the Permanent Secretary and one of the Junior Lords. He had also noticed that when reorganization schemes were submitted for Treasury consideration the department frequently omitted to state how many

[1] This clause excepted from the operation of the Order those departments connected with the Courts of Justice and the registration of legal titles and instruments, unless they had previously consented to be bound by it.

[2] Treasury to the Comptroller and Auditor-General, 18 October 1871, P.R.O. T.1/7143B/19698. A copy of the letter was sent to the CSC.

officers would have to retire, and what the increase in the charge for superannuation and compensation would be as a result of it.[1] Departments were now required, therefore, to provide more detailed information about the number of officers to be retired, their salaries, and the length of their service, in order that the Superannuation Committee could advise the Divisions whether those to be retired were entitled to compensation on loss of office on the ground that their retirement would lead to greater economy.

[1] At this time the cost of superannuation and compensation was about £200,000 more than it had been in 1868—the greater part of it due to the payments made to clerks retired in departmental reorganizations. See below Appendix V, Table 5.

8

TREASURY COMMITTEES OF INQUIRY

TREASURY committees of inquiry have their origin in the
revisions of the subordinate Revenue Departments which the
Treasury made occasionally in the first half of the nineteenth
century. In 1850 Trevelyan urged that they should be 'constant
and systematic instead of occasional and exceptional', and extended
to the Post Office, the Office of Woods and Forests, and other
departments as well.[1] It would be an advantage, he claimed, if
when deciding upon an increase of salary or establishment the
Treasury possessed an independent means of information because
'the statements furnished by the departments may be incomplete
either from defective knowledge or from an erroneous view of what
is required for a full consideration of the subject'.[2] Trevelyan had
just recently completed a successful inquiry at the Colonial Office,
where, it will be remembered, he claimed that the principle of the
division of labour had been first introduced; his success there may
have prompted him to make the proposal. The inquiries which
followed in 1853–4, of which he was an invariable member, were
the practical embodiment of the ideas expressed in 1850. Commending them to James Wilson in September 1853 he said that

The established mode of transacting the business of each Department
should from time to time be investigated and revised by the Treasury
as has been done of late years . . . with a view to adapt the number and
remuneration of the Persons employed to the actual state of the business,
to recast obsolete modes of proceeding, and to establish uniformity or
harmony of system throughout the Public Service.[3]

Two months later, appointing Trevelyan and Northcote to the
most widely known of all Treasury committees of inquiry, Gladstone described the tasks of the committees in similar terms.[4]
Thereafter if any justification had been needed (and none was) for

[1] Remarks by Trevelyan on *Confidential Memoranda on some branches of the
business of the Treasury*, 2 April 1850, Brit. Mus., G.P. Add. MSS. 44566.
[2] Trevelyan to Wilson, 13 September 1853, Bod., T.L.B., xxxii, 54–9.
[3] Ibid.   [4] See above, Introduction, p. xiv.

their continuation on a 'constant and systematic' basis ample precedent existed.

Trevelyan's estimate of the effect which 'constant and systematic' inquiry would have upon the control exercised by the Treasury, with which he justified his proposal in 1850, has an immediate relevance to those inquiries set up in the next twenty-five years; it is also a tribute to his prescience and to his influence upon the development of the committee of inquiry as an instrument of Treasury Control.

It would be found [he said] that the Superintending Department having taken this duty upon itself, and entered upon the full exercise of its office, would have, in the influence which naturally belongs to it, in its habitual intercourse with the departmental officers, and in the knowledge of passing transactions, progressive changes and prevailing wants which the transaction of the current business supplies, advantages which could not belong to any Commission. The working of these great establishments would be watched by the Treasury as a master-manufacturer watches his machinery: every redundancy would be supplied as soon as it was brought to light, and the inconvenience, waste and loss of power which at present arise from long periods of neglect, would be avoided.[1]

CHARACTERISTICS

After 1853 the committee of inquiry, now 'constant and systematic instead of occasional and exceptional', became the Treasury's most important and effective instrument for controlling establishments; in the twelve years following the Northcote–Trevelyan Report the Treasury investigated over forty different departments and sub-departments, thirteen of them on more than one occasion.

Both the Foreign Office and the Colonial Office escaped Treasury inquiry between 1854 and 1874. Precedent for a Colonial Office inquiry had been established in 1849 when Trevelyan looked at its organization, but the reforms which he inspired on that occasion, followed by two extensive internal inquiries in 1857 and 1859, may have made it unnecessary for the Treasury to inquire further—certainly the Treasury did not press the Colonial Secretary for another inquiry. The Foreign Office was one of the very few departments to avoid scrutiny by Trevelyan and Northcote in the period 1848–54, though in the latter year it introduced a

---

[1] Remarks by Trevelyan, 2 April 1850, op. cit.

modest reorganization of its own without outside help. There is no evidence that the Treasury felt the need of an inquiry there, although in 1872 it refused to review salaries unless the Foreign

TABLE I

Treasury Committees of Inquiry 1854–1865[1]

1853 Board of Trade; Department of Science and Art; Poor Law Board;
/54 Privy Council Office; Colonial Emigration and Land Office; Copyhold Enclosure and Tithe Commission; Board of Ordnance; Post Office; Audit Office; Board of Control; Office of Works; Organization of the Civil Service.

1854 Poor Law Board (Ireland); Office of Works (Ireland).

1855 *War Departments; Admiralty (Secretary's Department).

1856 *War Departments; Home Office; British Museum; Stationery Office.

1857 Fishery Board (Scotland); Duties performed by the Officers of the Order of the Bath; Register of Deeds (Ireland); Topographical and Statistical Department, War Office.

1858 Department of Science and Art; Queen's Remembrancer Office; Chancery Office (Scotland); Commissariat; Chancery Office (Ireland); Solicitor to the Board of Works.

1859 Account Branch, War Office; Poor Law Board; Ecclesiastical Commission; Constabulary Office (Ireland); Dublin Metropolitan Officers of Police; Mr. Permethorne's duties.

1860 Supplementary Clerks in the Civil Service; Home Office; Post Office (Circulation Department); Paymaster-General's Office; Record Office; Woods and Land Revenue Office; Receiver of Metropolitan Police (Financial duties).

1861 *Account Branch, War Office; Audit Office; Lunacy Board; Metropolitan Police Commissioners.

1862 *Account Branch, War Office; Paymaster-General's Office; Department of Science and Art; Royal Dublin Society.

1863 *Board of Trade; High Court of Admiralty (Ireland).

1864 *Board of Trade; *War Office; Ecclesiastical Commission; Constabulary Office (Ireland).

1865 *War Office; Admiralty; Fishery Inspectors; Department of Science and Art; Registry of Seamen; Patent Office; Registry of Deeds (Ireland); Duchy of Lancaster.

Secretary agreed to one. Another reason why they both escaped was their status *vis-à-vis* the Treasury. Together with the Home Office and the Treasury itself they were regarded as 'first-class' departments, each with a senior cabinet minister, and initiating an

[1] Based substantially upon *List of Reports of Committees of Inquiry into Public Departments in the years 1854–65*, prepared in the Treasury in 1866, P.R.O. T.1/6622B/6572. The earlier Trevelyan–Northcote inquiries discussed in Chapter 5 have been included. Where an inquiry was spread over more than one year it has been entered separately for each year and marked with an asterisk. The original Treasury list refers to a Board of Trade inquiry in 1857, omitted here because it was internal to the department and not a Treasury committee.

inquiry was a more difficult and delicate undertaking than in the case of one of those of the 'second rank', such as the Board of Trade or the Poor Law Board, or those subordinate to the Treasury like the Audit Office or the Office of Works. Besides this, the Treasury deferred more to the Foreign Office than to any other department, partly because of the political importance of the minister and his seniority in the cabinet, but also because the Foreign Office was inclined to be difficult or 'captious'.[1]

The inquiry was usually concerned with the work of a single department, rarely with a problem common to a number of them, although the precedent had been set by Trevelyan and Northcote in 1853, and followed later by the 1860 Treasury committee on the employment of Supplementary Clerks. This was largely due to the widely held belief that few administrative problems could be dealt with on a uniform basis in a Service comprising a number of disparate and semi-autonomous units. The problems of a particular department were generally considered by the Treasury, and even more so by the department itself, to be peculiar to it. Although for this reason most administrative reorganization was undertaken piecemeal, department by department, increasingly throughout the period 1854–74 the Treasury found that a solution adopted in one department could also be applied to a small number of other departments, and there began to emerge different groups of departments with a similar organization or pattern of establishment. The correspondence between the salary scales of the four 'first-class' departments in 1867 has already been commented upon; a different degree of uniformity was achieved in the salaries of the Superior Clerks in the War Office, Admiralty, Audit Office, and Paymaster-General's Office by the middle sixties. Similarly, sick-leave and superannuation rules drawn by the Treasury in individual cases were later applied uniformly throughout the Service.[2] For the Treasury the years following the Northcote–Trevelyan Report were a transitional period between dealing with each department separately, and dealing with the whole Civil Service on a uniform basis.

[1] In private both Trevelyan and Hamilton referred to the Foreign Office in such terms. In a memo to the Financial Secretary in November 1866 Hamilton wrote: 'Knowing how captious the FO are I thought it would be desirable to enter somewhat more fully than you had done into our reasons.' P.R.O. T.1/6640A/15321. See also above, Chapter 5, p. 130.

[2] See below, Chapters 13 and 14.

THE SETTING UP OF A COMMITTEE OF INQUIRY

Most inquiries were set up on the Treasury's initiative; a few, mainly those concerned with the War Office and Admiralty, were inspired by the department. Ministerial agreement was essential, but in practice it was difficult, particularly for the less important departments, to resist Treasury pressure for a committee of inquiry, especially when it was made a pre-condition of a salary revision or an increase to establishment—'no increase without inquiry' was a powerful and persuasive Treasury sanction. Questioned by a Select Committee, Hamilton would probably have denied that the Treasury ever took the initiative or brought pressure to bear upon a department, for he once told Gladstone that

With regard to our functions in reviewing other Establishments, I wish to observe that when a Department asks for an increased Establishment and the Treasury demurs—as it is its duty unless satisfied as to the necessity of such an increase, it is the Department asking for the increase which usually invites an inquiry—I am not aware that it is our practice to propose such inquiries ourselves.[1]

The evidence points to a different conclusion, however. Both the first and second committees set up in 1859 to inquire into the War Office Account Branch derived from the Treasury proposal 'shortly to institute an inquiry into the whole of the Establishment of the War Department';[2] while to the President of the Board of Trade Gladstone suggested 'that preliminary to any further revision, it would be advisable to have a further inquiry now, by a Committee, with regard to the working of the Establishment as organised in consequence of the Report of 1853'.[3] Three years later, in 1866, a further inquiry at the Board of Trade was similarly inspired by the Treasury, when replying to an application for an increase of two Assistant Secretaries in the Mercantile and Harbour Department, Hamilton himself wrote:

My Lords are of opinion that the present is a favourable opportunity for considering the whole question of the organisation of the Department with a view to the best distribution of the business and efficient

[1] Hamilton to Gladstone, 10 October 1860, P.R.O. *Hamilton Semi-official Correspondence*, i. As on this occasion Hamilton was resisting Gladstone's demand for an independent inquiry to investigate the Treasury Establishment it may have been special pleading on his part.

[2] Treasury to War Office, 15 February 1859, P.R.O. T.1/6180B/5016.

[3] Treasury to Board of Trade, 7 January 1863, P.R.O. T.1/6433B/13012.

working of the office and that they are unwilling to sanction any increase of staff until such question shall have been considered.[1]

On three separate occasions the Treasury proposed the setting up of a committee to inquire into the Admiralty Departments. Just two months before Hamilton assured him that it was not Treasury practice to propose committees of inquiry, Gladstone wrote privately to the First Lord of the Admiralty: 'I would therefore submit for your consideration that, according to the course which has been followed in other offices, a Committee might with advantage be appointed consisting of persons nominated partly by the Admiralty, and partly by the Treasury.'[2] Subsequently the Treasury pressed strongly for the establishment of this committee, but succeeded only in wringing from the Admiralty a grudging acceptance of the principle of amalgamating the Admiralty Departments at Whitehall and Somerset House, with which subject the committee of inquiry was to have been primarily concerned. The Treasury's next attempt, in 1867, led to the appointment of a committee, but its members, the First Lord of the Admiralty and Hamilton, did not report. Its origin can be traced to a memorandum written by George Ward Hunt, the Financial Secretary to the Treasury, in January 1867:

Write to the Admiralty that after further statements made to this Board by their Lordships [of the Admiralty] as to the position of the clerks in their Establishment My Lords are of opinion that it would be desirable that an inquiry should be instituted into the organisation of the staff. . . . My Lords will be prepared after the termination of the Parliamentary Session to appoint a Committee for the purpose of such inquiry. . . . In the meantime they must decline to give assent to any further changes in the position of the officers referred to in the Admiralty letter.[3]

This categorical refusal and the bald proposition to appoint an inquiry were deliciously underwritten in the official letter, no doubt to avoid the risk of unnecessary conflict. The proposal to appoint a committee of inquiry appeared in the following guise: 'Should their Lordships of the Admiralty think fit to invite this Board to

[1] Ibid., 16 August 1866, P.R.O. T.1/6671A/20139.
[2] Gladstone to the Duke of Somerset, 14 August 1860, P.R.O. T.1/6128A/11789. The Treasury file was headed 'As to a Committee of Inquiry into the Establishment of the Admiralty'.
[3] Memo by Hunt, 11 January 1867, P.R.O. T.1/6668B/19988.

assist in making an inquiry which would embrace the points above mentioned My Lords would be prepared to co-operate with them.' And the power to withhold sanction to the Admiralty proposals, nakedly exposed in Hunt's memorandum, was suitably clothed in the letter: 'It would appear to their Lordships better to postpone for the present further consideration of the matter especially as it would be possible to give retrospective effect to any alteration of salary which might hereafter be agreed upon.'[1]

An important factor in the Treasury's decision to appoint a committee was the 'spirit and object' with which an inquiry was undertaken, Hamilton told Gladstone.

An inquiry such as that which has recently been undertaken into the War Office Accounts, in which the Treasury officers felt that they might rely on the support of the Secretary of State, and which led to a detailed and *practical* investigation of the mode of conducting the business may do much good. An inquiry without such support, and without a resolute will, had better not be undertaken.[2]

Another factor was the time which had elapsed since the previous inquiry. It was felt to be a very bad precedent to appoint another committee to go over the same ground a short while after the previous one had reported, unless there had been a material change in the circumstances of the department in the meantime.[3] The authority of the committees could not be upheld if after their reports had been settled between the Treasury and the department they were liable to be reopened within a few months. 'It would really come to this', said the Financial Secretary rejecting the Department of Science and Art's request for another inquiry less than a year after the last, 'that where such a commission was appointed the Department affected would take all the rises of salary recommended and appeal to a fresh commission against all that had been decided against them.'[4] But expediency rather than principle dictated the Treasury's refusal in 1861 to accept the appointment of a Lord of the Admiralty and a Junior Lord of the Treasury to undertake an inquiry into the salaries of the Admiralty's Principal Officers. It would be 'impolitic and inconvenient',

---

[1] Treasury to Admiralty, 11 January 1867, P.R.O. T.1/6668B/19988.
[2] Hamilton to Gladstone, 18 August 1860, Brit. Mus., G.P. Add. MSS. 44096, ff. 194–7.
[3] e.g. Board of Trade 1863–6.
[4] Memo from Laing to Gladstone, 31 August 1859, P.R.O. T.1/6197B/13441.

Hamilton advised the Financial Secretary, believing that the purpose of such an inquiry would be to raise salaries by reference to those paid in the War Office, which he reminded him, the Treasury did not necessarily approve as a standard.[1]

COMPOSITION

Committees were appointed 'by concert between the departments', nothing was done without the concurrence of the departmental minister concerned.[2] Those which dealt with the civil departments followed the pattern of the earlier Trevelyan–Northcote inquiries, with two Treasury representatives to the department's one. Where there were exceptions to this general rule the Treasury secured at least equal representation, as on the Board of Trade inquiry of 1866; the Poor Law Board inquiry of the same year was somewhat unusual in that it was undertaken by the Financial Secretary to the Treasury alone. The Treasury appointed fewer members to the War Office and Admiralty inquiries: on the War Office inquiry of 1856 the Treasury representatives were outnumbered six to one, and on the Admiralty inquiry of 1865 by four to one; though those committees which examined the War Office Account Branch comprised, first, three members (all Treasury),[3] and, later, four, of whom three were Treasury and the other ex-Treasury.

The Treasury's minority representation on most of the military and naval committees was partly a function of their establishment. When the War Office or Admiralty, rather than the Treasury, proposed the setting up of a committee the Treasury were invited to nominate a fixed number of their people to sit on it; it would have been surprising had the department proposed that the Treasury should nominate more members than itself. The Treasury's minority representation was also partly a function of the size of the committees. With six or seven members, the Treasury would have had to nominate almost all its senior officials to secure even equal representation.

[1] Memo from Hamilton to Frederick Peel, 17 January 1861, P.R.O. T.1/6296A/3881.
[2] Gladstone to Duke of Somerset, 18 September 1860, Brit. Mus., G.P. Add. MSS. Letter Books, 1860–1.
[3] Sir Benjamin Hawes, Permanent Under-Secretary to the War Office, had written semi-officially to Sir Stafford Northcote, Financial Secretary to the Treasury, to say that he did not wish anybody from the War Office to serve upon it. Northcote to Hawes, 16 April 1859, Brit. Mus., I.P. Add. MSS. 50046.

Only rarely did a department subordinate to the Treasury appoint a representative when it was investigated. The inquiry which determined the establishment of the new Audit Department in 1861 was undertaken by Hamilton and William Anderson, the Treasury's Finance Officer; that which dealt with the Office of Works in 1857 comprised Sir Charles Trevelyan, George Arbuthnot, and Lord Duncan, one of the Treasury's Junior Lords.

The balance struck between Treasury and departmental representatives was important. While Hamilton saw no objection to Arbuthnot and Anderson being associated with five or six senior officers of the War Office in the general inquiry which preceded the consolidation of the War Departments, he very much doubted the expediency of a Treasury officer participating in the very much narrower inquiry proposed by the Admiralty in 1865. 'I have had experience of the inconvenience of it myself', he wrote to his financial Secretary. 'Either the Treasury Officer so appointed will be placed in a false position in the inquiry the numbers being four to one or the Treasury may be somewhat fettered afterwards in dealing with the recommendations.'[1] Important too, was the choice of those to represent the Treasury. Invariably they were drawn from the same small group of senior people: the permanent head of the department, the most senior of the Principal Officers, and occasionally the Financial Secretary or a Junior Lord.[2] Trevelyan, Hamilton, Arbuthnot, Anderson, and Stephenson were appointed time and time again, partly in acknowledgment of their seniority and experience, and partly because of their individual responsibility for the business of the department investigated. For example, Arbuthnot, whose division handled the business of the War Office and Admiralty was nominated to all but one of the War Office inquiries, and his successor, James Cole, to the Admiralty inquiry

[1] Memorandum from Hamilton to Childers, 8 November 1865, P.R.O. T.1/6579B/17150.

[2] While Financial Secretary to the Treasury George Ward Hunt served on at least three committees of inquiry. Besides the Poor Law Board inquiry of 1866 and the Board of Trade inquiry of the same year, he was a member of a committee appointed in 1867 to inquire 'into the question of the capabilities of the Inspectors and Sub-Inspectors of Factories to undertake additional work that the Legislature will impose upon them, and what addition should be made to their numbers and whether any change should be made in the amount of their remuneration'. Report of Committee of Inquiry, 9 December 1867, P.R.O. T.1/6754A/19895. A year later his successor, George Sclater-Booth served on a committee of inquiry dealing with the clerks of the Indoor Establishment of the Customs in the Port of London.

of 1865. With his knowledge and experience as Finance Officer, Anderson's services were relevant and valuable to the work of any committee. Significantly, he was appointed to all those which dealt with the War Office, which had the largest establishment and the heaviest expenditure of any department. Some of the factors which influenced the choice of Treasury representatives are evident in this memorandum which Arbuthnot sent to Gladstone in 1861 on the intended appointment of a committee to inquire into the Admiralty.

You will have to consider the constitution of the proposed Committee [he wrote]. It will obviously be desirable that some of the permanent officers of the Treasury should be upon it, in order that the labours of one year may not be lost on a change of Government, or even of the Parliamentary Officers presiding over the two departments. I am afraid that I ought to be one of them, as I hold the threads of the correspondence between the two departments. Mr. Anderson's aid would be invaluable if he can spare the time. If he cannot Mr Hamilton would probably not object to giving his aid. I would have suggested him at first, but he is so good that I feel sure that he would rather that the full strength of the Treasury in matters of Accounts should be represented by Mr Anderson, than that his own superior position as Assistant Secretary should stand in the way.

I think it very desirable, or rather essential, that we should have the support of the Parliamentary element in Mr. Peel.

A Committee so constituted, working cordially with the Secretary of the Admiralty, might I think render good service. Lord Clarence [Paget] would know best how the Admiralty part of the Committee should be constituted; but I would suggest for your consideration that himself with the A[ccountant] G[eneral] and perhaps the Civil Lord of the Admiralty should constitute the members.[1]

Arbuthnot also drew attention to the need for close co-operation with the Admiralty—a feature of the committee of inquiry procedure.

The heads of Departments and the Naval Lords should be taken into consultation when parts of the Estimates which affect the business under their direction come under review. The jealousy of the professional element in the Admiralty has often created difficulties in our correspondence, and, *if this is to be overcome, it can only be by co-operation*.[2]

[1] Memorandum from Arbuthnot to Gladstone, 14 October 1861, Brit. Mus., G.P. Add. MSS. 44096, ff. 250–3. The committee of inquiry was not set up.
[2] My italics.

The permutation of the top Treasury officials on the committees of inquiry had important consequences for the quality of control exercised by the Treasury generally over the Civil Service. First, each of the officials with responsibility for advising the Treasury ministers obtained a valuable insight into the working of those departments under his control, and, in consequence, had a first-hand knowledge of their organization and establishment. As a factor, not only in the control exercised by the Treasury in relation to the work of the committees of inquiry, but also in relation to the day to day control of establishments, the importance of this cannot be exaggerated. The opportunities provided for the acquisition of information sometimes proved embarrassing. Arbuthnot confessed to Gladstone that while a member of the War Office Account Branch inquiry he had 'been admitted rather more behind the scenes in the War Office than properly belongs to my position as a Treasury officer. The extent of my confidential information has sometimes been rather embarrassing for me'.[1] Secondly, the continuity in the relationship between a department and the Treasury representatives ensured a sympathetic, comprehending, and uniform approach to the organizational and peculiar difficulties of each department—continuity and uniformity were particularly important where a department was undergoing a series of extensive reorganizations such as the War Office in the fifties and sixties. Thirdly, it meant that those who participated in the inquiry also advised the Treasury ministers when the reports came before them officially. A settlement reached between the department and the Treasury representatives at least was assured of a sympathetic hearing, and at most obviated the need for further detailed consideration. And if the latter meant a 'rubber-stamping', it was not an abdication of control but an endorsement of that exercised earlier by experienced and trusted representatives. Fourthly, the practice of associating the 'top Treasury' with these committees of inquiry provided within the Treasury a rich fund of first-hand

[1] He had been thrown a good deal into contact with the officers attached to the outlying departments of the War Office and had learned much from them informally on questions connected with the organization and defects of their establishments. This, he admitted, went beyond the proper limits of the inquiry. Further, the Chairman of a recent Parliamentary Committee on Military Organization had communicated with him confidentially; and the Secretary of State had explained to him frankly the views by which he had been governed in carrying out the recommendations made by that committee.

knowledge and experience of current administrative practice in the public departments. Hamilton made extensive use of this, while Assistant Secretary he customarily referred almost all important, difficult or controversial establishments' problems to the inner-group of Arbuthnot, Anderson, and Stephenson for an opinion. On the latter leaving the Treasury to take up his appointment as Chairman of the Board of Inland Revenue Hamilton said to him: 'You have been usually consulted for many years on proposed alterations in Establishments—and we shall feel the loss of your experience and judgment in that as in other matters.'[1]

TERMS OF REFERENCE AND PROCEDURE

The Treasury did not worry too much about agreeing beforehand with the civil departments the precise limits of inquiry, confident that through its majority representation it could influence the scope and direction of the investigation once it had begun. The terms of reference drawn by the Treasury after consulting the department tended, therefore, to be wide, often vague: the committee appointed in 1856 was merely instructed 'to inquire into the conduct of the business of the Home Office', a term of reference wide enough to permit a thorough investigation of the whole organization; while that which examined the Board of Trade ten years later was asked simply to consider 'the whole question of the organization of the Department with a view to the best distribution of the business and the efficient working of the office'. Where the inquiry was initiated by the War Office or Admiralty the terms of reference were generally more carefully drawn, although even here it happened that a committee was instructed 'to make recommendations for the consolidation of the departments of the War Office'. It was more usual, however, for the War Office to seek Treasury agreement to more narrowly defined terms such as those given to the committee instructed 'to inquire into the organisation of the Central Office, the number and classification of the Clerks, the distribution of the duties in the several sub-divisions of the office and the regulations affecting promotion from class to class'. But even these were interpreted so widely that the committee produced four separate

---

[1] Memorandum from Hamilton to Stephenson, 4 December 1862, P.R.O. T.1/6395A/18140. This conclusion conflicts with the common view that the Treasury had little knowledge of the working of the departments before the passing of the Exchequer and Audit Act in 1866, but see below, Chapter 15.

reports dealing with the organization and administration of practically every sub-department, from the Accountant-General's to the Militia.[1]

The committee met in the department, never the Treasury, and its proceedings were informal and private. Before the inquiry began the Treasury usually asked the department to furnish a

> general sketch in writing of the nature of the duties in each Department of the Office, and of the manner in which each person on the Establishment is employed. Much time is saved to all parties by a preliminary statement of this sort; and as it is only intended to be a guide to further inquiry it may be prepared in a summary manner, and therefore without much delay.[2]

Statements were made to the committee, oral evidence heard, and witnesses occasionally called and examined, but more importance was attached to the informal investigations which were made in the department and private discussions with senior officials and ministers. After giving evidence at the Post Office inquiry, Sir Rowland Hill commented: 'Matters are conducted in a very pleasant, though discursive manner. As regards myself, it has been rather a conversation or discussion (as though I were a member of the Commission) than an examination.'[3] The committee which looked at the War Office in 1856 held several meetings, and

> Mr Monsell [M.P., Clerk of the Ordnance] afforded the Committee the benefit of his advice and assistance on several occasions. Before arriving, however, at any conclusions respecting the Duties of the Establishment of any particular Department or Branch of what is in future to be one great Department of State, presided over by the Secretary of State for War, the Heads of each Branch affected by the proposed consolidation of the War and Ordnance Departments, the War Office and the Commissariat were consulted and they afforded the Committee the valuable aid of their advice and co-operation. . . . The Committee examined each Department, or Branch of a Department in detail,

---

[1] The first report dealt with promotion; the second, with the separation of the Accountant-General's establishment from the general establishment; the third, with the Director of Works Branch, the Barrack Department, the Army Medical Department, the Store Branch, the Clothing Branch, and the Commissariat; and the fourth, with the Chief Clerk's Department, the Librarian, the Precis Writer, the Military Branch, the Ordnance Branch, the Contract Branch, the Militia, and the Volunteer Branch. P.R.O. T.1/6602A/19181.

[2] Trevelyan to H. W. Vincent, 20 February 1856, Bod., T.L.B., xxxvi. 103–4.   [3] G. B. Hill, *Life of Sir Rowland Hill*, pp. 221–2.

together with the nature and peculiarities of the business already or to be discharged.[1]

Northcote believed that a committee's investigations led to a 'great deal of heart-burning and intrigue' among the clerks and thought it wiser on this account 'to keep the intention to institute an inquiry secret until the last moment, and to proceed with it, when instituted, rapidly and vigorously'.[2] For this reason, most committees were able to complete their inquiries and to report within a few weeks of appointment.

REPORT

To make it easier to follow the successive steps from report to implementation, the examples used in this and the next section are drawn mainly from the same five inquiries: Home Office (1856), Board of Trade (1863 and 1866), and War Office (1856 and 1864–5).

Most committees introduced their report with a general appraisal of the department's efficiency, drawing attention to any fundamental defects or weaknesses of organization uncovered in their inquiries. The committee which looked at the Board of Trade in 1863, consisting of Hamilton, Arbuthnot, and the Secretary to the Board, began their report by criticizing the inadequate opportunities for promotion, the low salaries of the senior clerks, and the haphazard distribution of the clerks, attributing these weaknesses to the fact that the department had originally been designed for consultative purposes and had therefore been organized on a different basis from that of the more common executive departments.[3] Much the same conclusion was reached by the Financial Secretary to the Treasury and the Vice-President of the Board of Trade when they reported three years later.[4]

The difficulties usually experienced in recommending changes in the organisation of the Office have, in this instance, been increased by the

[1] Report of the Committee set up to make recommendations for the consolidation of the Departments of the War Department, 3 January 1856, P.R.O. T.1/6049/20946.
[2] Northcote to Disraeli, 2 August 1866, Brit. Mus., I.P. Add. MSS. 50015, fo. 150.
[3] Report of the Treasury Committee of Inquiry into the Board of Trade Establishment, 4 July 1863, P.R.O. T.1/6433B/13012.
[4] Report on the Board of Trade, 27 November 1866, P.R.O. T.1/6751A/19696.

two-fold nature of the functions performed by the Board of Trade, namely the consultative and executive, and by the double Secretariat designed to keep the working of those functions distinct but which has led to a want of cohesion in the staff of the establishment.

Within the two branches they found that the office had been broken up into separate, fragmentary sub-divisions 'the subjects under the control of each crossing and re-crossing each other in a manner which could only have been the result of temporary arrangements for the conduct of new business imposed from time to time upon the Office'. The executive functions now heavily outweighed those which were mainly consultative, in support of which the committee listed nineteen new functions acquired by the Board between 1863 and 1866.

The most important part of a report was the committee's recommendations. Probation, promotion, salaries, the size of the establishment—any, or all, of these might be touched upon, but primarily the report dealt with organization, and it was here that the scope and thoroughness of the investigations was most apparent. No facet of organization was beyond the committee's jurisdiction, no aspect of administration too delicate or personal for them to venture a criticism or make a suggestion for improvement. The great object of the War Office inquiry of 1864–5 was, according to Arbuthnot, 'to improve the efficiency of the Establishment by breaking it up into workable sections and getting the clerks to understand that they are paid for work and not for literary distinction'.[1] More biting still was the judgement passed on the Librarian's Department of the Home Office: 'The Registry of papers as at present conducted in the Department is really useless for any practical purposes', a 'useless encumbrance' which the committee thought should be abandoned and replaced by a system of Departmental Registers.[2] Their general remarks upon the merits of the two main registering systems used in the Civil Service are interesting:

Two different systems have been adopted in other offices with various success—in some a General Registry applicable to the whole Office

---

[1] Memo by Arbuthnot (one of the two Treasury representatives on the committee), 7 January 1865, P.R.O. T.1/6602A/19181.

[2] Report of the Committee of Inquiry set up in 1856 to inquire into the conduct of the business of the Home Office, 22 July 1856, P.R.O. T.1/6258A/13006.

and in others a Departmental Registry, each branch recording the letters relating to it. As a basic rule it may be said that in Offices in which the business is of a miscellaneous character not capable of marked classification the advantage of a General Registry predominates but that in other Offices, the business of which is of a contrary character, separate Departmental Registers are more useful.

Equally interesting, the present Police Department of the Home Office derives directly from a proposal made by the same Treasury committee that an additional division should be set up to deal with police and statistical business.

If the creation of six new administrative divisions was the most comprehensive organizational change proposed by the 1866 committee which looked at the Board of Trade, the recommendation that the office of Vice-President should be abolished was the most surprising, not simply because he was one of the two members of the committee, but because the office was a political one—further evidence of the apparently boundless limits of the jurisdiction of the Treasury committees. In the report it was referred to as the most striking of all the anomalies of the Board of Trade, and the description of the 'duties' of the office, presumably written by the Vice-President himself, bears this out.[1]

Whatever may have been the original position of the Vice-President he has now fallen into the unsatisfactory state of an irresponsible officer of almost equal rank with the President of the Office. In the absence of the President he is paramount. When the President is present he has no duties whatever, except as he may undertake by arrangement with the President. He may refuse to do anything or the President may refuse to allow him to do anything: and for these reasons perhaps, he has also to fill another office which bears no relation to the Board of Trade, namely that of Paymaster-General without salary.

If the office were abolished and replaced by a Parliamentary Secretary with carefully defined duties, one of the two permanent Joint Secretaries could be dispensed with, the committee recommended.[2]

One subject rarely dealt with by a committee was recruitment, not so much on account of the Treasury's reluctance to interfere—

---

[1] Report of the Committee of Inquiry into the Organisation of the Board of Trade, 27 November 1866, P.R.O. T.1/6751A/19696.

[2] The post of Vice-President was unpaid; the holder of it obtained a ministerial salary by combining the office with that of Paymaster-General.

though this was undoubtedly generally true before 1868—but more because both the department and the Treasury preferred to discuss recruitment independently of other establishment matters. Nevertheless, as the 1856 committee demonstrated, the Treasury did not hesitate to draw attention to abuses uncovered in the course of an inquiry. In the Home Office it was found that appointments were made without any preliminary examination, or the need to complete a period of probationary service. To bring it into line with the Treasury and other departments, the committee recommended examination by the Civil Service Commissioners and six months' probation after entry.

The committees of inquiry set up on Trevelyan's initiative between 1848 and 1854 had paid particular attention to the way in which the work was divided between the clerks, and to the pattern of establishment. In the next twenty years few committees found it necessary to make recommendations about either, although those which dealt with the Board of Trade, where the work had rarely divided in practice according to the principles laid down by Trevelyan and Northcote, could not avoid doing so. The size of the establishment always attracted much attention—on many occasions the demand for more posts was the principal reason for setting up the committee. In informal consultations with those responsible for directing the work of the divisions, as well as those actually doing the work, and without the need for both sides to maintain the elaborate formality of the written procedures, the committee could discover for themselves what was needed, and better estimate how many or how few clerks were wanted. Sometimes their inquiries led to very large increases, such as that proposed by the 1863 committee which recommended a 50 per cent increase in the Board of Trade establishment, from thirty-two to forty-eight; more rarely, to a substantial reduction, such as that which followed upon the second report of the 1864–5 War Office inquiry, the object of which to quote Arbuthnot was 'to inspire new vigour into the Department which ought to lead to a reduction of clerks and I think will. Some suggestions thrown out have already been acted upon, which, leading to economy of labour, must if followed up, lead to economy in Establishment'.[1] Shortly afterwards, thirty-four temporary clerks were discharged, all of whom had been first employed upon a 'temporary basis' in 1853–4. In their third

[1] Memo by Arbuthnot, 7 January 1865, P.R.O. T.1/6602A/19181.

report the same committee proposed extensive reductions in the Director of Works Branch, the Barrack Department, the Army Medical Department, the Store Branch, the Clothing Branch, and the Commissariat. Although such large reductions were uncommon, most committees usually found one or two posts which could be abolished if duties were redistributed or amalgamated. The significance of their work in this respect is best illustrated by two comments made by Arbuthnot after serving on the committee which inquired into the establishment of the Accountant-General in the War Office.

When we began our inquiry [he wrote] the War Office strongly urged upon us the alleged necessity for adding nine 1st Class Clerks to the General Establishment. By dealing with the Account Branch separately and proposing a moderate Establishment for that Department we have gained the admission that, at any rate, no increase of the general number of 1st Class Clerks is required.[1]

Arbuthnot attributed this to the support which the two War Office officials had given to the committee, which compared favourably with his recent experience at the hands of the Accountant-General of the Navy, Sir Richard Bromley. The temptation to point the moral was too strong to resist:

It shows that contrary to the dictum of Sir R. Bromley the Treasury may know, in some cases, better than the practical Heads of Departments what is really required. Sir Benjamin Hawes [the Permanent Under-Secretary] was at first disposed, and he had as much right to assume the position as Sir R. Bromley, that we must put faith in his practical experience and give him credit for not recommending more than he had satisfied himself to be absolutely necessary for conducting the business of the War Office.

Committees of inquiry also looked very closely at salaries. New scales were recommended for all the Home Office Superior Clerks in 1856, and revised salaries for all classes were introduced into the Board of Trade when the department was reorganized in 1863. The same classification and salary scales introduced into the Admiralty were also proposed for the reorganized War Office by the 1856 committee.

After the publication of the Northcote–Trevelyan Report in 1854 the Treasury encouraged departments to promote on merit rather

[1] Ibid., 19 June 1861, P.R.O. T.1/6333A/18167.

than seniority. The informal procedure of the committee of inquiry provided an excellent opportunity for canvassing the principle. Face to face with those at whose discretion candidates were promoted or passed over, the Treasury could exhort them to promote strictly on merit, and condemn abuse wherever it was uncovered. The 1856 committee did not hesitate to condemn the practice of promotion by rule of seniority which 'has invariably prevailed in the Home Office with one exception. . . . Merit and capacity should be the main consideration in governing promotion, seniority being regarded as one among other claims to advancement', they urged. 'As a clerk rises to the higher classes, the principle of selection on account of qualifications should acquire increased weight, and we recommend that in selecting officers for the charge of Departments their perfect fitness for that responsible duty should be the sole ground of preference.' The committee also recommended that a record of attendance and conduct should be kept in the department and referred to when considering the claims of rival candidates for promotion.

In the Board of Trade the 1863 committee were concerned not so much with the observance of the principle of promotion by merit as with the inadequate opportunities for promotion, and their proposals for reclassifying the clerks and redistributing the business were designed specifically to improve that situation. The 1866 committee dealt with a slightly different problem. They found that

As a general rule Clerks are retained in the particular Branch to which they are first attached, so that it becomes a matter of mere accident how many of each Class there may be in any one. In many instances, therefore, Senior Clerks are doing the work of Juniors and vice-versa. We think that the number of each Class in the different Departments should be settled at once: that the proportion determined upon should be established as soon as possible and strictly observed for the future, and that if there are any gentlemen who are unequal to the duties which may thus be imposed upon them, their places should be filled by others who possess the requisite qualifications.

The views of the committee on the desirability of moving clerks from branch to branch within a department are particularly interesting and have a contemporary relevance.

As to transfer of officers generally we may state that we are of opinion that the Junior Clerks should be moved from time to time from one

Department to another. We are aware that this practice is in every Office generally opposed by the heads of the Departments. When a Junior Clerk has become familiar with one class of business he saves his Superior Officer much trouble, and the latter is consequently averse to giving his place to another gentleman to whom that particular kind of work is new, but we see no other way of enabling the Junior Officers to become acquainted with the whole of the business and thus to fit themselves eventually for promotion to the staff appointments. Moreover it not infrequently happens that a gentleman when employed on a class of business for which he has no special aptitude, obtains but an indifferent character for ability, who, when transferred to another branch, and employed upon subjects of a different nature, displays a talent which had been before unsuspected by his superiors. It is only fair, in this view, that such constant transfers as we have suggested should take place. With regard to the Senior Clerks, we think that, as a general rule, that they should not be moved.

It is difficult to fault this enlightened and sensible recommendation; all too often similar pleas fell upon deaf ears.

For the first of their four inquiries the 1864 committee looked at the system of promotion introduced into the War Office in 1857. The Secretary of State had decided that promotion should take place on one general line throughout all the different branches of the new War Office, and that a vacancy in any one should be filled by promoting the clerk whose qualifications and experience were most suited to the duties of it, irrespective of the branch in which he was then serving, and the individual claims of other clerks. This rule had been rarely applied, the committee found; instead, promotion had been made the reward of general merit and not to accord with the actual requirements of the Service. In almost every instance the clerk with the strongest recommendation had been promoted without reference to the qualifications needed to fill the vacancy. He had rarely been transferred to that branch in which the vacancy had occurred but had remained in his own, with a higher rank and an increased salary, continuing to perform the same duties as before. The vacant post had remained unfilled, its duties now entrusted to a more junior officer.[1] Only three of the last thirty-seven promotions had been made to the branch where the vacancy occurred, the remainder had been given to clerks who continued to do the same work as before. Arbuthnot 'was as-

[1] As few transfers were made between branches, the number of unfilled vacancies tended to even out between different branches over a period of time.

tounded with the evidence . . . of the cool abuses which arise under the present system, if anything so foolish deserves the name of system, which is a burlesque of Trevelyanism'.[1] The committee's solution was to propose the substitution of separate lines of promotion for each branch of the War Office, as had been done in the Admiralty Departments in 1832. The report concluded with a scathing comment upon the quality and industry of the clerks.[2]

It was hoped that by excluding dunces and ensuring a sufficient but very moderate test of education the efficiency of the public departments would be improved, but it would seem that, so far from this end having been attained the character of the War Office is such that, if the clerks did their work with diligence 10 per cent of their number might be reduced.

The scope of the inquiries occasionally stretched farther still, to the scrutiny of discipline, attendance and other domestic arrangements which normally were left to the discretion of each individual minister. The 1856 committee criticized the Home Office for its inadequacy in 'enforcing discipline and encouraging exertion', and proposed that the head of each branch should furnish a monthly report to the Permanent Under-Secretary containing the record of attendance and conduct of each clerk for whom he was responsible.

IMPLEMENTATION

The committee's report was laid before the minister and a copy sent to the Treasury where his official observations were awaited before any further action was contemplated. The minister's comments usually consisted of a general appreciation of the report, together with suggestions for modifying some of the recommendations, and an indication of those (if any) which were unacceptable to him. While it was unusual for a report to be accepted without some modification, in practice few recommendations proved totally unacceptable—the Treasury was almost always prepared to approve the report as it stood. Given the close collaboration during the inquiry, the scope for fundamental disagreement at the report stage was not great. Nevertheless, a serious difference of opinion could arise over the implementation of some part of the

[1] Arbuthnot to Gladstone, 26 July 1864, Brit. Mus., G.P. Add. MSS. 44097, ff. 171–8.
[2] 1st Report of the Committee of Inquiry, 1864, P.R.O. T.1/6602A/19181.

report, as will be seen as we now follow the Home Office inquiry through to its conclusion.

The report signed by Arbuthnot, Brand (a Junior Lord of the Treasury), and the Parliamentary Under-Secretary of State at the Home Office was submitted to the Home Secretary, Sir George Grey, on 22 July 1856. Perhaps because it was in manuscript, no copy was made for the Treasury. This in itself was unusual; even more surprising, the subject of the inquiry was not raised in the Treasury for nearly two years, during which time no correspondence passed between the two departments concerning any part of the report. Nearly four years had passed before the Treasury examined it.

This strange and inexplicable oversight was brought to the Treasury's notice only on receipt of a letter from the Home Office in January 1858 in which, in requesting an increase of salary for four clerks, it was revealed that the report had not been adopted 'for some reason or other' and that objections had been made to it which had not met with any satisfactory answer. The next two years were spent in persuading the Home Office to part with a copy of it, to communicate the Home Secretary's views upon it, and to explain the objections which it was claimed had been raised to it. When the report was finally shown to the Treasury in February 1860 by Sir George Cornewall Lewis (who had succeeded Grey) it was merely to point out that his request to raise the salary of Everest, one of two clerks supernumerary to the 1st Class, had been proposed initially by the committee of inquiry.

Before replying to this request the Treasury prepared a memorandum showing how far the committee's recommendations had been carried out in the previous four years.[1] As reports were normally dealt with in the space of a few weeks this document is unusual, but interesting because it shows clearly to what extent the Home Office had adopted the committee's recommendations. Without prompting or discussion with the Treasury, twelve of the seventeen proposals had been adopted or implemented, including all those which related to organization. The department had been divided into four branches, one of which dealt with all police and statistical business; a new General Registry had been established; a Supplementary Establishment introduced to do copying and other mechanical work; the principle of promoting by merit had

[1] It is reproduced in full as Appendix IV.

been accepted; and all new entrants required to serve six months' probation. The most important of those recommendations which the Home Office had not adopted related to the salaries of the Superior and Supplementary Clerks.

On 25 February 1860 the Treasury wrote to the Home Office approving the proposed increase of Everest's salary to £900 on the understanding that he continued to hold rank as supernumerary to the 1st Class until his retirement, when his job would be taken over by one of the established 1st Class Clerks—in other words, the Treasury were insisting upon the prospective reduction of the number of 1st Class Clerks which the committee of inquiry had recommended. At the same time the Home Secretary was criticized for considering the claims of individual clerks by reference to the committee's overall scheme for the establishment without adopting the whole, or a modified version of it. This was inconsistent with the usual practice, the Treasury warned him, to which Cornewall Lewis replied that he was not prepared to recommend the adoption *in toto* of the committee's proposals, but was prepared to make certain arrangements on the impending retirement of Redgrave, the other supernumerary 1st Class Clerk: principally, the appointment of one of the 1st Class Clerks to succeed Redgrave as head of the new Police and Statistical Department; the increase of the 2nd Class from four to five; the reduction of the minimum salary of the 3rd Class from £150 to £100 (as recommended by the committee); and the introduction of the Board of Trade pay scales for the new Supplementary Establishment (as recommended also by the committee). To all these the Treasury gave its approval, but again upon condition that 'the number of 1st Class Clerks is to be reduced to three upon the occurrence of a vacancy'.

There were now prepared the ingredients of a major conflict, in which the extent of the Treasury's authority to control establishments—in this instance its power to enforce agreement to a prospective reduction—was to be debated and put to the test. Battle was joined with the receipt of Cornewall Lewis's tongue-in-cheek reply: 'As regards the number of Senior Clerks, some misconception has arisen at the Treasury. . . Sir G. Cornewall Lewis does not propose to reduce the present number of four Senior Clerks which in his opinion is by no means excessive for this Office.'[1]

[1] Home Office to Treasury, 2 April 1860, P.R.O. T.1/6258A/13006.

The Treasury's answer to this was drafted by Spencer Shelley, a Principal Officer who on several occasions in the fifties and sixties demonstrated his belief in the need for strict control. It was then forwarded to Arbuthnot who had served on the committee of inquiry, approved by him, and dispatched from the Treasury over the signatures of both Hamilton and the Financial Secretary. Great care was taken to restate the case for reducing the number of 1st Class Clerks on the lines set out in the committee's report, and to reiterate that the Treasury had approved the transfer of one of the established 1st Class Clerks to take charge of the Police and Statistical Department on Redgrave's retirement only upon condition that their number should be reduced to three on the occurrence of the first vacancy.

Urged once again to reconsider the matter Sir George Cornewall Lewis had 'nothing to add to his former communication. . . . It was not [his] intention to propose any change in the number of Senior Clerks and he sees no reason for departing from the view he has already expressed'.[1] An impasse had been reached. Significantly the first moves towards conciliation came from the Treasury and not the Home Office. Hamilton noted: 'I have endeavoured to frame a Minute which I hope will have the effect of inducing the Home Office to reconsider their last letter without . . . getting into collision with them.'[2] Regret was expressed that the Home Secretary wished to close an issue which it was the Treasury's duty to raise, and the reasons for the Treasury's insistence were carefully restated. But there now occurred a slight shift in the Treasury's original position. The condition that the number of 1st Class Clerks should be reduced to three on the occurrence of a vacancy was qualified by the addition of the phrase 'unless when that event should occur there may appear to be grounds for abandoning that part of the Committee's recommendations'.[3] In return for this concession the Treasury required an assurance from the Home Secretary that the whole question of the Home Office establishment would be gone into on the occurrence of the next vacancy. There was also a veiled reference to the ultimate power of the Treasury to withhold approval from the Home Office proposals,

---

[1] Ibid., 13 April 1860, P.R.O. T.1/6258A/13006.
[2] Memo from Hamilton to Laing (Financial Secretary), 18 April 1860, P.R.O. T.1/6258A/13006.
[3] Treasury to Home Office, 19 April 1860, P.R.O. T.1/6258A/13006.

but if this was a show of strength to awe the department its effect
was considerably diminished by the admission that the Treasury
would hesitate to deprive the clerk transferred to the Police and
Statistical Department of the salary to which he was entitled as
head of it, or to leave the number of 2nd Class Clerks insufficient
for the work of the Home Office. This was the only hint of a threat
throughout the entire correspondence, and in the qualified form
in which it was uttered it was hardly likely to persuade the Home
Secretary to change his mind—certainly it did not have that effect.

Sir George Cornewall Lewis remained unyielding, neither
impressed by the Treasury's veiled threat to withhold approval
nor disposed to accept the proffered concession as a way out of the
impasse. The Treasury threat was neatly blocked: if the Treasury
condition was essential the Home Secretary threatened to withdraw his application for a pay rise for the 1st Class Clerk transferred to the Police and Statistical Department. Cornewall Lewis
had manœuvred the Treasury into a very awkward position: to
insist upon the condition would cause him to withdraw his
application and deprive a deserving civil servant on an issue of
principle of what the Treasury had already conceded to be his due.
On the other hand, to forego it meant a withdrawal, and the loss
(temporarily) of a prospective reduction. But there remained a
loop-hole through which ultimately the Treasury was able to
wriggle without too much loss of face. While the Home Secretary
was unwilling to enter into an agreement binding upon his successors, he acknowledged the Treasury's competence to raise the
question of the establishment on the occurrence of the next
vacancy in the 1st Class, or on any other suitable occasion. But
before the Treasury accepted this solution, the line to be taken in
the face of the resolution shown by the Home Secretary had to be
argued out among the senior Treasury officials and the Financial
Secretary.

Predictably Spencer Shelley was against conceding either the
increase of salary or the additional 2nd Class Clerk without acceptance of the Treasury condition attached to them. His advice to
Hamilton is particularly interesting because of the assumptions
which underly it concerning the nature and purpose of Treasury
control. In a confrontation with a department Shelley was a 'hawk'
in a Treasury of 'doves', rejecting conciliation and flexibility in
favour of a strict interpretation of the Treasury's powers. On this

occasion, and on others where he advised similarly, his advice was disregarded by Hamilton; he wrote:

I hope you will be firm on this matter. Two of the members of the Committee of Inquiry of 1856 are now in the Treasury and can explain their views. Sir George Lewis says he cannot fetter a future Secretary of State. In that respect the Treasury has a great advantage for although the Board of Treasury goes out with a change of Government the office is more stable and not subject to one man's will, and the financial and administrative functions of the Treasury partake of that stability so that *we can insist on a persistent course whether the Secretary of State of the day likes it or not.* Sir George Lewis also considers that the peculiar qualifications of the principal clerks on the Establishment form a considerable element in organising the Office, thus introducing the maximum element of uncertainty, for peculiarities being personal they can neither have predecessors nor successors. Surely the better plan is to have a well-organised system of business and then train up the men to carry it out. This is what the Committee recommend and *it should be insisted on.*[1]

Hamilton next discussed the matter with the Financial Secretary, Samuel Laing, and together they decided to withdraw the condition. Hamilton informed Shelley of this in a short note:

Considering that we have already conceded the additional salary to Mr Leslie and the additional 2nd Class Clerk—subject only to a future reduction in the number of the 1st Class Clerks as recommended by the Committee and which reduction though Sir George will not now undertake to bind himself or his successor at a future time to make, yet he admits our right to make or create—I think we cannot go back without subjecting ourselves to the charge of being influenced by pettish feeling in refusing what we have admitted to be for the public interest.[2]

This was a sensible decision. While the course recommended by Shelley was entirely consistent with the recommendation made by the committee, which the Treasury had approved, if followed it seemed bound to lead to a deterioration in the relations between the two departments, upon the preservation of which, to a large extent, the effectiveness of the Treasury's control depended. This situation, however temporary, would affect not only establishments but other Home Office business too, with which the Treasury was daily concerned. For the effectiveness of its future control

[1] Memo from Shelley to Hamilton, 2 May 1860, P.R.O. T.1/6258A/13006. The italics in this quotation are mine.

[2] Undated memo from Hamilton to Shelley, P.R.O. T.1/6258A/13006.

the Treasury had more to lose by being insistent in circumstances such as these than the indignity suffered by the withdrawal of a condition and the sacrifice of a short-term economy. The wish on this occasion to avoid seeming 'pettish' again belies that reputation for parsimony, small-mindedness, and stringent control which the Treasury has inherited from the nineteenth century. Assent was now given unconditionally, although it was felt necessary to repeat to the Home Secretary the intention 'when the opportunity shall recur, unless reason shall then appear to the contrary, to give to the Public the advantage of the reduction and saving recommended by the Committee'.[1] The reduction was made eight years later without Treasury prompting as a result of recommendations made by an internal committee of inquiry which recommended the abolition of two superior and one supplementary clerkship and the introduction of writers to do the mechanical work.

As happened so often, the Treasury's anxiety to preserve good relations with a department had outweighed other considerations, and impelled it towards conciliation and compromise. When faced by a determined and unyielding minister it almost always preferred to accept an expedient and pragmatic solution rather than risk the precipitation of conflict by a doctrinaire and dogmatic insistence upon a cherished principle. On this occasion Cornewall Lewis's intransigence may have owed something to his familiarity with the practical limitations to the Treasury's powers while Chancellor of the Exchequer from 1855 to 1858.

It must be emphasized that the point at issue between the two departments was but a small part of the committee's report; most of their recommendations, and all the substantive ones, were not only accepted by the Home Office but carried out by it without any pressure from the Treasury. In this respect the implementation of the report followed the regular pattern, although most were settled between the Treasury and the department rather more quickly, in a matter of weeks after they had been submitted, and without serious disagreement. The Board of Trade disputed only one of the several recommendations made by the 1863 committee, but agreed promptly to a compromise worked out by the Treasury. There was no disagreement between the War Office and the Treasury over the 1856 report, despite the radical proposals for introducing a uniform classification of the clerks. Similarly, the four

[1] Treasury to Home Office, 9th May 1860, P.R.O. T.1/6258A/13006.

reports made by the 1864–5 committee, which dealt with almost every aspect of the organization and administration of the War Office, were accepted, with one exception, by both departments. The Secretary of State objected only to the proposal in the first report to alter the system of promotion. He denied that clerks employed in one branch were unfitted on promotion to take up duties in another, explaining that they had not been transferred to fill vacancies in other branches in accordance with the 1857 regulations because those in charge preferred to work with their existing staff and to wait their turn for promotion. With the Secretary of State firmly opposed to the introduction of separate branch promotion, the Treasury could do little more than 'suggest for the consideration of his Lordship the expediency of laying down defined rules for the future regulation of the promotion of clerks in the different sections of the revised Establishment'.[1]

Most reports were accepted and implemented without the need for further action by the Treasury. One which was not, and which provoked a bitter dispute, was that submitted by Hamilton and Anderson to the Commissioners of Audit in 1861.[2] 'Greatly dissatisfied', they proposed substantial modifications to the recommendations made by the two Treasury men. Their letter was forwarded by Hamilton to Peel, the Financial Secretary, who having gone 'into the whole question with the industry and discrimination for which he is so remarkably distinguished' proposed to accept almost all of them. This meant an increase of establishment greater than that suggested by Hamilton and Anderson in their report. Hamilton was told of Peel's decision on 23 September 1861 and instructed to draft a Minute, which together with the report and the papers connected with it were sent off to Gladstone for his approval. Two weeks later Gladstone replied from Hawarden:

I have read the Report on the Audit Office and the letter of the Commissioners. This will I apprehend require personal discussion with Peel and Anderson. . . . I shall be glad to know besides the matters expressly treated of something more of the causes of the large increase proposed by the Treasury Committee. . . . It is a very awkward arrangement for the public to start a new establishment with a large increase in view of a compensation of which the principle is not yet determined on. But if the

[1] Treasury to War Office, 5 April 1865, P.R.O. T.1/6602A/19181.
[2] Report of the Treasury Committee on the Audit Office, 4 July 1861, P.R.O. T.1/6334B/18313.

R

absolute wants and duties of the Office require the increase that is another matter.[1]

Subsequently a meeting took place in Downing Street between Gladstone, Peel, Hamilton, Anderson and Edwin Romilly, one of the Commissioners of Audit. Hamilton was largely instrumental in arranging it, for he had urged upon Gladstone and Peel 'the propriety of giving to Mr Romilly an interview in order that he might urge himself personally the views he entertained adverse to those contained in our Report'.[2] There then ensued 'a long and angry controversy between Mr. Romilly and Mr. Gladstone', the details of which are not known.[3] The decision which was come to consequent upon that meeting was Gladstone's own, as Hamilton had occasion to remind him two years later. Hamilton's draft Minute was cancelled, and Anderson was instructed to draft another embodying Gladstone's decision to affirm the recommendations of the Treasury committee, with the addition of a senior and a junior examiner beyond the numbers proposed in the report.

On 22 November Hamilton confided to Peel that he was afraid that some objection might be taken to the tone in which Anderson had dealt with the question in his Minute, and added 'I have therefore written a Minute embodying in more conciliatory language Mr Anderson's views'.[4] Anderson had not considered the two additional examiners necessary, but as Hamilton explained further to Peel, 'I fully understand Mr Gladstone to sanction that departure from our Report, and as on the whole we have borne rather hardly upon the Commissioners I think this small concession ought to be made.'

The Chancellor of the Exchequer was drawn into the case by both the Treasury (Peel) and the Audit Department. Earlier it was shown that when the Chancellor was consulted on proposals to increase the establishment either on appeal from the Treasury or a department, he almost always favoured conciliation, sometimes obliging the Treasury officials to revise or reverse a decision made previously. In this instance Gladstone was much firmer than either

[1] Gladstone to Hamilton, 5 October 1861, Brit. Mus., G.P. Add. MSS. Letter Books, 1861–2.
[2] Hamilton to Gladstone, 9 August 1863, P.R.O. *Hamilton Semi-official Correspondence*, ii.
[3] Memo from Hamilton to Hunt, 12 July 1867, P.R.O. T.1/6729B/17137.
[4] Memo from Hamilton to Frederick Peel, 22 November 1861, P.R.O. T.1/6334B/18313.

Peel or Hamilton, who were prepared to approve Romilly's proposals for additional examiners; but for the latter's insistence upon an interview with Gladstone, it is possible that he might have obtained many more than the two additional examiners which Gladstone allowed him. Once again Hamilton's anxiety to avoid needless offence and, on this occasion, the exacerbation of an already difficult situation, is apparent in his moderation of the tone of Anderson's Minute and his readiness to concede the increase to the department. His marked preference for conciliation is the more striking when it is known that he had little respect for Romilly,[1] and when it is remembered that he was here dealing with one of the Treasury's subordinate departments.

CONCLUSION

The Treasury achieved its most complete and effective control of the Civil Service through small committees set up from time to time to investigate and report on the organization of particular departments. The manner in which it did so adds a new dimension to the concept of Treasury control in the nineteenth century, for here decision was preceded by a careful and thorough inquiry in which the department co-operated closely with the Treasury. Control by committee of inquiry was no less than that 'joint working together in a common enterprise' enjoined upon the Treasury and the departments by a later age.[2]

This is an unusual picture of nineteenth-century Treasury control. Moreover, it bears little resemblance to the methods of day to day control examined in previous chapters. Yet the frequency with which these committees were established, the thoroughness of their investigations, and the extension of their inquiries throughout the whole administrative process, made their use by the Treasury the most important method of controlling the Civil Service. With a continuous growth in the area and volume of government activity, they provided an efficient, informal, prompt,

---

[1] See Hamilton's letter to Gladstone of 9 August 1863, op. cit.

[2] This phrase best conveys the nature of the relationship between the Treasury and the departments at these inquiries. In *Control of Public Expenditure*, Cmnd. 1432, July 1961, Lord Plowden said on behalf of his committee at paragraph 13 that the relationship between the Treasury and the Departments should be one of 'joint working together in a common enterprise: it should be considered not in terms of more or less "independence" of Departments from "control" by the Treasury, but rather in terms of getting the right balance and differentiation of function'.

and cheap method of making changes in the machinery of administration without the delay inherent in the establishment and proceedings of the more formal and elaborate public machinery (such as the Parliamentary Select Committee) for which there was always a need to secure a measure of support outside the administration itself. Shielded from the public gaze, there was less pressure upon senior officials to defend and justify the organization or establishment of their departments; and in the spirit of mutual self-help which usually prevailed (for different reasons both the department and the Treasury wanted to improve efficiency), departments were both receptive to proposals made by the committee, and willing to put forward their own for consideration by it.

The discovery of these inquiries makes it necessary to revise previous estimates of the nature of Treasury control at this time. In the light of the analysis of the previous chapters (and those which are to follow) it would be misleading and generally inaccurate to describe that control, as some have done, as 'the exercise of the maximum restraint with the minimum of understanding and knowledge', and the Treasury's attitude as distrustful of departments kept purposely at arm's length—here it would be a travesty. In this, its most important particular, the Treasury's control of the Civil Service was positive, informed and founded upon a close collaboration with the departments; its attitude, constructive, purposeful, and conciliatory.

PART THREE

CONTROL OF CONDITIONS OF SERVICE

9

SALARIES (I)

ANNUAL salaries paid out of monies voted by Parliament were an innovation of the early nineteenth century. Prior to this the principal source of income of many civil servants had been fees and revenue collected by the department, perquisites, and gratuities. The intervention of Parliament, in what had hitherto been a private contract negotiated between the individual civil servant and his department, brought with it not only public accountability but Treasury control of all salaries, pensions, and allowances. Despite this, the civil servant retained his traditional privilege of petitioning about pay or conditions of work. Customarily, he submitted his pay claim, or 'memorial', to the head of his department who decided whether to recommend it to the Treasury. Subject to the final authority of Parliament, the decision to approve or reject a pay claim rested with the Treasury. Some civil servants petitioned it directly, although the practice was officially discouraged, especially where the petitioner had persuaded his patron or a friendly M.P. to solicit the Treasury on his behalf.

With the reform of the Service in the fifties the procedure for obtaining pay rises became more firmly confined to the interdepartmental channels. The Treasury now refused to treat with anybody other than a head of department, although this did not put an end to private petitioning and the use of political influence. As late as 1866 it was necessary for the Treasury to make a formal Minute 'respecting the practice of subordinate officers in the Civil

Service memorialising the Treasury without permission of the Heads of Departments', and to reiterate the general rule that no application for increased pay would be entertained unless transmitted through them.[1] Far from declining, the use of political pressure appeared to be on the increase, for a year later the Treasury drew attention to the 'growing practice on the part of gentlemen employed in the public service, to endeavour to influence this Board to accede to their applications for increase of salary or additional retiring allowance, by means of the private solicitation of M.P.'s and other persons of political influence'.[2] Civil servants were again warned that the Treasury would listen only to representations made by the head of department. Later still, in 1873, William Baxter told a Select Committee that

> The most unpleasant part, as I find it, of the duty of the Financial Secretary to the Treasury is to resist the constant pressure brought day by day, and almost hour by hour, by Members of Parliament, in order to increase expenditure by increasing the pay of individuals, increasing the pay of classes, and granting larger compensations to individuals or to classes.

He agreed, however, that most representations were now made on behalf of classes of clerks, and few on behalf of individuals.[3]

In the special case of departments subordinate to the Treasury, such as the Revenue Departments or the Stationery Office, if the head of department refused to forward an application for a pay increase, the Treasury was prepared to receive it directly from the civil servant provided that it was accompanied by a copy or statement of the refusal. In practice, however, the Treasury would not seriously consider a petition from any department, subordinate or otherwise, unless it was supported by the head of that department. When the Home Office forwarded a memorial from their Supplementary Clerks in 1865 it was held to be insufficient on the grounds that 'the Secretary of State merely sends the paper for our consideration without expressing any opinion. This is not satisfactory and before making any concession I think we should write to the Home Office and inquire whether the Secretary of State is of opinion

---

[1] T.M. 26 February 1866, H.M.T., *Treasury Minutes and Circulars, 1831–1879*.
[2] T.M. 2 May 1867, H.M.T., *Treasury Minutes and Circulars, 1880–1889*.
[3] *Select Committee on Civil Services Expenditure*, 1873, qus. 4672, 4762–5.

that the scale of these clerks requires improvement'.[1] Sometimes the negotiations between the Treasury and the department proceeded semi-officially prior to the submission of an official application, as in 1864 when Lord Russell, the Foreign Secretary, wished to improve the salaries of the junior clerks in the Chief Clerk's and the Librarian's departments, but was 'unwilling to make a proposition regarding the officers of his Department if likely to be rejected by the Treasury'.[2] Instead it was submitted in 'demi-official shape' by the Permanent Under-Secretary, Edmund Hammond, who then spoke to Hamilton about it. When agreement had been reached between them acceptable to Lord Russell an official application was made to the Treasury in the ordinary way.

AD HOC COMBINATION

Petitioning was but little changed by the reforms of the middle fifties, although individual action, now less efficacious with the whittling away of patronage, began to give way to collective negotiation. The earliest formal departmental combinations appeared in the Revenue Departments; by 1858 there were two, the Surveyors Committee, the forerunner of the present-day Association of H.M. Inspectors of Taxes, and a central committee of officers of the Excise Branch.[3] The Treasury's attitude towards these and other *ad hoc* combinations of civil servants formed for the purpose of securing higher salaries and improved conditions of work was one of uncompromising hostility, and a steady refusal to treat with them.[4] Nevertheless the phenomenon of groups of civil servants petitioning for higher salaries became increasingly common. A combination of postal workers was formed in 1854–5 to protest against the Post Office economy drive which had resulted in men doing the same work for very different rates of pay. Groups of discontented Post Office employees continued to meet and submit memorials for the next fifteen years. Throughout the sixties Customs officers complained through the Board to the Treasury about the low rates of pay of 'out-door' officers in the provinces, and about the low level of salaries in the department generally

[1] Memo from Hamilton to Childers, 23 March 1866, P.R.O. T.1/6599B/18996.
[2] Memo from Hamilton to Frederick Peel, 8 June 1864, P.R.O. T.1/6519B/17518.
[3] See B. V. Humphreys, *Clerical Unions in the Civil Service*, Chapter 3.
[4] P.R.O. T.1/7143B/19698.

compared with those paid in the Inland Revenue. In 1867 they submitted to the Treasury a petition praying for an increase of salary signed by 530 officers.

In the late sixties there was growing discontent throughout the Service, especially among the lower-paid clerks, with the low level of salaries, many of which had remained unchanged for fifteen or twenty years. After a series of sporadic petitions, departmental dissatisfaction began to coalesce. *The Civil Service Gazette*, part leader, part agitator and propagandist, sounded the call to arms in July 1872, voicing sentiments which many in the Service began increasingly to share.

The time is rapidly coming when the Civil Service as a whole must do battle with Mr Lowe and his coadjutors for a general increase of pay. And we hope for its sake that the Civil Service will enter the contest *as a whole*, and will not allow departmental jealousies to interfere with concerted action. . . . The question to be decided, and that soon, is— union or disunion—victory or defeat.[1]

Soon after, the Civil Service Salaries Increase Movement was formed, which brought together in a central committee the representatives of a large number of different departments. Its aim was to secure a *pro rata* increase of salary for all civil servants to meet rising food, commodity and other prices. The '*Pro Rata Movement*', as it was known colloquially in the Service, attracted a large measure of support among civil servants. Outside the Service, most metropolitan and provincial newspapers, with the exception of *The Times*, supported the aims of the movement. In January 1873, the central committee submitted a petition to the Treasury praying for a general increase of salaries. It was the first occasion on which a body purporting to represent the whole Service had spoken on pay, though earlier, departments had united to secure the abolition of the hated superannuation abatements.[2]

The Treasury did not attempt to answer the careful arguments about the rise in the cost of living during the last twenty years, but simply objected to the principle of petitioning on behalf of the whole Service. It warned, however, that no such general increase of salary could be contemplated without a compensating reduction in the size of establishments. After such a rebuff, there was a danger that the tenuous base of the movement might disintegrate.

[1] Leading article, 27 July 1872.   [2] See below, Chapter 14.

Repeatedly *The Civil Service Gazette* urged its readers to preserve their solidarity and to support the central committee, and not to secede from the movement and petition separately as the Treasury wanted. In May, however, both the Customs and Revenue officers forwarded separate petitions to their Boards. Neither petition was endorsed, but they were sent up to the Treasury accompanied by statements of the Boards' refusal. Despite their impressive size —that of the Customs' officers was 38½ yards long and had been signed by almost 4,000 men, while the Inland Revenue petition had over 3,000 signatures—they were summarily rejected by the Treasury later that summer.

By August 1873, *The Civil Service Gazette*, pronouncing the central committee's policy of caution, moderation, and strict regard for orthodox procedures a failure, was calling for more militancy: it was 'now time for action'. Ignoring the Treasury Minute of 1866 warning civil servants against the use of political influence, it called upon the members of the *Pro Rata Movement* to petition Parliament before the end of the session, but an attempt to do so proved abortive. Throughout the remaining months of 1873 *The Civil Service Gazette*'s morale-boosting leading articles urged the Movement's members to remain united while plans were made for a thorough ventilation of the issue in the next Parliamentary session. Before these could be implemented, a general election ensued and a Conservative Government was returned. In April 1874 a Commission was appointed to inquire into the condition of the whole Service, and was asked specifically to examine 'the possibility of grading the Civil Service as a whole, so as to obviate the inconveniences which result from the differences of pay in different Departments'. The movement now collapsed, as hurriedly convened departmental groups vied with each other to present their particular grievances and suggestions for reform to the Commission.

The first essay in collective bargaining on a Service-wide basis had emphasized the difficulty of creating and sustaining an effective and lasting inter-departmental combination within the existing departmentalized structure of the Service. More effective action had to await changes in the structure of the Service and the introduction of common Service grades. The possibility and effectiveness of such combinations was illustrated by the experience of the Association of Civil Service Temporary Clerks and Writers formed in 1871. Drawn together by uniform conditions and grievances, they were the only group to appear before the Playfair Commission with mandated representatives.

Although the efforts of these early *ad hoc* combinations and associations represented 'an awakening of a trade union movement', their activities were little more than an extension of the traditional petition privilege.[1] Unions whose function was to constantly review working conditions and to negotiate with the employer on a regular basis did not emerge until the turn of the century.

PAY CLAIMS

Civil servants with appointments on Superior and Supplementary Establishments were paid salaries upon scales rising by fixed annual increments; the remainder holding permanent appointments independently of the general classification were paid either a fixed annual salary, or upon a scale.[2] The rest of this chapter is concerned with the Treasury's regulation of salaries paid to the former group, which comprised the bulk of the Civil Service; the latter are dealt with in the next.

A department submitting a pay claim to the Treasury had to provide details of the size and kind of rise required and to give reasons. The latter tended to be briefer and simpler than those given in support of an increase to establishment, less a careful argument purporting to demonstrate an increase of business or accumulation of new duties than a plea for a concession similar to that which had been extended previously to clerks elsewhere. About seven out of ten claims dealt with by the Treasury depended to a greater or lesser extent upon a comparison with a scale which obtained in another department. A comparison with a revision of Treasury salaries was the commonest basis for claims made by the other 'first-class' departments, the Foreign Office, Colonial Office, and Home Office. The Admiralty, always sensitive about its comparative status in the departmental hierarchy, laid claim on three separate occasions to parity of esteem with the 'first-class' de-

---

[1] Humphreys, p. 35.

[2] Salaries of all officers were traditionally paid quarterly. In the lower ranks this caused hardship, and *The Civil Service Gazette* campaigned relentlessly from its first issue for monthly payments. Some progress was made, but at the time (1867) the Treasury consented to test monthly payments in the War Office, quarterly payments were still the rule in most offices.

partments as grounds for an improvement of salaries. Occasionally other reasons were given. About one in ten claims contained some reference to the additional work or responsibility of the civil servants concerned. Less frequently, mention might be made that the opportunities for promotion were limited or diminished as a result of a revision of the establishment; or that the salary scales compared unfavourably with those received by other clerks in the same department. The cost of living was rarely mentioned before 1865; thereafter the rise in food and other prices led to several demands for pay rises. Lowe thought such claims inadmissible, founded upon a 'fallacious' and expensive principle.

It is quite true that living is more expensive [he said], and that money goes less way than it did; but I do not apprehend that that is a criterion by which the Government, or any employer of labour should go. The question is whether the species of labour which those clerks do is rising in the market. I think it is not; but, on the contrary, I believe it to be falling, owing to the spread of education and the increase of competition for these appointments. I do not think it is the duty of the Government to give higher wages in a falling market.[1]

PRINCIPLE AND PRACTICE

'We find uniformity is the usual plea for increased salaries, we disclaim comparisons and the plea of uniformity in such cases and I think rightly so', wrote Hamilton.[2] Throughout the whole of the period 1854–74 the Treasury declined 'to admit a comparison between the salaries of one Public Department and another as an argument in favour of an increase'.[3] Departments were constantly reminded that appropriate salaries for each class were determined not by a simple comparison between one scale and another, but after careful consideration of the nature and quality of the duties performed by the clerks, and the opportunities for their promotion and advancement.

It would be impossible [wrote Arbuthnot and Trevelyan in 1856] to come to any satisfactory arrangement for the conduct of the Public Service on any other principle, and, if arrangements adapted with these

[1] *Select Committee on Civil Services Expenditure*, 1873, qu. 4418.
[2] Memo from Hamilton to Childers, (?)March 1866, P.R.O. T.1/6599B/18996.
[3] Treasury to Admiralty, 30 November 1866, P.R.O. T.1/6668B/19988, and P.R.O. T.1 *passim*.

views are to be afterwards set aside, on representations regarding the comparative positions of gentlemen in other departments, the inconvenient practice would come into force of adapting the service to the claims or pretensions of individuals instead of fixing the appointments with reference to the requirements of the Service.[1]

Comparisons were disclaimed by the Treasury because the nature and quality of the duties, and the opportunities for promotion, were held to be peculiar to each department. Each case was judged on its own merits, James Stansfeld wrote to Algernon West, explaining why the Treasury invariably refused to listen to arguments founded upon comparisons with other departments.[2] As Hamilton explained on another occasion:

It is the duty of this Board to consider the case of each department 'per se' and giving due weight to all the considerations which belong properly to the Department or class before their Lordships, to assign such salaries as may appear to them just, on the one hand to the public, and on the other to the public servants upon whose case they have to decide.[3]

This attitude sprang from the rooted belief that the Civil Service was inherently heterogeneous, that there were 'scarcely any two departments quite alike or capable of being made alike'.[4] All who held office in the Treasury between 1854 and 1874—with the exception of Trevelyan, Northcote, and Childers—subscribed to that belief, and even Trevelyan expressly denied the validity of comparative claims as grounds for a pay increase. 'Logically speaking it is of course true—that persons rendering equal service in equal circumstances ought as far as possible to receive equal remuneration', Stansfeld admitted to West. But it was a logic in which neither he nor other Treasury ministers and officials (with the possible exception of Hugh Childers) yet fully believed, and the consequences of which they were unable to accept in principle. 'The doctrine that we cannot have two sets of men doing the same work on different conditions . . . is fatal to all retrenchment in the

[1] Treasury to Office of Works, February 1856, P.R.O. T.1/6041A/20465.
[2] Memo, 3 December 1869, P.R.O. T.1/6962B/3910. Stansfeld was Financial Secretary and West, Gladstone's private secretary.
[3] Treasury to Public Records Office, 27 January 1863, P.R.O. T.1/6395A/18140.
[4] Memo from Hamilton to Childers, (?)March 1866, op. cit.

salaries of large bodies of officers', Gladstone told a junior Treasury minister.[1]

The Treasury was unable to accept equality in principle, to acknowledge its acceptance in official communications with the departments, partly because it was thought impossible to achieve it given the character of the Civil Service at that time, and partly because it was feared that equality once conceded could be obtained only by raising salaries to the level of those received by the highest-paid clerks. This was a legitimate fear because it was possible to point to the demands of departments for the same (higher) scale of salary which obtained elsewhere. 'I am confident that if we yielded the Foreign Office all they ask', Trevelyan wrote to Gladstone, 'it would lead to a chronic state of discontent in other Offices, which could be remedied only by a general elevation of the standard of remuneration in the Offices which rank with the Foreign Office.'[2] On another occasion Gladstone communicated a similar anxiety to a junior Treasury colleague dealing with a pay claim from the Post Office:

Have you considered the effect which this augmentation may have on similar questions? A most formidable demand has just been made on me in the name of the body of out-door Customs officers. Are you sure that concession to the P.O. demand will not affect that still larger question? And that it will have no bearing on the Post Office pay out of London?[3]

The Treasury conceived its function to be to hold down expenditure, not to encourage it even though to do so might be more equitable. The consequence of any official departure from the rule which the Treasury quoted to the departments about the inadmissibility of comparisons was felt certain to be the encouragement and multiplication of pay claims laid before it.

An increase of the salaries of one Office as inevitably leads to a demand for a corresponding increase in other Offices, as an augmentation of the Pay of one branch of the Army would raise similar expectations in the other branches. For instance, the large Establishment of the Registrar General, the rate of remuneration of which is below that of the Public

[1] Gladstone to Frederick Peel, 22 August 1863, Brit. Mus., G.P. Add. MSS. Letter Books, 1862–63.
[2] Trevelyan to Gladstone, 28 April 1854, Bod., T.L.B. xxxiii. 179–81.
[3] Gladstone to Peel, 22 August 1863, op. cit.

Record Department, is at this moment under revision and it would be impossible to resist the pressure for an increase of salaries there, if it were conceded in the case of the Public Record Department, and it would then be taken up by other departments with the result that the standard of official remuneration would be generally and needlessly elevated.[1]

Professed principle was one thing, actual practice something quite different. In all important respects there was little correspondence between the principle insistently and constantly reiterated in official communications with the departments and the manner in which pay claims were dealt with inside the Treasury. In practice comparability was inescapable—indeed, it was the principal factor in the Treasury decision, although this was never disclosed to the departments. Paradoxically, while holding firmly that uniform salaries were unattainable and undesirable, the Treasury moved inexorably towards them by the manner in which it dealt with pay claims. Privately the Treasury acknowledged similarities between departments, and recognized (at least) four different groups of departments, partly upon the basis of the political importance of their ministers, and partly upon their similarity of function. The 'first-class' departments—Treasury, Foreign Office, Colonial Office, Home Office—comprised the most important group; a second, included the War Office, Admiralty, Paymaster-General's Office and (after 1861) the Audit Office; a third, but less coherent group, was made up of all the Revenue Departments; and the fourth, comprised all those departments employing Supplementary Clerks. Pay claims from other departments were frequently dealt with by the Treasury in relation to one or other of these four groups.

The Treasury's broad objective was to assimilate the classification and salaries of the clerks within each group, although this was never admitted to the departments, nor the existence of the groups alluded to in correspondence or informal discussion with them. A pay claim submitted by a department in one of them was largely decided by reference to the level of salaries and the general classification of the clerks of the others in the same group, or by its probable effect upon them if approved.

[1] Trevelyan to Sir George Cornewall Lewis, 4 June 1855, Bod. T.L.B., XXXV. 231–4.

COMPARABILITY

Comparability was the dominant theme of the Treasury discussions on the pay claims submitted by the 'first-class' departments.[1] Two decisions are dealt with here, the first shows the Treasury acquiescing in proposals made to it by the Colonial Office based solely upon comparisons with Treasury salaries and those in the other 'first-class' departments. The second case is an even more striking example of the extent to which the Treasury was influenced by considerations of comparability: proposals made by the Home Office were modified by the Treasury principally to achieve greater uniformity between the four departments.

The starting point for the Treasury discussion of the Colonial Office's pay claim in 1857 was the preparation of a *Statement of the Classes and Salaries in the Colonial Office, Home Office, Foreign Office and Treasury*, in itself a firm indication of the direction of Treasury thinking. Reproduced below, it shows the degree to which classification and salary structure had been assimilated in the four departments by that time.[2]

TABLE I

Salaries and Classification of Superior Clerks in the 'First-class' Departments, 1857

	Chief Clerk	Senior	Assistant	Junior	A/Junior
Colonial Office	£1,000×50 to £1,250	£600×25 to £1,000	£350×15 to £545	£150×10 to £300	£100×10 to £150
Home Office	£900	£600×20 to £800	£350×15 to £545	£150×10 to £300	—
Foreign Office	£1,000×50 to £1,250	£700×25 to £1,000	£350×15 to £545	£150×10 to £300	£100×10 to £150
Treasury	£1,000×50 to £1,200	£700×25 to £900	£350×20 to £600	£100×15 to £250	—

The Colonial Office's claim to increase the minimum salary of their Senior Clerks rested largely on the fact that a recent Treasury reorganization had led to an improvement of the salaries of the Principal Officers who now received the same minimum salary and annual increment as the Foreign Office Senior Clerks. It was

[1] Colonial Office and Treasury salaries were each revised twice between 1854–74, and those of the Home Office and Foreign Office once.
[2] Memo February/March 1857, P.R.O. T.1/6068B/10559.

also proposed to raise the maximum of the Assistant Clerks and to increase their annual increment 'thus assimilating [them] to the 2nd Class of Clerks in the Treasury'.[1] Finally the two classes of junior clerks were to be consolidated and the minimum of their scale raised to place them on the same footing as the Junior Clerks in the Home Office. None of these comparisons were resisted by the Treasury, it objected only to the proposed consolidation of the two junior classes but would not press it provided that the minimum salary was made £100 'which is the same as exists in the Foreign Office and the Treasury—the Home Office being the only exception, but for what reason my Lords are not aware'.[2]

In July 1865 the Home Office petitioned the Treasury to raise the salaries of two senior civil servants promoted to higher grades. Anxious to secure the implementation of recommendations made by a committee of inquiry in 1856 relating to these and other appointments, the Treasury seized the opportunity to raise the wider issue of the salaries and classification of the whole Superior Establishment. As a result of this, Baring, the Parliamentary Under-Secretary at the Home Office spoke informally to Hamilton and suggested to him the following classification and scales of salary:

Chief Clerk	£1,000 × 50 to £1,250
Senior Clerk	£700 × 20 to £1,000
Assistant	£550 × 20 to £650
Junior, 1st Class	£350 × 15 to £545
Junior, 2nd Class	£150 × 10 to £300

Hamilton commented on these proposals in a memorandum to his minister:[3]

i. I think £1,200 quite enough as the maximum of the CC and when a vacancy takes place in the Colonial Office I think £1,200 should be the maximum there—I should say the same as regards the Foreign Office. The salary of our Principal Officers here is £1,000 to £1,200. In short for Chief or Principal Clerks in the First Class Offices, Treasury and Secretaries of State might be all £1,000 by 50 to 1,200.

ii. I think the 3 Senior Clerks who have charge of Departments might go up to a maximum of 1,000 putting them on the same footing as

[1] Colonial Office to Treasury, 12 February 1857, P.R.O. T.1/6068B/10559.
[2] Treasury to Colonial Office, March 1857, P.R.O. T.1/6068B/10559.
[3] Memo from Hamilton to Childers, 8 December 1865, P.R.O. T.1/6599B/18996.

the 5 Senior Clerks in the Colonial Office and the 5 Senior Clerks in the Foreign Office.

iii. I would omit the intermediate class of 2 Assistants making the 2nd Class or Junior First Class whichever they please to call them 6 in number and the scale 350 by 20 to 600 as in the Colonial Office and as our Second Class Clerks. And the 3rd Class might be 100 by 10 to 300.

These extensive and important modifications depended in each instance solely upon a comparison with the level of salaries in the other 'first-class' departments. The objective criteria by which the Treasury professed to be guided—the nature and quality of the duties of the clerks and their prospects of promotion—were not even discussed. Hamilton's suggestions were taken up informally with the Home Office by the Financial Secretary who was told subsequently by Baring that the Home Secretary was prepared to accept them all.

These changes, and those made earlier in the Colonial Office, made the salaries and classification of the Superior Clerks in the four 'first-class' departments still more uniform than they had been in 1857. This is shown in Table II below.

The position remained unaltered until May 1870 when the Treasury triggered off a new round of pay claims, as it had done in 1856, by radically revising the classification and salaries of its own Superior Clerks. Two years later the Colonial Office followed suit, just as the previous reorganization fifteen years earlier had followed closely upon changes made in the Treasury. The old classification of clerks was swept away, replaced by the three new Treasury classes. The salary scale for the 2nd Class was made the same as that fixed for the Treasury on the ground that 'the inducement to enter the Colonial Office should at all events as regards the lowest grade not be less than that offered by any other Government Department'.[1] But for the other two classes strict comparability was expressly disclaimed, the Colonial Secretary thinking it unnecessary to pay his Principal and 1st Class Clerks quite such high salaries as those paid to their opposite numbers in the Treasury. To all his proposals the Treasury agreed without reservation. Once again there had been no discussion of the duties 'peculiar to each department', although it could be argued that this was implicit in the Colonial Secretary's rejection of Treasury

[1] Colonial Office to Treasury, 8 March 1872, P.R.O. T.1/7240A/17614.

S

TABLE II

Salaries and Classification of Superior Clerks in the 'First-class' Departments, 1866–1870

	Chief Clerk	Senior Clerk	Assistant	Assistant Clerk	Junior Clerk	A/Junior Clerk
Colonial Office	£1,000×50 to £1,250	£700×25 to £1,000	—	£350×20 to £600	£150×15 to £300	£100×10 to £150
Home Office	£1,000×50 to £1,200	£700×25 to £1,000	—	£350×20 to £600	£100×10 to £300	—
Foreign Office	£1,000×50 to £1,250	£700×25 to £1,000	£550×20 to £650	£350×15 to £545	£150×15 to £300	£100×10 to £150
Treasury	£1,000×50 to £1,200	£700×25 to £900	—	£350×20 to £600	£100×15 to £250	—

salaries for some of his clerks; nor had the question of promotion been considered.

The classification of the clerks in the two departments was identical, but there was now less correspondence between their salaries than there had been before 1870. The difference was greater still between them and the Foreign Office and Home Office. Because pay increases were conceded separately to each department, a period in which differences reappeared inevitably followed a period of relative uniformity, but as the other departments began

TABLE III

Salaries and Classification of Superior Clerks in the Treasury and Colonial Office, 1872–1874

	Treasury	Colonial Office
Principal	£1,000 × £50 to £1,200	£900 × £50 to £1,000
1st Class	£700 × £25 to £900	£700 × £25 to £800
2nd Class	£250 × £20 to £600	£250 × £20 to £600

to petition and receive the same or similar concessions the salaries of all four moved closer together again. Thus although the salaries of the 'first-class' departments were never raised simultaneously, a pay increase tended to be uniformly applicable. By raising the minimum salary on entry to the Treasury and Colonial Office from £100 to £250 junior clerkships in these two departments became financially (though not necessarily otherwise) more attractive under conditions of open competition than those in the Home Office and Foreign Office. Accordingly, the scales of salary introduced into the Colonial Office were conceded to the Home Office four years later, the only difference being that the minimum of the junior clerks was made £200 instead of £250. There is no evidence, however, that the Foreign Office petitioned the Treasury for the same concession.[1]

The contradiction between professed principle and actual practice was nowhere greater than in the settlement of War Office and

---

[1] Their failure to do so might have been a consequence of the Treasury's refusal in May 1872 to consider the improvement of salaries in the Treaty, Librarian's, and Chief Clerk's departments without prior inquiry to determine which posts should be open to competition. See above, Chapter 4, p. 96.

Admiralty pay claims. Replying to an Admiralty petition in 1866, James Cole wrote that 'they must decline to admit a comparison between the salaries of one Public Department and another as an argument in favour of an increase'.[1] Yet three weeks later, following the resubmission of the petition, he wrote in a memorandum to Hamilton that 'hitherto it has always been the custom to compare the Admiralty and the War Office'.[2] In 1856 the Treasury committee of inquiry set up to consolidate the different War Departments had proposed that the salaries of the new War Office should be assimilated with those of the Admiralty, and this had been accepted. The degree of assimilation was considerable; the classification and salaries shown in Table IV were identical with those of four of the eight Admiralty Departments; in the others there was either no second section to the 1st Class or a slightly lower minimum in the 3rd Class.

TABLE IV

Classification and Salaries of Established
Clerks in the War Office, 1856

1st Class, 1st section	£670 × £20 to £800
1st Class, 2nd section	£520 × £20 to £650
2nd Class	£315 × £15 to £500
3rd Class	£100 × £10 to £300

Shortly after the War Office reorganization the same classification and salaries were introduced into the Paymaster-General's Office;[3] and in 1861 very similar scales of salary, but not the same classification, into the Audit Office when its establishment was revised by the Treasury.[4] The salaries and classification of more than a thousand clerks were now very similar.

An important corollary of the decision to make salaries in these departments more uniform was that an increase conceded to one of them was generally applicable to the others. The Treasury never accepted this; at no time did it contemplate a general rise in salaries

---

[1] Treasury to Admiralty, 30 November 1866, P.R.O. T.1/6668B/19988.
[2] Memo from Cole to Hamilton, 22 December 1866, P.R.O. T.1/6668B/19988.
[3] Treasury to Paymaster-General, 18 April 1856, P.R.O. T.1/6035A/6052.
[4] Report of Treasury Committee on the Audit Office, 2 July 1861, P.R.O T.1/6334B/18313.

even in this limited number of departments. Within this and other groups of departments decisions about salaries were still made piecemeal. Even so the Treasury was apprehensive of the consequences which might follow the concession to one department of a pay increase, fearing that it would lead to a chain-reaction of demands from others. 'It will be necessary for them to satisfy themselves that that Establishment occupies an exceptional position and that any concession which may be made will not be quoted by other offices as a precedent for a similar request', the Treasury replied to a pay claim submitted by the Office of the Chief Secretary for Ireland.[1] As the Treasury's principal function was to keep public expenditure as low as possible these fears were understandable and well-founded. They are apparent in Cole's advice to Hamilton on an Admiralty pay claim comparing the salaries of their senior clerks unfavourably with those received by clerks in corresponding grades in other departments. Fearing the consequences of admitting such a claim, he was worried partly about the effect upon the War Office, but mainly about the effect upon a quite separate group of departments. 'If . . . what is asked by the Admiralty is conceded, the War Office can and with fairness—claim the same boon, and if granted to both the F.O., C.O. and H.O. have quite as much right to say our salaries have always been greater than the Admiralty and War Office and we have a right to have them increased.'[2]

This recurrent dilemma was never resolved. Nor could it be until the Treasury acknowledged openly that it resulted from the way in which it dealt with claims. A satisfactory solution was impossible until clerks in different departments were regarded as belonging to one class with the same conditions of employment. But neither the Treasury nor the departments were yet ready to admit the compelling truth of Stansfeld's 'logic', that clerks doing similar work were entitled to the same pay at the same time. Before that could happen the prevailing attitude towards the character and structure of the Civil Service had to be drastically revised. This change was presaged by developments such as those described above which tended towards a more uniform salary

[1] Treasury to Chief Secretary for Ireland, 22 December 1865, P.R.O. T.1/6600A/19062.
[2] Memo from Cole to Hamilton, 22 December 1866, P.R.O. T.1/6668B/19988.

structure; those like the administration of superannuation after the
1859 Act, the codification of sick-leave rules in the sixties, and
incipient trade union activity.[1] But the greatest impulse towards a
unified Civil Service was the introduction of open competition in
1870, itself a direct assault upon departmentalism and an instrument for forging greater uniformity in salaries and classification.

When a department was awarded a pay increase, others within
the same group (or outside) with an analogous salary structure and
classification were not automatically entitled to it. The Treasury
waited for each of them to submit a separate claim and make out a
case for the extension of the same increase. The consequences
which followed the pay award to the 3rd Class Clerks in the Admiralty, while foreseen by the Treasury, were not anticipated by an
offer to extend the same concession to the other three departments
in the same group. The new scale had been recommended by the
Treasury committee which inquired into the Admiralty in 1865,
and at the time both Rivers Wilson and Cole had warned Hamilton
that its adoption would lead to demands for its application
to the other three departments. Cole alone appeared to accept the
equity of this, writing to Hamilton he observed: 'I feel however
that once sanctioned the principle will have to be extended but I
believe that what with selection in the C.S. examination it is the
only way approaching fairness in which you deal with the C.S.
generally.'[2] Hamilton did not reply to this; nor was any attempt
made to apply the scale to the other departments. Only very
rarely did the Treasury suggest anything to a department without
first receiving a proposal from it—certainly there was no precedent
for volunteering a pay rise, and hence an increase of public
expenditure, where none had yet been requested. Control of
salaries was primarily concerned with holding down expenditure,
it was therefore unthinkable that the Treasury should volunteer
a general increase upon the basis of a principle to which as yet it
officially gave no cognisance.

Rivers Wilson's prognostication was soon fulfilled, the first
claim for a similar award arriving from the War Office in November
1866. Cole did 'not see how it can be refused for although it does
not appear to me that the relative position of these 3rd Class
Clerks is the same as that of the Admiralty their prospects are bad

[1] See below, Chapters 13 and 14.
[2] Memo from Cole to Hamilton, 18 January 1866, P.R.O. T.1/6668B/19988.

enough while the boon is not a very expensive one—on a rough calculation about £400, i.e. £5 to about 80 clerks'.[1] Thus even Cole, who alone of Treasury ministers and officials had admitted the fairness of a general increase, did not argue for the War Office claim on such grounds: he did not say that the salaries and classification of these clerks were assimilated largely on the Treasury's initiative with those of the Admiralty, and that on that account they should be given the same increase. Instead he compared the opportunities for promotion—which had been the *raison d'être* of the Admiralty increase recommended by the Treasury committee of inquiry—and the cost. Hamilton, influenced by considerations of comparability, wrote to the Financial Secretary that 'I think they establish an irresistible claim to have their 3rd Class Clerks placed on the same footing as those in the Admiralty', and appended a table showing the classification and salaries of the War Office and Admiralty clerks, pointing out to him 'that they are the same except as regards the minimum of the 3rd Class, £100 in WO and £90 in Admy'.[2] It was impossible, he continued, to compare the opportunities for promotion in each department 'because while the War Office appears one the Admiralty is divided into a number of sections in which practically I imagine promotion is confined to those in each section', but conceded that the War Office had established that promotion was 'inadequately slow' and on that ground did 'not see how in future we can refuse to do for that Department what we have done for the Admiralty'. The pay increase was approved towards the end of November 1866.

During the next eighteen months the same increase was claimed by the 3rd Class Clerks in the Paymaster-General's Office on the grounds of their strict analogy with the War Office and Admiralty. In May 1868 the Stationery Office submitted a similar claim on the grounds (which were neither apparent nor conceded by the Treasury) that their salaries had been fixed on the basis of scales which operated in the War Office. With even less justification, two other departments, the Poor Law Board and the Register Office, asked the Treasury for the same increase 'consistent with arrangements adopted in other Departments'. With the exception of the Stationery Office, where it was also alleged that there had been a

[1] Ibid., November 1866, P.R.O. T.1/6646B/17284.
[2] Memo from Hamilton to Hunt, 14 November 1866, P.R.O. T.1/6646B/17284.

rise in the cost of living since the previous revision, none of these departments argued their claims on grounds other than a strict comparison with another department or departments.

The Treasury allowed the claims of both the Paymaster-General's Office and the Register Office. The reasons for its decision, and that made earlier in the case of the War Office, were explained in the discussion between Treasury officials on the Stationery Office's claim. Sir William Clerke's view was 'that the principal reasons for making the change [in the scale] . . . was the very poor prospects which the clerks in the Admiralty, War Office, Pay Office and Register General's Office had of advancement from the lowest class'.[1] Hamilton, in a confused memorandum (he stated that the new scale was first introduced into the War Office and then extended to the Admiralty) agreed with Clerke: 'The reason, and the only good one, for making the change in the War Office and also in the Admiralty and the Pay Office was that the prospects of promotion from the lowest class was so remote as to amount to scarcely anything.'[2] But this statement was contradicted by the previous paragraph where he had written that 'we gave the same advantage to the Junior Clerks of the Admiralty and the Pay Office because their scale of salaries had been *avowedly framed according to the War Office*'.[3] Apart from the Admiralty where the unfavourable prospects of promotion had been the sole reason for the increase, it is probable that as with the War Office both comparability and the opportunities for promotion were factors in the Treasury decision to approve the same increase for the Paymaster-General's Office and the Register Office—in both the prospects of promotion were comparable with those in the Admiralty and the War Office.[4] Both Clerke and Hamilton were agreed that no similar concession should be extended to the Stationery Office clerks. Their memoranda expressed the fear alluded to previously: 'If the clerks in that Office are allowed to rise by £15 instead of £10 after 8 years service I don't see how the Treasury can refuse to make that scale general throughout the Public Service', warned Clerke.[5] The same anxiety troubled Hamilton too: 'We should cautiously avoid letting the arrangement become a precedent in other branches of the

[1] Memo by Sir William Clerke, 12 May 1868, P.R.O. T.1/6826B/18586.
[2] Memo by Hamilton, (?)May 1868, P.R.O. T.1/6826B/18586.
[3] My italics.
[4] See below, Chapter 12.
[5] Memo by Sir William Clerke, 12 May 1868, op. cit.

Public Service', he wrote.[1] The Stationery Office claim was rejected. For the same reason, and also because their salaries had been settled quite recently, the Poor Law Board was refused the increase in 1868 and again three years later.

The salary scale Trevelyan and Northcote proposed for the new class of Supplementary Clerks in 1853 was an essential element of the homogeneity which they envisaged for the class as a whole. The initial uniformity was short-lived, both the Treasury in 1855 and the Board of Trade two years later (with Treasury approval) adopted new and higher scales. Trevelyan justified the Treasury's own departure from the general scale on the grounds that 'it would be proper to allow a higher rate of remuneration than has been fixed for the Supplementary Clerks under the Committees of Council for Trade and Education and other offices',[2] yet less than a year later refused the Supplementary Clerks in the Office of Works an increase because 'it will be impossible to maintain the scale of pay of Supplementary Clerks in other Offices if clerks performing similar duties in the Office of Works are paid at a higher rate'.[3] This proved to be very true, but the concern to maintain uniformity here was belied by the earlier decision made in favour of the Treasury Supplementary Clerks and the unquestioning approval given to the new scales proposed by the Board of Trade in 1857. Other departments soon began to press for pay increases: in 1858 the Treasury Supplementary Clerks petitioned unsuccessfully for another increase; two years later the Home Office asked for the scales approved earlier for the Board of Trade, and temporary clerks in the War Office for a similar increase; while in the Poor Law Board and the Office of Woods and Forests an increment of £10 was substituted for the general one of £5. Thus between 1854–60 the Treasury under Trevelyan paid no more than lip service to one of the principal unifying factors in his and Northcote's conception of a general Civil Service class, and bore much of the responsibility for the confused situation which the Treasury's own committee found when it inquired into the employment of Supplementary Clerks in the Civil Service in 1860.

Subsequently the Treasury began to pay more attention to

[1] Memo by Hamilton, (?)May 1868, op. cit.
[2] T.M. 30 January 1855, quoted in letter from two Treasury Supplementary Clerks to Hamilton, 11 October 1859, P.R.O. T.1/6206B/15985.
[3] Treasury to Office of Works, 8 January 1856, P.R.O. T.1/6041A/20465.

uniformity, using the scales adopted for its own Supplementary Clerks in 1861 as a basis for comparison when revising those of the Home Office, Foreign Office and other departments. Although four years later the employment of Supplementary Clerks was officially discouraged outside the 'first-class' departments, Childers had also directed that to achieve greater uniformity throughout the Service the salaries and classification of clerks in different departments were to be assimilated wherever possible. Within two years very similar salaries and the same classification of the Supplementary Clerks had been introduced into the 'first-class' departments.

TABLE V

Salaries of the Supplementary Clerks in the 'First-class' Departments,
1867–1874

	1st Class Clerk	2nd Class Clerk	3rd Class Clerk
Treasury	£400 × £15 to £500	£250 × £10 to £350	£100 × £10 to £200
Colonial Office	£300 × £15 to £500	£250 × £10 to £350	£100 × £10 to £200
Home Office	£300 × £15 to £400	£250 × £10 to £350	£100 × £10 to £200
Foreign Office	£400 × £15 to £500	£250 × £15 to £360	£100 × £10 to £240

Salaries in departments outside the main groups recognized by the Treasury were frequently settled by reference to one or other of them. Comparability weighed as heavily with the Treasury in the consideration of their claims as it did elsewhere. Petitioning for an improvement in 1862 the Public Records Office drew a comparison between the salaries paid to their chief officers and those paid to officers of similar rank in other departments. In discussion within the Treasury it was argued not that such comparisons were invalid, but that the one drawn by the Records Office was 'delusive'. Stephenson, consulted by Hamilton, commented:

The nature of the work which the Records officers have to perform is not, I feel satisfied, to be compared in weight and responsibility with that of many of the higher officers, with which they compare themselves, in other Government departments. . . . It is not a class of work which puts them on a par with the superior officers of the Sects of State Depts., or one of the Revenue Boards.[1]

[1] Memo from Stephenson to Hamilton, 5 December 1862, P.R.O. T.1/ 6395A/18140.

No hint of these comparisons was betrayed in the letter rejecting the claim, which contained the inevitable reference to their inadmissibility.

OPPORTUNITIES FOR PROMOTION

Although less important than comparability, the Treasury could not afford to ignore the opportunities for promotion in each department, because clerks dissatisfied with their prospects tended to petition for a pay increase as compensation. Inevitably they tended to compare their own prospects with those of clerks in other departments. The Treasury did the same, while maintaining officially that the opportunities for promotion were governed by the nature and distribution of work, and hence peculiar to each department. On one occasion Cole pointed out to Hamilton that the proportion of Senior to Junior Clerks was more favourable in the Admiralty than in the War Office 'and even if one Senior Clerk is abolished as proposed they will be the same as the F.O.'[1]

Unfavourable prospects of promotion were sometimes the major consideration in the award of an increase; that made to the Admiralty 3rd Class Clerks in 1866, for example, where the proportion of 3rd to 1st and 2nd Class Clerks was held to be 'unfavourable'—it was almost 2:1. Exactly the same proportion—273:136—existed in the War Office when the same increase was extended to the 3rd Class Clerks, although there and in the Paymaster-General's Office and the Register Office where it was applied also there were other equally important factors. In the latter the proportion was the same, 30:14, while in the Paymaster-General's Office it was slightly more favourable to the 3rd Class Clerks, 33:23. The Stationery Office was refused the same increase because it was held that the prospects of promotion were unusually favourable, slightly better than 1:2.

Contingent or prospective advantages lost on the abolition of a post were disregarded, although the Treasury was occasionally asked to approve a pay increase on that ground. Such a loss incurred by a civil servant was to be taken 'as an incident to the Civil Service balanced by favourable incidents', Customs Office clerks were told when they claimed that their prospects of promotion had

---

[1] Memo from Cole to Hamilton, 22 December 1866, P.R.O. T.1/6668B/19988.

been diminished by the reduction in the number of senior officers following the alteration of the tariff in 1860.[1]

COST

The immediate cost of a pay increase was an additional but less important factor than those previously considered, because it excluded contingent costs. The Treasury well understood that the calculation of the real cost of an increase included an estimate of the probablity of other clerks in the same department or elsewhere pressing for the same or similar concessions. The insistent denial of the validity of comparisons was the official expression of the concern with that cost. In estimating immediate cost the Treasury usually calculated the average mean cost of the proposed salaries of the establishment and compared it with the existing average mean cost of that and other departments. The table shown below was prepared by the Treasury when the claim made by the Colonial Office in 1857 was considered.

TABLE VI

Average Mean Cost of the Colonial Office Superior Establishment, 1857[2]

	Min. salary	Max. salary	Mean	Total Mean
1 Chief Clerk	£1,000	£1,250	£1,125	£1,125
5 Senior Clerks	£700	£1,000	£850	£4,250
7 Assistants	£350	£600	£475	£3,325
11 Junior Clerks	£150	£300	£225	£2,475
24				£11,175

Average mean cost for the department $\dfrac{£11,175}{24} = £465$

The average mean cost was then compared with that of the Treasury (£459) and Foreign Office (£471), the comparison being held favourable to the Colonial Office. The precise weight given to it in the final decision is impossible to tell, but that it was a contributory factor there is no doubt.

Sometimes the mean costs of two alternative scales were com-

[1] Memo from Hamilton to Childers, September 1865, P.R.O. T.1/6559A/ 10351.   [2] P.R.O. T.1/6068B/10599.

pared, as in the discussion preceding the decision to approve the scales recommended by the Home Office rather than those proposed earlier by a committee of inquiry which were lower. Commending the Home Secretary's proposal to the Financial Secretary, Hamilton was able to show that there was 'very little difference in expense—means being as follows:

Committee of 1856:	Senior Class Mean £215	
	Junior Class Mean £130	
Home Office propose:	Senior Class Mean £225	
	Junior Class Mean £115'[1]	

There was no optimum average mean cost; here again there was no fixed objective standard, only a subjective, comparative one. Moreover, the calculation of the average mean cost was at best an extremely crude comparative cost analysis, bearing little relation to the real average cost of an establishment. No account was taken of the time taken to reach the maximum, nor allowance made for the period during which a clerk might be expected to remain in the class in question. For what it was worth, the average mean cost of an establishment in any particular year ought to have included the actual salary paid to each clerk, but not until 1884 is there any sign that the Treasury was aware of the limitations of mean cost calculations made in this way.[2]

One other factor, always considered and occasionally decisive, was the time which had elapsed since the last revision of the establishment. The Treasury particularly disliked disturbing arrangements which had been made after a careful inquiry by a Treasury committee, especially when they had been in operation for only a short time.

SCALES AND INCREMENTS

The question of what salary each clerk was to receive following the introduction of a new scale was resolved by reference to Treasury rules laid down in 1855.[3] Briefly, a clerk whose previous salary was

[1] Memo from Hamilton to Frederick Peel, 23 September 1861, P.R.O. T.1/6309A/11602.
[2] On 12 March 1884 a Treasury circular, 'Average Salary', was issued to all departments pointing out the 'inaccuracy of the common method of calculation' and suggesting how the mean salary of an office or class should be calculated in the future. P.R.O. T.1/7622A/16980.
[3] The rules are quoted in a Treasury letter to the Colonial Office, February 1857, P.R.O. T.1/6068B/10559.

less than the minimum of the class to which he was transferred on the new scale was entitled to the minimum immediately. Where his previous salary was more than the minimum, but less than the maximum of the new scale, he retained his old salary, and his annual increment was calculated from the same date as before but the rate of it and his maximum were now those of the new scale. If, however, his previous salary was equal to or higher than the maximum of the new class he kept it until by promotion he attained to a higher. Normally the Treasury refused to give retrospective effect to new scales of salary.

Annual increments became widespread in the service after the Napoleonic wars. Salary increased in proportion to length of service; extraordinary merit or the performance of higher duties were proper grounds for promotion and had nothing to do with reaching the maximum of a class, the Treasury told the departments.

An increment between the minimum and the maximum of a class whether annual or periodical, is to be regarded as the increased remuneration consequent upon an increased period of service faithfully performed. Whenever therefore a Civil Servant of the Crown either receives an immediate pecuniary advantage by being allowed to rise to a higher maximum than that already attained by such officer, the first increment will not accrue until a further service shall have been performed.[1]

Each head of department was required by Treasury Minute to make careful inquiry and certify in writing that a civil servant deserved his annual increment by virtue of his diligence and good conduct. The award, or the reason for withholding it,[2] was recorded in a book available to everybody in the department. These rules were laid down in 1855, but as their enforcement did not rest with the Treasury there was no guarantee that they were complied with in each instance.[3] From its inception in 1834 the Poor Law Board customarily calculated increments from the beginning of the financial year without reference to the date of appointment or promotion, continuing to do so until 1867, during the whole of which time the practice remained undetected by the Audit Office,

---

[1] Treasury to Audit Office, 13 December 1861, P.R.O. T.1/6334B/18313.
[2] For an example of this see P.R.O. T.1/6839D/19456.
[3] T.M. December 1855, H.M.T., *Departmental Arrangement Book*, iii.

as Hamilton was quick to point out to the Comptroller and Auditor-General.

Normally the Treasury refused to give retrospective effect to the increments of a newly approved salary scale, but it could occasionally be prevailed upon to do so when there had been unusual delay in the final settlement. A departure from the general rule was justified only by 'very peculiar circumstances' Hamilton told the War Office when they asked for authority to back-date the promotion of clerks on the newly revised establishment, but later Hamilton changed his mind, writing to his minister:

As the War Department urges the matter so strenuously I thought it desirable to ascertain the cost of it. I find that it is only £130. 12. 10. Perhaps therefore it might be expedient to make the concession on the grounds stated in the last letter of Sir E. Lugard it being understood that no claims for back-pay can be admitted.[1]

The Financial Secretary agreed, and retrospective effect was given to the clerks' promotion and hence their increments, a further illustration of the Treasury's disposition to subordinate principle to expediency when a department urged its case strongly, and the cost of doing so was not great.

SALARY ON PROMOTION

On promotion a clerk of the Superior or Supplementary Establishment received the minimum of the higher scale, although if his previous salary was greater he was allowed to retain it until he reached an equivalent point on the new scale. A temporary clerk or writer appointed to the establishment was entitled only to the minimum salary, for although that might be less than his previous earnings 'he acquires the advantage of an annual increment as well as the hopes of ultimate promotion and this affords a compensation for a temporary loss'.[2] The Treasury was often asked, and occasionally agreed, to relax both these rules. Twice within eight weeks the Colonial Office asked it to make an exception to the second. In August 1870 the Treasury refused to allow a copyist on his appointment to the Supplementary Establishment to receive £120 in consideration of his previous earnings in the department, and

[1] Memo from Hamilton to Frederick Peel, 6 September 1862, P.R.O. T.1/6392B/17889.

[2] Memo from Hamilton to Stephenson, 18 April 1860, P.R.O. T1/6280A/19564.

required him to start at £100, the minimum of the junior class. The month before the Colonial Office had had a similar request turned down, when a copyist who had served seven years in the department was not permitted to start at £200, the maximum of the junior class, on his appointment to the Supplementary Establishment. He gained 'an improved status by the change and my Lords must decline to agree to any departure from the established scale in order to make this particular promotion more favourable'.[1]

Thus far the two cases had proceeded similarly with the same result. On 2 December 1870 the second copyist's claim was resubmitted, the Colonial Office arguing that the payment of a salary of £200 would represent a saving on his previous earnings. Immediately before and after the receipt of the claim, Rivers Wilson, Lowe's private secretary, received semi-official memoranda from the Colonial Office urging and repeating the necessity for it. 'The CO have privately urged this strongly', he informed the Chancellor. 'It seems reasonable and it would certainly be hard to let Mr Adrian drop from £230 to £100. There are plenty of precedents.'[2] Lowe was concerned more with the way in which the clerk was to be recruited to the establishment than with his salary, and as soon as it was confirmed that the appointment had been recommended before the introduction of open competition he was quite prepared to allow him to start at £200. There is a striking contrast in these two cases between the official and semi-official pressure brought to bear by the Colonial Office. Through the usual official channels they failed to obtain Treasury approval, but by exerting discreet but persistent pressure upon Rivers Wilson who had the ear of the Chancellor, they succeeded in obtaining a reversal of the decision made originally in the more important and contentious of the two claims.

A serious and potentially damaging dispute between Hamilton and the Financial Secretary was provoked by a similar claim in 1869. It began with a request from the Copyhold and Tithe Commissioners to appoint a temporary clerk, Taylor, to a permanent clerkship on the establishment at a salary above the minimum of the scale. Taylor, whose annual earnings previously had been about £170, was unwilling to accept £100, the minimum of the

[1] Treasury to Colonial Office, 3 August 1870, P.R.O. T.1/7030A/22645.
[2] Memo from Rivers Wilson to Lowe, December 1870, P.R.O. T.1/7030A/22645.

junior class, and the Treasury were asked to approve payment of £130 on the grounds that it was in the public interest to retain his services because he had acquired valuable experience of the department's business. Hamilton and Sir William Clerke both supported the application, subject to the usual condition that Taylor should remain at £130 for two years by which time the annual increment of £15 would have brought him to that point on the scale. Curiously, Hamilton invoked the general rule relating to salary on transfer from one department to another to justify the claim in his memorandum to the Financial Secretary: briefly, that a civil servant transferred in the public interest should not suffer financially. But Taylor was here receiving an appointment in the same department, and previously, the general rule relating to salary on promotion had been applied (or relaxed) in similar cases. While it was possible to argue that the retention of Taylor's services was in the public interest, equally it could be argued as the Treasury had done many times before, that a permanent appointment and the expectation of a higher salary was adequate compensation for any immediate loss of income.

It was not on this ground, however, that the Financial Secretary, Acton Smee Ayrton, objected to the proposal; he was much more concerned with the principle of appointing a temporary clerk to the establishment without examination or any element of competition. 'I think this practice opens the door to very great abuse and I do not desire to encourage it', he wrote to Hamilton.[1] In a long memorandum the Permanent Secretary argued the case for the Commissioners' proposal, suggesting for Ayrton's further consideration whether his decision, if adopted as a general rule of the Service, would not be uneconomical and prejudicial. Instead of exercising their patronage and giving a nomination to a personal friend, the Commissioners had found a man in their own office who had acquired experience in the very business in which the new clerk was to be employed. Taylor with his six years' experience was better worth £130 than a novice with £100 for the first year and £115 for the second, he pointed out. Despite this persuasive pleading Ayrton drafted a letter refusing the request and stipulating that Taylor should start at the minimum salary.

On 11 May 1869 the Commissioners submitted the claim for the Treasury's reconsideration. Replying to it personally Ayrton now

[1] Memo from Ayrton to Hamilton, 14 April 1869, P.R.O. T.1/6878B/10528.

T

called for details of the work performed by Taylor and the clerk whose position he was to fill, which were supplied in a letter the following month. Again Hamilton commended the application to the Financial Secretary on the grounds that it would be 'both economical and advantageous for the public and only fair as regards [Taylor]'.[1] Ayrton's reply to this was unequivocal: 'I entirely dissent from the principle and practice involved in the proposals of the Commissioners.'[2] Hamilton's next step, without precedent in the previous fourteen years, was to appeal over the head of the Financial Secretary to the Chancellor of the Exchequer. 'I am sorry to intrude upon you', he wrote to Lowe, 'but being at issue with Mr Ayrton on a matter of some importance to the public service I am obliged to ask you for a decision.'[3]

The Chancellor's verdict was a personal triumph for Hamilton. 'There is much justice in what Mr Ayrton urges as to the principle of this transaction but it is so plainly for the public interest in this particular case that I am willing to aquiesce in the proposal of the Commissioners', Lowe wrote.[4] Hamilton's high-handed action in what was after all a matter of no great importance was probably undertaken in the knowledge that he was assured of a sympathetic hearing from Lowe, who in common with his senior advisers was finding Ayrton an increasingly irritating and irksome Financial Secretary.[5] Nevertheless, such an appeal and its consequences were not calculated to promote a better understanding between Hamilton and Ayrton, and had the latter remained much longer at the Treasury Hamilton's victory might have been bought dearly in terms of harmony and understanding at the top of the Treasury. A few months later, however, Ayrton was appointed First Commissioner of Works.[6]

It is interesting to compare this case with that discussed above:

[1] Memo from Hamilton to Ayrton, 6 July 1869, P.R.O. T.1/6878B/10528.
[2] Memo from Ayrton to Hamilton, 8 July 1869, P.R.O. T.1/6878B/10528.
[3] Memo from Hamilton to Lowe, 8 July 1869, P.R.O. T.1/6878/10528.
[4] Memo by Lowe, (?)July 1869, P.R.O. T.1/6878B/10528.
[5] See below, Chapter 15, pp. 336–7.
[6] 'Let us congratulate the entire service on the banishment of Mr Ayrton from the Treasury', commented *The Civilian*. 'It was not to be supposed that the only public man in England who has ever insultingly reproached our widowed Sovereign for her grief would show any sympathy for mere Government clerks. ... Insolent in demeanour, and as ignorant of the true functions of his office as he is unlearned in art, he scornfully rejected every application for the redress of grievances, no matter how powerfully supported by the most distinguished officials in his department.'

the problems, and the circumstances in which they arose, were almost identical, the Permanent Secretary different. Characteristically Hamilton, the arch-pragmatist, was quite prepared to relax the general rule, though his motives for doing so after Ayrton's first refusal may not have been wholly concerned with the public interest. Lingen's adherence to the general rule when faced by the same problem in similar circumstances was likewise typical of his more doctrinaire, uncompromising attitude towards other departments—at this time he was engaged simultaneously in trying to bring about greater uniformity in Civil Service recruitment and to stiffen the conditions governing the award of allowances.[1] Equally interesting is the fact that both cases were resolved by Lowe, who twice preferred expediency to principle. Although he did this on a number of occasions—sometimes (to their embarrassment) against the concerted advice of his Financial Secretary and senior advisers (though never in a matter concerning recruitment where he was even more inflexible than Lingen) —there are as many examples of his taking a firm stand in support of an established rule or cherished principle.

SALARY ON TRANSFER

Before 1860 the Treasury was guided solely by precedent and past practice in deciding the amount of salary to be paid to a clerk transferred to another department, but as this had led to some inconsistency it was thought desirable to establish a more regular procedure.[2] This was done, typically, not after abstract consideration of the general problem, but in a thoroughly empirical fashion by reviewing *ad hoc* decisions made in five previous cases, in much the same manner that sick-leave rules were codified by the Treasury a few years later.[3] From this review 'emerged' the rule that a civil servant transferred to another department for the convenience or advantage of the Public Service received his former salary and was placed in as good a position with regard to salary and increments as the circumstances of his new appointment permitted. If he chose to move voluntarily, having been nominated and then appointed, he was paid the minimum of the scale and had no claim to his old salary.

[1] See below, Chapter 11, p. 273.
[2] Treasury to Audit Office, 26 November 1860, P.R.O. T.1/6282A/19866.
[3] See below, Chapter 13.

Subsequently it was decided that a clerk transferred in the public interest was not entitled to the immediate benefit of annual increments when he retained his previous salary, although in practice this rule was interpreted very liberally by the Treasury. The rule governing voluntary transfer was not always applied literally either; in some cases the Treasury allowed clerks to keep their old salaries, and one, at least, was granted an increment immediately. The case of two others denied increments is rather more interesting. Three times the Treasury rejected their claim. On the fourth occasion the Poor Law Board submitted ten precedents purporting to support it, but the Treasury, who disliked departments quoting precedents in support of exceptional applications, denied the analogy of eight of them. Two alone were in point, it was conceded, and they were disposed of neatly: 'Admitting that an irregularity has in their case occurred it is obvious from the persistency with which they are quoted in support of this application that no further precedent should be sanctioned if the rule, which is applicable to the public service generally and has been in operation at least since 1852, is to be maintained at all.'[1]

Despite their persistent entreaties the Poor Law Board had obtained nothing, their strategy comparing unfavourably with that employed by the Colonial Office in the case discussed earlier. Whereas the latter had used private diplomacy to achieve their end, the Poor Law Board had embarked upon a major offensive. The pressure exerted by the Colonial Office had been discreet and shrewdly directed: the Poor Law Board had relied solely upon official channels, and, misguidedly, the weight of precedent. No attempt was made to argue the case informally by letter or in discussion with Treasury ministers or officials. While it is by no means certain that the Treasury would have been more willing to agree, there is no doubt that when a department approached the Treasury semi-officially it was more likely to obtain the reversal of a previous decision than when it relied wholly upon official channels.

CONCLUSION

Four general points may be made about the way in which the Treasury dealt with pay claims. First, salaries were settled by arrangement between the Treasury and the head of department,

[1] Treasury to Poor Law Board, 6 July 1868, P.R.O. T.1/6821B/17977.

to whom the individual clerk or (increasingly) groups of clerks addressed a petition praying for an increase. Second, a pay rise was never applied generally throughout the Service, or even to two departments simultaneously. To have done so without first receiving a claim from the department or departments concerned would have been contrary to the general practice of the Treasury at this time: only very rarely did the Treasury propose anything to a department without having first received an official communication from it—certainly the Treasury never volunteered an increase of expenditure. Third, in fixing salary scales there was little correspondence between the principles the Treasury professed to the departments in official dispatches and the manner in which salaries were settled in practice within the Treasury. Officially the Treasury maintained that salaries were determined only after a consideration of the nature and quality of the duties performed by the civil servants and their opportunities for promotion; as these were held to be peculiar to each department each pay claim had to be judged on its own merits. In practice neither the departments nor the Treasury subscribed to that doctrine, the former expressly repudiating it by their persistent pleas to have their pay claims judged by reference to salaries elsewhere. Among civil servants, now less dependent upon the support of an influential patron for advancement, the advantages of concerted action were becoming increasingly attractive, and groups in departments began, almost for the first time, to compare their duties and conditions of employment with those elsewhere. If as yet inter-departmental petitioning was not significant, growing discontent among the temporary clerks and writers, a class common to almost all departments, was to lead directly to the formation of the first formal Civil Service combination in 1871.

Repeatedly and insistently the Treasury denied the validity of comparability as a criterion in fixing salaries, but in practice, a consideration of it was the prime determinant in its own decisions. The contradiction is explained by the understandable and well-founded fear that if the validity of comparability was acknowledged it would inspire a 'multiplicity of demands' and trigger off a chain-reaction of pay claims. Paradoxically, the Treasury's private concern with comparability led to the recognition of groups of departments, within each of which salaries and classification were compared and roughly assimilated—though even here pay claims continued to be dealt with piecemeal and awards made separately.

Lastly, it was held generally in the Treasury (and by Hamilton in particular) that uniform salaries were unattainable given the character and structure of the Civil Service, and undesirable because likely to be achieved only by a general levelling up. Where a uniform scale existed, by virtue of its introduction separately into a number of different departments, the Treasury never for a moment contemplated preserving that uniformity by raising salaries simultaneously.

The Treasury's concern with salary did not end with the settlement of a pay claim, it had also to decide where each clerk was to be placed on the new scale. Other questions which arose from the payment of salary—the award of the annual increment and the amount of salary paid on promotion or transfer—were likewise subject to Treasury regulations. Some of these were precisely drawn, but most 'emerged' from precedent and past practice—all of them were interpreted loosely and applied flexibly and with great forbearance, relaxed almost as often as they were enforced. The main reason for this was explained by the Principal Officer of the Finance Division:

In all departments a change of scale or classification leads to individual cases of comparative hardship. . . . The difficulty in dealing with these cases is that if you make an exception in one instance it becomes difficult to refuse redress in other similar cases which are sure to be brought forward.[1]

[1] Memo by M. H. Foster, 2 November 1868, P.R.O. T.1/6826B/18586.

10

SALARIES (II)

THE salaries of senior civil servants—including the Permanent and Assistant Under-Secretaries, the Principal Officers in the War Office and Admiralty, and those with professional qualifications—were negotiated separately from those of the Superior and Supplementary Clerks. As a class they remained unorganized, petitioning the Treasury not as a group of 'higher civil servants' or professional officers, but individually through their departments. The procedure was very similar to that described in the previous chapter, with the important difference that the Treasury was sometimes asked to raise a civil servant's salary without altering the scale fixed for his post.[1] This type of pay increase is referred to hereafter as 'personal'.

REJECTION

One in five claims were rejected by the Treasury, most of them requests for a higher scale. Other things being equal, the Treasury was more likely to object to claims which entailed a permanent increase of expenditure such as these, than 'personal' increases whose cost was limited by the civil servant's tenure of office. None of the rejected claims was submitted for the Treasury's reconsideration, nor were they supported by semi-official representation to the Treasury ministers or officials. To overcome the strong objection or serious doubts which the Treasury entertained in each of these cases persistent entreaty, official and semi-official, would probably have been required, similar to that employed in support of those claims which were eventually approved by the Treasury after an initial refusal.

Most commonly claims were rejected because the department failed to prove to the Treasury's satisfaction that the work done by the civil servant had materially increased or become more ardu-

[1] Occasionally this was done for a Superior or Supplementary Clerk who had reached the maximum of his class but was ineligible for further promotion.

ous. In 1862 the Secretary of the Lunacy Commission was refused an increase because

It does not appear to their Lordships that the increase in the business transacted by the Commission which rendered it necessary to add to the working staff furnishes in the present case a sufficient reason for raising the salary of the Secretary. My Lords have to observe that there are attached to the Commission 6 Commissioners with salaries of £1,500 each, in addition to the Earl of Shaftesbury and other gentlemen who serve on the Commission gratuitously—under such circumstances by an arrangement of the business the duties and responsibility of the Secretary, it seems to my Lords, might be lightened, and they consider that the salary of £800 is adequate for the office.[1]

The fear of inconvenient (because expensive) precedent and the extension of a concession to a number of departments, referred to in the previous chapter, appeared in a similar form in the Treasury discussion of the salaries paid to senior civil servants. Petitions from the War Office and Admiralty, where there were a large number of senior civil servants with similar duties, were especially liable to evoke it. An example of this occurred in 1861 when the Admiralty argued that the salaries of their Principal Officers compared unfavourably with those received by officers in the War Office who did similar work. Discussing the validity of a comparison between the salaries of the two departments with Hamilton, Arbuthnot pointed out that it raised several difficulties 'and the fear of inconvenient precedent arises'.

Can we raise the salaries of the Heads of Departments in the Admiralty without increasing also those of the permanent Lords of the Admiralty? When we come to comparison with the W.O., difficulties accumulate. The salary of the Acct. Gen. at the W.O. is £1,200 p.a. without any increase. That of the Acct. Gen of the Navy is £1,000 p.a. besides an allowance of £300 p.a. for controlling the Naval Prize Fund, and a house of £300 p.a.—in all £1,600 p.a. . . .

. . . If the principle of comparison is to apply we could not raise the salary of the Acct. Gen. in the Navy without conceding the same increase to the Acct. Gen. in the W.O., an officer who, tho' not possessing the same ability as Acct. Gen as Sir R. Bromley, is efficient and very zealous, and could show claims, founded on extent of work and responsibility to have his office put on as good a footing as that of the Acct. Gen. of the Navy. Admit, however, his claim, and the Chief Clerk of the

---

[1] Treasury to Home Office (the Lunacy Commission was a subordinate department), 13 June 1862, P.R.O. T.1/6361/9955.

W.O., his superior in standing in the W.O. Establishment, and possessing, in the opinion of the Under-Secretary, at least, equal merits, would think himself hardly used if he did not obtain the same boon. A concession to him, however, would probably react as a precedent for some further increase in the Admiralty, and also create an invidious comparison with regard to the position of the Asst. Under Sect. of State. Then, as to the comparison between the heads of the Depts. It may be admitted that there does not appear to be any ground on which the Director General of the Medical Department in the Army should have a higher salary, viz. £1,500 p.a. than that of the officers of corresponding rank in the Admiralty, viz including house allowance £1,300 p.a. But is the former too much or the latter too little?[1]

Hamilton endorsed these views in a memorandum to his minister, and told him that the purpose of the inquiry which the Admiralty had proposed would be to raise salaries by a comparison with those in the War Office 'on the supposition that the scale of salaries in the War Department is such as we approve of as a standard'; but conceded that the Admiralty scales required amendment 'for we have since the large increase of the Army almost admitted by our decision that the head of a large department in the great services is to receive £1,500.'[2] Nevertheless, it was thought advisable to ask the Admiralty to provide more details of the Principal Officers' duties and responsibilities before deciding further. There the claim rested: no reply was received from the Admiralty; no change was made in salaries.

On some occasions it was not so much that the department had failed to make out a case to the Treasury's satisfaction, as that in its opinion no case could be made out. The salary of the Chief Clerk of the Foreign Office, for example, was higher than that of any other Chief Clerk in the Civil Service. Whatever the nature of his increased work and responsibility as represented by the Foreign Office, in no circumstances was the Treasury prepared to allow his salary to be raised further—it was an 'unreasonable application'.

MODIFICATION

Nearly half the claims made on behalf of senior administrative and professional officers were modified by the Treasury before

---

[1] Memo by Arbuthnot, 12 January 1861, P.R.O. T.1/6296A/3881.
[2] Memo from Hamilton to Peel, 17 January 1861, P.R.O. T.1/6296A/3881.

approval. The modification was the same in each instance, the substitution of a temporary 'personal' increase for a permanent change in the fixed salary scale. It was an expedient which commended itself to the Treasury, a compromise between its aim to resist all increases of public expenditure and the sometimes irresistible demands made upon it by departments anxious to secure an improvement of salary for a senior officer. From it the Treasury and the department derived some part of the different satisfac which each sought: the Treasury could take comfort that it not agreed to a permanent increase of public expenditure, while department had satisfied a discontented officer. In practice the Treasury usually gained very little; a civil servant's claim to receive the same salary and emoluments as his predecessor was difficult to resist; and in some cases the distinction between the fixed salary attached to the post and that paid personally to the office-holder became blurred, and the intention to return a successor to the fixed scale forgotten or disregarded.

Doubt or anxiety about the necessity for an increase was not by itself sufficient to prompt the Treasury to propose modification: what distinguished these applications from those which were rejected was the pressure put upon the Treasury by the departments. While the Treasury might remain unconvinced that the department had made out a satisfactory case, it gave way when it found it inexpedient to resist the pressure put upon it, or found that pressure difficult to resist. In many cases the compromise which resulted was both the expression of continuing Treasury uncertainty or anxiety and a tribute to the effectiveness of departmental pressure.

Sometimes the pressure was entirely official. Twice the Treasury declined to raise the salary of the Secretary for Military Correspondence at the War Office. Even after the third submission it remained unconvinced of the need to do so, but allowed him a 'personal' increase.

While my Lords retain their opinion as regards the proper salary to be attached to the Office of the Secretary for Military Correspondence as originally constituted and in its normal condition, yet considering the great increase which has taken place in the duties since [Col. Sir Henry Storks] was appointed to the situation and the important public advantage derived from his assistance my Lords do not feel justified in any longer withholding their consent from the proposed augmentation to his

salary... provided that it be clearly understood that £1,200 will
continue to be the fixed salary of the office and will be the amount
received by the holder's successor—the additional £300 being granted
as a special allowance with particular reference to the holder's claims.[1]

As the Treasury was reluctant to reverse a decision once made,
pressure could be applied more effectively and with greater assurance of success before the claim was officially rejected. Until the
Treasury had committed itself to a course of action there was
opportunity to argue the case, to meet objections and dispel
doubts. Some departments took advantage of this opportunity
to urge their case further in semi-official letters and memoranda
to the Treasury ministers and senior officials—but objections were
best discussed and reassurances offered in conversation. Sometimes
the Treasury granted an interview to the departmental minister or
one of his senior advisers; on other occasions the Financial Secretary or one of the senior Treasury men would go round to the
department to seek further information or to discuss privately
official objections. Hunt, the Financial Secretary, inquired personally at the Home Office about a proposal to raise the salary
of the civil servant in charge of the Roads Branch, spoke to the
Home Secretary about it, and came away with a detailed memorandum of the new business dealt with by him.

A promise of 'favourable consideration' or even unofficial consent was sometimes obtained from the Chancellor of the Exchequer
or the Financial Secretary before the application was submitted.
A written promise given privately by Gladstone to the Colonial
Secretary in 1860 obliged the Treasury to approve a pay claim of
the kind to which strong objection had been made on previous
occasions. But for Gladstone's prior agreement it seems certain the
Treasury would have objected to the increase and in all probability have rejected it—a 'personal' increase was as far as it dared
go without actually turning it down.

The kind of pressure employed by a department and its effect
upon the Treasury is apparent in the discussion of proposals
made by the Post Office in 1859. At first both the Financial Secretary and his senior advisers were agreed that an increase to the
salaries of the Assistant Secretaries and the Chief Clerk was unjustified. Hamilton thought the claim inadmissible, while Stephen-

[1] Treasury to War Office, September 1858, P.R.O. T.1/6155A/19493.

son argued that the reasons given by the Post Office were insufficient to justify such large increases, especially as their salaries had
been considered and settled five years ago by a Treasury committee of inquiry. Northcote, who with Trevelyan had reported on the
organization of the department at that time, was reluctant to disturb the arrangements which they had then made, feeling that there
was a 'good deal of objection to this sort of increase within so few
years of a careful revision of the Office. On the whole I fear we
cannot accede to the proposed increase without giving occasion
to similar requests from other departments, and possibly from
other officers in the Post Office'.[1]

Before submitting the application, the Secretary of the Post
Office, Rowland Hill, had mentioned it to Northcote, expressing
the hope that the Treasury would consent to the proposed increase, 'or that we would give him an opportunity of explaining it
before we decided against it'.[2] Northcote had promised a 'favourable consideration'. After the claim had been received by the
Treasury, Rowland Hill got in touch with Hamilton semi-officially,
sending him a memorandum 'which will I think afford the information you require'.[3] Despite all this it still seemed improbable
that the Treasury would agree to the increase. However, 'before
finally deciding on the adoption or rejection of the proposal I think
we had better send for Mr. Hill and see him together', Northcote
wrote to Hamilton, mindful of his earlier promise. At the meeting
Rowland Hill was able to persuade the two Treasury men that
there was a case for allowing some increase to the Assistant
Secretaries and the Chief Clerk, but not of the necessity for permanently altering the salaries of their posts. Northcote then wrote to
Hamilton:

Upon further consideration of the Post Office case, and after our
conversation with Mr. Rowland Hill I am disposed to think that there
is some reason for increasing the salaries of the present Assistant Secretaries upon whom no doubt very important and difficult duties have
devolved. . . . I think however, that the increase asked is both too large
in itself (due regard being had to the position and salaries of other officers
in the P.O. itself and in the other Revenue Departments), and to make

---

[1] Memo from Northcote to Hamilton, 8 March 1859, P.R.O. T.1/6188B/
9473.　　　　　　　　　　　　　　　　　　　　　　　　[2] Ibid.
[3] Semi-official letter from Rowland Hill to Hamilton, 25 February 1859, with
memo enclosed, P.R.O. T.1/6188B/9473.

it in the form of a permanent increase to the salary of the office is objectionable.[1]

He proposed to add £100 to the salary of each of the Assistant Secretaries, raising them to £1,100, and to give an extra £50 to the Chief Clerk. Before these increases were finally approved, a further semi-official letter was received from Rowland Hill giving an assurance that the increase would not lead to similar petitions from other Post Office clerks.

Some claims succeeded without departmental pressure because the Treasury was satisfied *ab initio* that the case argued by the department justified a 'personal' increase, though not a permanent alteration of the salary scale. Anderson thought that the Foreign Office's proposal to raise the salary of the Financial Clerk for Consular Accounts from £150 to £200 was a fair one in relation to the holder of the office, 'the reason being that increased labour and responsibility have devolved upon him in the first application of a new system and in assigning the detailed measure for working it'.[2] As that reason would not apply to his successors, Anderson advised that the salary fixed for the post should remain unaltered.

APPROVAL

It was more difficult to satisfy the Treasury that it was necessary to alter the scale of salary permanently, partly because it was more difficult to show that the duties or responsibility of a post would be permanently increased, and also because the Treasury was more reluctant to agree to a permanent increase of public expenditure. Where the Treasury objected, departments sometimes used semi-official pressure similar to that just described. Private discussion or arrangement between ministers or officials again could be decisive. The year after they had been given their 'personal' increases, the senior civil servants in the Post Office made a further claim. Although this was fiercely opposed by Hamilton and Stephenson, Laing, who had succeeded Northcote as Financial Secretary, thought that the demand should be acceded to on the ground 'that it is always true economy to have in the really responsible places in large departments as few men as possible but those as

[1] Memo from Northcote to Hamilton, 12 March 1859, P.R.O. T.1/6188B/9473.
[2] Memo by Anderson, December 1862, P.R.O. T.1/6397B/18450.

good as possible and liberally paid'.[1] As the application had been urged strongly in private by the Postmaster-General, his predecessor, and by Rowland Hill, Laing put it up for Gladstone's opinion. The Chancellor was 'averse to compliance', explaining his reasons in a characteristic memorandum:

i. I think Lord Elgin's [Postmaster-General] reasons for raising the question of increase at the present time unsound.
ii. The agitation for increase in the Dept. is on the point of time a decided objection.
iii. For the present Asst. Sects who have special allowances it seems strange to re-open the question unless on new grounds.
iv. Is the transfer of the Packet Service [from the Admiralty] such a ground? Is any office establishment or salary reduced at the Admiralty on account of this Transfer? Was any reduction made at the P.O. formerly when this business was taken away? How do we know whether another transfer will even justify the change, but pretty sure that if it is to afford ground for it, this can only be when it is at work and when we know by experience what its practical consequence and the respective shares of responsibility under it are to be.[2]

Gladstone, recently returned to the Treasury bent upon retrenchment, refused to allow the increase. The Post Office were informed that

The only ground they would be justified in assenting to the permanent augmentation of the salaries ... would be the increased labour and responsibility devolved on the officers in consequence of the transfer of the Packet business from the Admiralty ... and that this can only be ascertained after experience had been had of the working of the new system and of the practical results of the respective shares of responsibility under it.[3]

This condition seemed to rule out the possibility that the Treasury would agree in the near future to raise salaries in the Post Office, yet three weeks later the proposal to award a 'personal' increase to the Chief Clerk was resubmitted and approved. Agreement had been reached privately between the Chancellor of the Exchequer and his cabinet colleague, the Duke of Argyll, who was acting for the Postmaster-General while the latter was

---

[1] Memo from Samuel Laing to Gladstone, 30 April 1860, P.R.O. T.1/6253A/10656.
[2] Memo by Gladstone, 1 May 1860, P.R.O. T.1/6253A/10656.
[3] Treasury to Post Office, 2 May 1860, P.R.O. T.1/6253A/10656.

out of the country. That such pressure exerted unofficially could transcend the weight of Gladstone's personal objections without the prior fulfilment of the precise conditions written into the letter of rejection is further proof of the effectiveness of such pressure and of the practical limits to the control exercised by the Treasury.

11

ALLOWANCES

BESIDES salary some clerks, mainly those with permanent appointments, received allowances for services which their departments did not consider to be part of their ordinary duties. They were of two main kinds: allowances paid for a non-recurring service, such as the £25 paid to a War Office clerk in 1863 for his extra attendance while taking stock of articles in store in Pimlico; and those paid annually for the performance of a recurring service or duty, of which the commonest example was that paid to a clerk chosen as a private secretary to a minister or senior official.[1] The latter payments were provided for specially in each department's Estimates, while those for non-recurring services were made out of the Civil Contingencies Fund[2] or from the small fund voted to each department for 'Incidental Expenditure'.

In principle each new allowance required Treasury authority, but failure to obtain prior approval before making or promising payment was a common occurrence. To some departments it was not clear that it was necessary to obtain Treasury approval before using their funds for Incidental Expenditure, payments from which were not ordinarily subject to Treasury control; others merely disregarded the requirement. Many unauthorized allowances came to light only after the establishment of the Department of Exchequer

---

[1] The usual allowance was £150 p.a. in addition to salary. In some departments, however, 'private secretary' was an office held on establishment and the holder received an annual salary. In the Home Office the private secretary to the Secretary of State received an annual salary of £300, while in the Foreign Office the Precis Writer received a similar salary for work which consisted mainly of secretarial services for the Foreign Secretary.

[2] Advances were made out of the Fund by the Treasury either for new and unforeseen services, or to meet deficiencies on ordinary Votes. Sums advanced to supplement the ordinary Votes were repaid to the Fund out of the Vote taken in the following year, and Parliament was asked to vote money for the sum required to repay to the Fund the amount expended on unforeseen services for which no Vote had been taken. By this means the Fund was maintained constantly at £120,000.

and Audit in 1866, when the Comptroller and Auditor-General challenged the payment of allowances for which no Treasury authority had been obtained, refusing to pass all those for which departments pleaded merely custom or departmental usage.[1]

The Treasury's authority to control allowances (and salaries too) was disputed only by the Admiralty, whose claim to a unique relationship with the Treasury was argued in a correspondence towards the end of the fifties. Asked to account for an allowance of £300 p.a. paid to the Accountant-General of the Navy without prior approval, the Admiralty explained that the practice of submitting questions of small and detailed expenditure was a recent one; and, that it had decided to submit all those questions which involved '*any principle*' in connection with Naval expenditure.[2] They had no wish to disturb that practice, but great forbearance would be needed in referring matters to the Treasury which did not involve any point of principle 'but only some small and well-merited increase, which in the opinion of my Lords [of the Admiralty] it may be necessary to grant for the due execution of the Public Business', if difficulties and delays were to be avoided.[3]

The Admiralty's claim to control expenditure on allowances and salaries independently of the Treasury rested upon two grounds. Until recently it had been Admiralty practice to memorialize the Queen in Council for the required increases for the Naval Service without applying in the first instance for Treasury approval. In support of this it was claimed that there was still in force an Order in Council which empowered the Admiralty 'to increase salaries from time to time as shall appear to them necessary for the advantage of Her Majesty's Service'.[4] It was also argued that the Patent constituting and appointing the Lords of the Admiralty the Commissioners for executing the Office of High Lord Admiral of the United Kingdom specially empowered them 'to pay the Officers and Clerks employed under them such sums of money as they shall think reasonable or as shall be authorized by Order in Council, from time to time, to be made in reward for such services performed'. Although the Admiralty had no intention of exercising to the full the powers which it here claimed by prescriptive right,

[1] For an example of this see P.R.O. T.1/6943A/21356.

[2] Admiralty to Treasury, 18 October and 23 December 1858; and Treasury to Admiralty, 28 October 1858 and 6 January 1859, P.R.O. T.1/6168A/21041.

[3] Admiralty to Treasury, 19 February 1859, P.R.O. T.1/6178A/3106.

[4] Ibid.

U

most allowances could be construed by it as 'small and well-merited', raising no point of principle, and therefore free from the requirement of prior approval.

The Treasury did not contest the validity of the Patent or the Order in Council, although it asked for copies of both, but chose instead to rely on the overriding force of recent precedent, pointing out at the same time, however, that no such authority had been claimed previously by the Admiralty, and that in any case it was irreconcilable with the function imposed upon the Treasury by Parliament. Despite these arguments, the Admiralty continued to pay several allowances for which no Treasury authority was ever obtained. In the course of the Treasury inquiry of 1867 Hamilton and the First Lord of the Admiralty discovered 'a considerable number of allowances' which had been paid to clerks without Treasury authority, and were prepared to report strongly against the practice, but as they did not complete their investigation nothing was done until 1870, when the Admiralty volunteered a statement showing the allowances paid annually to clerks for special services, admitting that with very few exceptions they had been granted 'under the existing powers vested in the Board of Admiralty, and without reference to the Treasury'.[1] The Admiralty's willingness to surrender their putative authority now made it unnecessary for the Treasury to test its validity. The terms were unconditional, the Admiralty acknowledging that allowances should not be granted for the future without the concurrence of the department 'which controls and adjusts the salaries of the Civil Servants of the Crown'.

To avoid the possibility of further dispute, the Treasury now took steps to regularize its authority by formal Minute. The extent and nature of its authority to control the expenditure of the Admiralty (and the War Office) was carefully defined.[2] Paragraph five laid down that

The insertion in the Annual Estimates of any new classification of establishments, either as to numbers or rates of pay or of any new salary or allowance, or of any addition to any existing salary, rate of pay or allowance or gratuity of the nature of salary, is not to be considered an

---

[1] Admiralty to Treasury, 24 January 1870, P.R.O. T.1/7078A/11237.
[2] T.M. 24 November 1870, P.R.O. T.1/7044A/1609. The file contains a brief résumé of the former Minutes on the subject.

authority for the payment of the same unless they should have been submitted to and approved by this Board previously to their insertion in the Estimates.

Control was further strengthened by the stipulation that prior approval was necessary for any new salary or allowance or increase of salary or allowance whether inserted in the Estimates or not. Prior approval was also required for any new Order in Council, Warrant, Sign Manual, or Memorial to H.M. in Council. Other paragraphs dealt with the approval by the Treasury of the Annual Estimates; the submission to the Treasury at an early date of new charges to be inserted in the Estimates; the requirement that no additions were to be made to the numbers of any rank in the Navy and Army during the year without prior approval; that the Estimates for new works, improvements and repairs were to contain specific details; that prior approval was required for all urgent and unforeseen expenditure on all works not provided for in the Estimates in excess of £500; and that no transfer could be made between sub-heads of Votes without Treasury authority. The Minute also contained details of the Treasury's powers to carry surplus Votes to meet deficient Votes, and outlined the procedure for obtaining Votes on credit. Neither the Admiralty nor the War Office found any difficulty in accepting these conditions, for despite its apparent comprehensiveness the Minute represented much less a radical alteration in the balance of power between the Treasury and the two departments than the formal recognition of a relationship whose premises, derived from precedent and custom, had been previously largely unstated.

The Admiralty's belief in its authority to control its own expenditure on salaries and allowances partly explains the strained relations between it and the Treasury during the early sixties when Sir Richard Bromley, the Accountant-General of the Navy, clashed angrily with senior Treasury officials on several occasions. Most departments found Treasury control irritating and irksome when it led to the rejection of a favoured project, an increase of establishment, or a 'well-merited' allowance. But for the Admiralty it must have been especially galling to be denied an increase or obliged to justify the necessity of it to the Treasury, holding as it did until 1870 that Treasury authority to control its expenditure had no more substantial basis that its own acquiescence in that authority.

PRINCIPLE AND PRACTICE

Throughout the whole of the third quarter of the nineteenth century the Treasury was firmly opposed to the principle of granting allowances for extra or special duties, maintaining that the whole of a civil servant's time was at the disposal of the public service; that in times of pressure or emergency he ought to work beyond the usual office hours without expectation of additional pay, 'even an occasional attendance on Sundays under pressing circumstances ought not to lead to expenditure on gratuities'.[1] The Treasury not only objected to the principle, as contrary to the 'unwritten rules' of the Service, but feared also that any system of allowances was liable to abuse in practice: payments made for extra work performed out of office hours tended to encourage the accumulation of arrears in the expectation that they could be worked off by paid extra attendance, caused dissatisfaction among clerks who did not receive them, and were liable to become regarded as rights vested in particular appointments.

Despite these objections between 70 and 80 per cent of claims were approved. 'The rule is quite right but all rules admit of exception', Hamilton explained to one of his Principal Officers, Spencer Shelley, whose inclination was to enforce it strictly.[2] But the frequency with which the Treasury made exceptions to it gives cause to doubt whether for any practical purpose the rule could be said to exist. Nowhere was the inconsistency between principle and practice more marked than in the Treasury itself, where no fewer than forty-six different allowances were paid for extra or special services undertaken by the Treasury clerks.[3]

Gladstone's commitment to a reduction of public expenditure in 1868 induced both Treasury ministers and officials to interpret and apply the rule more strictly than they had done before. None was

[1] Memo by Hamilton, May 1868, P.R.O. T.1/6785A/8306.
[2] Ibid., February 1860, P.R.O. T.1/6261A/14291.
[3] Allowances were discontinued in the Treasury by a Minute of January 1855. Two years later, however, a clerk who had been appointed before that date was granted an allowance of £50 p.a. on the ground that the rule had not been intended to have retrospective effect. As all other clerks on the Supplementary Establishment had been appointed after 1855 no further occasion for relaxing the rule was envisaged, but in the same year a clerk on the Superior Establishment was awarded an allowance of £100 p.a. and in 1857 another Supplementary Clerk, an allowance of £50 p.a. for copying memoranda and semi-official correspondence for Sir Charles Trevelyan. By 1861 seven of the seventeen Supplementary Clerks were receiving allowances in addition to salary.

more eager to do so than the new Permanent Secretary, Ralph Lingen, who quickly made it known that he thought 'the whole principle of these special allowances bad' and that 'all uncertain and variable payments for extra time to salaried officers shall be got rid of'.[1] He had been no more than five days at the Treasury when he drafted a memorandum defining for the first time the conditions upon which allowances should be authorized as properly excepted to the general rule precluding them. The Treasury would not in future sanction allowances, and the salary attached to each post or class in the Estimates was to represent the entire amount which each officer was to receive 'for any duties whatever, which cannot be represented to the Treasury as: i. exceptional, ii. temporary, iii. likely to be less well performed by a person specially retained'.[2] The intention of the latter condition was that special or extra services should be performed ordinarily by clerks engaged specially for that purpose and not by those on the establishment. To merit an allowance extra duties had therefore to be both of an 'exceptional character' and 'of such a temporary nature as could not be foreseen', i.e. different in quality from ordinary duties or involving 'some altogether unusual increase in the annual average'.[3]

Allowances paid to clerks chosen as private secretaries were properly excepted from the rule. There were numerous acceptable precedents, and applications for their continuance or for the award of a new allowance were approved by the Treasury without much trouble, though it usually insisted that each allowance should be inserted in the Annual Estimates. But most allowances authorized by the Treasury could not be considered as legitimate exceptions to the rule: they fell outside the terms of Lingen's three conditions, or were not supported by an acceptable precedent. The Treasury agreed to them because it was unable, or deemed it inexpedient, to resist the demands made upon it. In each instance it declared its objection to the principle and practice of awarding allowances, informing the department that approval was given only on account of the 'special' or 'exceptional' circumstances of the particular case. Anxious to avoid the establishment of inconvenient precedents,

---

[1] Memo to James Stansfeld, 5 March 1870, P.R.O. T.1/7078A/11237, and to Baxter, 17 October 1871, P.R.O. T.1/7251A/18607.
[2] Memo by Lingen, 5 February 1870, P.R.O. T.1/7078A/11237.
[3] Treasury to Admiralty, 24 October 1871, P.R.O. T.1/7251A/18607.

care was also taken to impress upon the department that no similar application would be entertained. On one occasion the President of the Board of Trade was informed that

[The Treasury] cannot sanction the payment of the charge incurred by Mr Milner Gibson if it be intended to establish a precedent or lay down a principle. If however the Lords of the Commission will undertake to regard this as an exceptional case, not to be quoted hereafter and warranted only by the peculiar circumstances at the time when the charge was incurred, my Lords will not insist on their objection, and will authorise payment.[1]

Approval given to a 'very unusual and peculiar proposal' in 1872 was thought by all save Lowe to have established a very bad precedent. Briefly, the Foreign Secretary wished to reward the manager of a firm which did printing work for the Foreign Office with some extra payment for his good work, and on account of his ill-health and family commitments. With the exception of the Chancellor of the Exchequer, all in the Treasury agreed that 'the precedent of paying a contractor's workman would be a very serious one to admit'.[2] Lingen could 'see no way (except Secret Service)[3] of meeting such a proposal as a salary of £100 p.a. A gratuity of £100 might be authorized out of incidentals but even that would be mali exempli. Perhaps the Chancellor of the Exchequer will speak to Lord Granville. I would not have a correspondence'.[4] This and similar advice from his junior colleague was rejected by Lowe who authorized the award of an allowance of £2 per week. The Financial Secretary, convinced of the 'impolicy' of paying a contractor's workman, no matter how onerous and exceptional his work might have been, believed that a fixed sum of money was safer as a precedent and preferable as a matter of principle in rewarding another man's servant. But Lowe could not be persuaded to change his mind, although he agreed in principle that 'as a general rule it would be improper to pay a Govern-

---

[1] Treasury to Board of Trade, 4 December 1866, P.R.O. T.1/6654B/18692.

[2] Memo from Lingen to Baxter and Lowe, 6 April 1872, P.R.O. T.1/7177A/5460.

[3] It is not clear how Lingen meant this remark to be interpreted: he might have meant it ironically. On the other hand, he might have suggested the use of the Secret Service fund knowing that the charge would not be revealed in the Estimates or known to any other department, thereby confining an embarrassing precedent to the Foreign Office.

[4] Memo from Lingen to Baxter and Lowe, 6 April 1872, op. cit.

ment salary to the servant of a Government contractor—but he cannot disregard the testimony borne as to the exceptional claims of Mr Olding'.[1] This was an extraordinary and unparalleled decision: a man not employed in any capacity in the Civil Service was to be paid a weekly allowance of £2 from public funds on account of his long service, failing health, and the testimony of the Foreign Secretary. A proposal urged privately and personally by a cabinet colleague was always difficult to resist—even Gladstone was not proof against the persistent entreaties of senior ministers, witness his concession to the Post Office described in the last chapter.

The most striking characteristic of the relatively few claims turned down by the Treasury was their similarity to those approved on the grounds of 'special' or 'exceptional' circumstances. Thus Home Office clerks were refused allowances for their extra work at the time of the Fenian disturbances in Ireland, conditions analogous to those which had been rewarded in the Foreign Office in 1856 with an allowance of £2,000; earlier still Home Office clerks had been rewarded for their services during the Irish famine, while in 1867 clerks in the Office of the Chief Secretary for Ireland had been rewarded for their work in connection with the Fenian movement, and small gratuities given to clerks in the Office of the Quartermaster-General in Dublin. A clerk in the Irish Board of Works who acted as a shorthand writer was refused an allowance on the grounds that permanent extra allowances for particular duties were objectionable. This argument applied equally to the allowances received by several clerks in the Admiralty and War Office, but they were of long standing and their continuance was urged by cabinet ministers at the head of powerful departments; it was much more difficult for the Treasury to compel the discontinuance of an annual allowance there than to prevent a smaller department from awarding a new one.

If the rule had been enforced strictly it would have been necessary in very many cases for the Treasury to have insisted upon the repayment of allowances awarded without prior approval. Wisely it rarely attempted to do so, content to remind the department of the need to seek prior approval in all future cases. On one occasion, however, it did compel a clerk in the Science and Art Department

---

[1] Memo by Lowe's private secretary to Baxter's private secretary, 17 April 1872, P.R.O. T.1/7177A/5460.

to refund a £20 allowance paid to him without Treasury authority, but the decision appears to have been inspired rather more by the desire to discipline a department whose administration had lately been an embarrassment to the Treasury and Gladstone's Government, than the imperative need to uphold the rule relating to allowances. Lowe, in agreement this time with Lingen and Baxter, noted: 'The system of night attendance in a Department where such extra attendance is one of the conditions of the service is wrong and should be discontinued. It is liable to abuse especially when administered by the Science and Art Department. . . . The irregularities of this Department will never be checked if the Treasury on every occasion give way.'[1]

The divergence between principle and practice, and the apparent arbitrariness with which some applications were approved and others quite similar rejected, was due to the combination of several factors. The most important of these derived from the Treasury's pragmatic, flexible and essentially conciliatory attitude towards the departments described in previous chapters. Here also Treasury ministers and officials preferred to be guided more by expediency than principle. Principle was not completely ignored, but it was often subordinated because there were other factors of greater weight which had to be considered.

On many occasions the Treasury was presented with a *fait accompli*: either the service had been performed and already paid for, or the service had been performed with the expectation of some reward. In the former instance the Treasury could do little other than give authority for the payment, reiterate the general rule, and impress the department with the need to obtain prior approval in similar cases in future; in the latter, to withhold authority penalized the clerk for the department's failure to obtain prior approval. An enforcement of the rule in such circumstances would have been harsh, and as regards the large departments almost certain to give rise to an irritated correspondence. It is highly improbable that the Treasury would have contemplated (and had it done so whether it could ever hope to succeed) asking either the War Office or Admiralty, or the departments of the Secretaries of State, to refund an allowance paid without Treasury authority. Thus the rule could be applied efficaciously, with a minimum of hardship to the

[1] Memo by Lowe's private secretary, 7 February 1871, and by Lowe (?)February 1871, P.R.O. T.1/7159A/19851.

individual and with concern for the efficient management of the department, only when the Treasury was informed of a projected service. Then it could warn the department that the general rule precluded any extra payment for such a service. Rarely, however, was the Treasury notified before a service was begun or a payment made. Consequently, in exercising control it had to try to reconcile the public interest which the general rule was intended to protect, the claims of the clerks who had performed the extra duty, and the wishes of the heads of departments—an always difficult, sometimes impossible, task.

A further difficulty was the reluctance of some departments, especially the War Office and Admiralty, to give up long-established allowances. When their continuance was strongly urged by a minister, and supported by Treasury authority obtained some years before, it was almost impossible to persuade departments to forgo them. In earlier chapters it was shown how difficult it was for the Treasury to control establishments where a department was prepared to dispute Treasury authority, or where it refused to accept an adverse decision as binding or final. The most extreme example of this occurred after the Treasury had refused to approve the continuance of an annual payment of £200 to two War Office clerks for preparing the Estimates. On this occasion, however, the pertinacity of the department was matched by an equally determined and uncompromising Treasury.

The preliminary skirmishing which took place in the early months of 1871, resulted in an agreed Treasury decision to end the system the following year, and to extend the ruling to the Admiralty where allowances were paid for similar work. Protests were made by both departments, but not until the receipt of the fourth official War Office letter did the Treasury's resolve weaken. Surprisingly, Lingen was first to propose accommodation: 'I am not convinced but I doubt it being expedient to overrule in relation to an existing charge the strongly repeated opinion of a Secretary of State of Mr. Cardwell's experience. I should yield in such terms. Of course Admiralty goes as well', he wrote to Lowe.[1] But the Chancellor was not yet prepared to give way. Further letters were received from the two departments arguing for the continuance of the allowances, and both the Secretary of State for War and the First Lord of the Admiralty were granted formal inter-

[1] Memo by Lingen, 21 November 1871, P.R.O. T.1/7251A/18607.

views with Lowe. Baxter, the Financial Secretary, now capitulated: 'I think on the whole . . . that we ought not to contest this matter further', he noted. To Lowe he wrote:

It is impossible to defend these allowances in principle. The work is annual and regular and not at all of an exceptional nature: but a good deal is to be said in favour of the present system from the practical and economic side of the question, as if the allowances are stopped, the salaries might be increased and higher pensions given. On this account and because the heads of the War Office and Admiralty continue to urge the Treasury to give way I am quite prepared to do so.[1]

Lingen advised the Chancellor similarly:

There is nothing to be said about these cases, except that they ought to be brought to an end. I believe that the sound administrative rule would be, to maintain the decision already announced. On the other hand, there are the strongly expressed and persistently repeated opinions of the Ministers at the head of two of the principal Departments of the State, and the sums (£200 p.a.) are limited in amount and not large. If the concession is to be made, I would prefer to accept the present arrangement rather than invent a new one. There is no precedent for these charges in any other Department.[2]

Not for the first or last time Lowe disregarded the concerted opinion of his advisers: 'I would not give way. There may be some economy in these cases but the principle is an extravagant one and liable to much abuse and we cannot hope to maintain a better state of things in other Offices if we yield here.'[3]

In early January 1872 the War Office and Admiralty were told officially that the Treasury would stand by its earlier decision. Almost by return Cardwell wrote semi-officially to Lowe repeating the claims of his clerks to a continuance of their allowances, and warning him of the consequences of refusal. A week later he wrote semi-officially to Lingen, who advised Lowe to approve the allowances upon the condition that the War Office issued an order, subject to Treasury approval, stating that no Estimate Clerk would in future be allowed extra pay. Urged by his own advisers, and faced by a minister as intransigent and uncompromising as himself, Lowe finally gave way. Lingen's suggestion was now made

[1] (Second) memo by Baxter, 28 December 1871, P.R.O. T.1/7251A/18607.
[2] Memo from Lingen to Baxter and Lowe, 27 December 1871, P.R.O. T.1/7251A/18607.
[3] Memo by Lowe, 30 December 1871, P.R.O. T.1/7251A/18607.

a condition of Treasury concurrence, and both departments were required to make Orders in Council to the effect that duties in connection with the estimates were for the future to be considered part of the ordinary work of officers of the class employed upon them.

Only Lowe's determination prevented the Treasury from conceding the allowances sooner. Besides the persistent entreaties, official and semi-official, of his two cabinet colleagues, he disregarded the advice of both his Permanent Secretary (twice) and the Financial Secretary. It is significant that the Treasury was unwilling, even here when it was backed by a determined, powerful and iconoclastic Chancellor, to resist the recommendations urged repeatedly by two cabinet ministers. The sound administrative rule would have been, as Lingen said, to uphold the decision already made, but both he and the Financial Secretary explicitly questioned the expediency of refusing what was urged by ministers at the head of two of the principal departments. In a head-on clash the Treasury, not the department, was obliged to give way—yet again principle bowed to expediency. The kind of pressure brought to bear upon the Treasury—repeated official applications, semi-official correspondence with Treasury ministers and officials, interviews with the Chancellor—was not unusual, nor its success remarkable. On similar occasions other cabinet ministers employed the same tactics with equal success. As a consequence of this the extent and degree to which the Treasury could control the departments was circumscribed in practice.

The Treasury's ambivalent attitude towards the control of allowances is more readily understood when reference is made to Hamilton's views on the control of travel allowances. During Palmerston's administration he convened a meeting at the Treasury of the permanent heads of departments to discuss the advantages of classifying allowances paid to civil servants required to travel on duty, at which it was decided that it would be better and more economical to continue to pay them without classification. When the question was raised again a few years later he opposed the introduction of any system of classification, thinking it better 'to deal with each case as it arose on its own merits and in the light of the special circumstances of each case, rather than make any general rules for the whole of the Public Service'.[1] If allowances

[1] P.R.O. T.1/6930B.

were classified there would have to be a maximum scale, and he thought that this would lead to the maximum being applied rather more than the average amount which was the practice at that time.

Hamilton's concern for economy and expediency bears a striking resemblance to that expressed by Baxter when restraining Lingen from incurring an obligation to the Admiralty to concede allowances in exceptional cases by predetermining the circumstances in which the Treasury would be prepared to do so. Although it followed logically from the three conditions laid down in the 1870 memorandum, Baxter who had approved them, was not willing to go so far; 'it might commit us in cases where we did not wish to grant allowances', he confided to Lingen.[1] His attitude was shared by almost all Treasury ministers, who preferred to deal with each case on its own merits rather than to apply strictly (as Lingen wanted) general rules of which they approved in principle. Given the factors described above it made for more flexible, if sometimes uncertain, administration, and was better adjusted to the prevailing circumstances. Each department considered itself as special and its applications as exceptional; in the Treasury there was a disposition to treat them as such. Until the departments were regarded by the Treasury as different parts of the same single Service, and until it emphasized those elements of unity and similarity rather than those which were disparate, any attempt to apply Lingen's general rules was precipitate.

[1] Memo from Baxter to Lingen, 23 June 1871, P.R.O. T.1/7078A/11237.

12

PROMOTION

PROMOTION BY MERIT

The theory of the public service is, that the annual increase of salary from the minimum to the maximum of the class, is given as a matter of course as the reward of service, and with no reference to the comparative merits of the individuals; but that promotion from class to class is the reward of merit, or rather that it is regulated by a consideration of the public interests, and that those only are to be transferred from one class to a higher who have shown themselves capable of rendering valuable services in it.

THUS wrote Northcote and Trevelyan in 1853, adding that 'this salutary principle is, however, in practice often overlooked, and promotion from class to class ... is more commonly regulated by seniority than by merit'.[1] Not all who held office in the Treasury in the middle of the nineteenth century were such enthusiastic advocates of promotion by merit as Trevelyan, nor perhaps would have supported his claim that 'promotion according to qualification and merit is the life of Public Establishments. Without it they are inert masses. With it a general activity is diffused'.[2] He only just succeeded in persuading the Chancellor of the Exchequer, Sir George Cornewall Lewis, to formally acknowledge the Treasury's adherence to the principle when the department was reorganized in 1856. Trevelyan argued against his suggestion that no explicit reference should be made to it in the new written departmental rules on the ground that the subordinate departments, 'two-thirds of the Civil Service', had adopted the principle at the Treasury's insistence and looked to it for a lead. If promotion was not seen to be governed by merit in the Treasury they would consider 'the old regime of seniority-promotion and indifference to public duty reinstated'.[3]

---

[1] *Report of the Committee of Inquiry into the Organisation of the Civil Service*, 23 November 1853, P.P., 1854, XXVII.
[2] Trevelyan to W. Cooper, 12 November 1855, Bod., T.L.B., xxxvi. 5–6.
[3] Trevelyan to Lewis, 6 October 1856, Bod., T.L.B., xxxvi. 230–3.

Another Treasury sceptic, Lewis's Patronage Secretary, Sir William Hayter, had earlier attempted to intercede on behalf of a candidate for promotion in the Post Office, but had been unexpectedly rebuffed by Rowland Hill. Two years previously, Trevelyan's committee of inquiry had introduced promotion by merit and Hill now told Hayter: 'We really do mean to carry out the *Treasury* regulation as to promotion honestly and with an utter disregard of all conflicting interests, however potent'; and added that he did not intend to forward his application to the Postmaster-General, nor to allow it to influence him in any advice he gave to him.[1]

Before 1854 the Treasury had had little influence upon the selection of candidates for promotion in departments other than those immediately subordinate to it. Each had been free to make its own rules and to apply or relax them in individual cases without reference to the Treasury. After the publication of the Northcote–Trevelyan Report the Treasury took a much closer interest in the system used in each department, but it could not compel the acceptance of the principle to which it now subscribed, or secure its observance by those departments who professed to be guided by it. In practice it could do little other than exhort, where necessary admonish, and point to the example of its own establishment and those of the departments subordinate to it. Committees of inquiry could root out abuse and argue the case for promotion by merit, but even here the discretion of the minister was absolute; the Treasury could exhort, it could not command.

With regard to the subordinate departments there was no such limitation to the Treasury authority. Here it had the right, in some cases vested in it by statute, to influence the selection of clerks for promotion. Some time before 1854 the practice of interfering directly in the selection of candidates had been abandoned, although Arbuthnot, who joined the department in 1820, could remember when

The Treasury still retained generally considerable jealousy on the subject of promotions at the discretion of the Heads of Depts. The Customs for example were obliged to send up the names of 3 Landing Waiters for selection by the Treasury for each vacancy in the office of Landing

[1] Hill to Hayter, 27 December 1855, G. B. Hill, *Life of Sir Rowland Hill*, ii. 299.

Surveyor, and the Treasury interfered practically in the selection of officers for promotion to Collectorships and Controllerships.[1]

While the Treasury had no intention of reviving this practice 'it felt bound to see that the principle of selection of merit was strictly observed in the Departments under their control',[2] and throughout the whole of the period 1854–74 required them all to submit their recommendations for promotion for its approval. Generally these proved acceptable, but in 1863 there was a dispute with the Registrar-General. Although its origin is obscure, from Hamilton's admission that he spoke strongly to him 'as to the danger lest favouritism as regards promotions which formerly was exercised by Govt. for political purposes should under the new system be exercised for personal purposes by the Heads of Depts.',[3] it seems probable that a clerk had been promoted over the heads of better-qualified candidates. As a result Hamilton now insisted that the language of the recommendations submitted by departments should be carefully scrutinized to ensure that they stated explicitly that those recommended for promotion were the best entitled to it on the grounds of merit. 'It is the duty of the heads to form a judgment and state it', he said,[4] and was 'very particular' in seeing that they did not evade this responsibility. On one occasion he thought that the Irish Board of Works in recommending clerks for promotion 'rather shrank from saying they were the best entitled', and called upon them to furnish a specific statement of entitlement. A month later his private secretary, drawing the attention of the Secretary of the Poor Law Board to the omission in his letter of recommendation of any statement of merit, received a personal assurance that irrespective of the clerk's claim as senior of his class he was undoubtedly the person best fitted and most entitled to promotion, and the promise that in all future recommendations the grounds upon which the clerks were chosen for promotion would be clearly stated.[5]

The first promotion made after the revision of the Audit Office establishment in 1861 gave rise to a mild disagreement between Hamilton, Arbuthnot, and the Financial Secretary when it became apparent from the recommendation submitted for their

[1] Memo to Hamilton, 12 January 1864, P.R.O. T.1/6457B/17759.
[2] Memo from Hamilton to Frederick Peel, 27 November 1863, P.R.O. T.1/6463A/18235.   [3] Ibid.   [4] Ibid.
[5] Memo by Rivers Wilson, 5 December 1863, P.R.O. T.1/6466A/18407.

approval that three clerks eligible for promotion had been passed over. Hamilton urged an inquiry on the grounds that the procedure adopted by the Audit Office would be a precedent for the future, but was restrained by his colleagues.[1] It would create 'needless irritation', Arbuthnot warned him. The Financial Secretary agreed, and decided that on this occasion the promotion should be approved without comment. Arbuthnot felt some misgiving about Hamilton's general attitude towards the subordinate departments, arguing that control of promotions had 'subsided' since the days when the Treasury chose the clerk for promotion from among names submitted to it by the department; also, he believed that the Audit Office was less subordinate to the Treasury than some of the other departments. Peel's anxiety was altogether different, he was worried lest Hamilton's action should lead to a renewal of the dispute between the two departments which had taken place two years earlier—yet another illustration of the lengths to which the Treasury was prepared to go to conciliate a department, to avoid 'wounding its susceptibilities'.

Only in very exceptional circumstances did the Treasury reject a recommendation, such as those in which the promotion of a Stationery Office Clerk who had been a party in a court case was rejected on the ground of 'the public scandal of a person guilty of notorious profligacy and misconduct'.[2]

After the enthusiasm with which the Treasury hounded the subordinate departments in the early sixties there followed a period of relative calm in which approval was given more perfunctorily. Hamilton's intense concern, which had been the mainspring of the control, began to wane as he neared the end of his service as permanent head of the department and his successor, Ralph Lingen, never showed anything like the same interest. By then such close control may have become less necessary. While that exercised earlier did not guarantee that the best-qualified and most meritorious civil servant was always selected and recommended—more positive interference would have been necessary for that—the requirement of certificates of entitlement, the reitera-

---

[1] Draft Minute by Hamilton, 22 December 1863, later cancelled; and memo to Peel, 17 January 1864, P.R.O. T.1/6457B/17759.
[2] Treasury to Stationery Office, 11 May 1861, P.R.O. T.1/6333B/18192. For another example see T.M. 15 October 1872, H.M.T., *Departmental Arrangement Book*, v.

tion of the principle of promotion by merit, and the ever-present possibility that the Treasury might call for a more detailed explanation, probably had the effect then (and later) of deterring departments from recommending notoriously unfit or undeserving persons, as had sometimes happened in the past when promotion often depended upon a patron's influence, or was made with strict regard to seniority. Also, the propriety of exercising such a close control, which Arbuthnot had questioned in 1864, became more doubtful as those departments acquired greater independence with the introduction of open competition.

The Treasury had no similar authority to require other departments to submit their recommendations for promotion for its approval. Ordinarily the subject of promotion did not arise in correspondence with them, for they did not inform the Treasury when promotions were about to be made or who was to be promoted. Nevertheless, wherever possible the Treasury drew attention to the importance of upholding the principle of promotion by merit. For example, in the regulations governing salary scales which were drawn in December 1855 it was laid down that 'in case of a vacancy which is to be filled by promotion the merit and qualifications of each individual be carefully investigated, in order that the fittest person may be selected and recommended for promotion without regard to seniority, except where the merits and qualifications of the candidates are equal'.[1] Pressure of this kind could be exerted more effectively, and with less risk of provoking or offending the head of a department, when an establishment was revised or reorganized. Thus the Treasury agreed to the newly consolidated establishment of the War Office in 1856 partly upon the condition that 'promotion would be made on the ground of general merit'.[2] The extensive increases made to the Superior and Supplementary Establishments of the Board of Trade, and the introduction of new salary scales there, were approved 'provided that it be considered a fixed rule of the office . . . that promotion from class to class will be made on the ground of superior fitness for duties to be performed—seniority being regarded only in those cases in which the qualifications are equal'.[3] A similar recommendation was made in 1857 on the revision of the Colonial Office, and

[1] T.M. 24 December 1855, P.R.O. T.1/6276A/18982.
[2] Treasury to War Office, 18 February 1856, P.R.O. T.1/6049/20946.
[3] Treasury to Board of Trade, 10 March 1857, P.R.O. T.1/6057A/4581.

X

by the Treasury committees which inquired into the Home Office in 1856 and the War Office in 1865.

Occasionally it proved possible to uphold the principle in a more positive way. While the Treasury could not question the decision to pass over a clerk who was 'eminently qualified', when it was asked to compensate that clerk for the loss of promotion it could and did object. 'I think we have a perfect right and are bound to object', Hamilton claimed, when he learned that the Admiralty had passed over the most eligible candidate for promotion to the position of Deputy Accountant-General because his services as Auditor of Dockyard Accounts were indispensable to the introduction of a new system of accounts.[1] As compensation for the loss of this promotion the Admiralty now tried to persuade the Treasury to raise his salary to that received by the Deputy Accountant-General. To Arbuthnot the proposal looked like a 'job': that the Admiralty wanted to appoint another man to the vacancy but felt obliged to give the obvious candidate a 'sop' for his loss. Anderson and Hamilton agreed with him, the latter scarcely able to 'imagine the ground on which a man stated to be "eminently qualified" is to be passed over'.[2] The Admiralty's request was refused, the Treasury emphasizing the importance of adhering to the principle of promoting on merit. The slight inconvenience in completing the new system of Dockyard Accounts would not 'be so great an evil as the dereliction of principle which the proposed arrangement would involve'.[3]

In the development of the modern Civil Service the substitution of a system of promotion by merit and efficiency for one in which the criterion for advancement had too often been a strict regard for the claims of seniority or the persuasiveness of a political patron was an important and necessary step. After 1854 promotion by merit was increasingly accepted in principle by almost all departments, largely as a result of Treasury exhortation, the example of its own and the subordinate departments, and the use of indirect pressure such as that described above. But even so, promotion by

[1] In a letter to the Treasury, 24 March 1863, the Admiralty admitted that he was the best qualified candidate and that they had passed him over. P.R.O. T.1/6414A/4712.

[2] Anderson had written a Minute refusing the increase, but Arbuthnot while agreeing with the view expressed in it thought that 'his language is stronger than we ought to adopt'.

[3] Treasury to Admiralty, 28 March 1863, P.R.O. T.1/6414A/4712.

merit was not uniformly applied to all situations, even in the subordinate departments. Most witnesses before the Playfair Commission in 1874 testified that, although promotion to senior posts was by merit, in the lower classes it was best regulated by seniority, provided that the clerk in turn for promotion was qualified and deserving. Not all departments were perhaps as careful as the Board of Inland Revenue, where William Stephenson, an ex-Treasury man, would 'never scruple to pass over a man who was not reported by the responsible head of his department to be fitted for promotion'. In the Paymaster-General's Office weight was given to seniority, good conduct, efficiency, and promise, although even here seniority generally governed promotion in the lower classes.

Among civil servants promotion by merit was 'a greater source of heart-burning and remonstrance than any other grievance', and its introduction stoutly resisted. Less concerned with questions of efficiency than Trevelyan or Northcote, self-interest convinced them that the certainty and impartiality of a system of promotion by seniority was preferable to one in which advancement could be checked or halted at the pleasure of an unscrupulous or biased head of department. Reflecting this attitude, the paternalistic and vigilant *Civil Service Gazette* conducted a sustained and bitter campaign against promotion by merit, 'the perfection of iniquity as a working regulation'. Week by week it exposed and condemned alleged abuses, such as the case of a 4th Class Clerk in the General Registry and Record of Seamen's Office, who was promoted over the heads of the entire 3rd Class into the 2nd Class. Promotion, it suggested, should be governed by a different principle.

When a vacancy occurs the man next in seniority should be promoted if fit for the post; if not, he should at once be rejected. The principle of *rejection* is the only mode by which promotion can be safely and honourably regulated; that of *selection* affords an opening for jobbery and favouritism that poor human nature is too weak to resist.[1]

In the circumstances of a Service only slowly and painfully sloughing off patronage, this method was more realistic and practical than promotion by merit. It was the difference between selecting the fittest man, regardless of his service, and choosing the next senior if he was fit. In trying to introduce the former,

[1] Leading article, 16 August 1856.

Trevelyan was, as so often, trying to move too quickly. The transition from a system in which seniority was the prime consideration to one in which it was displaced by merit, could not be made overnight. There was a real danger, perhaps better appreciated among the rank and file, that those who had customarily used their patronage to appoint their own nominees would be unable to resist the temptation to evoke the new principle to justify the advance of their favourites.

Although the Treasury worked to secure the adoption of the principle throughout the Service, and grasped every opportunity to impress the departments with the desirability of applying it in practice, enforcement remained at the discretion of each head of department. Outside the subordinate departments the Treasury had only a very limited means of ensuring that departments such as those of the Secretaries of State, Admiralty or War Office promoted according to merit and qualification. Only on those few occasions when a promotion was brought to its attention indirectly could the Treasury influence the decision taken by the head of department. And while Treasury committees of inquiry provided a unique opportunity to check upon the system of promotion, the Treasury had no power even there other than to remonstrate, to exhort, and to recommend.[1]

OPPORTUNITIES FOR PROMOTION

The Treasury was concerned also to provide adequate opportunities for promotion within each department, less from the desire to provide favourable conditions in which the principle of promotion by merit could take root than a need to obviate demands for pay increases. Clerks who remained too long in one class, or at their maximum salary for too many years, or whose prospects of promotion were remote, became dissatisfied and demanded higher salaries in lieu of advancement, or an increase in the establishment of the higher classes. The Treasury, understandably anxious to avoid the precipitation of such demands, tried to provide reasonably rapid advancement from one class to the next—satisfied clerks were not only cheaper in the long run, they were also more efficient. This was well understood in the Treasury: in Hamilton's view there was 'nothing more important in the Civil Service with a view to economy and also in my opinion to efficiency than that

[1] See above, Chapter 8, pp. 211–14 and 221.

proper proportions should be as far as possible maintained as regards the numbers in the different classes'.[1]

'The discretion as regards ... the relative proportion of the numbers in each class has always been considered one in which the Treasury should have a voice', it was claimed.[2] Whenever, therefore, an increase or reduction in the size of the establishment was proposed which disturbed the ratio of one class to another it tried to secure a proportionate number of clerks in each class. This was done not by reference to an objective fixed standard, but by comparing the proportions with those in other branches within the department, and with those departments in the same group, i.e. the 'first-class' departments, the War Office/Admiralty group, and the Revenue Departments.[3] Thus the Treasury tended to object to a proposal the effect of which was to make the proportion between one class and another less favourable than that between similar classes in another branch within the same department, or in another department within the same group; and to object to a proposal which made the proportion between one class and another more favourable relative to others. For example, in April 1869 the Admiralty proposed a revision of the establishments of the Departments of the Storekeeper-General and the Registrar of Contracts, details of which are shown below in Table I.

TABLE I

Admiralty Establishments, 1869

Contract Department Establishment April 1869		Proposed	Storekeeper-General's Department Establishment April 1869		Proposed
1st Class Clerks	1	—	1st Class, 1st section	1	—
2nd Class Clerks	2	1	2nd section	1	—
3rd Class Clerks	4	10	2nd Class	5	3
			3rd Class	14	4

James Cole, the Principal Officer of the Treasury Second Division, objected to the proposal on the grounds that in the Contract Department there would be a much too large proportion of lower class clerks to the one senior clerk, i.e. that the opportunities for

[1] Memo by Hamilton, May 1869, P.R.O. T.1/6873B/8755.
[2] Memo by Cole, 4 June 1869, P.R.O. T.1/7069A/8920.
[3] There was of course a close connection between the fixing of salary scales and opportunities for promotion, see above, Chapter 9, pp. 247–8.

promotion of the ten 3rd Class Clerks would be very much less favourable. Conversely, in the Storekeeper-General's Department there would be too many 2nd Class Clerks compared with the number in the 3rd Class—the opportunities for promotion of the latter would be unusually favourable.[1] These judgements were based upon a comparison with the previous proportions in the two departments which had been assimilated with those in the other Admiralty departments. Hamilton warned the Financial Secretary that 'with a class consisting of 1 Second and 10 Third Class Clerks the inevitable result in a few years will be what has occurred in the War Office—complaints on the part of the 3rd Class Clerks of slowness of promotion and concession on the part of the then Government'.[2] The increase in the number of the War Office 3rd Class Clerks (from 119 to 140), to which Hamilton here referred, had taken place in 1862 despite strong Treasury objection. The consequences described by him were precisely those feared at that time. Arbuthnot had objected to 'the vast increase of an over-manned 3rd class, with remote hopes of promotion',[3] and drew the attention of the Secretary of State for War to the 'evil which un-doubtedly must arise from the admission of young men of ability and superior education to the bottom of an office with so remote a prospect as the proposed Establishment would afford'.[4]

A proposal to reduce the size of an establishment could draw a similar objection from the Treasury. Cole criticized a proposal to reduce the establishment of the Accountant-General of the Navy on the ground that it would raise the proportion of 3rd Class Clerks to the higher classes above the general average of two to one; he calculated that it would be raised as high as three to one 'and must certainly bring out in greater measure the dissatisfaction that follows as to the slowness of promotion'.[5] Hamilton agreed with him and anticipated that 'after some years the Treasury will be called upon to improve the proportions'.[6]

While in the War Office, Admiralty, Paymaster-General's Office,

---

[1] Memo by Cole, 6 May 1869, P.R.O. T.1/6873B/8755.

[2] Memo from Hamilton to James Stansfeld, May 1869, P.R.O. T.1/6873B/8755.

[3] Memo from Arbuthnot to Hamilton, 3 May 1862, P.R.O. T.1/6392B/17889.

[4] Treasury to War Office, 3 May 1862, P.R.O. T.1/6392B/17889.

[5] Memo by Cole, 4 June 1869, P.R.O. T.1/7069A/8920.

[6] Memo from Hamilton to James Stansfeld, 9 June 1869, P.R.O. T.1/7069A/8920.

and Audit Office the proportion of junior clerks to those above them was about two or three to one, in the 'first-class' departments it was much more favourable. In the middle fifties the Treasury had seven junior clerks and thirty clerks in the higher classes above them, a proportion of just over one to four in favour of the juniors; in the Foreign Office at about the same time it was more favourable still, but in the Colonial Office where it was least favourable the junior clerks were dissatisfied with their prospects of promotion. A 'state of discouragement' prevailed, four junior clerks had resigned within the space of a few years, no vacancy had occurred in the 1st Class for fourteen years, and the junior members of the 2nd Class had served for twenty years.

Provided that a department could satisfy the Treasury that an increase or reduction of establishment was necessary the Treasury was unable to sustain an objection to it solely upon the ground that it disturbed the proportion of the classes; none of the objections made to War Office and Admiralty proposals were sustained. Arbuthnot's firm opposition to the proposal to add twenty-one 3rd Class Clerks to the War Office Establishment in 1862 was overcome by the repeated avowals, privately and personally made to him, that the increase had been reduced to the smallest number 'scarcely admitting of leave of absence or illness—so that the amount of extra work thrown upon us by Parliament presses uncommonly hard upon us'.[1] He did not live to see his worst fears realized: in 1867 the 3rd Class Clerks pressed for and were awarded a pay increase on the ground of their slow promotion; four years later Cardwell and the Treasury Superannuation Committee wrestled with the insoluble problem posed by the hopeless position of these clerks who preferred 'the dismal certainty of their present prospects' to retirement on special terms offered by the Treasury.[2] On other occasions Treasury objections were overcome by the use of similar pressure.[3]

The Treasury's preoccupation with the provision of adequate opportunities for promotion was based largely upon economic self-

[1] Semi-official letter from Sir Edward Lugard to Arbuthnot, 7 July 1862, P.R.O. T.1/6393B/17889; later the two met at the War Office to discuss the official reply to the Treasury.

[2] Memo from Lord Lansdowne, a Junior Lord of the Treasury and member of the Treasury Superannuation Committee, to the Chancellor of the Exchequer, 4 March 1872, P.R.O. T.1/7120A/18249.

[3] See for example, P.R.O. T.1/6273B/18620 and T.1/6873B/8755.

interest: the need to hold down salaries. The departments, on the other hand, were very much less concerned to ensure that there were adequate opportunities, although occasionally the need to do so was given as a reason for requesting an increase of establishment, as for example when the War Office sought authority 'to recast the several classes of the Establishment as to afford the Secretary of State for War the same means of affording promotion and advancement as are now enjoyed by the Heads of like Departments of State'.[1] They were well aware that when their clerks became dissatisfied, dissatisfaction could be deflected towards the Treasury by endorsing petitions for improved salaries, and by themselves asking for an increase of establishment; that they did not hesitate to do so is clear from the claims submitted by the War Office and other departments after 1867.[2]

The Treasury could not have more effectively controlled the opportunities for promotion in each department, because (as was explained earlier) it was unable in the last resort to deny an increase of establishment which the department declared essential to its efficiency. But while it achieved no success in any particular instance where it objected to an application the opportunities for promotion within each group of departments were remarkably similar. The position in 1866, that is after the Treasury had objected unsuccessfully to large increases of establishment in both the War Office and Admiralty on the grounds that they disturbed the proportions between the classes, is shown in the following tables.

TABLE II

War Office/Admiralty Group
Numbers of clerks in each class, 1866

	Admiralty Depts.							Total	War Office	Audit Office	Pay Office
1st	11	9	2	4	1	2	1	30	41	9	7
2nd	13	39	5	11	4	4	2	68	95	34	16
3rd	23	104	14	25	9	10	4	195	273	69	35

[1] War Office to Treasury, 17 May 1860, P.R.O. T.1/6251A/9717.
[2] See above, Chapter 9, pp. 242–5.

TABLE III

War Office/Admiralty Group
Proportions of 2nd and 3rd Classes to 1st Class

	Admiralty	War Office	Audit Office	Pay Office
1st	1	1	1	1
2nd	2+	2+	4	2+
3rd	6+	7	7+	5

TABLE IV

War Office/Admiralty Group
3rd Class as proportion of other two classes

	Admiralty	War Office	Audit Office	Pay Office
1st/2nd	1	1	1	1
3rd	2	2	1·6	1·5

The situation in the four 'first-class' departments in 1866 is shown below in Table V.

TABLE V

'First-class' Departments
Numbers of clerks in each class, 1866[1]

	Treasury	Colonial Office	Home Office	Foreign Office
1st	7	5	4	8
2nd	13	13	9	27
3rd	7	7	2	6

The evidence points to the Treasury committees of inquiry as primarily responsible for the similarity in the proportions between classes in each group. Although their reports do not reveal the details of the discussion which preceded the revision of an establishment, there is little doubt that the proportion between one class and another was a factor considered by them. It was of course

[1] Clerks in the lowest class on the Superior Establishment have been counted as '3rd Class', those in the highest class as '1st Class', and the intermediate classes have all been counted as '2nd Class'.

only one factor—the requirements of the business was another, and probably more important on these occasions. But here too there was similarity. In the War Office, Admiralty, Audit Office, and Paymaster-General's Office, there was a great deal of accounts work requiring a large number of junior clerks relatively to those above them. Similarly, the functions of the three Secretariats and the Treasury were broadly comparable, requiring fewer junior than senior clerks.

When in 1856 the establishment of the Paymaster-General's Office was radically recast 'the number of Clerkships in each class was fixed as nearly as possible in the same proportions as in the War Department'.[1] The report of the War Office inquiry earlier the same year recommended the adoption of the classification and salary scales which obtained in the Admiralty; as the proportions between the classes of the new War Office establishment corresponded so closely to those in the Admiralty, it is reasonable to assume that the committee of inquiry had regard to them also.[2] A similar inference may be drawn from the degree of assimilation which was achieved between the Audit Office and the other three departments as a result of the implementation of the recommendations of the 1861 committee of inquiry. In the informal proceedings of an inquiry the Treasury could better urge the importance of providing adequate opportunities for promotion; and, before either side had committed itself officially, a reconciliation of the interests of the department and the Treasury, where these conflicted, could be more easily achieved.

---

[1] Treasury to Paymaster-General's Office, 18 April 1856, P.R.O. T.1/6035A/ 6052; and memo by Sir William Clerke, 12 May 1868, P.R.O. T.1/6826B/ 18586.

[2] In the Admiralty the proportions of the 2nd and 3rd Class to the 1st Class were 2·2 and 5·5; in the War Office they were 1·7 and 4·5. In both, the 3rd Class as a proportion of the other two classes was the same, 1·7.

13

OFFICE HOURS, LEAVE, AND DISCIPLINE

OFFICE hours, paid leave, and disciplinary regulations were fixed separately by each department free from Treasury control. Whether the Treasury could have acted differently had it wished to do so—to introduce greater uniformity for example—is doubtful, although Trevelyan claimed that the Treasury possessed the necessary authority.

If the power of making such Regulations be vested solely in the Head of each Department ... the consequences will be that conflicting principles will be introduced, and that it will be impossible to establish uniformity of administration in the conduct of the business of the Public.

Nor, indeed, can my Lords discharge the trust imposed upon them by the Parliament of regulating the numbers and the salaries of the several Public Establishments, unless they know that the time required to be ordinarily devoted by the members of those Establishments to their public duties will be equal to the fair measure of service required from public servants.

On the same principle proper securities in regard to attendance are required in reference to the grant of superannuation allowances. ... If this were not done, the Treasury would have to grant equal superannuation allowances to persons belonging to different Departments whose attendance might have been very different.

Although my Lords are quite prepared to admit that the enforcement of proper discipline in every office is the duty of the controlling Head of the Department, they cannot allow that it would be straining the authority which constitutionally belongs to the Treasury, to claim a right of concurring in the original adoption of regulations which are in a great degree common to all Departments.[1]

However laudable Trevelyan's intention, on this the occasion of the adoption by the War Office of a revised disciplinary code, it is more realistic to regard this statement as a declaration of what was desirable than as reflecting current Treasury practice, or even what was practicable at that time. There is no evidence that the Treasury

---

[1] Treasury to War Office, 22 February 1856, P.R.O. T.1/6049/20946.

ever referred to the number of hours worked by clerks when regulating the size or salaries of an establishment; pensions were awarded regardless of the number of hours worked each week, or the amount of paid leave permitted by the departments; and with the exception of the War Office in the case mentioned above departments were not required to obtain Treasury approval for disciplinary regulations.

Trevelyan's claim that the Treasury had authority to control departments in this respect was disputed by the Secretary of State for War, who argued (as most of his cabinet colleagues would have argued) that while the Treasury had a right and duty to exercise a financial control over all departments, such matters as these related 'entirely to the internal discipline of the Establishments placed under his Lordship's authority as Secretary of State, it rests with him to issue such regulations as he may consider necessary for the internal management of his Department, best calculated to maintain proper discipline in every branch of the Department'.[1] Therein lay the Treasury's difficulty: they were domestic matters arranged at the discretion of each head of department, and had the Treasury attempted to control them (and there is no evidence that it did on any other occasion) it laid itself open to the charge of interfering improperly in matters which fell solely within the minister's jurisdiction. Such criticism was levelled at it where there was a much better claim to control—the size of the establishment for example.

OFFICE HOURS

Most departments worked a six-hour day, six days a week; a few worked a seven-hour day.[2] Office hours were normally ten until four, in some of the larger departments, eleven to five, and in a few, ten to five. Treasury and Home Office clerks worked from eleven until five; in the Foreign Office 'the normal hours of attendance are as in other Offices, six. The Office, however, is not closed, nor are the clerks relieved from attendance till the work required, whatever may be its amount, is completed'.[3] Later hours were worked in the

---

[1] War Office to Treasury, 6 February 1856, P.R.O. T.1/6049/20946.

[2] The Playfair Commission was obliged to recommend two scales of pay for civil servants, one for those who worked in six-hour offices, and another for those who worked in seven-hour offices. *Civil Service (Playfair) Inquiry Commission*, P.P., 1875, XXIII.

[3] *Memo respecting the system under which the business of the British Foreign Office is conducted*, 1854, P.R.O. T.1/6971A/145.

Colonial Office than most other departments, from twelve until six, to provide for the daily mailing of urgent dispatches overseas.

The Treasury made no attempt to regulate office hours throughout the Service until 1887. Even then it did no more than draw attention to the subject by inviting departments to suggest regulations which might, if thought desirable, be made the subject of an Order in Council.[1] Two years later the seven-hour day was introduced throughout the lower ranks of the Service, although this had been urged by the Playfair Commission more than ten years before; the hours of the First Division Clerks (the old Superior Clerks) were not controlled until 1910 when a seven-hour day was imposed.

LEAVE

The annual leave entitlement was decided by each head of department. Eight weeks or forty-eight working days were allowed to the Clerks on the Superior Establishment of the Treasury. In the Foreign Office the allowance was the same, though they were 'not very particular as to occasional absence for a few days. We tax the clerks very severely at times, and therefore we are not very strict in other matters'.[2] In other departments annual leave varied from one to two months. Clerks in the War Office, Home Office, and Colonial Office had forty-eight days, those in the Audit Office seven weeks; while those in the Post Office only a month. Supplementary and 'inferior' clerks had less leave; in the Treasury and the offices of the Secretaries of State they were allowed thirty-one days.

Apart from the annual vacation there were 'no holidays properly so called, except Sunday, Xmas Day, Good Friday and the Queen's Birthday. In the Audit Office and perhaps in one or two other offices obsolete practices linger, but this is the general rule'.[3] Trevelyan, who believed that Treasury approval ought to be obtained before any alteration was made in the regulations governing leave, knew of only one department, the Board of Health, where the clerks were given a Saturday half-holiday, although the desirability of extending the practice throughout the Service was

[1] T.M. 5 September 1887, H.M.T., *Treasury Minutes and Circulars 1880–1889.*
[2] *Memo respecting the system under which the business of the British Foreign Office is conducted*, 1854, op. cit.
[3] The August Bank holiday was inaugurated in 1871.

discussed at a meeting of permanent heads of departments convened by Hamilton at the Treasury in 1865.[1] Half-holiday was perhaps an exaggeration, for it was proposed to 'surrender' no more than two hours on a Saturday afternoon. But even this minimum reduction in the working week was opposed by almost all the departmental representatives. Hamilton concluded, characteristically, that 'a general rule cannot be laid down but that there may be a question as to relaxation', and suggested that it would be better to leave it to be dealt with by each department, 'arrangement being better than rule'. Not until 1910 did a fortnightly half-holiday become general throughout the Service.[2]

SICK-LEAVE

Paid leave for absence caused by serious and prolonged illness was unknown in the Civil Service before 1857, although absence of a few days was recognized and caused no particular difficulty. When a civil servant fell ill and was not expected to return to work for some considerable time he was temporarily retired from the Service with a pension calculated upon the length of his service. To fill his place, or that created by the promotion of another clerk to it, an additional clerk was taken on strength. When the clerk returned to duty the departmental establishment remained one in excess of its complement until the extra clerk could be absorbed on the occurrence of the next vacancy.

This cumbrous and complicated procedure provided no safeguard for the Treasury that the extra clerk would be absorbed when a vacancy occurred and had the further disadvantage that while the clerk was temporarily retired an additional (non-effective) payment was made from public funds. Consideration of these factors when a Treasury clerk fell ill led to the abandonment of the system of temporary retirement and the introduction of the principle of paid sick-leave. The decision in this particular case marks the beginning of the control which the Treasury soon exercised over sick-leave throughout the Service. *Ad hoc* decisions made subsequently in individual cases contributed further to the development and refinement of the concept introduced for the first time in 1857, and in this way, empirically, there gradually evolved the

---

[1] *Memo of proceedings at a Conference of Heads of Public Offices held at the Treasury on Wednesday 5 July 1865*, Brit. Mus., G.P. Add. MSS. 44604, fo. 1.
[2] Order in Council, 10 January 1910.

principles, and the regulations derived from them, which distinguish sick-leave in the modern Civil Service.

The general principles by which the Treasury resolved to be guided in dealing with illness in its own department were explained briefly in a Minute drawn on 30 June 1857:

Leave of absence on full pay for the recovery of health should not exceed six months and if longer absence from duty should be necessary, not more than half salary should be allowed for a further period not exceeding six months by which time it may be expected that it will become apparent whether the officer can return to the effective discharge of his duty.[1]

No immediate attempt was made to introduce these principles into the Civil Service as a whole by issuing a general Treasury Minute or circular: at this stage the Treasury resolved only to be guided by them in similar cases in its own office and 'in other offices to which they may be applicable'. Because of its responsibility for superannuation this meant in practice that they were applied in all those cases where the Treasury was asked to retire a sick civil servant temporarily. Decisions made during the three years following the 1857 Minute served to explain and propagate the Treasury rules, and to refine them further. By 1860, as a result of a series of *ad hoc* decisions, the following 'unwritten' rules had emerged: first, in no case was temporary sick-leave to be granted unless it appeared that there was reasonable hope of recovery, attested by a medical certificate submitted to the head of department; secondly, having regard to the probability of recovery, it was at the discretion of the head of each department to grant sick-leave on full pay for a period not exceeding six months; and thirdly, at his discretion, sick-leave could be extended by a further period of six months, during which time the officer received half-pay, or such amount as he would be entitled to, supposing him then to be pensioned under the 1859 Act.[2]

One further refinement was made, again the result of considering the circumstances of a particular case. In 1860 the War Office applied to the Treasury for a ruling on the case of a clerk who had been absent on sick-leave for a total of eleven months and four days

---

[1] T.M. 30 June 1857, H.M.T., *Departmental Arrangement Book*, iii.

[2] See especially T.M. 1 September 1859, referred to in a letter to the War Office, 26 November 1860, P.R.O. T.1/6271A/17933; and T.M. 11 February 1860, P.R.O. T.1/6267B/16883.

during the previous three years. In the absence of any written Treasury directions, the War Office had assumed that the rules applied also to the sum of several short absences granted at intervals, and had continued to pay half-salary to the clerk during each period of sick-leave after the aggregate of his absences had exceeded six months.[1] The Treasury now decided that the rules related to continuous absence, and that twelve months' continuous absence was the maximum period during which any portion of salary could be paid. Frequent short absences were dealt with at the same time: 'When the aggregate time of unconnected absences from illness and with intervals between them shall exceed one-quarter of the period within which such absences may have been granted or of the extra period of active service, all salary during subsequent absences should cease.'

Treasury rules were intended more to place a limit upon the extent to which sick-leave ought to be granted than to ensure that civil servants received exactly the same sick pay. Within the limits set by the Treasury the head of each department was free to decide what benefit should be given having regard to the circumstances of each case. But even outside these limits the Treasury was always prepared to consider granting sick-leave in special circumstances. Although a civil servant unable to resume duty after twelve months' absence was considered permanently incapable and required to retire from the Service, the Treasury occasionally agreed to an additional period of leave (sometimes with, sometimes without pay) where it was anticipated that it would restore a 'valuable public servant' permanently to the Service, instead of compelling him to retire on a pension, or to return prematurely to active service. In one respect, however, the Treasury brooked no compromise. Departments were no longer permitted to obtain temporary assistance when clerks were absent through illness or other causes. With the introduction of sick-leave it became a rule of the Service that in such circumstances the duties of the absent clerk would be assumed by his colleagues, who if necessary, would be expected to work after office hours.

'GUARDIAN OF CIVIL SERVICE MORALITY'

'The public have a right to expect that a high moral standard should be maintained by the executive Government with reference

[1] War Office to Treasury, November 1860, P.R.O. T.1/6271A/17933.

to all civil servants of Her Majesty and especially those filling the higher situations', wrote Hamilton.[1] The Treasury's task was to preserve and reinforce that morality, he explained to Gladstone. In practice, however, the functions it performed in fulfilment of that self-imposed duty were few, although the manner in which they were discharged contributed to the development of an uncorrupt and incorruptible Service, and provided an important precedent for more ambitious disciplinary control in the future.

Only once did the Treasury succeed in introducing into the departments a general disciplinary regulation, and that was delayed for ten years because of the doubt and disapproval of Treasury ministers. Apart from this it made no attempt to secure the introduction of uniform disciplinary regulations or to prescribe a general code of conduct. Anxious as the Treasury was to uphold the 'honour and independence' of civil servants, it is perhaps not surprising that its only general disciplinary regulation dealt with those who got into financial difficulties as a result of improvidence or extravagance. Although drafted in 1858 it was not circularized until ten years later, despite the Prime Minister having approved and signed it. Disraeli, then Chancellor of the Exchequer, believing 'not in Thrift, but in Destiny',[2] 'had doubts about it and it stood over'.[3]

The Treasury's concern to uphold the morality of the Service and to prevent it suffering from 'the unworthiness of some of its members' was inspired partly by considerations of efficiency. An officer in financial difficulty was not an efficient officer:

An efficient performance of his official duty is not to be expected from any person involved in pecuniary difficulties as the time and thoughts of such a person, instead of being engaged in his official business, must necessarily be occupied in constant effort to meet the exigencies of the day, and further, it is highly inexpedient that any officer in such circumstances should be placed in a position of trust.[4]

Anthony Trollope, who began his official career as a £90 p.a. clerk in the Post Office, was 'hopelessly in debt' during the whole

[1] Treasury to Stationery Office, 11 May 1861, P.R.O. T.1/6333B/18192.
[2] Asa Briggs, *Victorian People*, p. 278.
[3] Memo from Hamilton to Sclater-Booth, 20 November 1868, P.R.O. T.1/6840A/19466.
[4] Minute of the Board of Stamps and Taxes, 23 June 1842, quoted in T.M. 30 November 1868, P.R.O. T.1/6840A/19466.

Y

of his seven years at St. Martin's Le Grand. 'Sheriffs' officers with uncanny documents, of which I never understood anything, were common attendants upon me. And yet I do not remember that I was ever locked up, though I think I was twice a prisoner.'[1] It was almost as though the Treasury had Trollope in mind when it thundered against young men who became involved in pecuniary obligations by putting their names to Accommodation Bills.

I rarely at this time had any money wherewith to pay my bills. In this state of things a certain tailor had taken from me an acceptance for, I think, £12, which found its way into the hands of a money-lender. With that man . . . I formed a most heart-rending but most intimate acquaintance. In cash I once received from him £4. For that and for the original amount of the tailor's bill, which grew monstrously under repeated renewals, I paid ultimately something over £200 . . . the peculiarity of this man was that he became so attached to me as to visit me every day at my office.[2]

A Foreign Secretary once gave a small dispatch bag addressed to one of H.M. Ministers abroad to a Civil Service friend who was in pecuniary difficulties so that he might leave the office by the back-door entrance, and so escape the vigilance of the bailiff who was waiting to meet him at the Downing Street entrance. On another occasion he instructed his office butler 'never to answer a knock at the door or a ring at the bell until he had put up the small chain, hung at the side of the hall door, so as to prevent the forced entrance of any undesirable visitors in the shape of a dun'.[3]

Financial embarrassment frequently led to absence from duty, either to avoid the importunities of creditors, such as the little man who dogged Trollope's heels, or to obtain protection under the Act for the relief of insolvent debtors. When, as often happened, a court order was made appropriating a part of the civil servant's salary for the liquidation of his debts 'the Public Service is damnified, the officer upon his return to duty is called upon to act very probably in a responsible situation, with diminished salary, disproportionately to the nature of the service required of him, and with a character in some manner impaired'.[4] To prevent this, and in order 'to maintain rigidly the moral standard of the Service and the independent position of its members', the Treasury drew

---

[1] Anthony Trollope, *An Autobiography*, p. 57.   [2] Ibid., p. 55.
[3] Hertslet, *Recollections of the Old Foreign Office*, pp. 17–18.
[4] T.M. 30 November 1868, op. cit.

up a set of rules closely modelled on those which had long been in existence in the Revenue Departments. Pecuniary embarrassment was punished with penalties of varying severity according to the culpability of the officer, from loss of promotion or annual incre- ment, to a threatened but indefinite 'summary and more severe punishment'. Suspension from duty and salary could be imposed for debt or bankruptcy, and reinstatement was guaranteed only if it was discovered subsequently that the civil servant's difficulties had been caused by unavoidable misfortune. Failure to inform the head of his department that he had been arrested for debt, or that he had applied to the Commissioners of Bankruptcy or Insolvency, could result in removal from the Service without expectation of reinstatement. These rules had been drafted in 1858, but held in abeyance until 1868 when Hamilton brought them to the attention of the Financial Secretary.

Many years experience convinces me [he wrote] more and more in the necessity of some definite rule being laid down, not to operate with unnecessary severity, but to prevent the scandal and feeling of injustice which must be created in the Public Service where an unfortunate man in the Inland Revenue is dismissed and sent with his family to beggary because he became a bankrupt from borrowing money to assist his Mother. While in the PO leave of absence is given to a man in order that he may become a bankrupt. I think such a rule as I have prepared in the present Minute is essential to the *morale* of the Civil Service.[1]

Copies of the Minute were sent out to all departments in Dec- ember 1868, but there was no question of the Treasury being able to secure the adoption of the rules throughout the Service. Con- scious of the limit within which it could operate, the Treasury merely invited their co-operation in giving effect to the views contained in the Minute; they should 'if possible be adopted as a general system'.

As the self-appointed guardian of Civil Service morality, the Treasury had one other function: in certain circumstances it awarded 'compassionate allowances' to civil servants who, dis- missed for misconduct, had neither pension nor gratuity. Authority to do so rested upon the will of Parliament to pass these payments; there was none under the 1859 Superannuation Act. Despite Hamilton's injunction that they 'ought to be as rare as possible

---

[1] Memo from Hamilton to Sclater-Booth, 20 November 1868, op. cit.

and to be watched vigilantly',[1] several examples are to be found in the Treasury files, among them awards to two War Office clerks, a clerk in the Stationery Office, and two clerks in the Treasury. The War Office clerks were dismissed for gambling with dice during office hours; two of the others were dismissed for borrowing money, and one for 'discreditable bill transactions'.

The decision to dismiss a clerk for misconduct rested with the head of department, and any claim for compassionate allowance subsequently had to be made by him on behalf of the dismissed man, and supported by evidence of destitution or great hardship. The allowances made by the Treasury, while invariably less than the man's pension entitlement, were generous in the circumstances, although there was reluctance to make any award to a clerk who had held a responsible position.

I have always thought it most important [wrote Hamilton] to maintain the morale of the Civil Service, and men in some authority who by example and influence and even by direct action ought to prevent such misconduct, are themselves guilty of connivance or encouragement, they ought to be severely dealt with. . . . I am unable to satisfy myself that where a man in authority is rightly dismissed for misconduct he can be regarded as a subject for a compassionate allowance.[2]

One of the two War Office clerks dismissed for gambling was the principal of a sub-division and because of that not recommended by the department for an award; the other, a 2nd Class Clerk, was supported, and the Treasury awarded him an allowance of £100 p.a. on the ground that he was less culpable than the principal. However, four years later, the latter applied through the War Office for an allowance. Hamilton opposed it but was overruled by the Financial Secretary who thought the principal 'may have been made the scapegoat for the sins of the WO'.[3]

The Treasury's attitude towards the award of these allowances was characteristically ambivalent. On the one hand there was the desire to uphold the public morality of the service, to make an example of the civil servant dismissed for misconduct; on the other, there was the wish to 'temper the severity' of the punish-

---

[1] Memo from Hamilton to Gladstone, 2 May 1864, P.R.O. T.1/6514B/16998.
[2] Memo from Hamilton to James Stansfeld, 4 November 1869, P.R.O. T.1/6912A/17948.
[3] Memo from James Stansfeld to Hamilton, 11 December 1869, P.R.O. T.1/6912A/17948.

ment (to use Hamilton's words). When, therefore, the conditions of diminished culpability and imminent destitution were fulfilled, the Treasury could usually be prevailed upon to award a compassionate allowance. In other circumstances the punishment meted out by the Treasury could be unusually severe. Borrowing money, especially from colleagues, was a serious offence (and for that reason necessitated the exceptional step of issuing a general regulation to deal with it). Lowe refused to agree to the award of an allowance to a clerk who borrowed money from those whose accounts he had been examining, because in doing so he had betrayed his employers and 'deserves condign punishment'. An extreme case was that of a clerk dismissed from the Treasury for using his position at the head of his sub-department to induce subordinates to join him in borrowing money. Hamilton admitted that he would not have been treated with such severity in other departments, but held that nothing short of dismissal would be sufficient to protect the public interest. 'If we were to allow one example of such public immorality as Mr. Miller's to be condoned in any way, in our own Department—I think we should become powerless in resisting such appeals which come before us.'[1] Nevertheless, the Treasury felt constrained even here to temper the severity of the punishment by awarding him a compassionate allowance of £130 p.a.

[1] Memo from Hamilton to Gladstone, 3 May 1864, P.R.O. T.1/6514B/16998.

14

SUPERANNUATION

INTRODUCTION

CIVIL SERVICE superannuation has its roots in a Treasury
Minute of August 1803, 'one of the great landmarks in
British social policy'.[1] More than a hundred years earlier
Martin Horsham, a landwaiter in the Port of London, who was
'so much indisposed by a great melancholy that he is at present
unfit for business', had received the first public pension granted by
the Government.[2] At first, office-holders provided personally for
their predecessors, but during the eighteenth century the principles
of public pensions were slowly evolved and refined, the search for
the equitable distribution of costs moving outwards from the individual to the group. Finally, the principle of collective responsibility was accepted and serving officers made regular contributions
to a Superannuation Fund.[3]

The enactment of the Treasury Minute in 1810 resulted in the
abolition of deductions from salaries and the establishment of the
first non-contributory superannuation scheme covering the whole
Service. But eleven years later, the heavy cost to the Exchequer led
to a demand that civil servants should contribute once again to a
Superannuation Fund. This was enacted shortly after, although
the new contributory scheme was short-lived, for it was soon discovered that abatement of salary was a violation of the terms upon
which civil servants entered the Civil Service, and in 1824 the
Government once again assumed sole responsibility for the cost of
public pensions.

---

[1] R. M. Titmuss, foreword to Marios Raphael, *Pensions and Public Servants*.
[2] Ibid.
[3] For the early history of Civil Service superannuation see Raphael, op. cit.
Developments in the nineteenth century are dealt with there and in the report of
the *Select Committee on Civil Service Superannuation*, 1856, P.P., 1856, IX;
in the report of the Commissioners appointed to inquire into the operation of the
Superannuation Act, P.P., 1857 (Session 2), XXIV, pp. v–xxxviii; and in Gerald
Rhodes, *Public Sector Pensions*.

The contributory scheme launched by the Act of 1834 was more firmly based. Deductions were made from the salaries only of those who had entered the Service after August 1829; those recruited before that date paid nothing. But it was no more popular with the civil servants, who in 1846 formed an association, with Richard Bromley (later Accountant-General of the Navy) as chairman, to petition the Government about the plight of widows left without pensions despite the deductions made from their husbands' salaries. For the first time civil servants combined on an inter-departmental basis to secure the redress of a common grievance. In 1853 an inter-departmental committee under the chairmanship of a Customs officer was set up to win public acceptance for the principle of an untaxed salary and a fair pension.

The main complaints of these bodies were that the Government was making a profit out of the deductions; that the surplus should be used to provide for officers' widows and children; that pensions should be increased, and calculated on annual instead of septennial terms of length of service; that those who contributed towards their pension received less generous awards than those whose allowances were calculated on scales fixed by earlier Acts; that salaries were inadequate after deducting the superannuation contribution; and that deductions were levied on civil servants who had no entitlement to superannuation under the Act. Besides these alleged inequities in the administration of the Superannuation Act, there was also the anomalous position of departments such as the Poor Law Board, which being established for a limited period, were not subject to the 1834 Act.

Some of these complaints were met by the provisions of the Bill introduced by Palmerston's Government in February 1856, although it did not deal with the question of deductions. It was greeted with considerable opposition in the House of Commons and the Government decided to refer it to a Select Committee. On 7 July the Committee reported to the House the evidence they had heard and submitted an amended version of the Bill. Their proposal to abolish contributions but requiring the Treasury to revise all salaries 'with a due regard to the amount of deductions remitted' was vigorously opposed by civil servants, a factor which contributed to the Government's decision to postpone discussion of the Bill until the following session. At the end of the year, however, a Treasury Commission was appointed to continue and com-

plete the inquiry into the operation of the Superannuation Acts
begun by the Select Committee. Its main conclusions were approval
of the principle of pensions, which they said safeguarded the
civil servant's independence; the abolition of deductions and the
Superannuation Fund, without corresponding reductions of
salaries; the extension of superannuation provisions to officers
of new departments; the lowering of the age of retirement from
sixty-five to sixty, and the introduction of compulsory retirement
at sixty-five; and the establishment of a new scale of pensions.
'The spirit behind these recommendations seemed to be the creation of a comprehensive system of superannuation provisions,
liberal enough to be accepted by the civil servants and sufficiently
extensive to cover the needs of a reformed Civil Service which was
then beginning to take shape. The fundamental argument throughout was the need to raise the efficiency of the Service.'[1]

The month following the submission of the Commission's report
to the Treasury a private member's Bill was introduced to repeal
that section of the 1834 Act which imposed deductions on civil servants. Despite Government opposition, the Bill became law in
August 1857, largely as a result of the campaign mounted by the
General Committee of Civil Servants for the Amendment of the
Superannuation Act of 1834 formed earlier that year. Twenty-
four departments were represented on the committee, which was
supported by a sub-structure of departmental committees.
Their petitions to Parliament, and their solicitation of the support
of back-bench members were described by Ayrton as an 'organised
conspiracy'. Ironically, six months later a report from the Government actuaries showed that deductions made from salaries did not
cover the costs of pensions, but it came too late to destroy the basis
of the case argued against deductions.

As *The Civil Service Gazette* was quick to point out, the successful campaign for the abolition of deductions had demonstrated the
strength and efficacy of collective action, but despite its constant
advocacy of unionism, it took another common and equally
deeply felt grievance, low salaries, to bring them together again.[2]
From its first issue in January 1853 until the passing of the Superannuation Act six years later, the paper placed before its readers
a ceaseless flow of information, commentary and discussion on
every aspect of the issue. Scarcely a week passed without a passion-
ate denunciation of the 'monster grievance', and its correspondence

[1] Raphael, pp. 156–7.   [2] See above, Chapter 9, pp. 227–30.

columns were filled with letters of complaint and suggestions for amelioration from serving officers. During this time it became the focus of opposition to the hated 'Superannuation Tax', whipping up enthusiasm and support for the activities of the campaign committees, and raising and sustaining morale in the months of inactivity. More than any other issue, it helped to establish the paper as the organ and voice of Civil Service opinion, the fearless and outspoken champion of the cause of all serving officers.

All the Commission's other proposals were incorporated in the Superannuation Act passed on 19 April 1859, with the exception of that intended to introduce compulsory retirement at sixty-five which was abandoned as a result of an almost accidental parliamentary bargain. Sixty became the recognized age of retirement. Together the Acts of 1857 and 1859 laid the foundations and established the principles which govern superannuation in the modern Civil Service.

The 1859 Act is significant in another respect: it required those who entered the Service after April 1859 to obtain a certificate from the Civil Service Commissioners in order to qualify for the award of a pension. This had important consequences for the control of recruitment by the Civil Service Commissioners and the Treasury. Much more important here, however, is the authority vested in the Treasury to regulate and control the award of superannuation allowances, and the almost unlimited discretion available to it in the exercise of that authority. It alone could make an award and decide who was entitled or ineligible. It could award pensions greater or less than the scales laid down in the Act, or refuse to make an award at all; and its decisions were final, not subject to any appeal.

Before the Treasury could begin to award pensions it had first to make regulations under the broad provisions of the new Act. Regulation and administration were inter-connected, however, and although the regulations drafted soon after the passing of the Act became the basis for the award of pensions subsequently, other regulations—some written but most of them unwritten rules which quickly became established as precedents—were added to them in the course of administering it. The main regulations were set out in two Treasury Minutes,[1] themselves based upon reports submitted by a Treasury Committee appointed on 30 May 1859, just six

---

[1] T.M. 14 June 1859, P.R.O. T.1/6269B/17680 and T.M. 24 August 1860, P.R.O. T.1/6270A/17757.

weeks after the passing of the Act, consisting of the newly formed Treasury Superannuation Committee (the Assistant Secretary and one of the Junior Lords), and the Principal Officer of the 4th Division who was responsible for the supervision of superannuation business.

THE TREASURY SUPERANNUATION COMMITTEE

Between 1831 and 1859 each pension claim submitted to the Treasury was scrutinized by two Junior Lords of the Treasury Board, 'who shall examine into its merits, and call for such information as they may think necessary, and report to my Lords the allowance which they consider just . . . and if there be any circumstances which may distinguish it from ordinary cases they are desired to state them in their Report'.[1] In practice most cases were seen by only one Junior Lord, assisted by the Principal Officer in charge of superannuation business who prepared the Minutes from the reports made by him.

Frequent changes in the composition of the Treasury Board had in the past militated against continuity in the administration of the superannuation regulations, especially important in this branch of Treasury business which required a close knowledge of precedents and past practice. To provide for it the Assistant Secretary was appointed a permanent member of the committee in May 1859. No change was made in the procedure for dealing with superannuation business, but from the formation of the new committee it was customary to select a 2nd Class Clerk from the 4th Division to prepare the superannuation cases for their consideration. C. C. Pullar, who served the committee from 1870–7, had 'so completely and systematically mastered the precedents and principles which govern this important and often difficult branch of administration that he has become a recognised authority upon the subject both within the Treasury and beyond it'.[2]

The Superannuation Committee would not consider a pension claim until the civil servant had left the Service. Preliminary communications or negotiations prior to retirement were discouraged on the ground that the committee's decision was semi-judicial. From time to time, usually in connection with projected

[1] T.M. 21 June 1831, P.R.O. T.1/6901A/15620.
[2] T.M. 22 November 1877, H.M.T., *Departmental Arrangement Book*, v.

schemes of departmental reorganization which involved the prospective abolition of office, the Treasury was invited to discuss the amount of compensation which a clerk would receive on retirement. The Chancellor of the Exchequer (Gladstone) and the President of the Board of Trade (Milner Gibson) discussed privately the amount of pension which might be awarded James Booth, Secretary to the Board, on his retirement. Gladstone referred the case unofficially to the Superannuation Committee for an opinion, but when Milner Gibson alleged that they were biased, Hamilton thought it time to remind Gladstone of the Treasury rule precluding prior discussion. Gladstone apologized to Hamilton:

Partly through deference to Milner Gibson (on every ground well deserved) and partly through want of carefulness to the importance of peculiar Treasury rules in this department of business, I have committed an error in letting this discussion proceed so far. I think it pretty plain that negotiations about superannuation anterior to resignation however fair they undoubtedly are in this case would, if they became a general rule, tend to demoralise and degrade the Civil Service.[1]

The concurrence of both members was not needed for every decision, but very special or unusual cases, or those in which doubt or difficulty arose, were seen by them both. Usually the Financial Secretary was consulted as well, and his judgement was sometimes decisive. A difference of opinion between the committee members was settled by reference to the Chancellor of the Exchequer.

RETIREMENT, DEATH OR RESIGNATION

For the purpose of awarding pensions in the normal circumstances of retirement, death or resignation through ill-health, the Treasury distinguished three categories of civil servants. Those who entered the Service after 1859 were awarded pensions on the scale set out in the Act, which provided for a maximum of two-thirds salary after forty years' service.[2] To qualify a civil servant had to serve continuously for ten years in an established capacity in the permanent Civil Service, although in practice the Treasury allowed civil servants to count temporary (unestablished) service, provided that

---

[1] Gladstone to Hamilton, 21 December 1864, P.R.O. T.1/6573A/15478.
[2] Those who had served between ten and eleven years were awarded an allowance equal to 10/60ths of salary and emoluments; those who had served between eleven and twelve years were awarded 11/60ths, and so on.

there was no break between it and subsequent established service. The other two categories—those who had entered before and after August 1829—were not provided for in the 1859 Act, separate regulations for each were drafted by the Superannuation Committee.[1]

A civil servant had to satisfy the Treasury that he had served in an established capacity in the permanent Civil Service, and that he had received salary or remuneration out of the Consolidated Fund, or from monies voted by Parliament. This latter requirement weeded out all those without *bona fide* claims and requires no further explanation. Service in the permanent Civil Service could be established by those who held an appointment directly from the Crown; by those admitted into the Civil Service with a certificate issued by the Civil Service Commissioners; by those belonging to a class already entitled to superannuation allowance; and by those belonging to a class in which, if the civil servant had been appointed to it subsequently to the passing of the 1859 Act, he would have been entitled to an allowance because he had been admitted into the Civil Service with a certificate issued by the Civil Service Commissioners.[2]

Difficulty arose mainly in the consideration of the claims of those who had entered the Service after 1859 without certificates, as *prima facie* they were disqualified from pension rights on retirement. 'The 17th section . . . makes it imperative for the purposes of the Act that every Civil Servant appointed after 19 April 1859 shall have been admitted into the Civil Service with a certificate from the Civil Service Commissioners', Hamilton wrote in 1863.[3] Nevertheless, it was thought inadvisable to lay it down as a rule that failure to obtain a certificate before appointment could not be remedied subsequently. While possesion of a certificate was essential, it could be (and was) obtained after appointment. 'The number of persons (especially in the Admiralty) who have obtained C.S. certificates some time after their appointment to established situations is very great', the Superannuation Clerk told Lingen.[4] But the Civil Service Commissioners could not be persuaded to

[1] See 1st Report of Treasury Superannuation Committee, 11 June 1859, P.R.O. T.1/6269B/17680.

[2] 22 Vic., cap 26, clause 17; and 1st Report of Treasury Superannuation Committee, 11 June 1859, op. cit.

[3] Letter to the Judges of the Landed Estates Court, Ireland, 30 May 1863, P.R.O. T.1/6455B/17607.

[4] Memo from Pullar to Lingen, 25 July 1873, P.R.O. T.1/7330/20175.

issue a certificate on every such occasion. To relieve hardship in deserving cases, the Treasury sponsored a Superannuation Amendment Act in 1873, enabling it to admit the claim to pension of any person who had been recruited to the Service after 1859 and before 4 June 1870 without a certificate, provided that the omission to comply with the 1859 Act had not been intentional.[1] To one of several submissions made by the Admiralty subsequently, the Treasury replied that the absence of a certificate showed such 'gross culpable negligence on the part of his superior officers that before making any order my Lords wished to know whether the Lords of the Admiralty would not in some way mark their sense of that negligence'.[2]

Possession of the Civil Service Commissioner's certificate was not the real test of eligibility, automatically qualifying the holder for a pension. Many certificated clerks were declared ineligible. In practice the Treasury distinguished between 'established' and 'non-established' service, and this definition of 'civil servant', drawn from a reading of clause 17 *and* clause 2 of the Act, which stated explicitly that pensions were to be granted to those 'who shall have served in an established capacity in the permanent Civil Service', excluded all the temporary clerks, copyists, writers, etc., from its benefits.[3] Most of them were engaged without examination, had no certificate, and could not establish a *prima facie* claim to a pension. Strictly, none of them should have been admitted without a certificate—under the 1855 Order in Council it was required for any employment in the Civil Service, permanent or *temporary*[4] —but few departments bothered to send their temporary clerks for examination; two who did were the War Office, where they were employed in greater numbers than elsewhere, and the Colonial Office. Because of this the Treasury was called upon to decide whether the possession of a certificate was in itself sufficient to qualify for a pension—clause 17 appeared to give them a good title. In April 1865 three temporary clerks admitted into the War Office with certificates issued by the Civil Service Commissioners,

---

[1] This was decided by the Treasury in each case after considering the replies to eighteen questions put to the department; a copy of the application form is enclosed in P.R.O. T.1/7330/20175.

[2] H. W. Primrose to J. G. Dodson, 6 January 1874, Bod., M.B.P., box 43.

[3] Memo from Hamilton to Frederick Peel, 13 April 1865, P.R.O. T.1/6558B/10183.

[4] See memo by Frederick Peel, 11 February 1865, P.R.O. T.1/6558B/10183.

submitted a legal opinion supporting their claim to a pension under the 1859 Act. 'There is not much in it', Hamilton advised Peel, because pensions were payable only to those who had served in an established capacity in the permanent Civil Service.[1] Temporary clerks were clearly excluded by this definition. Although they might 'be continued in the service for a considerable number of years and only retire from it through age or infirmity, yet from the uncertainty which must necessarily exist regarding the tenure of their appointments they cannot as a class be said to belong to the permanent Civil Service of the State'.[2] This interpretation was not arguable in law, for as Hamilton reminded Peel the Treasury's decision on all claims was final. The War Office was now informed of the new ruling: 'My Lords have no authority to treat the possession of a Civil Service Certificate or of a progressive salary as sufficient to establish a claim to Superannuation' under the 1859 Act.[3]

While this disposed of the claims of those temporary clerks who had been admitted with certificates, the claim to superannuation of the new class of writers introduced into the Customs in 1866 after an examination conducted by the Civil Service Commissioners appeared to rest on firmer ground. Hamilton disposed of it by ruling somewhat arbitrarily and speciously that the necessity for examination by the Civil Service Commissioners arose from the 1855 Order in Council, whereas the necessity for a certificate for superannuation arose from the Act of 1859. 'Because a person appointed after 1859 to the Civil Service cannot receive superannuation of retirement unless admitted by Civil Service certificate it does not follow that the admission by the Civil Service Commissioners entitled a man to superannuation allowance.'[4]

In the light of this evidence generalizations about the restrictive nature of the 1859 Act and its effect upon recruitment now require some qualification. It is no longer true to say that 'its benefits were restricted to civil servants who had entered the service with the certificate of the Civil Service Commissioners'.[5] Many who entered with certificates were denied allowances by the Treasury, while some who had entered without a certificate, but who ob-

---

[1] Hamilton to Frederick Peel, 13 April 1865, P.R.O. T.1/6558B/10183.
[2] Treasury to Colonial Office, 13 May 1863, P.R.O. T.1/6466A/18399.
[3] Treasury to War Office, 13 April 1865, P.R.O. T.1/6558B/10183.
[4] Memo by Hamilton, (?)June 1866, P.R.O. T.1/6628B/10734.
[5] R. Moses, *The Civil Service of Great Britain*, p. 97. This is the general view of those who have written on the nineteenth-century Civil Service.

tained one subsequently, were declared by the Treasury to be eligible for the award; others still who had no certificate were superannuated by the Treasury under clause four of the Act.[1] Much more important for the development of a modern unified Service was that by making the crucial distinction between 'established' and 'non-established' service the Treasury had produced the first working definition of 'civil servant'.

Unless the head of department testified that the clerk had served with 'diligence and fidelity' the Treasury awarded less than the full amount of pension. It found 'according to the conscience or caprice of the head officers who certify every variety of qualification to the complete certificate'.[2] Those considered unsatisfactory, of which the Treasury was the sole judge, were marked by making a deduction from the full superannuation entitlement; it was customary to do so in every instance of misconduct, however slight. For example, if the certificate stated that a clerk had been suspended or degraded thirty years previously for carelessness, but that his conduct had been exemplary since, the Treasury made a nominal deduction to comply with the Act. To do so, said Hamilton, had a salutary effect because 'every man knows that a recorded fault whether of omission or commission will have a result upon his superannuation. If in slight or remote cases we ignore it altogether, the expectation will spread'.[3] Although the rule was applied very strictly, deductions were generally very small and the civil servant suffered no great financial loss.

In normal circumstances the Treasury would not grant a pension to a civil servant who retired under the age of sixty unless he produced a medical certificate testifying that he was incapable from infirmity of mind or body from carrying out his duties. There had to be a probability that the infirmity would be permanent.

SPECIAL SERVICES

In certain special circumstances the Treasury could award a higher pension than that normally permitted under the Act. Provided that the amount was not greater than the salary and emoluments received at the time of retirement, and the reasons for making the

---

[1] See below, p. 324.
[2] Memo from Hamilton to James Stansfeld, 18 November 1869, P.R.O. T.1/6907A/17125. [3] Ibid.

award stated in a Minute laid before Parliament, its discretion was unlimited. Early on, however, Gladstone ruled that ordinary duties however well performed, were insufficient to establish a claim for a special pension; to which Lowe added later that: 'If a man possesses in however high degree the qualities which we have a right to expect from a good clerk, he is not by that entitled to a pension for special service. If he has qualities different in kind from the ordinary qualifications of a clerk and uses them so as materially to benefit the public service, I think he is entitled.'[1]

Awards were made mainly to three kinds of civil servants: first, to those permanent heads of departments who had not served long enough to qualify for a pension commensurate with their position and responsibility. This happened quite frequently, for people were still appointed to such posts from outside the Service. Sir Rowland Hill had been a civil servant intermittently for a period of twenty years and on retirement was entitled to a pension of only £568 p.a. Exercising its discretion under the Act the Treasury awarded him £2,000 p.a., a sum equivalent to his salary, the maximum which he could receive. Secondly, pensions for special services were awarded to distinguished high-ranking officers whose service while long did not provide them with a sufficient reward for their services to the State. Sir Richard Bromley, the Accountant-General of the Navy, had served for thirty-three years, his salary was £1,300 and his superannuation entitlement, £715; he retired on £1,000 p.a. Thirdly, and most commonly, special pensions were awarded to senior officers who had served with distinction for a very long time, normally between forty and fifty years, in order that their long and meritorious service could be brought to the notice of Parliament. All of them had entered the Service before 1859, and their ordinary entitlement under previous Acts closely approximated to their salary on retirement; in such cases it was considered necessary to mark the recognition of their special services by only a small addition. Charles Crafer, a Principal Clerk in the Treasury, had served for forty-seven years and was entitled to £1,100 on retirement, only £100 less than his salary; his special services were acknowledged by the addition of £50 p.a.

Before agreeing to an award the Treasury required a strong recommendation from the head of the department, a testimonial of

[1] Memo by Lowe, 1872, P.R.O. T.1/7281B/3067.

character, service, and merit, and evidence that the civil servant
had performed some special service, or had performed his duties in
an exceptional manner, or had some special claim to consideration
under the ninth clause. Crafer had broken down from overwork,
and in Hamilton's opinion 'these are precisely the cases in which
in my judgment a special recognition is not only just—but gives
a most useful encouragement to every gentleman in the Civil
Service'.[1] On a number of occasions Hamilton maintained that the
Treasury very rarely awarded an allowance equal to full salary,
yet several civil servants received such a sum, among them Sir
Rowland Hill, Secretary of the Post Office; Pressley, Chairman of
the Board of Inland Revenue; and Antonio Panizzi, Principal
Librarian and Secretary of the British Museum. Pressley's services
were unusual even among special services: 'Sir Robert Peel in
Parliament attributed to him mainly the success which attended
the introduction of the Property Tax, and every Chancellor of the
Exchequer knows the value of his services in the preparation of the
Budget.'[2] Pensions for special services had to be approved by the
Chancellor of the Exchequer, but only once did he reject the Super-
annuation Committee's recommendation.

The superannuation of James Booth, Secretary to the Board of
Trade, illustrates the difficulties which could arise under the
ninth clause where the head of a department urged the award of a
pension greater than the Superannuation Committee was prepared
to recommend. Gladstone had been urged privately by the President of the Board of Trade, Milner Gibson, to authorize the award
of full salary. While Hamilton and Sir William Dunbar, the two
members of the Superannuation Committee, agreed that the ordinary rules of superannuation were inapplicable, neither felt able
to recommend the award of more than two-thirds. Later, in conversation with Hamilton, Gladstone agreed that Booth should
not be allowed full salary, but after further private talks with
Milner Gibson, thought that the Treasury might go as high as
three-quarters. Writing to the Financial Secretary Hamilton
then said: 'He will sanction 2/3 if on consideration we think it
should be limited to that but I cannot doubt that his own judgment

[1] Memo from Hamilton to J. Bagwell (Junior Lord and member of Treasury
Superannuation Committee), 26 November 1859, P.R.O. T.1/6215A/18322.
[2] Memo from Hamilton to Sir William Dunbar (Junior Lord and member of
Treasury Superannuation Committee), 1 December 1864, P.R.O. T.1/6573A/
15478.

z

leans to 3/4. As it is entirely discretional with him and as I think he estimates Mr Booth's services somewhat more highly than we do I incline to think we ought to sanction 3/4.'[1] Milner Gibson then called twice on Hamilton at the Treasury to urge Booth's claim to full salary, later alleging that it had not been considered impartially. Answering this charge Hamilton remarked to Peel that 'there is just as much impartiality inside as outside the Treasury—perhaps in cases like Mr Booth's our bias is sensibly rather in his favour than in favour of the public—and I freely confess, as Sir William Dunbar very well puts it, the suggestion I ventured to offer that we might possibly go as far as 3/4 was rather in deference to what I believed to be Gladstone's view, than in accordance with my own judgment'. Peel agreed that the Treasury was not justified in going beyond three-quarters. At Gladstone's request the Superannuation Committee now re-examined the claim in the light of Milner Gibson's further representations, but its opinion remained unchanged and Booth was awarded a pension equal to three-quarters of his salary.

The Treasury could also use the ninth clause to reduce a pension for demerit. It did so on three occasions where the head of a department refused to certify that the civil servant had served with 'diligence and fidelity'. Lowe dealt personally with two of the cases and made substantial reductions.[2]

ABOLITION OF OFFICE

The Treasury could also award a special pension where a civil servant retired voluntarily on the abolition of his office, or was removed from the Service 'for the purpose of facilitating improvements in the organisation of the department to which he belongs, by which greater efficiency and economy can be effected'.[3] The Treasury's discretion was subject only to the condition that the pension could not exceed two-thirds of the salary and other earnings at the time of retirement, but even this limitation was disregarded in certain circumstances. Compensation on loss of office was awarded on a special scale drawn by the Superannuation Committee shortly after the passing of the 1859 Act, providing for a

---

[1] Memo from Hamilton to Frederick Peel, 23 November 1864, P.R.O. T.1/ 6573A/15478.
[2] One pension was reduced from £877 to £650, the other from £1,050 to £980.   [3] Clause seven, 22 Vic, cap 26.

maximum of ten years to be added to actual service for those who had served twenty years or more. Sixty-five was regarded by the Treasury as the proper age for retirement, although legally there was no fixed age-limit, Parliament having expressly rejected a clause in the 1859 Act requiring retirement at that age.[1] The Superannuation Committee's practice was to award only a proportion of the additional ten years to those over the age of fifty-five who had served twenty years; a civil servant aged sixty was awarded five extra years, and a clerk of sixty-four, one.[2]

Abolition of office was discretionary with each department, but each claim for pension had to be supported by details of service and salary together with the usual certificate of diligence and fidelity. As far as possible the Treasury tried to ensure that those recommended by the departments were over sixty and thus ineligible for recall into the Service under clause eleven of the 1859 Act. It also tried to prevent departments retiring efficient officers, although in the War Office reorganization of 1864–5 this condition was disregarded and some efficient civil servants well below the age of sixty were retired.[3] Particular attention was paid to the requirement under the Act that the retirement of officers to facilitate improvements in departmental organization should result in 'greater efficiency and economy'. It was not enough that 'the public service will not suffer disadvantage'; nor would the Treasury allow a civil servant to retire with compensation for loss of office if it was intended that somebody else should take his place. The Assistant Accountant-General of the War Office was not permitted to retire although the retirement was recommended by his department and desired by him. The immediate abolition of his office was not essential to the reorganization of the Account Branch, and his age (forty-four) and the testimony borne to his ability were proof of his continuing fitness for useful service, the Treasury said. But after personal representations made to him by the War Office, Hamilton changed his mind and advised his minister to

[1] Witnesses examined by the *Select Committee on Civil Services Expenditure* in 1873 all agreed that sixty-five should be the age of compulsory retirement throughout the Service.

[2] This was an 'unwritten rule' of the Treasury applied 'with almost uniform strictness to a very large number of cases probably hundreds', superseding a T.M. of 17 December 1864 which fixed the age limit at sixty. For this whole issue see P.R.O. T.1/6520C/17582 and T.1/7072A/9803.

[3] Memo from Cole to Hamilton, 25 November 1865, P.R.O. T.1/6602A/19181.

superannuate under the seventh clause: 'It cannot be denied that the more usual course has been to permit persons to retire under somewhat similar circumstances.'[1] (The Superannuation Clerk had prepared a list showing that the Treasury's usual practice had been to award compensation to clerks of similar age, despite the condition that clerks eligible for recall into the Service should not be retired on abolition of office.) The Financial Secretary would not agree, however, and retirement under clause seven was refused: 'It would be a very bad precedent to superannuate an Assistant Accountant-General [of his] age on the ground that he has "no knowledge of book-keeping".'[2] This extraordinary admission by the War Office was thought no more than 'strange' by Childers, while Cole and Hamilton were concerned only to get rid of him. It is possible, of course, that the War Office's statement was merely a pretext for pensioning-off somebody personally objectionable.

The most extreme use of the Treasury's discretionary power, to the extent even of relaxing conditions laid down in the 1859 Act, was its offer of special pension terms under clause seven to encourage the speedy reduction of establishments. This 'temporary departure from the usual application of the Superannuation Acts'[3] provides a further illustration of the empirical way in which rules, which later became generally applicable, emerged from the Treasury's response to the circumstances of a particular case. While after 1868 the Treasury was anxious to reduce the size of establishments as part of the general retrenchment of expenditure, it had no intention initially of assisting departments by offering them pension terms more favourable than those ordinarily allowed on the abolition of office. More generous terms were offered for the first time to the Admiralty in response to a suggestion made by it in 1869, the offer remaining open for a year on the understanding that the Admiralty would work out a scheme for the reorganization of the department 'on the basis of an economic but efficient fulfilment of the real requirements of the Service'. A year later similar terms were offered to the War Office in response to its initiative, and in August 1870 they were made generally available throughout the Service.

[1] Memo from Hamilton to Childers, 15 December 1865, P.R.O. T.1/6602A/19181.
[2] Memo from Childers to Hamilton, 12 January 1866, P.R.O. T.1/6602A/19181.
[3] Memo by Lord Lansdowne, 20 April 1871, P.R.O. T.1/7120A/18249.

The difficulties encountered by Cardwell in persuading clerks to retire from the War Office were described earlier.[1] Only with the greatest reluctance had the Treasury agreed to extend the time during which the special pension terms were on offer. Cardwell's later suggestion that the ordinary terms of retirement on abolition of office should be offered without limitation of time was turned down flat. Lowe, in a memorandum to Lord Lansdowne, a member of the Superannuation Committee, who after repeated representations from the War Office was proposing concession, pointed out that the intention of the Superannuation Act was that a civil servant should hold his office on the terms of not retiring with a pension unless over sixty or incapacitated by ill-health; and that abolition of office should be the act of the department and not the clerk. This latter condition was clearly a reference to the necessity for enforced retirement—the War Office had of course 'shrunk from clearing off by compulsory abolition'.[2] Both intentions of the Act, Lowe told Lansdowne, would be frustrated by the War Office's proposal.

I can on no account accede to it. . . . It is for the heads of Departments to consider whether the advantage of a change is counter balanced by the hardship it inflicts. I cannot agree that they are to make these changes, reduce their estimates and get credit for small establishments and then expect us to redress the hardships by straining Acts of Parliament and making bad precedents.[3]

Lowe's impatience with the War Office now led to a significant change in Treasury policy. Where a general invitation to retire did not result in a reduction of the establishment to the level contemplated in the reorganization, some civil servants would be compulsorily retired. As Lingen explained in further correspondence with the War Office, liability to removal from the Service was necessary if it was to be accommodated to changing circumstances. It was

simply impossible to treat section seven of the Superannuation Act of 1859 as if it constituted an offer unlimited in respect of time instead of being what my Lords hold it to be, a statutory power conferred upon the

[1] See above, Chapter 7, pp. 186-8.
[2] Memo from Lord Lansdowne to Baxter, 20 April 1871, P.R.O. T.1/7120A/18249.
[3] Memo by Lowe, 6 March 1872, P.R.O. T.1/7120A/18249.

Treasury, acting in concert with the authority of whatever other Department of the Public Service may be from time to time under reconstruction, to remove officers whose removal has become necessary
without fault of their own for the introduction of greater economy and
efficiency into their Departments.[1]

Other departments contemplating reductions were similarly
warned that if sufficient clerks did not retire voluntarily upon the
special terms offered, the Treasury, in consultation with the head
of the department, would take steps to enforce retirement.

TEMPORARY CLERKS

Despite the ruling that temporary clerks, writers, copyists, and
other clerks employed on day or weekly wages were excluded from
the benefits of the Superannuation Act, the Treasury awarded
gratuities and, in certain circumstances, pensions to those discharged
after several years' continuous service. Precedent for such payments had been established some years before the Act. In 1857
the Treasury told the Admiralty that there was an unwritten rule
that temporary clerks who were not entitled to a pension were
awarded gratuities calculated at the rate of two months' pay for
each three years of service, with an additional month's pay for the
termination of employment, provided that the department testified
to the zeal and efficiency of the clerk. Those who retired voluntarily even after long service received nothing.

There was no statutory authority for these payments before or
after the passing of the 1859 Act. While clause six empowered the
Treasury to award gratuities of one month's pay for each year of
service to those civil servants who had not served the ten years
necessary to qualify for a pension, the Treasury's definition of
'civil servant' excluded temporary clerks from its benefits. After
the passing of the Act the practice of giving gratuities to temporary
clerks rested on precedent alone, a precedent which appeared
to be explicitly repudiated by its terms.

There was not even the authority of precedent for a decision
made in 1865, when pensions calculated on the scale prescribed
in the 1859 Act were awarded to several temporary clerks who had
served continuously for fifteen years in the War Office. A month
later the Treasury ruled that temporary clerks with or without
certificates issued by the Civil Service Commissioners were in-

[1] Treasury to War Office, 29 May 1872, P.R.O. T.1/7211B/13876.

eligible for pensions under the Act. Although the effect of this was to deny a prescriptive right to a pension, the practice of awarding pensions in certain special circumstances founded upon the earlier precedent continued until 1872. Thereafter those already in the Service had to satisfy the Treasury that the expectation of a gratuity had entered into the terms of their engagement, while those without such expectation, and those who entered the Civil Service after that date, were entitled neither to pension nor gratuity.[1]

After the introduction of the writer class throughout the Civil Service in the early seventies, the difficulties which arose from prolonged temporary service, particularly the expectation of a gratuity or pension on discharge, were considerably diminished. Writers could now be obtained only from the Civil Service Commissioners who were solely responsible for their pay and conditions of service. There remained only those temporary clerks who had entered the Service before the introduction of open competition, who were permitted either to remain in the Service upon the same terms they accepted on entry, or to retire with a gratuity calculated under clause seven of the 1859 Act; those who chose to retire were eligible for re-employment under the new conditions for writers.[2]

PROFESSIONAL CIVIL SERVANTS

Some appointments, legal assistant, inspector, medical officer, for instance, required extra-Service experience and professional or special qualifications, and those appointed tended to enter at a much later age than those recruited to the clerical classes. Their late entry meant that their pension entitlement, calculated on length of service, was smaller. The Act provided specially for them by empowering the Treasury to declare certain offices or classes of offices 'professional' or 'special' and to superannuate the holders of them although they might not have served the minimum period of ten years. To compensate for their late entry the Treasury could add up to twenty years to the actual period of service, but decided upon a maximum of ten for all those offices declared

---

[1] 'Gratuities Not to be Granted to Temporary Clerks on Retirement', Treasury circular, 30 May 1872, P.R.O. T.1/7176A/5135.

[2] T.M., 27 June 1872, P.R.O. T.1/7240A/17614.

'professional' or 'special' which it placed in the 1st Class; those in the 2nd Class had seven years added, and those in the 3rd, five.

Under the fourth clause the Treasury had an unlimited discretion in awarding these pensions; it had only to declare an office to be 'professional' or 'special' and the holder could receive a pension even though he might not hold his appointment from the Crown or have obtained a certificate from the Civil Service Commissioners. There was a danger here that the benefits of this dispensation would be extended to persons appointed without a certificate to positions which had not been previously scheduled by the Superannuation Committee as 'professional' or 'special'; or used to pension those 'jobbed' into the Service at a mature age. To guard against this the Committee warned from the beginning that offices brought within the fourth clause should be defined strictly according to 'right principles', and the terms of service prescribed before the civil servant entered the Service.[1] But the process of bringing departments under the 1855 Order in Council was a gradual one, and people were admitted into some departments without a certificate throughout the whole of the period 1854–74. After 1859 they were of course *prima facie* ineligible for a pension, and on several occasions the Treasury was subjected to considerable pressure to extend the benefits of the fourth clause to them. The number and type of posts scheduled 'professional' or 'special' was carefully watched. 'We have been very jealous and I think rightly so with regard to placing offices under the 4th section of the Superannuation Act of 1859', Hamilton wrote to his colleague on the Superannuation Committee.[2] Despite this, and the insistence that the clause was not applied to individual cases, but only to offices or classes of offices previously scheduled, Lowe admitted in 1872 that the clause had been 'a good deal stretched already to applying it to persons applying for a pension'.[3] Here, as elsewhere, the Treasury was sometimes obliged, or could be persuaded, to relax its rules in 'special circumstances'.

CONCLUSION

The 1859 Act replaced the 'chaotic, inequitable and disparate system' in which the Treasury had exercised a 'capricious discretion

[1] 2nd Report Superannuation Committee, 19 October 1859, op. cit.
[2] Memo from Hamilton to Lord Lansdowne, 30 July 1869, P.R.O. T./1 6944A/21400.   [3] Memo by Lowe, 22 October 1872, P.R.O. T.1/7221B/15469.

in making awards' by one in which an attempt was made to reduce decisions to the application of a number of fixed and known rules uniformly applicable to the whole Service.[1] To a quite remarkable extent the Treasury succeeded very quickly in establishing regulations covering all civil servants in all departments, although it was much less successful immediately in applying those regulations uniformly. Besides the regulations prescribed in the Act which applied to all civil servants who joined after 1859, the Treasury drew up rules for awarding pensions to all those who had entered at an earlier date and made them known throughout the Service; those whose office was abolished after 1859 knew on what scale they would be compensated, previously the amount had been entirely discretionary with the Treasury; the special pension terms offered to the departments in the seventies to enable them to make reductions were notable not only for the Financial Secretary's decision to define more precisely the discretion which the Treasury would exercise in each case, but also for his insistence that the same terms should be offered to each department; and, finally, the Treasury's unlimited discretion to award pensions to professional civil servants was quickly reduced to a number of fixed and known rules.

The Treasury's control of superannuation was different from that of the size of the establishment, pay, or allowances, where acting as the public's watch-dog it was primarily concerned to resist the spending of public money. This concept of Treasury control was inappropriate and irrelevant to the control of superannuation. Parliament had decided that all established civil servants were to receive a pension on retirement from the Service. The Treasury's task was not to resist payments, but to decide how large they were to be. It was not guardian of the public interest, rather it stood between the public and the civil servant protecting both interests. 'I have always considered that the exercise of the powers vested in the Treasury by the Superannuation Act is strictly judicial', said Hamilton. 'The Act defines our duties and we stand between the public and the retiring Civil Servants to do impartial justice to both.'[2]

But Treasury justice was not a wholly impartial justice. Where it had discretion it tended to exercise it in favour of the civil servant

---

[1] Memo from Hamilton to James Stansfeld, 22 February 1869, P.R.O. T.1/6907B/17186.   [2] Ibid.

rather than the public; it was concerned less with economy than ensuring that civil servants were adequately, even amply, rewarded. Once a claim to benefit under the ninth clause had been admitted— and few proposed by the departments were rejected—generous pensions were awarded. Those entitled under the ordinary pro- visions of the Act to only a small pension were often handsomely, occasionally excessively, rewarded; and there were sufficient examples of retirement on full salary to suggest that the practice was not as exceptional as Hamilton claimed. While the rules relating to diligence and fidelity were interpreted very narrowly and deductions made for every misdemeanour, however slight and inconsequential, they were intended to have a mainly exemplary effect and did not cause any real hardship. Compensation on the abolition of office was generous: civil servants were permitted to retire well below the age of sixty despite the existence of a written rule to the contrary; the scale of additional years was liber- al, and even the firm age-limit of sixty-five was relaxed from time to time to enable those near to it to add several years to their actual service. The special terms offered to the Admiralty and War Office clerks and, later, the whole Civil Service, were more generous still, to the point where their application to those who had entered the Service before 1859 was a contravention of the condi- tions laid down by Parliament in the Act limiting the pension on abolition of office to two-thirds salary. And if, as seems probable, Parliament had intended abolition of office to be the act of the department and not of the individual clerk, then the condition upon which a large number of War Office and Admiralty clerks were permitted to retire voluntarily was invalid. After ruling that tem- porary clerks were ineligible for pensions or gratuities under the Act, the Treasury continued after 1859, as before, to rely on the force of precedent to reward those discharged after long service with a month's pay for each year's service, and, in certain circum- stances, to award a pension. Finally, civil servants without claim to benefit under the ordinary conditions prescribed by the Treasury were sometimes pensioned by stretching the special provisions made for professional officers.

The beneficence and flexibility with which the Treasury applied the superannuation regulations was largely attributable to two inter-connected and reinforcing factors. In the first place there was pressure from the departments to relax rules in 'special circumstances'. They were almost always willing to press the claims of their clerks to exceptional treatment.

Owing to pensions not being a charge on departmental estimates there is no sort of departmental conscience against pressing for them: on the contrary every one feels that he has a personal interest in breaking down the hedges before his own turn comes to enter.[1]

Some justification for special consideration could be found in almost every case. In a moment of disillusionment Lingen observed:

As no two cases are ever completely identical, 'special circumstances' are a necessary feature in each. I doubt most extremely whether . . . equal or impartial justice is possible . . . from the application of properly classified scales for retirement and superannuation. It is a self-evident condemnation of the scales in force that they require so many exceptions, which the Treasury has only the most imperfect and unsatisfactory means of deciding.[2]

Secondly, 1854–74 was a transitional period, between a system characterized by lack of uniformity, uncertainty, and the exercise of an arbitrary Treasury discretion, and one in which the administration of superannuation was governed by fixed and known rules. In these difficult circumstances it was necessary for the Treasury to adjust rules to special cases, and to leave a wide margin for the exercise of discretion even where the rules had been precisely drawn. To deal fairly and equitably with those civil servants who had entered the Service at different times, under different regulations, some with and some without a certificate, the Treasury had necessarily to retain and use the power to deal with special cases on their own merits without the application of prescribed rules, and often in contravention of those rules. To create a uniform system (which was the Treasury's avowed intention) from the chaos which existed previously, and to bring all departments and all civil servants within that system required time: time for the departments to be brought under the regulation of the Civil Service Commissioners and to obtain certificates for all their clerks on entry (the Treasury was reluctant to penalize a civil servant for his department's failure to obtain a certificate, hence the sponsorship of the 1873 Superannuation Amendment

[1] Memo by Lingen, 2 August 1871, P.R.O. T.1/7143B/19698.
[2] Ibid. 19 March 1870, P.R.O. T.1/6975B/9208.

Act); time for the conditions for awarding pensions under the 1859 Act to become generally known and understood in the Service; and time for those civil servants recruited before 1859, with strong claims to special treatment, to disappear from the Service. It could have been done more quickly, but only by the exercise of a more stringent, more niggardly control. Unquestionably a strict application of the Treasury rules would have caused hardship in some cases and general dissatisfaction in the circumstances immediately following the passing of the 1859 Act, and would have been very difficult to enforce.

PART FOUR

CONCLUSIONS

15

TREASURY CONTROL OF EXPENDITURE

A STEADY increase in civil expenditure, and the continuance of a high level of naval and military expenditure after the end of the Crimean War, led to demands throughout the period 1854–74 for economy and the more efficient control of public expenditure. In twenty years government expenditure nearly doubled. In 1874 the Government asked Parliament for £43·5 million; twenty years earlier it had asked for £23·1 million.[1] Expenditure on Civil Services in 1874 was twice that of 1854, £11·2 million compared with £5·2 million. Departmental establishments cost nearly £2 million in 1874, twice the 1854 sum. The Revenue Estimates had risen from £4·0 million to £7·5 million; those for naval and military expenditure were running at an annual figure of between £20 and £25 million, twice the pre-war amount.

The mid-Victorians disliked government spending. Benthamite individualism and *laissez-faire* liberalism fostered the belief that 'control ought to be directed to watching, criticizing, and, above all keeping down expenditure',[2] an attitude sustained and nourished by the tradition which Gladstone inherited from Peel that 'to take care of the pence was policy enough'. Applying the principles of this tradition—'that money should be left to fructify in the

---

[1] Estimates of civil and military expenditure are given in tables in Appendix V.
[2] Basil Chubb, *The Control of Public Expenditure*, p. 33.

pockets of the taxpayer', and that 'the cost of any particular service should be the decisive factor in deciding upon its desirability'— Gladstone became the champion and epitome of Victorian financial prudence and economy; he was at the Treasury as First Lord or Chancellor for more than a dozen years between 1854 and 1874. Because of this the period was essentially one in which governments were concerned with the retrenchment of public expenditure.

From the basic premise of Victorian finance that public expenditure had to be kept at a minimum it followed that all additional expenditure on establishments had to be shown to be both justified and necessary. This the Treasury did on behalf of Parliament largely through the requirement of prior approval. With the main exception of some allowances, very little establishments' expenditure was incurred without prior Treasury authority. The effectiveness of Treasury control in limiting public expenditure, therefore, depended more upon the control exercised after a department had applied for authority when the Treasury was 'doing its duty in criticizing and in insisting upon some reasonable proof in support of the propositions for increased expenditure' which were submitted to it.[1]

Judged by this criterion, it was not very successful. Where control was directly related to the spending of money—numbers, salaries, allowances, sick-leave and pensions—it was marked by the relatively few instances in which departmental proposals were rejected or even modified by the Treasury. It is not true, of course, that control of expenditure is effective only where it results in the rejection or modification of a proposal. If, after critical examination, the Treasury was satisfied that an increase was both justified and necessary, it discharged the responsibility laid upon it by Parliament for controlling public expenditure. However, departments were rarely refused requests for additional staff so that it cannot be claimed that the Treasury achieved any great degree of success in restricting expenditure on establishments. Moreover, agreement was often secured despite the Treasury's opposition, or without it being satisfied. It is, therefore, clear that to this extent control of expenditure was ineffective.

A similar tendency is apparent elsewhere. Few departments failed to obtain pay rises for their clerks when application was

---

[1] Memo from Lingen to Lowe, 1872, P.R.O. T.1/7253A/18718.

made to the Treasury, where it was found difficult to resist giving
to one department what had been granted to another. The most
common method of dealing with the pay claim of a senior civil
servant was to allow him a personal increase without altering the
scale fixed for his post. This was an effective long-term limitation
of expenditure only if those succeeding to the office could be denied
the salary paid to their predecessor. The Treasury was rarely able
to do this. As Sir Stafford Northcote pointed out: 'Salaries of this
kind are often raised in consequence of the special merits of and
the great services rendered by particular officers; and once raised,
they never go back again.'[1] Control of allowances was singularly
ineffective: nearly 80 per cent of all the applications made to the
Treasury were approved despite a firm rule precluding their award
except in very special circumstances. The Treasury's discretion to
award pensions under the 1859 Act favoured the civil servant
rather than the public's interest in limiting expenditure. Sick-
leave payments were authorized by the Treasury for 'valuable and
deserving' civil servants beyond the limits it had itself set, and for
others neither valuable nor deserving.

Retrenchment was scarcely more successful. Before 1864 the
political and administrative climate made Gladstone's cabinet
colleagues unsympathetic to his pleas for a reduction of establishments, and without their co-operation he admitted that the Treasury could do little. Substantial reductions were made later, but
were dependent more upon the agreement and willingness of the
individual minister than the persuasiveness of Treasury argument.
Economies were largest in the Admiralty and War Office which
were in the hands of Childers and Cardwell, two of the ablest
administrative reformers of the day; nowhere outside the Treasury
were there two stauncher advocates of the policy of retrenchment.
But here and elsewhere economy was often expensive. To get rid
of redundant clerks at once the Treasury had to offer inducements:
pay reviews for those departments willing to revise their establishments, and compensation for those civil servants who retired
voluntarily or compulsorily. Outside the Admiralty, War Office,
and Customs—where retrenchment was not an unqualified success
—results were much less spectacular, although despite the smaller
size of the economies the civil departments responded well to the
Treasury's blandishments.

[1] Northcote to Hamilton, 12 March 1859, P.R.O. T.1/6188B/9473.

To explain the limited effectiveness of Treasury control as a restraint upon expenditure, especially in those fields of establishments where the opportunities for economy were apparently greatest, it is necessary to examine the criteria upon which Treasury decisions were based, and then to explain the Treasury's attitude towards the exercise of control and towards the departments.

THE CRITERIA OF TREASURY DECISIONS

The three main sources of authority for Treasury decisions were statutes, orders in council, and other formal ordinances; written fixed regulations such as Treasury Minutes and Circulars, some of which were to be found in the reports of the Public Accounts Committee; and 'unwritten' rules, i.e. precedents, principles, etc. Statutes and other formal ordinances gave the Treasury authority to control some aspects of establishments, for example recruitment or superannuation, but were not in themselves the bases of Treasury decisions. Neither the provisions of the Orders in Council of 1855 and 1870, nor the Superannuation Acts, provide an accurate and adequate explanation of the scope of Treasury control of recruitment and superannuation between 1854 and 1874—still less are they a guide to the kind of control exercised by the Treasury. It is the Treasury's interpretation of these formal authorities which is important to an understanding of Treasury control: the rules which were made, and how and when they were applied.

Few Treasury establishments' rules were written and issued as general Minutes or Circulars, although the latter were used occasionally to obtain information, for example the Circular of December 1869 asking departments for their views on the introduction of open competition, but even for this purpose they were used sparingly for they 'always breed questions'. Fewer Treasury Minutes still were issued generally to the departments; those that were issued more often asked a department to comply with a recommended course of action than prescribed the limits of future Treasury control. In 1855 Treasury rules governing the introduction of new salary scales were printed and published as a Parliamentary Paper, but scarcely anything else of comparable significance was made generally available to all departments.

With the exception of recruitment after 1870, there are very few examples of Treasury decisions governed by fixed, written regula-

tions known simultaneously to all departments. When it became
necessary to prescribe rules regulating the scope of a department's
future conduct in a particular field, they were not made generally
available to all other departments, although the same or very similar rules might be applied to them as well. *means - notes*

Written regulations were eschewed in order to discourage public
expenditure. Pains were taken to foster the impression that all
increases to expenditure were *prima facie* undesirable, justified
only in 'special and exceptional' circumstances. To have prescribed and issued regulations which authorized expenditure when
certain conditions were fulfilled would have been to acknowledge
the legitimacy of such expenditure; to admit that pay claims were
settled on the basis of comparability was to invite departments
to claim rises awarded elsewhere; to establish conditions was to *not want to be*
invite departments to comply with them. Written regulations *limited by*
would also have limited the Treasury's discretion to apply, relax *written*
or vary them in particular cases. If conditions had been prescribed *rules*
it would have been difficult to refuse a pay rise or allowance when
those conditions were met. The Treasury did not want to be
inevitably committed to a decision. As Baxter explained to Lingen
when restraining him from establishing a fixed rule for the award
of allowances: 'It might commit us in cases where we did not wish
to grant allowances.'[1] Also, to prescribe fixed rules was to admit
that the Civil Service could and should be dealt with uniformly.
Childers apart, Treasury ministers and officials displayed little
sympathy for Northcote's and Trevelyan's insistent belief that the
Civil Service could and should be made more uniform. Lingen
was keen (as was Hamilton) to establish general rules for some
aspects of establishments, such as allowances or superannuation,
but neither he nor Lowe, even when dealing with open competition, pursued the larger purpose of making a single, unified Service. Hamilton, whose influence stretched through two-thirds of
the period 1854–74 maintained that 'there are scarcely any two
Departments quite alike or capable of being made alike'. With this
view tacitly affirmed by most who held Treasury office, it was not
to be expected that the establishment of fixed rules uniformly
applicable throughout the Service would attract much support in
the department.

Nevertheless it is clear from the previous chapters that the

[1] Memo from Baxter to Lingen, 23 June 1871, P.R.O. T.1/7078A/11237.

Treasury made constant reference to a number of well-defined, but 'unwritten' rules: to principles and precedents, which emerged not after abstract discussion of a general problem but in response to the circumstances of a given situation. Control of numbers, salaries, allowances, sick-leave and, to a lesser extent, pensions, was essentially pragmatic, originating very largely in particular *ad hoc* decisions and developing subsequently in an empirical fashion as the Treasury responded to the circumstances of similar situations. Decisions made in particular cases became precedents which were invoked in analogous cases. Later, as it became necessary, those precedents were embellished or amended to provide for circumstances which had not been anticipated. The result was the establishment of a number of 'unwritten' rules which could be applied uniformly in almost all ordinary circumstances. The *locus classicus* was the emergence of a sick-leave code from principles established by the Treasury after consideration of the factors of a single case. Similarly, rules for the introduction of new salary scales were formulated after consideration of a number of separate decisions made in particular cases. Basic principles became 'unwritten' rules which were applied (or relaxed) subsequently. Control of numbers and salaries both depended upon principles rooted in precedents established in particular cases.

While these 'unwritten' rules provide a guide to Treasury decisions, they are not a complete explanation of what Treasury control was in practice. The recurring theme of many of the previous chapters has been the contradiction between principle and practice, and the subordination of principle to expediency in the exercise of day to day control. In resolving pay claims the Treasury had constant recourse to the expedient of comparability, while maintaining the fiction that its decisions were determined largely by the nature and quality of the duties performed. Many increases to establishment were approved while the Treasury remained 'unsatisfied' because for political or administrative reasons it was more expedient to do so; the 'unwritten' rule prohibiting the payment of allowances was almost lost to view beneath a welter of 'special and exceptional' circumstances; and the hedges of the superannuation rules were so frequently broken down that a despairing Lingen doubted whether equal and impartial justice was possible from the application of properly classified pension scales.

Paradoxically the guiding principle of Treasury control was often expediency. Time and again Treasury ministers and officials (especially Hamilton) preferred 'to deal with each case as it arose on its own merits and in the light of the special circumstances of each case'; what John Stuart Mill called 'the dogmatism of common-sense'. It was not exclusive to administration; Lord Robert Cecil made much the same comment when writing about politics in 1858:

The tacit unanimity with which this generation has laid aside the ingenious network of political first principles which the industry of three centuries of theorists have woven, is one of the most remarkable phenomena in the history of thought. In politics at least the old antithesis of principle and expediency is absolutely forgotten; expediency is the only principle to which allegiance is paid.

and Walter Pater, in an essay on Coleridge, in 1866:

Modern thought is distinguished from ancient by its cultivation of the 'relative' spirit in place of the 'absolute'.... To the modern spirit nothing is or can rightly be known, except relatively and under conditions.[1]

To understand why the Treasury was unwilling or unable in a large number of cases to apply well-defined rules and principles, why it frequently found expediency more attractive than principle, it is necessary to explain the Treasury's attitude towards the control of establishments, and to discuss the practical limitations to its authority.

THE TREASURY'S ATTITUDE TOWARDS CONTROL

The Treasury's attitude towards the control of establishments belies its mid-nineteenth century reputation for parsimony and the exercise of an inflexible and 'despotic' control.[2] The greater the Treasury's discretion the more it tended to exercise it in favour of the civil

---

[1] Quoted in W. L. Burn, *The Age of Equipoise*, p. 55.
[2] Thus K. B. Smellie, writing in *A Hundred Years of English Government*, p. 165, 'The system of audited accounts inaugurated by the Act of 1866 had taken away the unlimited discretion which the Treasury had in the past enjoyed and blindly used. An enlightened tyrant replaced a capricious despot.' Smellie draws heavily upon Durell's *Parliamentary Grants* published in 1917, an authoritative account by a former Chief Paymaster of the War Office based mainly upon the evidence given before inquiries and commissions.

servant rather than the public's interest in limiting expenditure. Pensions awarded on loss of office were generous, so much so that a few civil servants not yet into middle age had to be restrained from retiring voluntarily in order to benefit from them. Many others below sixty were permitted to retire on the abolition of their offices despite an 'unwritten' rule to the contrary. Special services were amply rewarded; those of Sir Rowland Hill to the development of postal administration, and Antonio Panizzi to the British Museum were perhaps no more than adequately rewarded by the receipt of full pension on their retirement, but the attitude which inspired these and similar decisions (where some of the civil servants were less deserving) is not that most obviously associated with candle-end saving. However, the Treasury did not bow inevitably before departmental pressure, Hamilton's resolution in the case of the retirement of the Secretary of the Board of Trade is proof against such a notion; here, interestingly, it was Gladstone who proposed the concession to Booth of three-quarters salary.

From the same beneficence sprang the Treasury's unwillingness to deny an allowance to a clerk who had performed a special service with the expectation of some reward. Here it is Lowe's harsh decision enforcing repayment of an allowance already made which is marked out as exceptional, balanced nicely by his equally extraordinary decision to allow a payment to a non-civil servant when both his junior minister and officials alike had been unable to find any justification for it and feared the establishment of a most unwelcome precedent. There was a similar reluctance to withhold a pay increase from a civil servant strongly supported by his minister. Sick-leave rules were relaxed for 'valuable and deserving' civil servants.

Beneficence was combined with flexibility. Treasury ministers were rarely unbending or concerned to apply rules rigidly, though here again Lowe's attitude towards the application of examination regulations is exceptional. Nothing is more striking between 1854 and 1874 than the isolation of two men whose attitude towards controlling expenditure was inconsonant with the general view held by other Treasury ministers and officials. Ayrton's overbearing zeal for economy made him one of the most unpopular members of Gladstone's ministry, and his inflexibility and persistent 'cutting back' was too much even for Lowe, who took some trouble to have him removed from the Treasury on that account.[1] If he had stayed longer, Lowe told Gladstone, he would have demoralized the whole department.[2] On Hamilton's suggestion Lowe advised Gladstone to move him to the Office of Works where he would be 'quite in his element wrangling about coals, candles and furniture'.[3] Such wrangling it might be thought would have been appreciated in a Treasury committed to saving candle-ends, but even allowing for Lowe's dislike of Ayrton there is little doubt that the latter's attitude did not match the temper of the department. For it was Ayrton with whom Hamilton crossed swords earlier, and from whose decision he appealed to the Chancellor of the Exchequer. On that occasion it will be recalled that Hamilton had recommended, as had the Principal Officer, that a Treasury rule relating to the application of salary scales should be relaxed on the grounds of expediency—that it would be 'both economical and advantageous to the public and only fair as regards [the civil servant]'.[4]

Ayrton was a junior minister for only a few months, Spencer Shelley was a Principal Officer for eight years; his interpretation of the Treasury's authority to control expenditure was even more at variance with that of the department generally. Reference has been made on several occasions to Hamilton's rejection of the advice tendered by Shelley as a Principal Officer, advice which usually emphasized the need for firmness in dealing with departments. His most important statement and Hamilton's reply to it are worth repeating here as illustrative of the basic difference of attitude. Urging upon Hamilton the need to insist upon the Home Office's compliance with a recommendation made by the Treasury committee of inquiry which reported in 1856, Shelley wrote: 'I hope you will be firm on this matter, . . . we can insist on a persistent course whether the Secretary of State of the day likes it or not . . . it should be insisted on.'[5] Rejecting his advice Hamilton replied that the Treasury could not follow such a course of action without subjecting itself to the charge of being influenced by 'pettish' feeling in refusing what had previously been admitted to be for the public good.

[1] Lowe to Gladstone, 7, 9, 15 and 23 August 1869, Brit. Mus., G.P. Add. MSS. 44301, ff. 63–72.
[2] Lowe to Gladstone, 7 August 1869, op. cit.
[3] Ibid. 9 August 1869, op. cit.
[4] See above, Chapter 9, pp. 252–4.
[5] Memo from Shelley to Hamilton, 2 May 1860, P.R.O. T.1/6258A/13006.

Control by the Treasury was rarely niggardly or small-minded. At times Arbuthnot became insistent in his dealings with the War Office and Admiralty, but these two departments were generally acknowledged to be the most difficult to deal with. His exasperation that they 'seemed to resent any proposal for a modification of a suggestion made by them' was not altogether surprising or unwarranted in the circumstances.[1] His excesses and occasional immoderate language were generally checked by Hamilton, though on one occasion a bitter dispute between the Treasury and the Admiralty was ended only by the intervention of the Chancellor of the Exchequer and the First Lord of the Admiralty and the subsequent withdrawal of letters on both sides.[2]

Towards the departments generally the Treasury showed a willingness to accept the judgement of the minister and a wish for agreement and accommodation wherever possible. In this respect its attitude conflicted with the basic assumption of Treasury control at that time, namely, that public spending had to be resisted. This could not be left to the departmental ministers; nor was it their proper function anyway. 'The primary object of every Minister is and must be to place his own Department and the interests committed to him in the greatest state of efficiency— the cost I venture to state will be necessarily secondary', Hamilton admitted.[3] But in place of the suspicion and distrust which that assumption should have bred and fostered, there was instead a disposition to agree, an anxiety to accommodate the departmental minister, and above all the desire to avoid conflict and collision. The Treasury's fear of collision was a real one; it was inconvenient, detrimental to the public service and discreditable.[4] Before a decision was made the probable consequences of Treasury action were carefully weighed and, if possible, conflict anticipated and avoided. 'I have endeavoured to frame a Minute which I hope will have the effect of inducing the Home Office to reconsider their last letter without actually getting into collision with them', Hamilton wrote on one occasion to his minister.[5] On another, he

---

[1] See above, Chapter 6, p. 158.   [2] P.R.O. T.1/6313A/13238.

[3] Hamilton to James Stansfeld, 21 October 1869, P.R.O., *Hamilton Semi-official correspondence*, iv.

[4] Hamilton to Gladstone, 9 March 1863, P.R.O. *Hamilton Semi-official correspondence*, ii.

[5] Memo from Hamilton to Laing, 18 April 1860, see above, Chapter 8, p. 217.

was restrained by Arbuthnot and the Financial Secretary from a particular course of action because they feared that what he proposed would unnecessarily provoke the Audit Office and exacerbate the difficulties of communication between the two departments at that time.[1] Before issuing a circular on the reduction of the estimates, Gladstone suggested to Childers, his Financial Secretary, that it should be sent in draft to any departments 'where the difficulty lies. For if any of them raise difficulties in an official correspondence, the impediment will be harder to overcome'.[2]

The desire for conciliation and the avoidance of dispute is apparent in the relative lack of serious conflict between the Treasury and the departments, despite the inevitable and natural suspicion, resentment and irritation with which those who were controlled regarded the Treasury. 'Arbuthnot has had to bear so much of the brunt of the anti-Treasury feeling in high quarters', Hamilton told Gladstone in 1862.[3] But departmental intransigence—of which there was a good deal—was rarely matched by a similar show of determination on the part of the Treasury. Faced by a resolute department, and often subjected to intense official, semi-official, and private pressure, the Treasury almost always gave way. Where it dug in its heels—and there were really only two notable occasions in the whole of the period—it yielded ultimately. In the dispute with the War Office and Admiralty over the abolition of allowances in 1871–2 it was only Lowe's determination (obstinacy?) which prevented an earlier Treasury capitulation; both Lingen and the Financial Secretary had proposed concession long before.

Because the Treasury did not, and often could not, impose control directly, the amount and quality of the control which it exercised through its committees of inquiry assume a special significance. They were the most important and effective means by which the Treasury controlled establishments between 1854 and 1874. At the same time they epitomized the willingness of the Treasury to seek agreement with the departments, the desire to co-operate with them, which is apparent in the day to day control. Privately and informally the Treasury could explain and argue its

[1] See above, Chapter 12, pp. 283–4.
[2] Gladstone to Childers, 12 September 1865, Brit. Mus., G.P. Add. MSS., Letter Books, 1865.
[3] Hamilton to Gladstone, 20 August 1862, Brit Mus., G.P. Add. MSS. 44192, fo. 46.

view. Both sides had no longer to maintain the tiresome, elaborate posturing enjoined upon them in their official communications; that ritual which made it impossible for the Treasury to give up lightly a position adopted officially 'at least not without the conventional honours of war expressed by a further skirmish'.[1] In private the frustrating and irritating conventions of proposal and demur, resubmission and modification, scrupulously observed in the official relationship, could be discarded. Control could be exercised at its most effective point—before a proposal took official shape. Here after detailed inquiry Arbuthnot could secure the admission of the Permanent Under-Secretary at the War Office that a rearrangement of the business now made it unnecessary to ask the Treasury for nine additional 1st Class Clerks. Economies such as these which accrued from greater efficiency remained 'invisible'.

LIMITATIONS UPON TREASURY CONTROL

The Treasury's attitude towards civil servants and departments described above was reinforced by its acknowledgement of important practical limitations to its control which derived mainly from the independence, influence and departmental autonomy of a nineteenth-century cabinet minister. 'Each department under each Minister is almost a little kingdom in itself', Lingen told the Select Committee on Civil Services Expenditure in 1873.[2] Even Gladstone was led to justify his advising Clarendon how best to avoid the importunities of Lowe and the Treasury by the desire to uphold 'our respective autonomies'.[3] Most of the ministers with whom the Treasury dealt were in the cabinet, one, Russell, had been Prime Minister. It was not easy for the Treasury led by the Financial Secretary, to resist proposals made above the names of powerful ministers whose autonomy was widely recognized and respected, especially when senior civil servants rarely hesitated to involve them directly in a negotiation with the Treasury, even over quite minor matters.

This was particularly true of the 'first-class' departments, those of the Secretaries of State, whose superior status was

---

[1] Memo from Lingen to Lowe, 6 April 1871, see above, Chapter 6, p. 173.
[2] qu. 2911.
[3] Gladstone to Clarendon, 31 December 1869, see above, Chapter 4, p. 83.

recognized by the Treasury and acknowledged in the greater deference shown to them than to other departments. Trevelyan once criticized Gladstone for his 'willingness to do for the Foreign Office more than [was] done for any office, viz. to adopt their proposals on minor points because they are their proposals, although much reason could be shown for a contrary conclusion'.[1] The Select Committee on Miscellaneous Expenditure commented in 1848 that the offices of the Secretaries of State used better quality paper than the Treasury or Admiralty; the Foreign Office and the Home Office 'used nothing but the finest description of paper of a very expensive kind'. Asked by the Committee whether 'remonstrances' had been made, Trevelyan replied that the Treasury had been in touch with them about it, 'but the Secretaries of State have been held in a degree of respect by the Treasury, and we have not felt that we had precisely the same control over them in matters of this sort as over the other offices'.[2]

Privately the Treasury admitted that a minister could not really be refused what he represented to be essential and necessary to the efficiency of his department—and ministers were quite prepared officially and semi-officially on paper, and privately in conversation to testify to that. Thus Lingen could write to Lowe: 'I am not convinced, but I doubt it being expedient to overrule in relation to an existing charge the strongly repeated opinion of a Secretary of State of Mr. Cardwell's experience.'[3] Lowe himself was obliged to admit that 'when a Secretary of State upon whom the responsibility for the work rests urges so strongly the necessity [of an increase of establishment] the Treasury can hardly with propriety refuse assent'.[4] A similar sensitivity to the minister's position *vis-à-vis* the Treasury permeated discussion within the Treasury and official dispatches with other departments. Care was taken not to embarrass the head of the department, to avoid 'wounding the susceptibilities' of the Secretary of State for War, for example; and to ensure that Treasury letters were civil, sober and moderate. 'I would ask you to read as an example of wolf and lamb, this correspondence which on the part of the Treasury is studiously civil and is occasioned principally by the slip-shod

[1] Trevelyan to Gladstone, 28 April 1854, Bod., T.L.B., xxxiii. 179–181.
[2] *Select Committee on Miscellaneous Expenditure*, 1848, P.P., 1847–8, XVIII, qus. 1139, 1189–90.
[3] Memo by Lingen, 21 November 1871, see above, Chapter 11, p. 277.
[4] Memo from Lowe to Lingen, 4 April 1871, P.R.O. T.1/7142A/19621.

style in which the proposal first came from the W.O.', Lingen once wrote to Lowe.[1]

The importance of ministerial influence and pressure in securing Treasury approval has been a recurring theme of previous chapters. Departments were encouraged to see the Chancellor, the Financial Secretary, or a senior official when contemplating a major change in establishments 'and to avoid writing until the subject was nearly matured'. Doubts or uncertainties were often stilled, though not always dispelled by their semi-official and private representations. At the lowest level this took the form of an exchange of memoranda or a meeting, between a Treasury Principal Officer and the Permanent Secretary or other senior official of the applicant department; at the highest, the conversation or exchange of notes between the Chancellor of the Exchequer and his cabinet colleague, personally or through the network of private secretaries. The commonest pressure was exerted mid-way between, upon the Financial Secretary and Assistant Secretary. The exchange of semi-official letters with either, or more effective still, informal discussion, was rarely unsuccessful for a department. In many cases it is clear that such communication served to clear up a misunderstanding, to elucidate a point, or to explain more fully the necessity for a pay rise or allowance, or the award of a pension. Nevertheless the Financial Secretary was at a distinct disadvantage when treating with cabinet ministers, as Northcote shrewdly pointed out to Disraeli.[2] Both he and Gladstone favoured an increase in the authority of the Financial Secretary, who, as they said, had responsibility without authority. Face to face with a senior minister, who was also head of a great department and a leading politician of the same party, it was additionally difficult for the Financial Secretary to refuse what was represented as necessary and essential. Nor was such pressure exceptional. When the Treasury demurred, the department's case was almost always supported thereafter by some form of semi-official and private pressure. It was not to be expected that a cabinet minister would be willing to accept an unfavourable decision made by Treasury officials and junior ministers upon a matter which affected the organization of his department, without frequently attempting to use what influence

[1] Memo from Lingen to Lowe, 1872, P.R.O. T.1/7253A/18718.
[2] Memo from Northcote to Disraeli, 29 June 1866, Brit. Mus., I.P. Add. MSS. 50015, fo. 135.

he had with his Treasury colleagues; or that the officials of other departments were always prepared to accept an unfavourable decision without sometimes attempting to bring unofficial pressure to bear upon their opposite numbers in the Treasury. It would be unrealistic to assume that the expectation of such pressure, as well as its use, had no effect upon the way in which the Treasury exercised its control.

Further, the Treasury's attitude towards the departments was influenced by their own behaviour towards the Treasury, and in some respects was a response or even anticipatory to it. Both the War Office and Admiralty smarted under the requirement of prior approval: they seemed to 'resent any proposal for a modification of suggestions made by them'. This attitude, which was by no means peculiar to these two departments, is well summarized in an exchange between Sir Benjamin Hawes, Permanent Under-Secretary at the War Office, and Sir Stafford Northcote. Replying to Hawes, Northcote said:

In the present case, you really place us in a very strange position. You send us a plan for the organisation of a new Corps and enclose for our 'consideration and approval' the rates of pay which you proposed. We demur to those rates of pay; and you reply that they have been fixed by a competent Board of Officers, and are adopted by the Secretary of State; and you imply that, whether our objections have anything in them or not, we have no business to make them. If that be so, why should you ask our approval?[1]

It was not so much that departments avoided prior approval, as that they tended to object to any decision which was not entirely favourable. In other words, to them Treasury control represented interference, acceptable when it led to the exercise of a favourable judgement, intolerable when it led to an unfavourable one. They were generally loth to accept a refusal from the Treasury, disputing not only the judgement but the Treasury's authority to control establishments, and its competence to decide the requirements of the department better than the minister himself.

This attitude towards the Treasury was expressed in a slightly different form by the Foreign Office. Hamilton described it as 'captiousness'; Trevelyan had run up against it in 1854. 'Although

---

[1] Northcote to Sir Benjamin Hawes, 2 May 1859, Brit. Mus., I.P. Add. MSS. 50046.

344   *Conclusions*

that Office assumes to itself an exclusive and superior position, this pretention is by no means admitted by the Treasury' he remarked to Gladstone. It seemed to him

entirely unreasonable and improper that the Foreign Office should submit an arrangement for the revision and approval of the Treasury and then reject any decision which does not award to them all they have asked for. If the Treasury has a discretion and responsibility on the matter, its judgment ought to be accepted. If it has not the matter ought not to be at all referred to the Treasury.[1]

Even after 1866, when the Exchequer and Audit Act laid it down that expenditure not approved by the Treasury was not properly chargeable to Parliamentary Votes, the Treasury's most difficult task was to get departments to acknowledge the discretion and responsibility conferred upon it by Parliament, and to accept its authority and judgements. Not until 1870 did the War Office and Admiralty formally acknowledge the Treasury's authority to control their establishments' expenditure. Throughout the previous sixteen years (and earlier) they tended to dispute the right to do so when the Treasury objected to an increase of expenditure. The scope of the Treasury's authority was carefully defined in a printed Treasury Minute, paragraph five of which dealt with civil establishments.

All new Civil situations to be created in either branch of the Service, whether the same are to be included in the Annual Estimates under Establishments, New Works, or otherwise, are to be submitted for the consideration and approval of the Treasury before the same are filled up; and no new salary, nor increase of any existing salary, nor any allowance, whether in money or kind, gratuity nor other form of remuneration of persons employed, either permanently or temporarily, in the Civil Branches of the two Services, is to be granted without the previous sanction of this Board.[2]

Control of naval and military expenditure was the Treasury's largest and most difficult task. Arbuthnot with all his experience and diligence 'had scarcely been able to master the great Departments of the War Office and Admiralty . . . our warfare with these Departments is perpetual', Hamilton told Gladstone in 1865.[3]

[1] Trevelyan to Gladstone, 28 April 1854, Bod., T.L.B., xxxiii. 179–81.
[2] T.M. 24 November 1870, P.R.O. T.1/7044A/1609.
[3] Hamilton to Gladstone, 2 August 1865, P.R.O. *Hamilton Semi-official Correspondence*, ii.

Their agreement to the conditions prescribed by the Treasury in 1870 did not make the task of control easy, but at least it ensured that discussion was at last freed from arguments about the Treasury's authority to control their expenditure with which Arbuthnot had had to contend. Their agreement meant also that in the field of public expenditure Treasury hegemony was complete and undisputed; the circle of internal financial control had been closed, just as earlier the establishment of the Public Accounts Committee and the appointment of the Comptroller and Auditor-General had closed the ring of Parliamentary control of finance.

THE EFFECTIVENESS OF TREASURY CONTROL

Within these limitations, three general points may be made about the effectiveness of Treasury control as a restraint upon expenditure. First, the requirement of prior approval, a precondition of effective control, was generally well observed. Secondly, there were many occasions when without prompting the departments provided the Treasury with adequate information to enable it to make a 'mature judgement'; no mean achievement, for departments did not relish having to justify their actions and decisions to another department. Thirdly, by insisting upon the condition that a case had to be made out to its satisfaction the Treasury demonstrated to the departments that approval was not to be had easily; even where the Treasury was unsuccessful in obtaining satisfaction it had usually caused the department to resubmit its application. When the Treasury demurred, approval was rarely obtained easily or quickly, even if it was nearly always obtained in the end. Departments were obliged to fight for it; that they did so was taken to be some indication of the necessity for the expenditure. In this connection, mention should be made of the use of the demur as a tactical weapon in the larger strategy of restraining expenditure on the supply side. Delay in approving increased or new expenditure on departmental projects was a clumsy, though often the only effective, Treasury weapon of control. To ministers, few of whom held office for any length of time and who were anxious to do things fairly quickly, a delay of several months was exasperating and often critical. By linking delay on the supply side with delay in approving expenditure on establishments, the Treasury was able to exert still greater pressure on a department.

Few opportunities were missed to impress upon departments

5555555

that approval of additional expenditure was a concession not to be had lightly. The effect of the intentional creation of an atmosphere of reluctance, in which approval was given in the manner of a concession grudgingly bestowed, may well have been that departments refrained from submitting applications to the Treasury unless they were convinced that they were absolutely necessary, and were prepared to defend them on that ground. By fostering this impression, and by obliging departments to fight for their additional expenditure when the Treasury was not satisfied that it was necessary or desirable, while it was unwilling or unable in the last resort to prevent it, the Treasury may well have prevented many proposals from progressing beyond the stage of preliminary discussion in the department. Goschen, Chancellor of the Exchequer in Salisbury's Administration, thought that

> The first object of the Treasury must be to throw the departments on their defence, and to compel them to give strong reasons for any increased expenditure, and to explain how they have come to have to demand it. This control alone contributes to make the departments careful in what they put forward.[1]

Earlier, William Baxter, Lowe's Financial Secretary, had stated to a Select Committee that Treasury control was 'the means of preventing a great many proposals for increase which are never heard of outside'.[2]

An indirect control like this, rather than direct Treasury control was more important, perhaps more effective, Hamilton thought. The control which the Treasury should be expected to exercise

> is not a mere technical control or criticism like that of the Audit Office—whose business it is to question the details of an amount—but a moral, quite as much, or perhaps even more than an official control. In my judgment the value of the Treasury in this point of view is that it exercises a moral rather than an official control over the Secretaries of State and all other public functionaries. A great deal of the good we do in this world might perhaps be properly measured by the evil we prevent, and I cannot help thinking that it is both wholesome and convenient to a Secretary of State, perhaps even to a Lord Chancellor, when subjected to influential pressure to be able to fall back upon the Treasury

[1] *Report of the Committee on War Office Organisation*, 1901, Cd 580, qus. 3204–5.
[2] *Select Committee on Civil Services Expenditure*, 1873, qu. 4671.

and that by the operation of this moral control we have prevented much evil without being conscious of it.[1]

It is impossible to estimate the extent to which the threat of Treasury control deterred departments from putting up certain proposals, or caused them to modify others. An examination of the discussions which preceded the submission of a formal application to the Treasury would reveal only those instances where the threat of control was an explicit factor in the decision; where it was implicit, or discussed verbally, the papers would provide no guidance. Given the general attitude towards the Treasury of such departments as the War Office, Admiralty, and Foreign Office, the degree of self-restraint was probably not great. Nevertheless, the Treasury's insistence upon a *prima facie* case being made for each proposed increase of expenditure meant that departments were obliged initially, or after the Treasury had demurred, to present a strong case. Because of this all departments had to be selective to some extent in what they put up to the Treasury; in the case of a reforming and economizing minister like Childers, the extent of selectivity might be considerable. As Secretary of State for War in Gladstone's second administration, he did all he could 'to curtail expenditure, and to enforce sound financial principles, and of the proposals for expenditure which come forward I think I may safely say that not one of a hundred reaches the Treasury'.[2]

One of the most effective means of limiting Imperial expenditure in the seventies and eighties was the Treasury's indirect influence as a potential check on excessive colonial demands, and its 'moral suasion' strengthened by Parliamentary support for an economic colonial policy.[3] Here, it is argued, the existence of an external financial authority, which demanded that a *prima facie* case be made for each item of increased expenditure, acted as a deterrent. 'An Office like the Colonial Office, beset as it was with a multitude of demands from needy communities, would be thus encouraged to forward only those applications which were most pressing'. Moreover, by invoking the threat of Treasury control, the Colonial

[1] Memo from Hamilton to James Stansfeld, 21 October 1869, P.R.O. *Hamilton Semi-official Correspondence*, iv.

[2] Childers to Gladstone, 5 December 1880, Brit. Mus., G.P. Add. MSS. 44129, ff. 109–11.

[3] Ann M. Burton, 'Treasury Control and Colonial Policy in the late Nineteenth Century', *Public Administration*, Vol. 44, Summer 1966, p. 173.

Secretary was, himself, able to resist some of the demands made by colonial governments for increased expenditure. 'It was not uncommon for the Colonial Office to refuse peremptorily a request on the grounds that it would be folly to consult the Treasury.' Hamilton approved this. Defending the retention of the Treasury's control of colonial expenditure he argued that 'the firmness and virtue of the Secretary of State should be supported by the unseen authority of My Lords'.[1]

It is probable that Hamilton's views of the effectiveness of a 'moral control' were derived from an earlier discussion with Gladstone when the Chancellor had argued the need for an independent inquiry into the Treasury establishment.[2] What the Treasury needed in order to discharge its important duties of control over other departments, he told Hamilton on that occasion, was an unimpaired moral authority, 'without which mere *power* will never enable it to do its duty'.[3] He developed the argument further before the Select Committee on Civil Services Expenditure in 1873 when he was asked whether the Treasury exercised a direct and effectual control over the expenditure of the different departments. 'We are only one department side by side with others, with very limited powers; it is more after all by moral suasion and pointing out things that our influence is exercised, than by any large power we have.'[4] He went on to deny that the Treasury had any direct power to regulate and control public expenditure:

I am afraid that the other departments would consider that we were erecting a sort of tyranny over them if we got that power; this thing is certain; that we have not got it; that the Treasury have never possessed it, and that we have gone on very well without it.[5]

To the suggestion that the House of Commons would check the danger of any Treasury tyranny, he replied:

I almost doubt whether one department, which probably is neither wiser nor better than its neighbours, should be entrusted with such powers; we are all equal as Members of the Government, and it would make one a sort of king over the others; but I only point it out, because we are often being found fault with for not being that which we really have not the power to do.

[1] Hamilton to James Stansfeld, 21 October 1869, P.R.O. *Hamilton Semi-official Correspondence*, i.

[2] Gladstone to Hamilton, 4 October 1860, P.R.O. *Hamilton Semi-official Correspondence*, i.   [3] Ibid.   [4] P.P., 1873, VII, p. 669.   [5] qus. 4491-6.

Gladstone was right in thinking that the Treasury would be unable to exercise such an effective control by mere power. For it was not power but co-operation, understanding, and mutual respect which enabled the Treasury to exercise its most effective and complete control of establishments through the unofficial committees of inquiry. By their concern for greater efficiency, indirectly these committees were more successful in limiting expenditure than the day to day control where the Treasury relied mainly upon the requirement of prior approval.

THE MACHINERY OF CONTROL

While the systematic use of committees of inquiry was the Treasury's outstanding administrative innovation, other changes in organization and practice contributed to the development of a more effective machine for controlling public expenditure. The profound reorganization of 1856, completed fourteen years later, gave the department its modern shape. The separation of intellectual from mechanical work, the creation of two hierarchies of clerks each with its own route of entry and conditions of service, the introduction of executive divisions and a slowly emerging functional distribution of business, the introduction of improved work methods and the elimination of wasteful and obsolete procedures—all these, and the adoption of open competition, promotion by merit and other principles prescribed by Northcote and Trevelyan, contributed to the evolution of a smaller, specialized, and more efficient department. Overshadowing all these developments was the dominant and dominating position achieved by the Assistant Secretary. To give him greater weight in his dealings with other departments, his authority and status were deliberately enhanced, formalizing a process of aggrandisement begun by Trevelyan. This, and Hamilton's assumption of responsibility for the organization of the whole Civil Service, transformed the office from that of a senior executive official to one in which the roles of policy-adviser, manager, and co-ordinator were combined.

Despite the procedural and organizational changes which were made throughout the period 1854–74, the top of the department remained remarkably stable, due mainly to the continuity of service of the senior people, details of which are given in Table I.

BB

TABLE I

Continuity of Service in the Treasury, 1854–1874

	Years of Service in the Treasury	Years in senior posts (Principal Officer and above), between 1854 and 1874	Retired/resigned, etc.
Trevelyan, C. E. T.	18 (1840–58)	4 (Assistant Secretary)	Resigned
Hamilton, G. A.	12 (1858–70)	12 (Asst. Sec./Perm. Sec.)	Retired
Lingen, R. R. W.	15 (1870–85)	4 (Permanent Sec.)	Retired
Arbuthnot, G.	45 (1820–65)	11 (Auditor of Civil List)	Died in office
Stephenson, W.	35 (1827–62)	8 (Principal Officer)	Appointed Chairman of Board of I.R.
Anderson, W.	13 (1854–67)	13 (Principal Finance Officer)	Appointed Assistant Comptroller and Auditor-General
Crafer, C. L.	47 (1812–59)	5 (Principal Officer)	Retired
Seton, W.	26 (1834–60)	4 (Principal Officer)	Died in office
Law, W.	43 (1838–81)	14 (Principal Officer; Auditor of Civil List and Asst. to Secs.)	Retired
Stronge, C. W.	47 (1833–80)	12 (Principal Officer)	Retired
Shelley, S.	37 (1830–67)	8 (Principal Officer)	Superannuated
Cole, J. H.	45 (1843–88)	10 (Principal Officer)	Retired
Clerke, Sir W.	39 (1843–82)	7 (Principal Officer)	Died in office
Foster, M. H.	8 (1855–59; 1867–71)	4 (Principal Finance Officer)	Retired
Welby, R. E.	38 (1856–94)	3 (Principal Finance Officer)	Resigned

Turnover at the top of the department was low. In twenty years only fifteen people held the six senior posts. Six men, Hamilton, Arbuthnot, Anderson, Law, Stronge, and Cole, each served for more than half that time in a key post. Those who left the Treasury did so after long and continuous service, like Charles Crafer, who retired with failing eye-sight after forty-seven years in the department. Trevelyan resigned after eighteen years as permanent head of the department in order to return to India; Hamilton retired at the age of sixty-eight after a life-time of Parliamentary and public Service; Arbuthnot and Seton died in office. Only Stephenson and Anderson of the senior men were transferred to other departments.[1]

[1] See above, Chapter 1, p. 16.

Stability and continuity of service, together with the increased specialization and concentration of responsibility in the heads of divisions which resulted from the organizational changes made in the department, contributed to the emergence of an influential, informed, and highly experienced *élite* of top Treasury officials upon whom ministers relied increasingly for advice on policy. Their accumulated knowledge and experience of what was going on in other departments, much of it obtained at first-hand through numerous committees of inquiry, ensured that the Treasury was better informed about the work of the departments and current administrative practice, better able to make 'mature judgements' on proposals submitted to it, than it had ever been before.

All these factors contributed to the greater effectiveness of Treasury control. To them must be added the appointment of a Comptroller and Auditor-General and the establishment of the Public Accounts Committee, which together ensured that departments were less likely to risk avoiding the requirement of prior approval, statutorily enacted in the Exchequer and Audit Act of 1866; or where they did risk it, that they were less likely to go undetected and uncensured.

16

THE TREASURY AND THE
DEVELOPMENT OF THE CIVIL SERVICE

WRITING to Lyon Playfair in 1875, Sir Stafford Northcote said that 'the Civil Service has been undergoing a great transformation of late years: indeed it may be said to have been in the crucible for the last twenty'.[1] Many important changes had taken place: the Civil Service Commission had been set up, entry by examination had become universal, and Lowe and Lingen had thrown open the Service to talent. The Service was open, but socially and educationally stratified. Superior Clerkships were open to all those who had the knowledge and ability to pass literary examinations modelled closely on the revised Oxford and Cambridge syllabuses, which effectively excluded all those who had not had public school or university education. Similarly, Supplementary Clerkships were open to those who had profited by a secondary or commercial education.

Most opponents of open competition had feared that it would mean the replacement of the aristocracy by a lower social class.[2] But the reformers' intention was to work a meritocratic and elitist revolution, not a social one: to weed-out the 'incapable and indolent' and 'to invite the flower of our youth to the aid of the public service'.[3] Trevelyan had no doubt who the latter were, and where they were to be found:

Who are so successful in carrying off the prizes at competing scholarships, fellowships, etc, as the most expensively educated young men? Almost invariably, the sons of gentlemen, or those who by force of cultivation, good training and good society have acquired the feelings and habits of gentlemen. The tendency of the measure will, I am confident, be decidedly *aristocratic*.[4]

[1] 27 January 1875, reproduced in 1st Report of the *Civil Service* (*Playfair*) *Inquiry Commission*, P.P., 1875, XXIII.   [2] Morley, i. 511.
[3] Trevelyan, 'Thoughts on Patronage', 17 January 1854, Brit. Mus., G.P. Add. MSS. 44333, fo. 91.
[4] Marginal comments by Trevelyan on a paper by Capt. H. H. O'Brien, Editor of *Quarterly*, 18 January 1854, Brit. Mus., G.P. Add. MSS. 44333, fo. 103.

Northcote was equally certain:

The advantages which an University training would give in the competition would almost ensure the selection of a large majority from among those who have received it; and there is no kind of education, so likely to make a man a gentleman, to fit him to play his part among other gentlemen and to furnish him forth for the world, as that of an English University.

and attributed his own success:

entirely to the power of close reasoning which a course of Thucydides, Aristotle and Mathematics, etc engenders or develops, and to the facility of composition which arises from classical studies.[1]

The higher Civil Service was to be open, but socially and educationally exclusive, as Lowe made plain. The Supplementary Class was probably best adapted to the needs of the public service, he admitted to the Select Committee on Civil Services Expenditure, but the members of it lacked breeding and education and would be at a disadvantage with those with whom they were brought into contact. If the Civil Service were made more open, by recruiting only to the Supplementary Class, the 'public service would suffer for want of that sort of freemasonry which exists between people who have had a certain grade of education'.[2] Here was a very early formulation of the elitist argument based upon education which was to dominate thinking about recruitment to the higher Civil Service for a hundred years.

The education of public schools and colleges and such things, which gives a sort of freemasonry among men which is not very easy to describe, but which everybody feels; I think that is extremely desirable: there are a number of persons in those offices who are brought into contact with the upper classes of this country, and they should be of that class, in order that they may hold their own on behalf of the Government, and not be overcrowded by other people. . . .

Supplementary Clerks might be found wanting in the very things to which I attach great value in the upper class; perhaps he might not pronouce his 'h's or commit some similar solecism, which might be a most serious damage to a department in a case of negotiation.[3]

By 1874 the principle of dividing intellectual and mechanical

---

[1] Marginal comments by Northcote on O'Brien's paper, op. cit.
[2] *Select Committee on Civil Services Expenditure*, 1873, qu. 4937.
[3] Qus. 4544, 4548.

work was no longer questioned; the three schemes of examination introduced in 1870 had been based upon it. Echoing Trevelyan twenty years earlier, the Playfair Commission affirmed that the division of labour was the key to the whole organization of the Service; unlike him they were supported by most of the witnesses who appeared before them. Their proposal to divide the Service into a Higher and Lower Division was an attempt to achieve a more practicable division of work.

But little progress had been made towards a satisfactory and permanent solution to the problem of dealing with the rapidly increasing amount of purely mechanical work, particularly the copying of letters and other documents. In ten years the number of documents received and registered by the Home Office rose from 18,659 to 30,047, while the number issued, all of which had to be copied at least once, increased from 14,784 to 25,698. Between 1840 and 1869, the number of letters received and dispatched in the Colonial Office had increased by nearly 60 per cent. Copying and other mechanical work was still done in 1874, as it had been twenty years earlier, almost wholly without mechanical aid. Experiments with letter-presses in a few departments in the sixties were not very successful, and complaints were made about the poor quality of the copies, and about their cost. Nevertheless, the Select Committee on Civil Services Expenditure recommended in 1873 that the use of such 'machines' should be obligatory. The typewriter, the use of carbon paper, and the employment of shorthand writers were not widespread in the Service until the end of the century.

Fewer established clerks were now employed on copying as a result of the acceptance of the principle of dividing work than when Northcote and Trevelyan wrote their report, but the recruitment and employment of a special class of writers brought with it fresh problems. While the Civil Service Commissioners' register reduced the possibility of 'back-door' entry to the Service, there was nothing to prevent a department employing a registered writer on work other than copying. Employed on an hourly basis, with no certainty of employment, no prospects of advancement or establishment, and no pension entitlement, writers were a depressed and discontented class throughout the seventies.

In 1874 the rigid departmentalism which had characterized the Service throughout the nineteenth century was under constant attack. Many witnesses who gave evidence to the Select Committee on Civil Services Expenditure in 1873 and to the Playfair Commission a year later criticized the lack of a general classification of salaries. Sir William Stephenson, Chairman of the Board of Inland Revenue, and an old Treasury man, thought that a general classification 'would prevent a great deal of . . . individual clamours for increase of salary'.[1] The different branches of the service rivalled and vied with each other, and had nothing by which to compare themselves and very little knowledge of each other's work. 'One man thinks that his merits are just as great as another's, and he does not see any reason why one particular department should be paid better than another.' Against this, it was still argued that a general classification might lead to a universal movement to increase salaries, and would encourage the growth of union activity. It would be more difficult for the Treasury to resist an application submitted on behalf of all the 3rd class clerks in the Service, than a number of separate applications from departments upon different footings.

The introduction of open competitive examinations based upon a formal division of work had pointed the way towards general classes, and made their attainment a more practicable proposition. The Playfair Commission, asked to consider the possibility of grading the Civil Service as a whole, recommended the creation of 'two separate and distinct grades of clerks', a Higher and a Lower Division. Only the latter was created, but by providing for recruitment to it by open competitive examination under Regulation II, and by introducing uniform salary scales, departmentalism, rudely shaken by the 1870 Order, began to crumble. By 1888 there were three thousand Lower Division Clerks, who in association acted 'practically like one man'. The integration of the other half of the Service took longer. Playfair's abortive proposal for a Higher Division became a reality in 1890 as a result of the Ridley Commission's recommendations, but while entry to the new First Division was upon a common basis, the introduction of uniform salary scales was delayed until the turn of the century.

By the middle sixties Hamilton was claiming, with some exaggeration, that the principle of promotion by merit had been generally accepted throughout the Service, although its acceptance did not ensure that merit rather than favouritism always prevailed.

[1] Qu. 4122.

At about the same time, the rules which govern the administration of sick-leave in the modern Service were gradually emerging as the Treasury assumed for the first time control over this aspect of establishment; and all departments were being brought within the scope of new, uniform pension rules. Office hours and annual leave continued, with one or two exceptions, to vary from one department to another, and to remain beyond Treasury influence. Discipline was left similarly to the minister's discretion, although the Treasury's concern for financial probity, which had led to the issue of a circular on bankruptcy and insolvency in 1866, was an important precedent for more ambitious disciplinary control in the future. Similarly, the Treasury's assumption of the role of 'guardian of Civil Service morality' was an important contribution to the development of an uncorrupt and incorruptible Service.

Perhaps more important than any structural or organizational change was the growth of corporatism among civil servants in different departments. 'Within the memory of men who are yet scarcely gray the term Civil Service was hardly known. People used to talk of "men in Government Offices", of so-and-so being in the War Office, and some one else in the Treasury; but the idea of the "Service" in the generic application of the word was undeveloped.'[1] The Civil Service had acquired 'an educational status' and had 'taken rank as a liberal profession'.[2] The greatest impetus to unionism was provided by the *ad hoc* departmental and inter-departmental combinations of civil servants which were formed during the period 1854–74 to secure the redress of common grievances, like the abolition of superannuation deductions. These movements towards greater unity were encouraged and reinforced by the publication of the first Civil Service newspapers.

The earliest formal departmental combinations appeared in branches of the Customs and Inland Revenue, where salaries tended to be low and conditions of service tended to vary from one port to another, and from one local tax office to another. In 1858 the Tax Surveyors set up a central committee to present grievances to the Board of Inland Revenue, to petition M.P.s, and to appeal to the public. Eleven years later revenue clerks of all grades co-operated in the publication of a weekly journal, *The*

---

[1] *The Civil Service Gazette*, 15 May 1869.
[2] Trevelyan to C. P. Measor, Hon. Sec. to the Committee of the Civil Service College, printed in *The Civil Service Gazette*, 27 May 1867.

Civilian, to voice their ideas and grievances. Commenting upon this 'tendency which did not exist in former years to combine as a body', Earl Granville pointed out in 1867 that civil servants had their own newspaper, *The Civil Service Gazette*, their own athletic sports, and their own social club.[1] There was also a Volunteer Corps, and a cricket club; and, in the teeth of fierce opposition, the Civil Service had begun trading co-operatively for the benefit of its members.

Encouraged, exhorted and often led by their own newspaper, civil servants began slowly to think and act as a unified profession. *The Civil Service Gazette* began publication on 1 January 1853, the first in a long and distinguished line of Civil Service newspapers and journals; within five years it had a weekly stamped circulation of 74,072.[2] Its aim was 'to make the employees of the State know themselves, and to make the public know and properly estimate their servants'.[3] In twenty or thirty closely printed pages it commented and argued each week on the great and small issues which affected the daily working lives of its readers, and kept them informed of vacancies, appointments, promotions, and other Service news. Through its correspondence columns, civil servants were enabled for the first time to exchange views and opinions on issues of common interest.

Missionary in fervour, strident in tone, militant and radical in outlook, it urged and encouraged its readers to think and act as a great and unified profession, 'to lay aside individual dislikes and sectional prejudices, and to combine rationally . . . for the improvement and advancement of the collective body'.[4] Deprecation of the fragmentary character of the Service, the lack of uniform conditions of employment, and the need to seek the redress of common grievances through concerted action, were reiterated themes of its leading articles. Looking back in 1872, the editor commented:

Having an organ in the press, free, fearless and independent, the Civil Service soon became aware of its own importance and strength. What was before a concourse of atoms, with no adhesion, no moving spirit, no apparent vitality, became a living mass with a giant's power.[5]

[1] Quoted in *The Civil Service Gazette*, 1 June 1867.
[2] Figures for stamped circulation were only a part of the circulation of a metropolitan newspaper. The actual circulation was probably three or four times this number.   [3] Leading article, 23 January 1858.
[4] Leading article, 2 January 1858.   [5] Leading article, 6 January 1872.

It showed them how to organize, to co-operate and to exercise legitimate influence. In the successful organized resistance to the abatement of salaries in the fifties it played a major role, passionately and furiously denouncing week by week the 'iniquitous tax', and drawing public attention to the plight of officers' widows, who were not entitled to a pension despite their husbands' contributions. For six years it provided a forum for the discussion of the issue, and informed its readers of the multifarious activities of the various campaign committees. With equal enthusiasm it campaigned tirelessly for a general increase of salaries in the late sixties, when rising food and commodity prices led to considerable discontent throughout the Service, and eventually to the emergence of the '*Pro Rata* Movement', which on behalf of the whole Service petitioned the Treasury for a *pro rata* increase of salaries.

As a 'union' newspaper, *The Civil Service Gazette* was particularly concerned with the conditions of work, terms of employment, and career prospects of the serving officer. To the Treasury, to heads of departments, and to the Government as a whole, its exposure and condemnation of departmental 'abuses', inefficiency or favouritism, and its championing of the cause of an aggrieved individual or group of officers, was a constant source of irritation and embarrassment. Its commitment to the cause of the serving officer influenced the stand it took on wider issues of improvement and reform. Radical in outlook, it agitated for the abolition of patronage and all forms of ministerial influence, but nevertheless remained sceptical of the need and efficacy of literary examinations open to all. One of the most persistent and perceptive critics of open competition, it ridiculed the Government's claim that the 1870 Order enabled the peasant's son to compete with the peer's son for a Treasury clerkship. As it rightly perceived, competition under Regulation I was open only to those who had had a public school or university education. It opposed promotion by merit, arguing, rightly, that it afforded the means for unscrupulous heads of departments to promote favourites over the heads of their seniors. Like most civil servants, it preferred a system in which promotion went to the senior qualified man. On the other hand, it never wavered in its attack upon departmentalism, and urged the introduction of uniform leave and disciplinary regulations, and the classification of grades and salaries.

Few of the changes in structure and conditions of service

described above were under way by 1854; none when Trevelyan entered the Treasury in 1840. To a great extent they were inspired by the Treasury's changing attitude towards the Service. Before 1854 it had been primarily concerned with controlling conspicuous establishments expenditure—pay, allowances, pensions and numbers. The prevailing idea in 1834, Trevelyan explained to Gladstone twenty years later, had been *'economy pure and simple.* Now we are beginning to see that there can be no real economy which is not combined with efficiency, and that the highest efficiency is generally the best economy'.[1] Concern for efficiency led the Treasury into other fields of establishments, such as recruitment, organization, and promotion, where customarily it had rarely exercised influence outside its own subordinate departments. For this more purposeful, constructive control the instrument of prior approval was supplemented by 'constant and systematic' committees of inquiry in which the Treasury collaborated closely and informally with the departments.

Trevelyan and Northcote had prescribed the conditions for a more economic and efficient Service, but not all in the Treasury accepted the corollary of this—that the Service could or should be made more uniform by the acceptance and implementation of those conditions in every department. While the two reformers, together with Childers, were committed to making the Service more unified, and under their guidance Treasury control of particular aspects of establishments was usually directed to the achievement of that larger purpose, many more, among them Hamilton, Lingen, Arbuthnot, and Anderson of the officials, and Lowe and Peel of the ministers, were primarily motivated by the desire for cheaper and more efficient administration. (Trevelyan, Northcote, and Childers wanted that too, of course.) Childers saw the introduction of the writer class in the late sixties as a means of unifying the Service, whereas Hamilton thought such unity undesirable and unattainable in practice. Nevertheless, he was prepared to support their introduction because he believed that a division of work between three separate classes was the most economical and efficient arrangement. Similarly, he canvassed promotion by merit mainly because he believed it to be more efficient and economical than any other method. Trevelyan believed that too, but saw in it also a means to make the Service

[1] 6 February 1856, Bod. T.L.B., xxxvi, 87–8.

more unified. Sick-leave and pension regulations were made more uniform under the guidance of Hamilton and Peel, not from any desire to make the Service more unified, but because to do so made for simpler administration and brought order and regularity to a system which had been chaotic, inequitable and largely uncontrolled. The series of *ad hoc* decisions in which the status of 'civil servant' was defined for the purpose of awarding pensions was an important contributory factor in the development of a single, unified Service, but neither Hamilton nor Peel, who were primarily responsible, did more than react to the immediate problem with which they were faced.

To the extent that the Civil Service was transformed between 1854 and 1874 it was accomplished largely without the preconceived notion of a unified Service. Hamilton, and those who thought like him, believed the Civil Service incapable of unification, and that this was in any case undesirable because likely to prove more expensive (*pace* the argument about the levelling-up of salaries if the principle of comparability were publicly accepted). But in practice they contributed to it by their insistence on economy and efficiency which led them to advocate the introduction of general rules in certain establishment sectors. Trevelyan's contribution was more theoretical: with Northcote he laid down the standards—division of labour, promotion by merit, open competition, transferability, uniform conditions of service—the basis of the modern Service. Hamilton and Lingen his two immediate successors, together with Lowe, were principally responsible for the first attempts to translate these principles into practice, albeit without the vision of a unified Service which had inspired the framers of the *Report on the Organisation of the Civil Service*.

By 1874 the Civil Service was far from unified, but the basis had been established from which unification could proceed. By this time it was very much less difficult than it had been twenty years earlier to conceive of the Civil Service as one Service—as is apparent from the evidence of witnesses who appeared before the Playfair Commission in 1874. To talk in terms of finding common solutions to problems common to most departments was not greeted with cries of heresy as it had been when Trevelyan had given evidence before the 1848 Select Committee; and many, where previously there had been few, now gave their support to a general classification of all civil servants, to uniform salaries, and to transfers between departments. Indeed, one of the four instructions given to the Commission was the exploration of the possibility of grading the Civil Service as a whole to obviate the inconvenience which resulted from the variations of pay in the different departments. By 1874 continued development along the paths indicated by Trevelyan and Northcote was ineluctable: the process of change had gone too far to be halted or reversed. Above all, the conditions had been created for the emergence of the new Service: the transition had been made. The complete acceptance of their principles, and the practical application of them, was to take much longer and to command the attention and energies not only of the Treasury, but of three Royal Commissions.

APPENDIX I

THE TITLE OF PERMANENT SECRETARY TO THE TREASURY

Treasury Minute No. 10369 dated 10 May 1867

'Treasury Establishment, Alterations in the constitution of.'

The First Lord and the Chancellor of the Exchequer state to the Board that they have had under consideration the present organisation of the Treasury Establishment, with reference more particularly to the excessive pressure of business which has of late years devolved upon the Financial Secretary and the Assistant Secretary.

The necessity of affording assistance to these Officers was noticed by Mr Childers the late Financial Secretary, in his Memo of 5th July 1866 and has been confirmed by the experience of Mr Hunt since that period. Lord Derby and Mr Disraeli are of the opinion that the best and most convenient mode of rendering that assistance will be by taking advantage of the present vacancy in the office of Auditor of the Civil List and reviving it as a separate office and constituting the gentleman who may be appointed to fill it Assistant to the Secretaries.

They are further of opinion that the Financial Secretary should be afforded additional assistance in the Department of his Private Secretary.

Lord Derby and Mr Disraeli also state to the Board that in their opinion it is desirable that the position of the office held by Mr Hamilton should be better defined and that its title should be changed to that of Permanent Secretary.

My Lords entirely approve of the recommendation of the First Lord and the Chancellor of the Exchequer.

With reference to the Office now held by Mr Hamilton their Lordships observe that in the Minute of 19th August 1805 when that Office was originally constituted it is recited and described as that of an additional Secretary as well as Assistant Secretary, and in subsequent Minutes as that of Third Secretary. By the arrangement of the Treasury Minute of 4th July 1856 the character and position of the Office was altered by having duties belonging to a Division attached to it, which duties were, however, withdrawn from it by the Minute of 14th December 1859. Since that period the functions which have devolved upon the Financial Secretary having increased greatly both in their extent and importance, the work and duties cast upon the Assistant Secretary have necessarily been more onerous and responsible. Under these circumstances My Lords are of opinion that the Office shall now be given a more substantive character than that of Assistant Secretary and they are pleased to direct that its title shall be that of 'Permanent Secretary of the Treasury'.

It will be the duty of the Permanent Secretary to exercise a general supervision over the business of the office, to keep himself well informed regarding all subjects which come before the Treasury, so as to be able at all times to furnish information and advice to the Board and to the Political Secretaries as may be required on all matters before them.

He will have particular regard to all increases of Establishments and Salaries in the Public Service. He will see that Orders and regulations and Minutes of the Board are duly carried out and generally undertake such duties as one of the Secretaries of the Board, as My Lords through their Financial Secretary, or by Minute shall prescribe.

With regard to the assistance to be given to the Secretaries, My Lords are pleased to direct that there shall be attached to the Establishment of the Treasury the Office of Auditor of the Civil List, with a salary of £1,500 a year being the amount named in 56 Geo 3, c 46 under which that Office is constituted and assigned as the salary of the Office in the Treasury Minute of 28th August 1865 (13280) and that in addition to the duties prescribed by the Act for the office of Auditor of the Civil List, the Gentleman filling that Office shall undertake the duty of assisting the Secretaries with the title of Assistant to the Secretaries.

He shall rank next in the Office to the Permanent Secretary and take his place in his absence, he shall sign such letters and take charge of such papers and business, as from time to time shall be assigned to him by the Secretaries, and deal with such papers in such manner as they shall direct, and generally shall take such a part in the business of the Office as shall be committed to him by them.

My Lords are pleased to appoint Mr William Law, at present the Principal Clerk in charge of the Third Division, to the Office of Auditor of the Civil List and Assistant to the Secretaries.

And in selecting him, Their Lordships adopt the words of the Board of Treasury in the Minute of 15th February 1815, when, under circumstances somewhat similar, Mr W. Hill was appointed to relieve the Secretaries from a part of the detailed business of the Office.

In making this selection, 'My Lords (it is stated in that Minute) desire to hold out to the several clerks in the Treasury an example of the honour and advantage to come to them from the assiduous and able discharge of their duties and it is their Lordships intention, upon any vacancy that may hereafter arise in their Office to appoint such person as from their Lordships knowledge and experience they may deem most competent to discharge the duties of it.'

With a view to the additional assistance which is required for the Financial Secretary, My Lords direct that a Third Class Clerk shall be assigned to him for that purpose and that a special allowance of £50 a year shall be given to the gentleman whom the Financial Secretary may select.

The present Establishment of the Treasury being constituted under the Minute of 24th December 1859, of five Divisions with a Principal Clerk in charge of each, My Lords are of opinion that by a redistribution of the business the Divisions may be reduced to four and one of the offices of Principal Clerk abolished.

It will be necessary to fill up the office vacated by Mr Law's appointment, but understanding that Mr Shelley, the Principal Clerk of the Fifth Division is willing to retire, My Lords will be prepared, on his retirement to abolish the Fifth Division distributing the business among the others, and to consider Mr Shelley's claim for Superannuation under the 7th Section of the Superannuation Act of 1859.

My Lords direct that the Permanent Secretary shall consider and make a Report to the Board as to the distribution of business and the alteration in the organisation of the Department which the changes now made may require.

Let the usual Report be made under the Treasury Minute of

cc

1st October 1856 as to the promotions consequent upon the advancement of Mr Law.

              (Signed)   G. A. Hamilton, 6th May.
                                  (Assistant Secretary)

                                  G. W. Hunt, 10th May.
                                  (Financial Secretary)

APPENDIX II

A NOTE ON THE TITLE OF OFFICIAL HEAD OF THE CIVIL SERVICE

It has been generally assumed that the Treasury Minute of 10 May 1867 conferred upon the permanent head of the Treasury not only the title of Permanent Secretary but that of Official Head of the Civil Service as well. The original of that Minute has been lost or destroyed. However, a copy of it is to be found in the Treasury *Departmental Arrangement Books* and it is clear beyond any doubt that the title of Official Head of the Civil Service was not conferred by it.

From time to time other evidence has been cited in support of the claim that the title was introduced at that time. There are two main sources. The first of these is the statement made by Robert Lowe in the House of Commons on 8 April 1872. Lowe was at that time Chancellor of the Exchequer and in the course of a debate on the Civil Service Estimates he interjected: 'that the Secretary of the Treasury was not an Under-Secretary of State, he was at the head of the Civil Service'. From this remark it has been inferred that the Permanent Secretary of the Treasury was also the Official Head of the Civil Service. At that time the Commons were discussing the salary of the Permanent Secretary and comparing it with that received by other permanent heads of department. A more probable explanation of Lowe's remark is, therefore, that he was seeking to justify the higher salary of the Permanent Secretary of the Treasury on the ground that he was at the head of the Civil Service, i.e., he stood first in his profession, at the head of the most important department. If not, why did he not say that the Permanent Secretary was the Official Head of the Civil Service, or simply Head of the Civil Service, both of which would have been more felicitous and unambiguous descriptions of the Permanent Secretary's position?

The second source of evidence is less reliable even than this. In the second edition of Alpheus Todd's *On Parliamentary Government* published in 1887 the office of Permanent Secretary of the Treasury is described as 'the official head of the Department and of the whole Civil Service'. From this it has been inferred that between the publication of the 1st edition in 1867, which contained no reference to that title, and the 2nd, the office had been transformed and had acquired the title. One of the merits of Todd's work is that his statements are supported by reference to contemporary sources. When these are examined it is found that he rests his case, firstly, upon Lowe's interjection in the 1872 debate, secondly, upon the use in a debate in the House of Commons of the title of Permanent Secretary, and, thirdly, upon evidence given before the Select Committee on Civil Services Expenditure in 1873. There are three references to the latter, one to the statement that the Permanent Secretary was permanent head of the Treasury, another to the title of Permanent Secretary, while the third appears not to be a reference to the office at all. Todd's evidence, therefore, adds nothing new. We are thrown back upon Lowe. Unsupported by other evidence his ambiguous statement is insufficient to confirm the existence of the title at that time.

There is no reliable evidence that the title was afforded official recognition before 1919 when a Treasury Minute of 4 September provided that the Permanent Secretary should act as the Permanent Head of the Civil Service and advise the First Lord of the Treasury on appointments made to the Service. If the title had existed officially before that date it seems unlikely that it would not have come to light. No mention of it is to be found in the exhaustive Civil Service Inquiries of 1873, 1875, 1887–90, and 1912–16. And it has been said that neither Welby, nor Mowatt, nor Murray, who held the office of Permanent Secretary in succession to Lingen, ever claimed the title. Despite this, it is clear that the *de facto* position of the Permanent Secretary was that of Head of the Civil Service from at least 1856. Charged specially with the regulation of salaries and establishments throughout the Civil Service the Permanent Secretary assumed in practice the wider responsibility for the organization of the Service. At the time of his retirement in 1870 Hamilton stated that he had presided over the Civil Service for 13 years and referred to the office as 'almost the keystone of the whole Civil Service'. The manner in which he and his successor discharged their responsibilities support this description of the office.

APPENDIX III

COMPETITIVE EXAMINATIONS

TABLE I

Limited Competitions, 1 January 1862–30 June 1868
Proportion of Qualified Candidates to Vacancies

(a) In competitions for single vacancies

Number of limited competitions in
which the proportion of qualified
competitors to vacancies was:

Less than equal	38	(6·7)
Less than two to one	106	(18·6)
Less than three to one	133	(23·4)
Less than four to one	248	(43·6)
Less than five to one	26	(4·5)
Five or more to one (as recommended)	18	(3·2)
	569	(100)

(b) In competitions for plural vacancies

Number of limited competitions in
which the proportion of qualified
competitors to vacancies was:

Less than equal	24	(8·3)
Less than two to one	84	(29·0)
Less than three to one	102	(35·3)
Three or more to one (as recommended	79	(27·4)
	289	(100)

(c) Percentage of limited competitions in which the proportion of candidates to vacancies was as recommended by the 1860 Select Committee on Civil
Service Appointments:

1862	10 per cent
1863	12 per cent
1864	9 per cent
1865	12 per cent
1866	14 per cent
1867–8	11 per cent

Appendix III

TABLE 2

Open Competitions under Regulations I and II, 1870–1874

22 August 1871	Reg 11	66 competitors for 20 vacancies
23 January 1872	Reg 1	22 competitors for 10 vacancies
14 May 1872	Reg 11	119 competitors for 21 vacancies
15 October 1872	Reg 11	155 competitors for 39 vacancies
4 March 1873	Reg 11	146 competitors for 52 vacancies
10 June 1873	Reg 1	46 competitors for 10 vacancies
24 June 1873	Reg 11	169 competitors for 44 vacancies

In addition to these competitions a number of examinations were held for single posts, or for a number of special posts. In February 1872, an open competition for the situation of 2nd Class Assistant of Excise in the Inland Revenue attracted 738 competitors for 100 vacancies.

APPENDIX IV

TREASURY MEMORANDUM ON THE HOME OFFICE INQUIRY OF 1856

Memorandum showing how far the recommendations of the Committee of 1856 have been carried out in the Home Office[1]

Recommendations made by the Treasury Committee of Inquiry	Treasury Comments
(i) Clerks after obtaining certificate of qualification to be admitted only after a probation of six months;	Adopted
(ii) Monthly reports of the attendance of the Junior Clerks to be furnished to the Under-Secretary;	Adopted
(iii) Promotion of Junior Clerks to depend on regularity of attendance and efficiency and not on seniority alone;	Adopted
(iv) Annual addition to salaries of Junior Clerks to be allowed only on certificate of satisfactory conduct;	Adopted
(v) Heads of Departments to be selected on account of qualification which should form the sole ground of preference;	Adopted
(vi) Office to be divided into four instead of three departments;	Carried out
(vii) Everest and Redgrave to be placed on the Establishment as Supernumerary Clerks of the 1st Class;	So employed but not so classed
(viii) Extra or supplemental clerks to be employed in copying or other mechanical work on a scale of pay adopted in other Departments;	They are so employed as well as upon the general business of the office, but the scale of pay recommended which is superior to that which they receive has not been adopted.
(ix) Details of Office arrangements to be under the direction of the Permanent Under-Secretary assisted by the Chief Clerk;	Adopted
(x) Separate Departmental Registers of paper to be established and the general Register to be abolished;	Adopted
(xi) Clerk attached to Librarian to be transferred to Domestic Branch;	Clerk transferred

[1] P.R.O. T.1/6258A/13006.

(xii) One Clerk of the Second and one of the Third Class to be attached to Mr Redgrave's Department together with a sufficient number of extra or supplemental clerks;

Carried out

(xiii) Domestic Branch to be in charge of one Senior, three Second and Three Third Class Clerks;

?

(xiv) One clerk of the Second and two of the Third Class always to be attached to the Criminal Branch;

This arrangement existed when the Report was made and exists still

(xv) Future Establishment to consist of 1 Chief Clerk, 3 1st Class, 6 Second Class, 7 Third Class and 1 Librarian;

Not yet carried out

(xvi) Salaries
Chief Clerk—£1,000
1st Class including Redgrave and Everest
£650 by £20 to £900
2nd Class £350 by £15 to £600
3rd Class £100 by £10 to £300

This scale has not been adopted generally. The max. of the Chief Clerk had been fixed at £1,000 as he was just attaining it at the time of report. The salary of the 1st Senior Clerk had also been previously fixed and he has risen to his max., since the date of the report. Mr Redgrave has since been raised to the max. of £900 but the salary of Mr Everest at the head of the Criminal Dept. has not been raised to £900

(xvii) Extra or supplemental clerks
£80 by £5 to £180 and by £10 to £350.

Not adopted

APPENDIX V

PUBLIC EXPENDITURE, 1854–1875[1]

TABLE 1
Public Expenditure Estimates, 1854–1875

	Civil Services £	Rev. Depts. £	War Depts. £	Admiralty £	Total £
1854–5	5,294,915	4,052,803	6,287,486	7,487,948	23,123,152
1855	6,506,062	4,870,645	13,721,158	10,716,338	35,814,203
1856	6,740,648	5,082,927	34,998,504	12,148,641	58,970,720
1857	7,465,878	5,182,216	11,247,235	8,109,168	32,004,497
1858	7,239,795	4,723,149	11,538,387	9,140,127	32,641,458
1859	7,880,182	4,741,453	11,568,060	9,813,181	34,002,876
1860	7,492,329	4,932,432	14,842,275	12,802,200	40,069,236
1861	7,665,377	4,778,574	14,606,751	12,029,475	39,080,177
1862	7,848,297	4,752,795	15,302,870	11,794,305	39,698,267
1863	7,805,277	4,720,641	15,060,237	10,736,032	38,322,187
1864	7,622,117	4,692,092	14,844,888	10,432,610	37,591,707
1865	7,624,872	4,656,760	14,348,447	10,392,224	37,022,303
1866	7,856,836	5,824,862[2]	14,095,000	10,388,153	38,164,851
1867	8,202,953	5,852,429	14,752,200	10,926,253	39,733,835
1868	9,173,032	6,057,447	15,455,400	11,177,290	41,863,169
1869	9,530,158	6,065,580	14,230,400	9,996,641	39,822,779
1870	9,989,545	6,426,720[3]	12,975,000	9,250,530	38,641,795
1871	10,725,544	6,644,255	15,851,700	9,756,356	42,977,855
1872	10,651,824	6,865,222	14,824,500	9,508,149	41,849,695
1873	11,067,757	7,351,941	14,416,400	9,872,725	42,708,823
1874	11,286,978	7,513,683	14,485,300	10,179,485	43,465,446
1875	12,656,132	7,706,680	14,677,700	10,784,644	45,825,156

[1] All the tables in this appendix are based upon the annual estimates of expenditure submitted to the Treasury, and laid before Parliament. Their purpose is to show the annual trends in public expenditure as they appeared to the Treasury, rather than the actual amounts spent by the Government in each year. The latter included not only the amounts voted by Parliament which were subject to Treasury Control, but also those sums charged on the Consolidated Fund which were paid without annual appropriation and over which the Treasury had no control. In the expenditure accounts of the salaries and expenses of the public departments provision was also made for the deduction of fees, fee-stamps, and other receipts paid into the Exchequer during the year; these sums were offset against the totals spent from the votes and the Consolidated Fund.

Only the initial estimates submitted by the departments are included here; no allowance has been made for supplementary estimates made before or after appropriation by Parliament. The totals do not, therefore, necessarily show the total grant asked for each year. In some years, 1854–6 for example, there were very heavy supplementary estimates.

[2] Post Office Packet Service transferred to Revenue Votes.

[3] Post Office Telegraphs transferred to Revenue Votes.

TABLE 2

Estimates of Expenditure on Civil Services, 1854–1875

	Class I £	Class II £	Class III £	Class IV £	Class V £	Class VI £	Class VII £	Class VIII £	Civil Contingencies £	Total £
1854–5	815,829	1,094,786	1,478,851	722,812	333,460	213,079	536,098	—	100,000	5,294,915
1855	746,760	1,315,390	2,245,287	831,670	328,344	218,342	704,969	15,300	100,000	6,506,062
1856	802,000	1,513,903	2,257,083	876,937	320,265	226,199	449,573	104,688	100,000	6,740,648
1857	918,888	1,599,117	2,637,129	996,722	382,215	239,689	682,118	—	100,000	7,465,878
1858	781,469	1,480,565	2,462,472	1,126,307	368,762	242,331	677,889	—	100,000	7,239,795
1859	793,844	1,413,495	2,544,650	1,328,453	428,710	242,794	1,028,236	—	100,000	7,880,182
1860	621,990	1,413,503	2,565,301	1,305,912	484,012	253,610	723,001	—	125,000	7,492,329
1861	773,974	1,449,062	2,673,458	1,358,996	689,283	349,638	295,966	—	75,000	7,665,377
1862	692,215	1,473,625	2,763,308	1,410,114	937,400	338,896	229,739	—	—	7,848,297
1863	960,123	1,490,887	2,780,341	1,386,417	611,396	327,643	248,470	—	—	7,805,277
1864	857,518	1,548,518	2,859,945	1,311,620	558,357	347,479	138,620	—	—	7,622,117
1865	799,370	1,580,185	2,897,515	1,362,821	476,106	339,107	169,768	—	—	7,624,872
1866	993,906	1,580,056	2,875,344	1,387,515	508,408	344,766	166,841	—	—	7,856,836
1867	942,535	1,703,230	3,026,942	1,487,554	499,280	359,558	183,854	—	—	8,202,953
1868	1,266,782	1,661,179	3,581,586	1,618,527	486,277	426,825	131,756	—	—	9,173,032
1869	1,223,806	1,733,681	3,712,426	1,628,170	643,500	457,401	131,174	—	—	9,530,158
1870	1,378,924	1,712,960	3,985,380	1,689,790	620,593	512,916	88,892	—	—	9,989,545
1871	1,461,121	1,854,535	3,995,660	2,266,324	579,606	500,413	69,884	—	—	10,725,544
1872	1,350,246	1,803,008	3,992,911	2,392,160	544,297	525,801	34,401	—	—	10,651,824
1873	1,331,762	2,003,383	4,136,585	2,440,442	601,674	527,674	26,237	—	—	11,067,757
1874	1,297,178	1,933,356	4,322,607	2,577,398	586,763	528,196	31,480	—	—	11,286,978
1875	1,430,439	2,489,379	4,818,251	2,824,474	537,502	526,755	29,332	—	—	12,656,132

Note: Class I   = Public Works and Buildings.   Class V   = Consular, Colonial and other Foreign Services.
       Class II = Salaries, etc of Public Departments.   Class VI   = Superannuation and Charities.
       Class III = Law and Justice.   Class VII = Misc., Special and Temporary Objects.
       Class IV = Education, Science and Art.   Class VIII = Miscellaneous.

TABLE 3

Estimates of Expenditure on Salaries, etc., of (selected) Public Offices

	Treasury £	Home Office £	Foreign Office £	Colonial Office £	Privy Council £	Board and Trade £	War Office £	Admiralty Office £	Exchequer and £	Audit £	Paymaster-General £	Works and P.B. £
1854–5	55,146	27,552	72,372	40,550	68,660		—		7,295	47,736	23,850	20,124
1855	54,400	27,595	83,849	35,897	75,733		—		7,314	46,421	25,211	21,595
1856	52,095	24,204	68,241	28,452	61,067		191,817[1]	136,467	6,483	30,361	24,594	23,313
1857	53,171	24,466	67,169	29,160	66,426		184,909	140,469	6,218	38,575	17,510	26,614
1858	54,000	24,799	76,900	29,134	13,832	54,015	182,977	138,399	6,255	36,768	17,198	26,575
1859	54,600	25,911	82,800	30,178	15,593	53,942	185,594	134,217	6,898	32,466	17,762	29,746
1860	53,095	25,687	62,145	29,208	18,730	54,129	196,224	140,439	6,630	33,118	17,500	30,559
1861	53,173	25,753	62,715	30,449	20,508	59,595	201,833	142,957	6,640	33,092	13,550	30,333
1862	52,363	25,856	64,319	30,748	20,566	59,787	209,901	160,280	6,565	32,931	19,800	30,839
1863	51,730	26,263	72,325	31,047	20,637	62,181	213,177	161,157	4,923	34,060	19,640	30,857
1864	53,147	26,883	72,015	31,421	24,306	65,543	223,384	170,832	4,928	35,512	19,491	31,903
1865	53,488	27,118	66,885	31,658	20,842	68,523	212,800	165,322	5,048	36,559	20,391	32,148
1866	52,432	26,471	63,840	32,124	20,739	65,285	212,800	168,605	5,558	36,866	20,558	32,226
1867	52,836	27,308	67,410	33,250	30,423	68,386	218,600	175,957	38,000		20,200	32,463
1868	52,609	89,410[3]	74,453	32,990	42,585[4]	97,725[5]	224,600	173,655	38,500		19,526	34,700
1869	59,275[2]	85,696	70,413	34,884	41,413	101,033	223,400	176,018	37,324		20,417	34,222
1870	59,193	87,032	64,814	34,933	47,249	100,114	222,300	182,364	37,349		21,432	34,028
1871	54,964	88,430	64,674	31,249	55,885	97,390	194,000	168,704	37,533		22,166	38,741
1872	55,269	82,024	63,985	31,402	52,397	98,235	196,800	159,368	38,256		24,841	40,257
1873	56,213	92,830	62,085	31,582	31,675	101,778	200,500	163,499	43,676		25,506	42,072
1874	57,058	85,212	61,713	32,290	31,276	109,916	205,900	173,767	39,819		22,327	44,159
1875	57,016	87,872	61,792	33,238	35,052	126,631	210,900	174,983	45,325		22,861	44,590

Admiralty Office additional: 178,066 (1874), 183,916 (1875).

[1] War Department and H.Q. Military Department.
[2] From 1869 includes office of Parliamentary Counsel.
[3] From 1868 includes estimates for subordinate departments of Factories, Mines, Fisheries, Superintendent of Roads South Wales, Local Government Act Office, Inspectors of Burial Grounds, Inspectors of Constabulary, Inspectors of Prisons, and Inspectors of Reformatories.
[4] From 1868 includes estimates for subordinate departments, e.g. public health, quarantine, cattle plague department.
[5] From 1868 includes estimates for subordinate departments, e.g. General Register and Record of Seamen, Designs Office.

TABLE 4

Estimates of Expenditure of the Revenue Departments, 1854–1875

	Customs £	Inland Revenue £	P.O. £	P.O. Packet Service £	P.O. Telegraphs £	Total[1] £
1854–5	840,785	1,154,594	1,525,335	—	—	4,052,803
1855	835,182	1,365,950	1,638,861	—	—	4,870,645
1856	840,001	1,459,207	1,740,483	—	—	5,082,927
1857	855,482	1,429,133	1,868,181	—	—	5,182,216
1858	849,285	1,362,258	2,026,031	—	—	4,723,149
1859	857,155	1,349,864	2,051,213	—	—	4,741,453
1860	855,200	1,490,813	2,108,581	—	—	4,932,432
1861	750,000	1,440,000	2,050,000	—	—	4,778,574
1862	750,000	1,382,274	2,084,687	—	—	4,752,795
1863	754,154	1,351,771	2,098,920	—	—	4,720,641
1864	771,473	1,313,467	2,114,616	—	—	4,692,092
1865	773,009	1,284,157	2,121,478	—	—	4,656,760
1866	798,493	1,295,645	2,436,061	821,164	—	5,824,862
1867	801,623	1,332,707	2,438,929	807,428	—	5,852,428
1868	1,024,653	1,574,210	2,369,235	1,089,349	—	6,037,447
1869	1,008,343	1,604,616	2,362,841	1,089,780	—	6,065,580
1870	989,837	1,592,751	2,376,979	1,107,153	360,000	6,426,720
1871	979,888	1,625,625	2,470,355	1,148,387	420,000	6,644,255
1872	976,468	1,644,308	2,609,814	1,134,632	500,000	6,865,222
1873	983,015	1,678,236	2,745,342	1,130,348	815,000	7,351,941
1874	1,013,246	1,681,013	2,882,423	998,662	938,339	7,513,683
1875	996,896	1,697,172	3,036,210	878,688	1,097,714	7,706,680

[1] Includes charge for superannuation and pensions; and for the Coast Guard until 1857, and the Revenue Police, Ireland, until 1858.

TABLE 5

Estimates of Expenditure for Superannuation and Retired Allowances
1854–1875
(Civil Establishments only)

	Civil Depts. £	Revenue Depts. £	Admiralty £	War Depts. £	Total £
1854–5	135,722	479,857	148,798	38,000[1]	802,377
1855	138,609	484,694	149,558	38,700[1]	811,561
1856	146,537	494,183	147,685	124,264	912,669
1857	159,842	483,150	147,682	124,000	914,674
1858	162,889	485,575	160,481	130,410	939,355
1859	166,989	481,221	163,416	133,903	945,529
1860	177,713	477,838	173,030	136,837	965,418
1861	185,140	538,574	180,397	138,151	1,042,262
1862	184,706	535,834	194,282	143,364	1,058,186
1863	176,462	515,796	194,932	144,964	1,032,154
1864	183,280	492,536	193,983	136,332	1,006,131
1865	179,382	478,116	208,033	131,000	996,531
1866	185,888	473,544	213,837	135,900	1,009,169
1867	197,035	471,741	218,915	136,000	1,023,691
1868	255,867	467,812	223,498	135,200	1,082,377
1869	290,377	420,279	222,566	132,000	1,065,222
1870	398,283	447,382	287,134	148,300	1,281,099
1871	387,972	433,809	312,237	162,900	1,296,918
1872	416,472	433,879	309,185	167,600	1,327,136
1873	423,996	451,608	296,448	172,100	1,344,152
1874	430,957	449,494	288,670	172,100	1,341,221
1875	430,359	449,926	284,529	167,500	1,332,314

[1] Does not include Ordnance Office and other War Departments.

BIBLIOGRAPHY

This bibliography is not exhaustive but it includes all the manuscript collections to which reference has been made in the preparation of this study, and all the printed material which has been found useful.

The material is arranged under the following heads:

      A. Manuscript Collections
      B. Official Papers
      C. Newspapers and Periodicals
      D. Works of Reference
      E. Biographies
      F. Works on the Treasury and the Civil Service
      G. Other Works

A. MANUSCRIPT COLLECTIONS

1. *H.M. Treasury*

Departmental Arrangement Books
  Six bound volumes of manuscript for the years 1805–1900.

Treasury Minutes and Circulars
  Two bound volumes of manuscript for the years 1831–89.

Treasury Establishment
  Bound volume of manuscript containing the Blue Notes for 1879–80, a manuscript analysis of the saving in the work of the Treasury in 1850 as compared with 1821; three memoranda on Treasury organization; and Establishment Lists for 1851 and 1856 and for frequent dates thereafter down to 1895.

2. *Public Record Office*

Treasury Papers
  (i) In-letters and files
    Treasury Board Papers, 1557–1920 (T.1).
    Register of Papers, 1777–1920 (T.2).
    Skeleton Registers, 1783–1920 (T.3).
    Subject Registers, 1852–1909 (T.108).

(ii) Out-letters

Admiralty, 1849–1920 (T.5/2–7).

Colonial Affairs, 1849–1921 (T.7/5–18).

Foreign Affairs, 1857–1920 (T.12/1–7).

Home Office, 1835–1920 (T.13/4–10).

War Departments, 1855–1920 (T.24/1–9).

(iii) Miscellaneous

Minutes: Minute Books, 1667–1870 (T.29/554–619).

Establishments Registers, 1794–1856 (T.41).

Superannuation, 1857–1920 (T.21/1–21).

Papers of Sir Edward Hamilton: (*a*) Financial Notes, 1870–1913; (*b*) Vade Mecum, 1879–1905 (T.168).

Semi-official Correspondence of George Alexander Hamilton: Four bound volumes of manuscript for the period 21 July 1858 to 2 February 1870 (T.168).

The Trevelyan Papers: 23 boxes of papers, mostly on the administration of the Irish famine relief (T.64/362A–370c).

Admiralty Papers

Record and Establishment Books, 1857–73 (Admiralty 115).

Board of Trade Papers

Establishments: Correspondence and Papers, 1865–1930 (BT 13).

Registers of Correspondence (BT 14).

Foreign Office Papers

Letters and Papers relating to the administration and establishment of the Foreign Office (FO 95/592).

Foreign Office Establishments, Treasury correspondence, 1853–74 (FO 366/368).

Foreign Office Establishment, Distribution of Business, 1799–1903 (FO 366/368).

Granville Papers

Letters to Lowe (P.R.O. 30/29/66).

Cardwell Papers

Correspondence with Lowe, 1868–74 (P.R.O. 30/48/22–4).

Russell Papers (P.R.O. 30/22).

Hammond Papers (P.R.O. 391).

3. *British Museum*

Gladstone Papers

(i) Series A. Correspondence

Special Correspondence (Add. MSS. 44086–351).

Letter Books (Add. MSS. 44527–51).

(ii) Series B. Official Papers, including memoranda prepared for the use of the cabinet, 1834–95, 73 volumes mostly printed (Add. MSS. 44563–635).

(iii) Series C. Cabinet Minutes (Add. MSS. 44636–48).

Iddesleigh Papers
  (i) Series B. Special Correspondence (1857–67, Add. MSS. 50015).
  (ii) Series D. General Correspondence (1847–61, Add. MSS. 50034–5).
  (iii) Series F. Letter Books (January 1859 to March 1867, Add. MSS. 50046).

Palmerston Papers
  Private Letter Books, 1853–65 (Add. MSS. 48578–83).

Sir Edward Hamilton's Papers
  Letters to W. E. Gladstone and family (Add. MSS. 48607–9).

Halifax Papers (Sir Charles Wood)
  General Correspondence, 1832–58 (Add. MSS. 49554–60).
  Admiralty Letter Books (Add. MSS. 49562–70).
  Papers relating to Naval Estimates, 1855–8 (Add. MSS. 49582–6).

4. *Bodleian Library, Oxford*

Trevelyan Papers
  Semi-official correspondence of Sir Charles Trevelyan: thirty-eight volumes of Letter Books, 1840–59.

Monk Bretton Papers
  Private Papers of J. G. Dodson, 1st Baron Monk Bretton.

5. *Other Museums, Libraries and Record Offices*

Disraeli Papers (Hughendon Manor)
  Correspondence with G. A. Hamilton and Sir Stafford Northcote (Box 13).

Cornewall Lewis Papers (National Library of Wales)
  Correspondence with Lord Palmerston, 1855–7 (C/2146–8).
  Correspondence with Gladstone, 1855–7 (C/2856, C/1229, and C/1231).

Welby-Allington Papers (Lincolnshire Archives Office)
  Official and personal papers of R. E. Welby, Lindsay Deposit (24/5/1–3).

Ward Hunt Papers (Northamptonshire Record Office)
  Semi-official correspondence, July 1866 to December 1968 (2 volumes).

B. OFFICIAL PAPERS

1. *Hansard's Parliamentary Debates, Third Series*, vols. CXXXVI–CCXXVII.

2. *Parliamentary Papers*

(i) *Reports of the Civil Service Commissioners*, 1856–75.

(ii) *Reports from the Committee of Public Accounts*, 1861–75
General Index of the *Reports from the Committee of Public Accounts* (1857–87), P.P., 1888 LXXIX.

(iii) Reports of Select Committees, Committees of Inquiry, etc.

2nd Report from the Select Committee on Public Income and Expenditure 1828, P.P., 1828 V.

Report from the Select Committee on Miscellaneous Expenditure, 1848, P.P., 1847–8, XVIII.

Report of the Committee of Inquiry into the Organisation of the Civil Service (Northcote–Trevelyan), 23 November, 1853, P.P., 1854, XXVII.

Reports from the Committees of Inquiry into Public Offices and Papers connected therewith, 1854, P.P., 1854, XXVII.

Papers on the Re-organisation of the Civil Service, P.P., 1854–5, XX.

Report from the Select Committee on Superannuation Allowances, P.P., 1856, IX.

Report from the Commissioners appointed to inquire into the operation of the Superannuation Acts, P.P., 1857 (session 2), XXIV.

Reports from the Select Committee on Public Monies, 1856–7, P.P., 1856, XV; 1857 (session 1) II; 1857 (session 2) IX.

Report from the Select Committee on Civil Service Appointments, P.P., 1860, IX.

Reports from the Select Committee on Civil Services Expenditure, 1873, P.P., 1873, VII.

Report from the Select Committee on Civil Service Writers, P.P., 1873, XI.

Reports of the Civil Service (*Playfair*) *Inquiry Commission*, 1875, P.P., 1875, XXIII.

1st Report from the Royal (*Ridley*) *Commission on Civil Establishments*, P.P., 1887, XIX.

2nd Report, P.P., 1888, XXVII.

3rd Report, P.P., 1889, XXI.

4th Report, P.P., 1890, XXVII.

1st and 2nd Reports from the Royal (*MacDonnell*) *Commission on the Civil Service*, P.P., 1912–13, XV.

3rd Report, P.P., 1913, XVIII.

4th Report, P.P., 1914, XVI.

Select Committee on Estimates, Sixth Report, 1957–8 (Treasury Control of Expenditure), 1957–8, H.C. 254–I.

Control of Public Expenditure (Plowden Report), July 1961, Cmnd 1432.

(iv) Returns, lists, etc.

Return of Establishment of Secretary's Department, Admiralty, between 1854–1888, P.P., 1888 LXXX.

Return of the Accountant-General's Department, Admiralty, 1854–1886, P.P., 1888, LII.

Temporary Clerks, Number employed with date of employment, age, salary, etc., 1860, P.P., 1860, XLI and 1861, XXXVI.

Return of Establishments in the Admiralty at Somerset House and Whitehall, P.P., 1861, XXXVIII.

Return of Temporary, Copying or Extra Clerks in Admiralty and War Office, P.P., 1862 XXIX.

Return of salaries, allowances, etc. of Lords of the Admiralty, of the two Secretaries, and salaries of clerks, P.P., 1866, XLVI.

Return of Establishment and Salaries, Board of Trade, P.P., 1871, XXXVII.

Return of all persons employed in the various public departments who have during the three years from the 1st day of April 1868 been placed on the superannuation or redundant list in consequence of re-organisation, reduction or abolition of office, 1871, P.P., 1871, XXXVII.

Comparison of Civil Establishments, Admiralty, 1868–69 to 1872–73, P.P., 1872, XXXIX.

Return of all offices vacancies in which are to be filled by open competitive examinations under schemes I or II, 1873, P.P., 1873, LII.

Abstract of an Account of every Increase and Dimunition which has taken place, in the year 1854, in the number of persons employed, or in the salaries, emoluments, allowances and expenses of all public offices and departments, P.P., 1854–5, XXX; 1856, XXXVIII; 1857 (2), XXV; 1857–8, XXXIV; 1859 (1), XIV; 1860, XXXIX; 1861, XXXV; 1862, XXX; 1863, XXIX; 1864, XXII; 1865, XXX; 1866, XXXIX; 1867, XXXIX; 1867–8, XLI; 1868–9, XXXIV; 1870, XLI; 1871, XXXIV; 1872, XXXVI; 1873, XXXIX; 1874, XXXV.

Return of all names of all persons and the offices to which they have been appointed in the Civil Service under the seventh rule of the Order in Council of 4th day of June 1870, since the issue of the Order, 1882, P.P., 1882, XXXVII.

(v) Annual Estimates of Public Expenditure, P.P., 1853–75.

C. NEWSPAPERS AND PERIODICALS

1. *Newspapers*

   The Civil Service Gazette   *The Civil Service Review*

Daily News
London Gazette
Morning Advertiser

Morning Post
The Civilian
The Times

2. *Periodicals*

Atlantic Monthly
American Journal of Education
British Quarterly
Canadian Magazine
Chambers Journal
Contemporary Review
Cornhill Magazine
Dublin University Magazine
Eclectic Magazine
Edinburgh Review
Fraser's Magazine
Fortnightly Review
Journal of the Statistical Society
Lakeside Monthly
Leisure Hour
London Quarterly
McMillan's Magazine
Mind
Nation
National Review

Nature
Nineteenth Century
North American Review
North British Review
Old and New
Penn Monthly
Popular Science Monthly
Princeton Review
Quarterly Review
St. James
Saturday Review
Scribner's Magazine
Spectator
Tait's American Magazine
The Economist
Unita Review
Victoria Magazine
Westminster Review
Western

D. WORKS OF REFERENCE

1. *General*

Annual Register.
British Imperial Calendar and Civil Service List.
Burke's Landed Gentry.
Burke's Peerage, Baronetage and Knightage.
Dictionary of National Biography (to 1900), ed. by Sir Leslie Stephen and Sir Sidney Lee, London, 1885–1901.
Index to Periodical Literature, W. F. Poole and W. I. Fletcher, London, 1882.
Men of the Time, ed. Thompson Cooper, 9th edn., London, 1875.

2. *Civil Service*

A Complete Practical Guide to the Civil Service, London, 1860.
A Guide to Civil Service Examinations, London, 1856.
Admission to Government Appointments, London, 1861.

EWALD, A. C.: *Civil Service Guide*, London, 1869.
Examinations for the Civil Service, London, 1855.
Guide to Employment in the Civil Service, London, 1866.
HALL, J. P.: *Civil Service Guide*, London, 1860.
Handbook of the Civil Service, London, 1860.
Handbook to Government Situations, London, 1866 and 1871.
HURST, J. C.: *A Complete Guide to Government Appointments*, London, 1856.
JOHNSTON, R.: *A Civil Service Guide*, London, 1869.
—— *A Guide to the Army and Civil Service*, London, 1873.
LETHBRIDGE, E.: *Civil Service Appointments*, London, 1866.
MORELL, J. D.: *A Guide to Civil Service Employment*, London, 1882.
Our Home Civil Service, London, 1862.
PARKINSON, J. C.: *Under Government: An Official Key to the Civil Service*, London, 1st and 2nd edns, 1859; 3rd edn, 1862; 4th edn, 1865; 5th edn, 1869.
WALFORD, E. D.: *The Handy-book of the Civil Service*, London, 1860.
WHITE, H.: *A Guide to the Civil Service*, London, 1867.

E. BIOGRAPHIES

(arranged in order of subjects)

ABERDARE, 1ST LORD: *Letters of the Rt. Hon. Henry Austin Bruce, G.C.B., Lord Aberdare of Duffryn*, 2 vols., privately printed, Oxford, 1902.
BAGEHOT, WALTER: *Biographical Studies*, by Walter Bagehot, ed. R. H. Hutton, London, 1881.
BARRINGTON, E. I.: *The Servant of All*, by E. I. Barrington, London, 1927
BEACONSFIELD, EARL OF: *Life of Benjamin Disraeli, Earl of Beaconsfield*, by W. F. Monypenny and G. E. Buckle, 6 vols., London, 1910–24.
—— *Disraeli*, by R. N. W. Blake, London, 1966.
BLATCHFORD, 1ST LORD: *Letters*, ed. G. E. Marindin, London, 1896.
BRIGGS, ASA: *Victorian People*, by Asa Briggs, London, 1954.
BRYCE, JAMES: *Studies in Contemporary Biography*, London, 1903.
CARDWELL, EDWARD: 'Edward Cardwell at the Colonial Office, 1864–66', by G. J. Sellars, unpublished B.Litt. thesis, Oxford, 1958.
CHADWICK, SIR EDWIN: *The Life and Times of Sir Edwin Chadwick*, by S. E. Finer, London, 1952.
CHILDERS, HUGH CULLING EARDLEY: *Life and Correspondence of the Right Hon. Hugh C. E. Childers, 1827–1896*, by Spencer Childers, 2 vols., London, 1901.

CLARENDON, 4TH EARL OF: *Life and Letters of George William Frederick, Fourth Earl of Clarendon*, by Sir Herbert Maxwell, 2 vols., London, 1913.

FISHER, SIR WARREN: 'Sir Warren Fisher and the Public Service', by Sir H. P. Hamilton, *Public Administration*, xxix, Spring 1951.

GLADSTONE, WILLIAM EWART: *Life of William Ewart Gladstone*, by John Morley, 2 vol. edn., London, 1905.

—— *Gladstone: A Biography*, by Sir Philip Magnus, London, 1954.

—— *Gladstone as Financier and Economist*, by Francis W. Hirst, London, 1931.

GRANVILLE, 2ND EARL: *Life of Granville George Leveson-Gower, Second Earl Granville, K.G.*, by Lord Fitzmaurice, 2 vols., London, 1905.

HAMMOND, EDMUND: 'Edmund Hammond, Permanent Under-Secretary of State for Foreign Affairs, 1854–73', by M. A. Anderson, unpublished Ph.D. thesis, London, 1955.

HARRISON, SIR GEORGE: 'Sir George Harrison and the growth of bureaucracy in the early nineteenth century', by John Torrance, *The English Historical Review*, LXXXIII, Jan. 1968.

HELPS, SIR ARTHUR: *Correspondence*, ed. by E. A. Helps, London, 1917.

—— 'Sir Arthur Helps and the Art of Administration', by B. B. Schaffer, *Public Administration*, xxxviii, Spring 1960.

HILL, SIR ROWLAND: *The Life of Sir Rowland Hill*, by G. B. Hill, London, 1880.

HUGHES, PHILIP: 'Memoirs of Philip Hughes, 1797–1883', by Philip Hughes, unpublished manuscript in the possession of Professor C. J. Hughes.

IDDESLEIGH, 1ST EARL OF: *Life, Letters and Diaries of Sir Stafford Northcote, First Earl of Iddesleigh*, by Andrew Lang, 2 vol. edn., Edinburgh, 1890.

JOWETT, BENJAMIN: *The Life and Letters of Benjamin Jowett*, by Evelyn Abbott and Lewis Campbell, 3 vols., London, 1897.

—— *Jowett: a portrait with a background*, by G. Faber, London, 1957.

KAY-SHUTTLEWORTH, SIR JAMES: *Life and Work of Sir James Kay-Shuttleworth*, by F. Smith, London, 1923.

KEKEWICH, SIR GEORGE W.: *The Education Department and After*, by Sir George W. Kekewich, London, 1920.

KEMPE, SIR JOHN ARROW: *Reminiscences of an Old Civil Servant, 1846–1927*, by Sir John Arrow Kempe, London, 1928.

LEWIS, SIR GEORGE CORNEWALL: *Letters of the Right Honourable Sir George Cornewall Lewis to Various Friends*, ed. by Sir G. F. Lewis, London, 1870.

MACAULAY, 1ST LORD: *Life and Letters of Lord Macaulay*, by Sir George Otto Trevelyan, 2 vols., London, 1876.

MALLET, SIR LOUIS: *Sir Louis Mallet: a record of public service and political ideals*, by Sir Bernard Mallet, London, 1905.

MERIVALE, HERMAN: *Memoir of Herman Merivale*, by C. Merivale, London, 1884.

NIGHTINGALE, FLORENCE: *Florence Nightingale*, by Cecil Woodham-Smith, London, 1950.

NORTHBROOK, 1ST EARL OF: *Journals and Correspondence of F. T. Baring, Lord Northbrook*, 2 vols., privately printed, London, 1902–5.

PAGET, LORD CLARENCE E.: *Autobiography and Journals of Lord Clarence E. Paget*, ed. by Rt. Hon. Sir Arthur Otway, London, 1896.

PEEL, SIR ROBERT: *Sir Robert Peel from his Private Papers*, ed. by C. S. Parker, 3 vols., London, 1891.

PLAYFAIR, 1ST LORD: *Memoirs and Correspondence of Lyon Playfair, First Lord Playfair of St. Andrews*, by Sir T. Wemyss Reid, London, 1899.

PRESTON-THOMAS, H.: *Work and Play of a Government Inspector*, London, 1909.

RUSSELL, 1ST EARL OF: *Later Correspondence of Lord John Russell*, ed, G. P. Gooch, 2 vols., London, 1925.

SHERBROOKE, VISCOUNT: *Life and Letters of the Right Honourable Robert Lowe, Viscount Sherbrooke*, by A. P. Martin, 2 vols., London, 1893.

—— *Robert Lowe, Viscount Sherbrooke*, by J. F. Hogan, London, 1893.

SPEARMAN, SIR ALEXANDER: 'The Rt. Hon. Sir Alexander Spearman, Bart. (1793–1874)', by Sir John Winnifrith, *Public Administration*, xxxviii, Winter, 1960.

STANSFELD, JAMES: *James Stansfeld: A Victorian Champion of Sex Equality*, by J. L. and Barbara Hammond, London, 1932.

SIMON, SIR JOHN: *Sir John Simon*, by Royston Lambert, London, 1963.

TROLLOPE, ANTHONY: *An Autobiography*, by Anthony Trollope, London, 1883.

—— *The Three Clerks*, by Anthony Trollope, London, 1857.

VICTORIA, QUEEN: *The Letters of Queen Victoria*, ed. by A. C. Benson and Viscount Esher. 3 vols., London, 1908.

WEST, SIR ALGERNON: *Recollections, 1832 to 1886*, by Sir Algernon West, 2nd edn., 2 vols., London, 1899.

—— *Private Diaries of Sir Algernon West*, ed. by H. G. Hutchinson, London, 1922.

WILSON, SIR CHARLES RIVERS: *Chapters from my Official Life*, by Sir C. Rivers Wilson, London, 1916.

YATES, EDMUND: *His Recollections and Experiences*, by Edmund Yates, London, 1884.

F. WORKS ON THE TREASURY AND THE CIVIL SERVICE

1. The Treasury

BAXTER, STEPHEN B.: *The Development of the Treasury, 1660–1702*, London, 1957.

BEER, SAMUEL H.: *Treasury Control*, 2nd edn, Oxford, 1957.

BRIDGES, LORD: *Treasury Control*. The Stamp Memorial Lecture 1950, London, 1950.

—— *The Treasury* (New Whitehall Series), London, 1964.

BURTON, ANN M.: 'The influence of the Treasury on the Making of British Colonial Policy, 1868–1880', unpublished D.Phil. thesis, Oxford, 1960.

—— 'Treasury Control and Colonial Policy in the Late Nineteenth Century', *Public Administration*, xliv, Summer 1966.

HAMILTON, SIR HORACE: 'Treasury Control in the Eighties', *Public Administration*, xxxiii, Spring 1955.

HANHAM, H. J.: 'Political Patronage at the Treasury, 1870–1912', *The Historical Journal*, Vol. 3, No. 1, 1960.

HART, JENNIFER: 'Sir Charles Trevelyan at the Treasury', *English Historical Review*, LXXV, No. CCXCIV, Jan. 1960.

HEATH, SIR T. W.: *The Treasury*, London, 1927.

WINNIFRITH, A. J. D.: 'The Treasury, Whitehall—I and II', *Country Life*, 7 and 14 Nov. 1957.

—— 'Treasury Control of Establishments', *Public Administration*, xxxvi, Spring, 1958.

WOODS, SIR JOHN: 'Treasury Control', *Political Quarterly*, XXV, No. 4, Oct.–Dec. 1954.

2. The Civil Service

ADMINISTRATIVE REFORM ASSOCIATION, *Official Papers*, London, 1855.

AYLMER, G.: *The King's Servants: The Civil Service of Charles I, 1625–42*, London, 1961.

BROWN, LUCY: 'The Board of Trade and the Tariff Problem, 1840–42', *English Historical Review*, 68, No. 268, July 1953.

—— *The Board of Trade and the Free Trade Movement, 1830–42*, Oxford, 1958.

CLARK, G. KITSON: 'Statesmen in Disguise: Reflexions on the History of the Neutrality of the Civil Service', *Historical Journal*, ii, 1959.

COHEN, EMMELINE: *The Growth of the British Civil Service, 1780–1939*, London, 1941.

DALE, H. E.: *The Higher Civil Service of Great Britain*, London, 1941.

EATON, DORMAN B.: *Civil Service in Great Britain*, New York, 1880.

GREG, W. R.: *The Way Out*, London, 1855.

GREGOIRE, ROGER: *The French Civil Service*, Brussels, 1964.

HALL, H. L.: *The Colonial Office*, London, 1937.

HERTSLET, Sir E.: *Recollections of the Old Foreign Office*, London, 1901.

HUGHES, EDWARD: 'Civil Service Reform, 1853–55', *History*, XXVII June–Sept. 1943. (Reprinted in *Public Administration*, xxxiii, Spring 1954.)

—— 'Sir Charles Trevelyan and Civil Service Reform, 1853–5', Parts I and II, *The English Historical Review*, LXIV, Nos. 250–1, Jan. and April 1949.

—— 'Postscript to the Civil Service Reforms of 1855', *Public Administration*, xxxiii, Autumn 1955.

HUMPHREYS, B. V.: *Clerical Unions in the Civil Service*, Oxford, 1958.

KELSALL, R. K.: *Higher Civil Servants in Britain*, London, 1955.

KNOX, B. A.: 'The Provision of Legal Advice, and Colonial Office Re-organisation, 1866–67', *Bulletin of the Institute of Historical Research*, XXV, No. 92, Nov. 1962.

LAMBERT, R. J.: 'Central and Local Relations in Mid-Victorian England: The Local Government Act Office 1853–71', *Victorian Studies*, vi. 2, 1962.

MARVIN, CHARLES: *Our Public Offices*, London, 1879.

MARTINDALE, HILDA: *Women Servants of the State, 1870–1938*, London, 1938.

MOSES, ROBERT: *The Civil Service of Great Britain*, New York, 1914.

NORTHCOTE and TREVELYAN: 'Report on the Organisation of the Civil Service', 23 November 1853, *Public Administration*, xxxiii, Spring 1954.

PROUTY, R.: *The Transformation of the Board of Trade*, London, 1957.

PUGH, R. B.: 'The Colonial Office, 1801–1925', in *The Cambridge History of the British Empire*, iii, Cambridge, 1959.

RAPHAEL, M.: *Pensions and Public Servants: A Study of the Origins of the British System*, Paris, 1964.

RHODES, GERALD: *Public Sector Pensions*, London, 1965.

ROY, N. C.: *The Civil Service in India*, Calcutta, 1935.

STACK, J. H.: *Our Government Offices*, London, 1855.

SYMONDS, R.: *The British and their Successors*, London, 1966.

STRUTT, SIR AUSTIN: 'The Home Office: An Introduction to its Early History', *Public Administration*, xxxix, Summer 1961.

TILLEY, SIR JOHN and GASELEE, S.: *The Foreign Office*, London, 1933.

TROUP, SIR CHARLES: *The Home Office*, London, 1925.

WEBSTER, C. K.: 'Lord Palmerston at Work, 1830–1841', *Politica*, i, 1934–5.

WILLSON, F. M. G.: 'Ministries and Boards: Some Aspects of Administrative Development Since 1832', *Public Administration*, xxxiii, Spring, 1955.

390   *Bibliography*

YOUNG, D. M.: *The Colonial Office in the Early Nineteenth Century*, London, 1961.

G. OTHER WORKS

ANDERSON, OLIVE: *A Liberal State at War*, New York, 1967.

ANSON, SIR WILLIAM: *The Law and Custom of the Constitution*, 2 vols., Oxford, 1886.

BAGEHOT, WALTER: *The English Constitution*, London, 1867.

BINNEY, J. E. D.: *British Public Finance and Administration, 1774–92*, Oxford, 1958.

BRIGGS, ASA: *Age of Improvement*, London, 1959.

—— *Victorian Cities*, London, 1963.

BURN, W. L.: *The Age of Equipoise*, London, 1964.

CLARK, G. KITSON: *The Making of Victorian England*, London, 1962.

CHUBB, BASIL: *The Control of Public Expenditure*, Oxford, 1952.

DICEY, A. V.: *Lectures on the relation between law and public opinion in England during the 19th Century*, London, 1905.

DICKENS, CHARLES: *Little Dorrit*, London, 1857.

DURELL, COL. A. J. V.: *The Principles and Practice of the System of Control over Parliamentary Grants*, London, 1917.

HANHAM, H. J.: *Elections and Party Management*, London, 1959.

HOUGHTON, W. E.: *The Victorian Frame of Mind, 1830–70*, London, 1957.

LOWELL, A. LAWRENCE: *The Government of England*, rev. edn, New York, 1914.

MACDONAGH, OLIVER: *A Pattern of Government Growth, 1800–1860*, London, 1961.

—— 'Delegated Legislation and Administrative Discretion in the Fifties: A particular study', *Victorian Studies*, ii. 1958.

—— 'The 19th Century Revolution in Government: A Reappraisal', *Historical Journal*, i, 1958.

PARRIS, HENRY W.: *Government and the Railways in Nineteenth-Century Britain*, London, 1965.

—— 'The 19th Century Revolution in Government: A Reappraisal Reappraised', *Historical Journal*, 3, 1960.

PETRIE, SIR CHARLES: *The Powers Behind the Prime Ministers*, London, 1958.

RICHTER, MELVIN: *The Politics of Conscience*, London, 1964.

SABINE, B. E. V.: *A History of Income Tax*, London, 1966.

SMELLIE, K. B.: *A Hundred Years of English Government*, 2nd rev. edn, London, 1950

TAYLOR, SIR HENRY: *The Statesman*, London, 1836. (Reprinted with an

Introduction by H. J. Laski, Cambridge, 1927; reprinted with an Introduction by Leo Silberman, Cambridge, 1957.)

TODD, ALPHEUS: *On Parliamentary Government in England*, 2 vols., London, 1867–9.

TODD, ARTHUR HORATIO: *On Parliamentary Government in England*, 2 vols., 2nd rev. edn, Ottawa, 1887.

VINCENT, JOHN: *The Formation of the Liberal Party*, London, 1966.

WALLAS, GRAHAM: *Human Nature in Politics*, 3rd edn, London, 1914.

WOLFE, HUMBERT: *Dialogues and Monologues*, London, 1928.

WOODHAM-SMITH, CECIL: *The Great Hunger*, London, 1962.

WOODWARD, SIR LLEWELLYN: *Age of Reform*, 2nd edn, Oxford, 1962.

YOUNG, G. M.: *Portrait of an Age*, 2nd edn, London, 1953.

—— *Victorian Essays*, London, 1962.

INDEX

Aberdeen, 4th Earl of, xxvii; and reform of the I.C.S., 57

Administrative Reform Association, 64

Admiralty, Treasury control of allowances in, 269–71, 277–9; increase of establishment in, 144–6, 151–3, 154; proportions between different classes in, 292–3; recruitment to, 312–13; reductions of establishment in, 178–81; writers substituted for clerks in, 136–7, 183–4, 186; Treasury control of naval expenditure, 344–5; pay claims of general classes in, 239–45; pay claims of Principal Officers in, 260–1; special pension terms to facilitate reductions of establishment in, 320; promotion in disputed by Treasury, 286; opportunities for promotion in compared with other departments, 289–94; redundancy in, 104–5, 182; secondment of clerk to Foreign Office, 105; Treasury committee of inquiry into, 182, 199–201; admission into without C.S.C. certificate 312–13

Anderson, Sir William, 24–5, 36n., 160–1; service on Treasury committees of inquiry, 202–3; and the Treasury inquiry into the Audit Office, 221–3

Arbuthnot, George, xxii, xxxi, 36n.; authority on currency and banking, 20 and n.; death of, 24; opposition to Northcote–Trevelyan Report, 61; and division of labour in Treasury, 112; on report of Treasury committee of inquiry into division of labour in Civil Service, 122–3; on Admiralty application for increase of establishment in 1861, 158–9; service on Treasury committees of inquiry, 202; on the composition of Treasury committees of inquiry, 203; on the efficacy of Treasury committees of inquiry, 211; on promotion in the Civil Service before 1854, 282–3

Arnold, Matthew, xxxiv

Audit Office, xxv, xxvi; implementation of Treasury committee of inquiry report, 221–3; promotion in, the cause of Treasury disagreement, 283–4; proportions between different classes of clerks in, compared with other departments, 292–3; annual leave in, 297; also under Exchequer and Audit Department

Ayrton, Acton Smee, biog., 46n.; division of responsibility with Junior Lords of Treasury, 51–2; dispute with G. A. Hamilton, 252–4; egregious behaviour as Financial Secretary, 336–7

Aytoun, Sinclair, 84

Baring, Sir Francis, xx, 111

Baxter, William E., 45, 278, 280

Booth, James, 317–18

Bridges, Lord, on recruitment to the Treasury, 17n.

British Museum, 94

Bromley, Sir Richard, 158; awarded special pension, 316; chairman of association of civil servants in 1846, 307

Brooksbanks, T. C., xxxi

Bruce, H. A. (1st Lord Aberdare), and the introduction of open competition, 83–4, 89–90, 94–5

Cabinet, and the decision to introduce open competition in 1854, 62n.; and in 1869, 80–1

235–9; average mean cost of the Superior Establishment, 248; relaxation of Treasury rules for payment of salary on promotion, 251–2; office hours in, 297; leave in, 297; Treasury control of Imperial expenditure through deterrence, 347–8; documents received and despatched, 354

Comptroller and Auditor-General, 104–5, 191, 268–9, 351

Copyhold and Tithe Commission, 252–4

Crafer, Charles L., 316

Crafer, Edwin, xxxi

Crimean War, xiii, 64, 329

Customs, Board of, xxiv, xxvi, 91–3; redundancy in, 104–5; reductions in, 181; substitution of writers for permanent clerks in, 136–7; complaints of civil servants in about pay, 227–8, 356; petition Treasury, 229; pay claim, 247–8

Delane, J. T., xv, 59

Delves-Broughton, V., 32

Disraeli, Benjamin (1st Earl of Beaconsfield), and the title of Permanent Secretary to the Treasury, 38–9; as Chancellor, 48; delays issue of Treasury Minute on financial probity in Civil Service, 301

Dodson, J. G. (1st Lord Monk Bretton), 47n.

Dunbar, Sir William, 104–5, 317–18

East India Company, 54–5

Education Department, 75; transfer of redundant clerks to, 104

Exchequer and Audit Act, 1, 344, 351

Exchequer and Audit Department, introduction of open competition in, 84; transfer of redundant clerks to, 104–5; Treasury committee of inquiry into, 202; failure of to detect irregularities in the Poor Law Board, 250–1; Comptroller and Auditor-General checks the payment of allowances in the Civil Service, 268–9

Excise Department, 91–3

Expenditure, Public, increase of between 1854–74, 329; Victorians' dislike of increase, 329; principles of control of, 329–30; estimates of (1854–75), 373; estimates of, on Civil Services (1854–75), 374; estimates of, on salaries, etc. (1854–75), 375; estimates of, on the Revenue Departments (1854–75), 376; estimates of, for Superannuation and Retired Allowances (1854–75) 377

Expenditure, Select Committee on Civil Services (1873), Lowe and Gladstone in evidence to on Treasury's authority to enforce reductions, 176–7; Gladstone's evidence to on Treasury's powers of moral suasion, 348; Lowe's evidence to on need for social and educational exclusiveness in an open Civil Service, 353; recommends use of letter-presses in the Civil Service, 354; criticizes excessive number of civil servants, 140–1

Expenditure, Select Committee on Miscellaneous (1848), xiii, 110–11

Expenditure, Select Committee on Public Income and (1828), 3

Fawcett, Henry, 78, 84

Finance, Select Committee on (1818), 3

Foreign Office, xxxii–xxxiii; relations between ministers and civil servants in, xxviii–xxix; 'young gentlemen' in, xxxii; introduction of open competition in, 82–3, 89–90, 94–7; Treasury deference to, 96, 129–31; applies for increase of establishment 147–8, 153; transfer of redundant clerk to, 183; opposition to reduction of establishment and substitution of writers, 184; reductions in after 1870, 189–90; Treasury committee of inquiry into, 195–6; applies for pay increase, 226–7, 265; pays an allowance to a private contractor, 274–5; office hours in, 296; annual leave in, 297; Secretary of State of and financial embarrassment, 302; 'captiousness' of, 343–4

Fortescue, Chichester P. (1st Lord Carlingford), 89

tion of two-tiered establishment into, 115; pay claims in, 123, 235–9; application of for increase of establishment, 149; and transfer of redundant clerk, 183; reductions in after 1870, 190; Treasury committee of inquiry into, 208–9, 215–20, 371–2; setting up of Police Department in, 209; recruitment, promotion and discipline in, in 1856, 210–14; office hours in, 296; leave in, 297; documents received and registered in, 354

Hunt, George Ward, 25n., 26; and change of the Assistant Secretary's title, 38–9; and Treasury committees of inquiry, 199–202

Inland Revenue, Board of, xxiv, 99; petition of revenue officers to for pay rise, 229; promotion in, 287; Tax Surveyors' central committee, 356; revenue clerks co-operate to publish *The Civilian*, 356–7
Ireland, Office of the Secretary for, 99

Jelf, Dr., 59
Jeune, Dr., 59
Jowett, Benjamin, and the appointment of the Civil Service Commission, 53–4; and the campaign for reform of I.C.S., 54–5; and the campaign for reform of the Civil Service, 56–65

Kekewich, Sir George, 1st Bt., 75
Kempe, Sir John Arrow, 1st Bt., xxxii, 19
Kimberley, 1st Earl of, and the reorganization of the Colonial Office 189

Lansdowne, 3rd Marquis of, and the Treasury Superannuation Committee, 321
Law, William, 25; appointment as Auditor of the Civil List and Assistant to the Secretaries, 27
Lewis, Sir George Cornewall, 10, 48, 63; and the implementation of the Treasury's report on the Home Office, 216–20

Liddell, Dr. Henry, and the reform of I.C.S., 57
Lingen, Ralph Robert Wheeler (1st Baron Lingen), biog., 35n., 42; xxx, 43, 59, 75; and right of appeal to the Chancellor of the Exchequer, 47; and the implementation of the 1870 Order in Council, 88–96; and the control of open competitive examinations, 97–102; influence on recruitment to the Civil Service, 107–9; appointed to Committee of Inquiry into Supplementary Clerks in the Civil Service, 120; attitude towards Treasury control, 225; formulates rules on payment of allowances in the Civil Service, 273; and allowances in the War Office and Admiralty, 277–9
Local Government Act Office, 173
Lowe, Robert (1st Viscount Sherbrooke), xxx, 42–3, 55; as Chancellor, 48; and the division of work among the Treasury Junior Lords, 51–2; and the introduction of open competition in the Civil Service, 74, 77, 79–85; and the implementation of the 1870 Order, 88–96; and the control of open competitive examinations, 97–102; and the power of dispensation under the 1870 Order, 103–4; influence on recruitment, 107–9; on the Treasury's lack of authority to enforce reductions of establishment, 176–7; and Treasury policy on reductions, 183–5; and the offer of special pension terms to civil servants, 187–8; attitude towards Treasury control, 255; and the need for firmness in controlling allowances, 277–9; authorizes the payment of an allowance to a private individual, 274–5; impatience with departments in reducing the size of their establishments, 321; intention to make the Civil Service open but socially and educationally exclusive, 353
Lunacy Commission, 260

Maberley, Col., xxxiii–xxxiv
Macaulay, Thomas Babington (1st

x21FR2

1a# 402 Index

Science and Art Department, 200, 275-6
Scully, Vincent, 65
Secret Service, the head of, 165
Shaw Lefevre, J. G., 54, 57n., 59
Shelley, Spencer, 25; enforced retirement of, 26-7; and the need for strict Treasury control, 217-20, 337
Shuttleworth, Sir James Kay, xxx
Simon, Sir John, xxx
Spearman, Sir Alexander, 43, 111
Spring-Rice, Stephen, 17, 19
Stansfeld, James (jnr.), 44, 46n., 51, 232
Stationery Office, pay claim of clerks in, 243-4; recommendation for promotion in rejected by Treasury, 284
Stephen, Sir James, xxviii-xxix, 59, 62
Stephenson, Sir William H., 43, 63; service on Treasury committees of inquiry, 202; consulted by Hamilton on establishments' matters, 205; on promotion in Board of Inland Revenue, 287

Taylor, Sir Henry, xxviii, xxxiv-xxxv
Taylor, Col. T. E., 41-2
Taylor, Tom, xxxv
Temple, the Rev. Frederick, 54
Times, on open competition, 78, 91-2; 228
Trade, Board of, relations between ministers and civil servants in, xxviii-xxix; Treasury committees of inquiry into, 113, 128-9, 135, 198-9, 207-10, 212-13; separation of intellectual and mechanical work in 113; difficulty of maintaining the separation, 116-17, 128-9; reductions of establishments in, 189; duties of Vice-President of, 209; promotion in, 212-23
Treasury,
— accommodation in, 6
— Assistant/Permanent Secretary to: functions and responsibilities of, 33-43; attendance at Board meetings, 7; duties in 1854, 8; salary, 11; responsibility for establishments, 20; relieved of a division, 21-4; relations with the Financial Secretary, 34-7, 44-7, 252-4; change of

title of, 37-40, 363-6; claim to title of Official Head of Civil Service, 40-1, 367-8; right of appeal to Chancellor, 39-41, 46, 252-4; functions and responsibility of new office of Permanent Secretary, 41; appointed permanent member of Treasury Superannuation Committee, 310; transformation of office between 1854-74, 349
— Auditor of the Civil List, in 8, 11, 24-5
— Board of, 6-7, 9
— building and physical location of, 4-5
— Chancellor of the Exchequer in, attendance at Board meetings, 7; relations with Financial Secretary, 45-6, 47-9
— committees of inquiry of: importance of in controlling Civil Service, 204-5, 211, 223-4, 339-40, 349; Arbuthnot on the efficacy of, 211; origin of, 194-5; Trevelyan on the need for, 194-5; Gladstone on the purpose and functions of, 114; characteristics of, 195-7; numbers of, 196; setting up of, 198-201; composition of, 201-5; Arbuthnot on composition of, 203; terms of reference and procedure of, 205-7; report stage of, 207-14; implementation of reports of, 214-23; and the Colonial Office, 112, 195-6; and the Board of Trade, 113, 128-9, 135, 198-9, 207-13; and the War Office, 180-2, 198, 201, 204-14; and the Admiralty, 182, 199, 201; and the Home Office, 208-12, 215-20, 371-2; and the Audit Office, 202, 221-3; and other departments, 113; and division of work, 118-24, 210; and promotion, 211-14, 221, 293-4; and salaries, 211
— development of Civil Service and, 352-61
— establishment of:
— — Accountant in, 14, 31
— — continuity of service of senior men in, 16, 349-50
— — division of labour in, 9-10, 33-4, 111-12, 115